Coffee with Matt & Joe
Following Jesus One Step at a Time

Dr. Jim McClaren

Coffee with Matt & Joe: Following Jesus One Step at a Time
Copyright © 2010 James E. McClaren. All rights reserved.
www.coffeewithmattandjoe.com

Printed in the United States of America

ISBN 9781612150345

All rights reserved solely by the author. The author guarantees all contents are original and do not infringe upon the legal rights of any other person or work. No part of this book may be reproduced in any form without the permission of the author. The views expressed in this book are not necessarily those of the publisher.

All scripture quotations, unless otherwise indicated, are taken from the Holy Bible, New International Version®, NIV®. Copyright ©1973, 1978, 1984 by Biblica, Inc.™ Used by permission of Zondervan. All rights reserved worldwide.

Scripture quotations from **THE MESSAGE**. Copyright © by Eugene H. Peterson 1993, 1994, 1995, 1996, 2000, 2001, 2002. Used by permission of NavPress Publishing Group.

Scripture taken from the Contemporary English Version © 1991, 1992, 1995 by American Bible Society. Used by Permission.

THE SPIRIT OF THE DISCIPLINES:UNDERSTANDING HOW GOD CHANGES LIVES by DALLAS WILLARD. Copyright © 1989 by Dallas Willard. Reprinted by permission of HarperCollins Publishers.

THE DIVINE CONSPIRACY by DALLAS WILLARD. Copyright © 1998 by Dallas Willard. Reprinted by permission of HarperCollins Publishers.

Reprinted or adapted from *Bold Love*. © 1992 by Dan B. Allender and Tremper Longman III. Used by permission of NavPress, Colorado Springs, CO (www.navpress.com). All rights reserved.

Reprinted by permission. *We Are Driven*, Robert Hemfelt, Frank Minirth, Paul Meier, 1991, Thomas Nelson Inc. Nashville, Tennessee. All rights reserved.

Adapted by permission. *Uprising: A Revolution of the Soul*, Erwin Raphael McManus, 2003, Thomas Nelson Inc. Nashville, Tennessee. All rights reserved.

Taken from **Becoming a Contagious Christian** by BILLL HYBELS; MARK MITTELBERG. Copyright © 1994 by Bill Hybels and Mark Mittelberg. Used by permission of Zondervan. WWW.ZONDERVAN.COM

Taken from **Boundaries** by JOHN S TOWNSEND TRUST; HENRY CLOUD. Copyright © 1992 by Henry Cloud and John Townsend. Used by permission of Zondervan. WWW.ZONDERVAN.COM

Illustrations taken from **Boundaries** by JOHN S TOWNSEND TRUST; HENRY CLOUD. Copyright © 1992 by Henry Cloud and John Townsend. Used by permission of Zondervan. WWW.ZONDERVAN.COM

Taken from **Sacred Pathways** by GARY L. THOMAS. Copyright © 2000 by Gary L. Thomas. Used by permission of Zondervan. WWW.ZONDERVAN.COM

Taken from **Just Walk Across the Room** by BILL HYBELS. Copyright © 2006 by Bill Hybels. Used by permission of Zondervan. WWW.ZONDERVAN.COM

Excerpt from THE GREAT SANTINI by Pat Conroy. Copyright © 1976 by Pat Conroy. Reprinted by permission of Houghton Mifflin Harcourt Publishing Company. All rights reserved.

Adapted and reprinted from THE POWERS THAT BE by Walter Wink, copyright © 1998 Augsburg Fortress. Used by permission.

Quotation from The Little Engine That Could by Watty Piper, TM & © Penguin Group (USA) Inc. Used by permission.

www.xulonpress.com

What our readers are saying...

As a business and executive coach, I try to stay informed on the latest management, motivational, leadership, and positive psychology books as they are published to continually bring new ideas to the table for each of my clients. In my profession, I'm lucky enough to also bring my faith into my client sessions quite often. *Coffee with Matt & Joe* brings all of those topics to bear with real life issues and solutions to those issues. You will not find another book that deals with more <u>real life issues and solutions for those issues</u> than this one. Whether you are a seasoned veteran and servant for Jesus Christ for many years or someone who has never picked up a Bible, you will find comfort, solace, and solutions for the issues in life we encounter daily. And, if you are someone new to Jesus Christ, you have just picked up a book to take you into a new life of patience, contemplation, comfort, and joy. —Robert C. Meyer, MBA, CBC, President, Executive Strategies, Inc.

This book is a teaching tool, written for those who would rather learn discipleship through story and conversation instead of the unfriendly step-by-step methods. *Coffee with Matt and Joe* allowed me to pull up a chair and experience a better understanding of how to share faith with others. —Cathy Hasek, Freelance Writer

For anyone working in Corporate America, the faith journey of Matt and Joe will give new insights into how you can fulfill your God-given purpose in the business world. Jim McClaren's story provides a great perspective on how we can more closely experience God's grace as well as contribute to Kingdom living, now and beyond the grave.—KB Kleckner, Vice President, Manufacturing and Product Supply, Mohawk Industries Inc, Home Division

Coffee with Matt & Joe allowed me to first establish, then build, and finally strengthen my relationship with God on a daily basis. The course provided me with the teachings and life skills that transformed me from a "fifty minutes on Sunday worshiper" to an "all day, everyday follower" of the Lord Almighty. A perfect mix of the life experiences of Matt & Joe, the Book of Matthew, and the eight Beatitudes, the course allowed me to grow in Spirit and realize that joy and harmony in family, career, and life come from commitment, trust, and faith in God.—Kevin McKeigue, Marketing, Life Safety

Coffee with Matt and Joe provided the best insight into the Gospel of Matthew we have ever experienced. Other books and study groups did not give the in-depth and real-life explanations that are packed into this book. The teaching of Jesus, from the book of Matthew, is broken down and presented using today's language and experiences and provides straightforward ways to apply these disciplines to your own life.—Paul Slebodnik, Vice President of Hospital Operations, and Judy Slebodnik, Appraisal Research Assistant

We are all called to the Great Commission—to see others come to the saving knowledge of Christ. This book offers practical yet eye-opening ways to not only effectively share the Gospel but also challenges the readers to take a look at their own lives and begin to make changes in the process. It impacted me in a profound way in my walk with the Lord and took me to a deeper level of ministry.—Cindy Hirch, Volunteer Staff, City Mission

Through studying *Coffee with Matt & Joe*, we have learned: The kingdom of God is here and now because the kingdom is where Jesus is, and Jesus is now in our hearts; the true significance of Jesus' Sermon on the Mount as he has taught us through the Beatitudes; how to apply the spiritual disciplines in our everyday lives, providing guidance to live as Jesus would want and to be more mindful of the needs of others.—David Gray, Consulting Engineer, and Darla Gray, Medical Adviser

Reading *Coffee with Matt & Joe* gave me new insight into how Jesus wants us to live as Christians. It was an intense study that was both encouraging and overwhelming. I liked delving into passages I knew from childhood, but it made me realize that studying is not enough. God expects us to share His "good news." Having the book as a reference is great. It is life changing but only if I put what I learned into action. The book provides a path for me to do so.—Tess Anderson, Volunteer

Coffee with Matt & Joe is a life relevant read. It allowed us to reassess early life teachings to an adult point of view. The book had us doing a lot of soul searching.—Jean Johnson, Master Gardener-Horticulture Teacher, Cleveland Municipal School, and Bruce Johnson, Retired Accountant, LTV Steel

Life happens one step at a time, and Matt & Joe are blessed to have each other to share joys, sorrows, and insights on our Great God and His Kingdom. Pull up a chair and bring a friend. I learned to let go of anger, to live humbly, and that you grow best in community.—Nancy McCormick

For me, *Coffee with Matt & Joe* is a spiritual psychoanalysis and treatment plan. It made me aware of the walls I had erected which kept me from developing a personal relationship with God. It gave me the tools, strength, courage, and support to dismantle the wall and build on a new foundation. I continue to use the spiritual disciplines and continue to grow in an intimate relationship with my God who is always near.—Dottie Tabar, Registered Nurse

Coffee with Matt & Joe is Life Coaching. I look at the thirty sessions like drawing a picture from thirty dots on a paper. After the study sessions and the dots are connected, you see a heart change.—Bob L. Fortune, Retired YMCA Director

Coffee with Matt & Joe is a positive experience in spiritual growth. I feel closer to God since reading the book.—Cecilia A. McClaren, Retired Nurse

The book helped me realize that the only self-help book I need is the Bible, specifically Jesus' teachings in the book of Matthew.—Jenny McKeigue, Marketing Consultant

Coffee with Matt & Joe opens discussions centering around some difficult real life situations. It gave us a peace and understanding of how to live better lives and how to be the followers of God we were meant to be.—Russ Gordon, Compliance Director, Skylight Financial Group, and Sherri Gordon, Outside Sales Representative

What an engaging story of real life struggles and how to get the kingdom resources you need, here, now, and forever. It is a unique Bible study providing boundaries for the Christian soul along with a plan to live each day with the only audience that counts—the audience of one. Having brokenness in my past, this study helped me get rid of the negative tapes that ran in my head when I felt unworthy as well as deal with my stuff personally, emotionally, and spiritually.—Corky Salloum, Labor Relations/Human Resources Management

Acknowledgments

I want to thank the congregations I served while developing this material: Montrose Zion United Methodist Church and River of Life United Methodist Church. Their participation in Matthew Groups, their response to the material, the change that occurred in their lives, and the encouragement they gave made this work possible. I also want to thank those at Fields United Methodist Church who participated in Matthew Groups and who continued the encouragement to publish.

I want to thank my wife, Gail, who did the hard part. I just wrote the book. She edited it, launched an exhaustive search for and massive communications with publishers and authors, and handled details with Xulon Press. Without her help and hard work, the book would still be just a manuscript full of left out words, typos, and grammatical errors.

I want to thank all of the writers I have quoted in this book. I have attempted to give them all the respect they so rightfully deserve.

I want to thank Jacquelynn Hongosh and Lynne R. Karr for their expertise in creating our front cover.

I want to thank Matthew, the tax collector, whose work, The Gospel According to Matthew, is the foundation of this book. Without Matthew's ears to hear and his unique understanding of what Jesus was doing, I would have nothing to say.

This book is dedicated to Jesus of Nazareth, the Christ, whom I'm trying to follow one shaky step at a time.

CONTENTS

Introduction xv

Phase I—Sermon on the Mount—Matthew 5-7 ... 19

Prelude 21
1. The Kingdom of Heaven 27
2. The Beatitudes 37
3. Salt & Light 58
4. Jesus' Sending Instructions 70
5. Anger 78
6. Sexuality 93
7. Yes & No 108
8. Turn the Other Cheek 124
9. Love Your Enemies 141
10. Prayer & Worship 158
11. Fasting & Other Spiritual Exercises 177
12. Jesus & Treasures 198
13. Dynamics of Change 215
14. The Rule of the Kingdom: Ask 232
15. Houses of Rock or Sand 253

Phase II—Sending into Ministry—Matthew 10 ... 265

16. Sending Instructions 267
17. Holy Spirit 282
18. Holy Spirit: Gifts & Fruit 299

19. How to Share the Gospel 316
20. Questions & Objections to the Gospel 336

Phase III—Parables—Matthew 13 . . . 359

21. Seeds, Sowing, & Soils 361
22. Weeds, Seeds, Treasures, & Nets 373

Phase IV—Getting Along With Each Other
—Matthew 18 . . . 389

23. Life Together: Child Care 391
24. Life Together: Offense & Togetherness 408

Phase V—Until the End—Matthew 24-25 . . . 423

25. Until the End: Part I 425
26. Until the End: Part II 442
27. Until the End: Part III 456

Phase VI—The Great Commission
—Matthew 28:18-20 . . . 469

28. The Great Commission 471

INTRODUCTION

A group of 120 Jesus followers, led by 12 men, turned the world upside down. The movement they started 2,000 years ago has become the largest in human history and still today captures the hearts and minds of men and women. Roughly one-third of the world's population claim allegiance to this movement in some way, shape, or form.

As best as I can tell, there was nothing special about those 120 or the 12 that led them. There are only three things I find noteworthy about this group: The first is the activity of the Holy Spirit in their lives that began on Pentecost as recorded in Acts 2. That is a story for another book. The second is that these 12 men who led the group spent 3 years with Jesus. That is the story of this book. The third is the dedication of those people to live out what they learned from Jesus. I hope that can be true of us too.

One of those 12, a man named Matthew, formerly a tax collector, wrote down what he saw, heard, and experienced in those years he and the others spent with Jesus. What he wrote was not a journal or remembrances to be shared with his grandchildren. What Matthew wrote was a record of the change that Jesus brought into the world. Jesus called the change "the kingdom of heaven." Matthew wrote what Jesus said this change looked like and felt like. He wrote what Jesus said about how to get this change into one's life. He wrote what Jesus said about how to use this change to change the world.

It is my belief that what Matthew recorded, about Jesus and the change he brought, is still potent today. The change Matthew recorded is still available, still changing lives, and still changing the world today. It is my belief that if we take seriously the words of Jesus and the change he brought, and apply them to our lives, then we too, with the help of the Holy Spirit, can turn our worlds upside down.

This book is my attempt to unpack those words of Jesus, recorded by Matthew, so we, like those first followers of Jesus, can have the change happen to us, in us, and through us.

Working with this material over the last few years, I have been amazed at the change that actually has occurred in the lives of the people who have committed to living out what Matthew recorded for us of Jesus. Greg Kennedy, who went through an early version of what is in this book, wrote:

> I began to understand my vision of that kingdom (the kingdom of heaven) was upside down. I was so focused on the idea of a *coming* kingdom that I couldn't see Jesus had brought it to this world. I was so fixated on Jesus' death that I couldn't see what he taught us while he was alive. I was so focused on my faults and failures that I couldn't see the power to change that Jesus offered. Since studying what Matthew recorded of Jesus, I have learned the kingdom of heaven is indeed near. By following Jesus' way of life, I can live in it each day, right here, right now.

I have been amazed at the brilliance of Jesus. Let me say that again. I have been amazed at the brilliance of Jesus. From his announcement of the nearness of the kingdom of heaven to his last words to his followers to go into all the world, Jesus was and is brilliant. His understanding of the human heart, of relational dynamics, of change, of what God wants to do in us and how God works is so deep, so concise, so accurate, so hopeful that I'm dazzled every time I approach it.

I have been amazed at how Jesus touches every area of our lives. He lays bare our hearts. He touches our anger, our sexuality, our dysfunctional relationships, our struggles with forgiveness and love, and our fears and doubts about God. Jesus leaves us nothing to hide and no place to hide it.

I have been amazed at how difficult this all is. The change the kingdom of heaven brings is completely opposite to how we are wired. The change Jesus brings is 180 degrees from how we normally act. The concepts are difficult because they are so different from how we think and live. Putting them into practice is even more difficult. Greg, who was quoted earlier, would be the first to state that all this is impossible to do.

He is right. But the good news is that the very first thing Jesus teaches all who want to follow him is that we must ask for his help to be able to do what he asks. With Jesus' help, the impossible becomes possible, but more about that later.

Disclaimer: If you proceed, Jesus will mess with your life. This is not a typical Bible study or theological work. This is about getting the change Jesus brought into you, letting it change you, and then allowing it to challenge you to change the world. You may struggle. You may have to stop and go get help to deal with some issue or another and then come back. You may be angry with Jesus about some of his expectations. Some expectations may be hard to understand. Some may be beyond you to do. Others you may not want to do. Some, you may claim, will not work in the real world. At some point, you may be tempted to quit. A brief word of encouragement: Don't!

If you are still reading, let me say this book is best used in a group. I wrote it for group use of thirty weekly sessions. In a group, you can share your experiences, pray for one another, support one another, practice the spiritual disciplines together, and be partners in mission projects. Group materials, including session guides and leaders' guides, will be available in the near future. Check our website for details:

www.coffeewithmattandjoe.com

Author's confession: While I have enjoyed writing this, I have been in over my head with a lot of what Jesus had to say. To the extent that what is written here is helpful, I thank the Holy Spirit for guiding me. To the extent that what is written here is not helpful, I ask for your forgiveness.

As you turn the page, you will meet Matt and Joe. Get a cup of coffee, pull up a chair, and join them as they work at understanding Jesus and following Jesus one step at time.

Let the change begin.

PHASE I

SERMON ON THE MOUNT

MATTHEW 5-7

PRELUDE

Joe's mood was as black as the cup of coffee into which he was staring. He and his wife, Sue, had just had a soul-wrenching, emotion-draining, gut-wrenching fight. His self-esteem was still bleeding from the verbal scratching he had received, and Joe was sure that Sue's emotions were covered with large bruises from the verbal body blows he had given her. Her fault, his fault, money, in-laws, children, work, time away from home, blame, and issues didn't matter anymore. Joe felt he was on the verge of losing his family. He was feeling unwelcome at home and found himself trying to avoid being there. He didn't like living this way. He didn't like the fights he and Sue got into. He didn't like his job, his inability to say no to his boss, and the extra hours he put into his job. He didn't like looking in the mirror at what was in his own eyes. They haunted him.

Joe thought, "I'm halfway through my life. I have a good-looking wife who loves me and beautiful children. I have a nice house in a good neighborhood, and the kids go to a good school. We have new cars, a large screen TV, and a manicured lawn. My golf game is good, the company I work for is strong, and they pay very well. I should be on top of the world. Why do I feel so bad?"

Joe thought of a friend of his whose life wasn't much different. This guy would say, "I must be the world's greatest magician—everything I touch turns to crap." That was exactly how he felt.

But the worst part for Joe was the helplessness he felt. He didn't want to keep living this way. He wanted to change, but he didn't know how. He didn't know what to do differently, and even if there were a different way, he wasn't sure he could pull it off. The patterns, routines, assumptions, and emotions that brought him to this point were so much a part of him he didn't know where the switch was to turn them off. The helplessness bred hopelessness. The hopelessness was beginning to breed despair. Joe was beginning to think his future was going to be as black as his coffee. He was beginning to smell a gathering doom.

Trying to snap out of the darkness, he swirled the coffee in his cup. He was hoping that like the magic black eight ball he had as a child, the cup of coffee would cause a pithy saying to appear that held the answers for him. But no answers came. He started to wonder if maybe instead of leaving the home battle zone for coffee he should have sought out a bottle of whiskey for some comfort. At least he would be numb by now. But numbness had no answers either.

"Hello."

The voice startled Joe. He looked up. It was Matt. Matt was a guy whose son played on the same soccer team as Joe's boy. They had talked some on the sidelines during the season about the weather, professional baseball, and how the soccer refs always let the other teams get away with too much.

Joe managed a "hello" in return.

Matt sat down and said sympathetically, "You don't look like things are going your way. Are you finding any answers in that cup of coffee?"

"No," was all Joe said in return.

Matt allowed a couple of minutes of silence to pass. When Joe didn't say any more, Matt figured he didn't want to talk about whatever it was. Matt gently said, "I've been through some rough times too. I found some help at church. If I can do anything, let me know. I just want to tell you that you don't have to be alone."

Joe muttered, "Thanks," as Matt got up and went back to a table halfway across the coffee shop where he was sitting with a couple of guys Joe didn't recognize.

Church? That was a new idea to Joe. He didn't know if it was a good idea, but it was a new idea. Joe had never really done the church thing. His family went to church occasionally on Christmas or Easter when he was growing up. He and Sue had gone less than that with their own family. Joe didn't think it could hurt. Or even if it did hurt, it wouldn't hurt as much as a bottle of whiskey hurt the next morning. By this point, Joe was just desperate enough to give church a shot. As Joe looked back down in his coffee cup, he thought he saw a flicker of light in the dark liquid. Then it was gone, if it were ever there.

Two weeks later, Joe found himself rummaging through the drawer under the phone looking for the roster for his son's soccer team that would have Matt's phone number on it. Joe thought things had been bad that night in the coffee shop, but now he found himself wishing things could be as good again as that night in the coffee shop. He was close to moving out because he was afraid he was going to hurt someone. He now felt like a stranger in his own skin. He needed to do something fast or his whole life was going to explode and leave a mess that could never be repaired. He thought of what had happened to his own father and dialed Matt's number as quickly as he could. He didn't want to end up like his dad.

"Hello, Matt? How are you? Fine. Which church did you say and what time? Thanks. Sure." Joe's hand was trembling as he hung up the phone. The darkness in his soul was being stirred by uncertainty. Maybe tomorrow he would find some help at church.

When he left the house Sunday morning, Sue asked him where he was going. Joe shouted back from the garage, "What do you care?" *Nice*, Joe thought, *real nice*. Then, for the first time, Joe looked toward heaven and said, "God, if you're still in the miracle business, I'm going to need one bigger than the parting of the Red Sea to save my sorry hide." While Joe didn't consider it a prayer, God must have, because for a brief instant there was hope in Joe's soul.

"So that was church?!" Joe said somewhat astonished. "It wasn't what I was expecting."

"What were you expecting?" asked Matt.

"I'm not sure. I've never really been to church before," Joe replied, "but I didn't expect a pep rally for Jesus. The place was packed. The people were excited. The music rocked. People were clapping and singing. I saw several people I knew who I had no idea went to any church let alone this church. When the guy stood up and thanked the congregation for praying, I was floored. Was he really in intensive care last week, the church prayed, and the next day they sent him home unable to find anything wrong?"

Matt nodded.

Joe went on, "And when it was prayer time, I could actually feel the people praying with the woman up front like they really thought God was present and listening. I don't know, maybe he is. The guy who talked—what do you call that?"

"A sermon," Matt said.

"Yeah that. Was he on the level about that stuff?"

"Which stuff do you mean?" asked Matt.

"He seemed to have a lot to say about what Jesus called 'the kingdom.'"

"Our pastor talks a lot about what Jesus called 'the kingdom of heaven,'" Matt responded.

"That guy, your pastor, said some amazing things. Is this kingdom of heaven really here, available to us now? I know a lot about the kingdom of hell. It feels like I live in it most of the time. Is there really help from God available to someone like me? Is it really true that in the end the kingdom of heaven wins? Is this heaven stuff really stronger than the hell that has a hold of me? Is everything really going to be alright? Does God, can God really care about a guy like me? Is God really interested in something other than adding to my misery? Was your pastor on the level about that stuff?"

"Yes, he was," Matt replied.

"So you mean there might be hope for a guy like me? Hey, thanks for inviting me. Would it be alright if I came back again some time?" Joe asked.

"We do this every week," Matt said. "I'll save you a place."

"Thanks," said Joe, and he was gone.

Over the course of the next several weeks, Joe came back to church. He asked Matt lots of questions about what the pastor said about Jesus and the kingdom of heaven. Joe wanted what the pastor was talking about, but he didn't know if it was available to a guy like him. He thought the only thing worse than living in hell would be to hear that heaven was real and then be turned away at the door. Matt continued to tell Joe that heaven was real and that Jesus had turned no one away at the door. In fact, Matt said the dynamic was working the other way. It was heaven that was knocking on the door of Joe's heart, hoping that Joe would open the door so that heaven could come in and free him from the hold of hell.

One Sunday, Joe couldn't take it anymore. As soon as the service was over, he grabbed a hold of Matt and said, "I want it. I want what your pastor has been talking about. How do I get it?"

"There are two things you need to do," Matt replied.

"Tell me what they are, and I'll do them," Joe said.

"The first thing you need to do is make an invitation. Jesus is knocking at the door of your heart and wants to come in even more than you want to let him in, so you need to open the door and invite him in."

"How do I do that?" Joe wanted to know.

"You pray this prayer: 'Jesus, please come into my life. Forgive me for the things I've messed up. Free me from the hell that has a hold of me. Help me, by your Spirit, to live differently with you.'"

"That's all I have to pray? When can we do that? I'm ready now," Joe said.

"Just wait a minute. Let me tell you about the second thing. The second thing you need to do is make a commitment to be a disciple of Jesus."

"What do you mean by that? Just what is a disciple?" Joe asked.

"A disciple is someone who spends time with Jesus to learn his teachings and to apply them to his life."

"Isn't that what I've been telling you I want to do? Can we pray that prayer now? Help me get started. I've never done anything like this before," Joe said.

"Okay," Matt said, "Here we go. I'm going to start the prayer and then ask you to follow along: Jesus, my friend Joe wants you and your kingdom of heaven in his life. He wants to invite you in, so I'm going to lead him in prayer, and he's going to ask you to come in.

"Joe, please pray after me: Jesus, I want you in my life. Please come into my heart."

Joe prayed, "Jesus I hope you hear me. I want you in my life. Please come into my heart."

Matt continued, "Forgive me for the things I've messed up."

Joe followed, "Please forgive me for the things I've messed up. And you know I've really messed up. There's so much stuff I can't fix. I've tried. But I can't. Please forgive me."

Matt led on, "Free me from the hell that has a hold on me."

Joe continued to follow, "Free me from the hell that I'm in and the hell that is in me. I can't take it anymore. I can't get loose of it on my own. Please free me."

Matt prayed some more, "Help me, by your Spirit, to live differently."

Joe followed, "Jesus, I'm not sure what that means, but help me, by your Spirit, to live differently. If that means change, I want it."

As Matt thanked Jesus for hearing their prayer and entering Joe's heart, Joe started to weep. After a few moments, Matt asked Joe if he was alright. Joe said, "I've never felt anything like that before. It was like love and forgiveness and acceptance and hope all at once in the deepest part of me. It was like God saying he's rooting for me and everything is going to be alright. This is so cool. No wonder people write songs about it. Now what's that other thing you said I needed to do, something about committing to be a disciple of Jesus? When can I start, and how do I do it?"

"Can you meet me tonight at seven o'clock, and we'll get started?" Matt asked.

"Sure," said Joe. "Do I need to bring anything?"

"Do you have a Bible?"

"Yeah. One of my mom's relatives gave it to me a few years back. I've never opened it, but I've got one," said Joe.

"Good," Matt replied. "Bring it. You'll need it."

Joe embraced Matt and left not quite sure what to expect but convinced that whatever was going to happen had to be better than anything else that had happened so far in his life.

CHAPTER 1

THE KINGDOM OF HEAVEN

When Matt arrived that evening, Joe was already there with a cup of coffee and a Bible in front of him. Matt got a cup of coffee and came over to the table with Joe. Before Matt had a chance to say "hello," Joe said, "Where do we start? How do we begin? How do I become a disciple?"

Matt replied, "It's good to see you too. Let me tell you again what a disciple is. Disciples are people who spend time with a teacher for the purpose of learning his teaching and putting it into action in their lives. Being a disciple is not simply an academic exercise in acquiring head knowledge and new pieces of data. Being a disciple is about acquiring information from a teacher in order to bring about transformation in the life of the disciple. The teacher we're going to disciple with is the most brilliant teacher ever to have walked the face of the earth. He is Jesus of Nazareth. The people who have been his disciples, those who have learned his teachings and applied them to their lives, have been changed in ways they never thought possible, and as a result of the change that has happened in them, they have transformed the worlds in which they have lived. I want to warn you that you're going to be pushed and stretched to the core of your being in ways that will change the fabric of your life and effect every moment of your day 24/7. Some of what Jesus has to say may be comforting and hopeful. Some of it may make you angry. Some of it may challenge your assumptions about what life is and cause you to call into question a lot of what you have worked for and are working for. Some of it may bring you face to face with your fears and demons, and some of it may bring you face to face with the fears and demons of others around you. It won't be easy being a disciple of Jesus. Are you sure you want to get started?"

"Listen," said Joe, "I figure I've got nothing to lose. My life is a mess. You know that. I do what I think is right, and it blows up in my face. There are things in my life I'm not proud of. I live with a lot of pain, not so much physical pain, but pain from my relationships and actions. If being a disciple of Jesus means there's hope for my life to be different, and if there's hope that what I felt this morning, when I prayed with you, can be an ongoing part of my life, I'll risk the rest. So to answer your question, let's get going.

"But," Joe continued, "I have a question of my own. If being a disciple is being with a teacher to learn from that teacher and to apply his teachings to my life, how are we going to be with Jesus? He lived two thousand years ago. How are we going to be with him?"

"That's precisely where we're going to begin," Matt said. "We're going to be following Jesus through his teachings in the Gospel of Matthew. Matthew has recorded for us what Jesus taught his first twelve disciples. Before meeting Jesus, Matthew was a tax collector. In Matthew's Gospel, we see some of Matthew's accounting mind. He laid out in neat columns what Jesus said and in other columns what Jesus did. Matthew gave us five columns of teaching that Jesus gave to his disciples. Some of this teaching occurred while the crowd was listening, and some of it occurred in private with his disciples. How do we know this? Matthew has been good enough to tell us who was listening when Jesus was speaking. These five columns are:

- The Sermon on the Mount, Matthew 5-7, is where Jesus described the Kingdom lifestyle.
- Humans are basically Sending into Kingdom Mission, Matthew 10, is where Jesus told us our mission, gave us marching orders, and equipped us for the mission.
- Kingdom Principles, Matthew 13, is where Jesus told several parables to help us understand how God works in kingdom mission and what we can expect from God and the mission.

- Kingdom Community, Matthew 18, is where Jesus told us how to get along with each other and to work out our differences, disappointments, and hurts with each other.
- Using Time for the Kingdom, Matthew 24-25, is where Jesus told us about the end and what we are to be doing between now and when the end comes.

In addition to these five columns, Matthew gave us an introduction and a conclusion. The conclusion is Matthew 28:18-20, called, The Great Commission. The introduction is Matthew 4:12-17, which is Jesus' initial preaching and teaching about the kingdom."

"Okay," said Joe, "I got all that, even though I don't know anything that's in Matthew's columns. But you still haven't answered my question. How are we going to be with Jesus?"

"The way we're with Jesus is being together," Matt responded.

"I don't understand."

"Let's turn in your Bible to Matthew 18:20 where Jesus is speaking. Read out loud what it says," Matt prompted.

"'For where two or three come together in my name, there I am with them.'"

"There are two of us here, we're gathered in his name, and we're going to be learning from his teachings. That means Jesus is here with us right now, tonight, in this coffee shop," Matt said.

"I don't see him," said Joe.

"Before the night is done, you will be aware that Jesus has been here with us. Let's get some more coffee."

When they returned to their table, Matt said, "Joe, let's turn to Matthew 4:12-17 and see what Jesus had to say about the kingdom of heaven. Why don't you read that?"

> When Jesus heard that John had been put in prison, he returned to Galilee. Leaving Nazareth, he went and lived in Capernaum, which was by the lake in the area of Zebulun and Naphtali—to fulfill what was said through the prophet Isaiah:
>
> "Land of Zebulun and land of Naphtali,
>   the way to the sea, along the Jordan,

>   Galilee of the Gentiles—
> the people living in darkness
>   have seen a great light;
> on those living in the land of the shadow of death
>   a light has dawned."
>
> From that time on Jesus began to preach, "Repent, for the kingdom of heaven is near."

"I can't say those names either," Matt said, "Author and theologian, Andrew Greeley, summarizes Jesus' teaching about the kingdom of heaven in five points:

1. Change your life, for the kingdom of heaven is at hand.
2. The day of salvation has dawned.
3. The principle sign of the kingdom and its salvation is God's loving mercy.
4. The kingdom will triumph.
5. Since we have heard about the Good News, we must rejoice.[i]

"Slow down," Joe said. "I can't write that fast, and besides, I have no idea what those five things mean."

"Let's go over them one at a time," Matt responded. "The first one is this: Change your life, for the kingdom of heaven is at hand. That last verse you read records Jesus as saying, "Repent, for the kingdom of heaven is at hand." That word *repent* means *to change direction*. Jesus is telling us there are now new possibilities for life. We can live differently. We can respond differently. The basic structures of our lives can be transformed. Jesus was telling us something was happening that would make the old ways of responding to life obsolete and would make a new response possible. We can take a different road and be different people."

"Change is what I want," said Joe. "But how does this change happen? I write resolutions every January 1, and by the middle of January, I can't even remember what the resolutions were, let alone live differently. There are cycles in my life where I find myself doing the same things over and over. I don't want to do those things, but I can't stop doing them. I've been in some therapy, and I've read the self help books. I agree with my therapist and the books, but I can't stop. I want to believe that change is possible. That's why I'm here. But what does Jesus bring, what does Jesus have that makes him any different, that would make this kind of change possible?"

"What Jesus brings," Matt responded, "is the kingdom of heaven. Jesus comes to announce that God is doing a new thing. Because God is doing a new thing, we can be different. Look at Luke 4:18-19. In Luke's Gospel, these are Jesus' first public words. He was in his home town of Nazareth, in the synagogue, and was asked to read the scripture for that day. He was handed Isaiah's scroll and unrolled it to this passage. Would you read it?"

"The Spirit of the Lord is on me,
because he has anointed me
to preach good news to the poor.
He has sent me to proclaim freedom for the prisoners
and recovery of sight for the blind,
to release the oppressed,
to proclaim the year of the Lord's favor."

"The prophet wrote that passage," Matt continued, "some 400-500 years before Jesus stood before the synagogue, and the people of Israel had been waiting ever since for it to come to pass. Now look closely at what Jesus said when he finished the reading. Every eye in the synagogue was fixed on him. Read verse 21."

"'Today this scripture is fulfilled in your hearing,'" read Joe.

"In Jesus, God is going to give good news to the poor, free the prisoners, release the oppressed, and announce that now is the time to ask for help from God, and it will be granted. God is doing a new thing, and that new thing is called the kingdom of heaven. The kingdom of heaven is God's action to create a new order where there is good news from God for those who are poor, where God himself is releasing those who are in prisons of whatever kind, where it is God who frees the oppressed and the oppressor from their dysfunctional relationship, where God opens blind eyes and shows his favor to any who will receive it. As the kingdom of Heaven comes to our lives, God makes change possible through the power and availability of his kingdom resources."

"So what you're telling me," Joe wanted to know, "is that heaven is not someplace out there somewhere. It's not about if I'm good enough or lucky enough, so when I die I'll get to go there, and everything will be wonderful. You're telling me that all that stuff we hope for in heaven is here, now, available, today, and that it's found in Jesus. Is that what you're saying?"

"Yes," said Matt.

"That's huge," Joe said, "I mean if that's true, it changes everything, doesn't it."

"It does. But I want you to know that Jesus isn't done yet." Matt continued, "Point two of Jesus' teaching about the kingdom of heaven is that *now* is the day of salvation. John the Baptist, who pointed Jesus out as the One, was imprisoned. While in prison, John began to have some second thoughts about who he claimed Jesus was. John sent some of his disciples to ask Jesus, 'Are you the one who was to come, or should we expect someone else?' Jesus responded by quoting that Isaiah passage again saying, 'The blind receive sight, the lame walk, those who have leprosy are cured, the deaf hear, the dead are raised, and the good news is preached to the poor.' You can find that exchange in Matthew 11:1-6. Jesus said the change is now. Now is the day. Now is the time God is acting to do his new thing. Once again, the time is not far away—yesterday or some long hoped for tomorrow. The time is now, today. The place is not halfway around the world, but the place is here.

"Point three of Jesus teaching is the principal sign of the kingdom, the principal sign of God's action in human life on planet earth, is loving mercy. God has not drawn near in anger and judgment to deliver punishment. God has not drawn near to curse us but to bless us. God has drawn near because he loves us, so he can love us and help us. Everywhere Jesus went, he was healing someone, or helping someone, or feeding some crowd, or teaching someone, or confronting someone, all because he loved them. When questioned, Jesus claimed he was just doing what he saw the Father doing. Greeley highlights four of Jesus' parables to make this point. Three of the parables are in Luke 15, and they are: The Prodigal Son, The Lost Sheep, and The Lost Coin. The fourth parable is what Greeley calls The Parable of the Good Employer, found in Matthew 20. In these parables, we humans act in incredibly foolish ways.

"In The Prodigal Son, the father welcomes back the prodigal who has squandered the father's estate and good name on wine, women, and song. The father throws a huge party and welcomes the son back into the family. The only one who doesn't seem to know the son should be thrown out, or at least received back on probation or a greatly reduced role, is the father. What kind of father would throw (waste) the party of a lifetime on that kind of son? Only a crazy father.

"In the Parable of the Lost Sheep, a shepherd, who has one hundred sheep, notices one of them is missing. What does he do? He leaves the ninety-nine and goes looking for the lost one. What kind of shepherd would do such a thing? Only a crazy shepherd. No sane, responsible shepherd would leave ninety-nine sheep unattended, unguarded, or unwatched to search for one run away who might, even as the shepherd begins the search, already have become lunch for some wolf. Then when the shepherd finds the sheep and wants his friends to rejoice with him, I can see them shaking their heads and saying to themselves, 'When will he learn to act responsibly?'

"In the Lost Coin, we have the same dynamic going on. A woman turns her house upside down for one lost coin. She has nine, but she becomes obsessed with finding the lost one. At the end of the day, when she has finally found the coin, she excitedly tells her friends she found her lost quarter. They ask how long she spent looking for it, and when they are told she spent all day, they look at each other wondering if more than a quarter is lost. No sane person spends all day looking for a lost coin.

"In the Parable of the Good Employer, a land owner goes to the town square to hire some day labor to harvest his crops. They agree on a good wage for the day. The laborers go to work. Three more times during the day, including an hour before quitting time, the land owner goes back to the square and hires more workers. He offers to pay them the exact same amount as the laborers who worked all day. Now if that isn't bad enough, the land owner pays off the workers all at the same time, starting with those who have worked the least. When those who worked all day question the land owner about this, the land owner seems shocked. He tells them he paid them what he agreed to pay them, and if he wants to be generous with his money, that is his affair. The labor unions are still upset with this guy. The question comes back, who in their right mind would pay those who only worked an hour the same as the ones who worked all day. Only a crazy man.[ii]

"In these stories and others, Jesus seemed to indicate that not only does God love us, but that perhaps God loves us too much. I can see this played out on an afternoon talk show, 'Next: The God Who Loves Too Much.' God is sitting in the guest chair saying, 'Yes, it's true. I welcomed back the prodigal without any punishment. I forgave the woman caught in adultery without giving her a lecture about her lifestyle. I turned all that water into wine at a wedding reception when the party was nearly over and almost everyone was drunk anyway. I healed everyone who came and asked without checking their theology. I can't help myself. I love too much.'

"As I have thought about God's actions, I wonder if it is we who are crazy. God's love for us is much greater than our love for ourselves. We don't love ourselves, or anyone else for that matter, as much as God loves us, so these actions just seem crazy. We know that we're not worth that kind of effort or worthy of such gifts. It makes us uncomfortable. God's love for us, or God's capacity to love us, is greater than our capacity to be loved, to receive love. But what if it's true? What if God really does love me, love us all, in this way?"

"Whoa!" said Joe. "You're frying my circuits here. You're telling me that in Jesus, God has made the kingdom of heaven available here, now, today, and that the reason God has done this is because he is crazy in love with me, with a love for me that I can't even begin to comprehend?"

"Yes," replied Matt, "that is exactly what I'm trying to say."

"This whole thing is 180 degrees from what I've always thought, felt, and how I viewed the world. I always thought God was way out there somewhere, either unconcerned about us or angry with us, and if God could be reached, it was only with great risk and as a last resort for some dire emergency. Most of the time God's response is about as effective as a Hail Mary pass at the end of a football game. But it's not like that?"

"No, it's not, and there's more," Matt said.

"Let me catch my breath. Okay, I'm ready. Let's do some more."

"Point four of Jesus' teaching about the kingdom and the God who is king is that in the end, this God and his kingdom win, which means everything is going to be alright. In the Parables of The Sower, The Mustard Seed, The Leaven in the Loaf, all found in Matthew 13, and The Patient Farmer, found in Mark 4, the kingdom is presented as winning. As surely as seed grows and produces a crop, or leaven works through a loaf and causes it all to rise, or a small seed grows into a tree for birds to build their nests in, or the farmer, regardless of his activity, sees the seed grow, so the kingdom wins. In the end, the kingdom wins. Greeley says we can no more stop the triumph of God and his kingdom than we can stop the sun from rising.[iii]

"All the stuff I face now from my own flaws and failing, financial reverses, relational crises, cancer, addiction, whatever, is going to be alright. Nothing I do, and nothing anyone does to me, is fatal. In the end, the kingdom wins."

Before Joe could respond, Matt continued on with the final point.

"In light of all this, there is only one response—Rejoice! Jesus told two other parables in Matthew 13. One is the story about a man who finds buried treasure in a field. He sells all he has and buys the field. The other is about a merchant, who finds a pearl of great price, sells all he has, and buys the pearl. Both are ecstatic about their find and their purchase. Neither can believe the bargain, for what each purchased was worth far more than the price either paid.

"Greeley sums it all up this way:

> Again we are forced to note the extreme simplicity of the message of Jesus. An old era is done. God is intervening to begin a new age. It is an era of incredible generosity. One must change one's life in order to benefit from the generosity, but so great is the payoff in accepting the abundance of

the new age that our [change] ought not to be one of sorrow and sacrifice, but of wonder and rejoicing.[iv]

"This is all incredible stuff," Joe said. "And even though my circuits are completely fried, I'm starting to get the picture. After church, when you led me in prayer, what I experienced was a taste, a touch of the kingdom, wasn't it? And if all this that you have been telling me is true, then all kinds of changes are possible for my life. In light of all this you have just told me about the kingdom, 90 percent of what I worry about just went up in smoke. And if all this is true, then very soon my life is going to start to look a whole lot different.

"I can't handle any more tonight. Can we get together again soon and do some more?"

"Sure," said Matt. "If you have the time, let's meet each Sunday night here at seven o'clock."

"Works for me," Joe said. "Is there anything I should do to get ready for next week?"

"I'm glad you asked that," Matt responded, "Based on what we talked about tonight, write a description of the kingdom of heaven. Each day read a Psalm, starting with Psalm 120, and write a short reflection on it. Read Matthew 5:1-11. That passage begins the Sermon on the Mount, where Jesus painted a picture of what life in the kingdom of heaven can look like for us. Also, think about this: Jesus' first words in the Sermon on the Mount, his first words of teaching to his disciples were, 'Blessed are the poor in spirit, for theirs is the kingdom of heaven' (Matthew 5:3). If we don't get these words, nothing else Jesus said will make sense. Let's pray."

Joe and Matt prayed and, each in his own words, thanked God for their time together and the presence of Jesus with them, and asked for a fuller understanding of what God was getting ready to do in their lives. As they said goodbye, Joe knew for sure that he was in over his head. How far over, though, he had no idea.

Suggested resource:
Andrew Greeley, *The Jesus Myth*, Image Books, 1973.

CHAPTER 2

THE BEATITUDES

The next Sunday evening Matt was again surprised to find Joe all fired up and ready to go when he got there.

"So I didn't scare you off last week?" Matt asked.

"No, you didn't. I'm back for more. I spent the week thinking about what we talked about. I'm way behind the curve. I yelled at my daughter last week for scraping the back fender of the car on the side of the garage when she backed out. If you had listened to me, you would have thought it was the end of the world, and before last week, I would have thought it was, but the next day, all this kingdom stuff we talked about last week surfaced again. If it's true my life can be different because God is doing a new thing, bringing the kingdom of heaven to my life with all its resources and possibilities, that God loves me far too much, that in the end the kingdom wins, and I can rejoice because of this activity of God in my life—this kingdom of heaven stuff—is a huge bargain, then what is a scraped fender? I found myself going to my daughter and apologizing for going off on her about something as insignificant as a fender. My daughter looked at me like I was crazy. I guess it must have seemed that way to her. I go off on her all the time, and rarely do I apologize. I think she liked the apology though.

"What I mean about being way behind the curve is this: I asked Jesus to come into my heart last week, and he did. I asked him to help me live differently, and I learned all this kingdom stuff. So how come I still went off on my daughter, and it took me a full day to realize I messed up?"

"It sounds to me," Matt said, "like you've made huge strides. You went from rarely apologizing to your daughter when you get angry at her to being able to apologize a day after the event. That sounds big to me. It may not be where you want to be, but it's a long way from where you were. It's hard to get these teachings of Jesus about the kingdom of heaven off the page and into our heads. It's even harder to get these teachings from our heads to our hearts. The process of getting it from our hearts to our hands is just as difficult. I suffer from time lapses of being in a situation, responding poorly, and then becoming aware of the kingdom response sometime later; but there are times when the kingdom response is the one I act on in the situation, and I'm amazed. In a few weeks, we'll talk about what we can do to shorten the time lapse from situation to kingdom reaction. So did you write a description of the kingdom of heaven?"

"I tried," Joe said, "but it was rough. Here it is: The kingdom of heaven is the place where God does lots of good things for us. Jesus told us the kingdom of heaven is here, now, today. Jesus is where we find the kingdom of heaven here, now, today.

"It's not very polished, but it's the best I can do."

"That's good," Matt said. "Sometimes I describe it this way: The kingdom of heaven engulfs us in the outlandish love of God that loves us regardless of who we are or what we have done, a love that cannot be taken away, a love that brings with it all the resources, possibilities, and opportunities of the kingdom to protect, secure, and heal us in the course of this life. It is a love that fills us and overflows into the lives of those around us.

"I have a friend who describes it this way: Being in the kingdom is being in the zone with God. It's kind of like playing basketball and finding yourself in the right place at the right time to make the right plays, and every shot falls, and you can do no wrong. Being in the zone with God is like that, being able to flow with God and do the right thing at the right time for the right reason with the right people and having all the resources available to pull it off. It's like feeling a nudge from God, acting on it, and seeing God show up and do something incredible and unexpected.

"The kingdom of heaven is hard to describe, but once you experience it, you're hooked. Tell me, did you read the Beatitudes this week in Matthew 5:1-11?"

"Yes," Joe said, "but I can't make head nor tail of them. I'm not really sure what Jesus means by blessed. It's not a word I use. I remember my grandma used to say someone was blessed when something that was both nice and unexpected happened to him. I think she said that when my aunt and uncle found out my aunt was pregnant, and they were in their late forties. Not everyone thought it was a good thing or something they wanted to happen to them, but Grandma said they were blessed.

"So I think being blessed is a good thing, but I'm not at all sure when Jesus said blessed it was a good thing. Poor in spirit, mourning, meekness, and being persecuted don't sound all that good to me. That's like being blessed by having a plate full of lima beans as opposed to having nothing at all. I like what Jesus said these blessed people receive—they will find comfort and mercy, inherit the earth, be satisfied, and the rest. I hope you can help me with these."

"I'll give it a try," said Matt. "*Blessed* is a word we don't use much these days. We talk about having it made or being lucky. Dallas Willard, who did some research on the word and the concept, says that being blessed 'refers to the highest type of well-being possible for human beings, but it is also the term the Greeks used for the kind of blissful existence characteristic of the gods.'[i] So if being blessed is the highest type of well-being possible, who is someone today you think is blessed?"

"Maybe the young professional athletes," said Joe. "They're young, they have millions of dollars, they're successful, and they have their whole careers in front of them. The sky's the limit for people like that. So why didn't Jesus profile guys like that? Blessed are those who have millions of dollars and athletic talent, are young, and can do whatever they want?"

"Let's take a closer look at who Jesus did profile, and then maybe you can tell me," Matt replied. "The first people Jesus called blessed were the 'poor in spirit, for theirs is the kingdom of heaven' (Matthew 5:3). You're right. On the face of it, it doesn't sound very promising, but look a little closer. Those who are poor in spirit know they need help. Those who are poor in spirit know they can't make it on their own. Those who are poor in spirit have tried will power, self-help, money, positive thinking, and all the rest and still can't get it done. Those who are poor in spirit have something in their lives that is broken, and they can't fix it, some barrier they can't overcome, some hurt they can't heal, some dream they can't attain. They just can't make it happen, and they know it."

"It doesn't sound very blessed to me," Joe said.

"Oh, there's one other thing about being poor in spirit," Matt said. "They're poor enough to receive. They have no pride. They're poor enough to ask. They're often desperate. Those who are poor in spirit receive the kingdom of heaven, its King, and all its resources. They call out to God, 'We need your help. We can't make it alone.' They call out to God, 'Please do for us what we can't do for ourselves.' They call out to God because they can't make it, and if God doesn't act, they won't make it.

"Now watch closely. As soon as they call out, the kingdom of heaven becomes theirs. God hears, and God responds with all the resources of God's kingdom. God and all God's resources are more than enough to meet and overcome any situation we might find ourselves in. As long as we think our money, our technology, our science, our medicine, our education, our initiative, our can-do, pull-myself-up-by-the-bootstraps mindset can get us through, we won't call out to God for help. When we don't call out to God for help, he doesn't help us. Jesus didn't say, 'God helps those who help themselves.' Jesus did say here that God helps those who are desperate enough to cry out to him for help.

"One of the reasons for twelve-step recovery groups' success is that they are built on this Beatitude. They recognize that addiction is a problem over which they are powerless. They need help from a power higher than themselves. They ask for help, and help comes."

"I think I'm starting to understand," said Joe. "When you helped me pray the first time, I was desperate. My relational world was a wreck. My wife wanted to take me to marriage counseling because she said she didn't know whether to hurt me, help me, or holler at me. She cycled through hoping I wouldn't come home, leaving me, or dreaming that we could get through this and live happily ever after. My kids avoided me because they said I yelled at them all the time and expected them to be perfect. I haven't spoken to my dad in years. My financial world crashed with the market as my investments went south, and now I have more debt than I can live with. My work world just took a nosedive as the company I work for was bought. They said it was a good thing, but I'm seeing signs that say the shark might be happy, but the outlook for the fish is not so good. All this was causing me to stop at the bar on the way home far too many nights, and you know about my health. It was like the whole world was caving in on me at once. Everything I had ever been taught about how to deal with life failed me. I didn't know what to do or where to turn. I couldn't sleep, and I hated looking at myself in the mirror, so when you invited me to church, I thought however bad church might be, it couldn't make things any worse. When I heard your minister talk about help from God, and when you told me how God had helped you, I knew I couldn't make it myself. I needed God's help.

"When you helped me pray, God was there. God's love, God's mercy, and God's help were there. I still have the problems, but now I have some peace and some hope and support to get through. I'm starting to sleep again, and I can look in the mirror again. It feels like a whole new world is opening up to me. I'm hoping this stuff Jesus talked about is going to make the difference, but until I was poor in spirit, as Jesus said, I got no help from God because I didn't ask. I wouldn't have accepted help from God if he had offered it because I didn't need his help or anyone else's. I could handle it myself. I'm beginning to see that there is no one poorer than the person who thinks he doesn't need any help. Becoming poor in spirit was a painful process, but if being poor in spirit is the condition necessary to receive God and God's help, then being poor in spirit is a good thing to be. It might even be blessed."

"You're starting to get it," Matt responded. "Let me tell you two other things about poor in spirit before we move on to the next one. The first is that once you have become poor in spirit and call out for God's help, you don't have to wait for desperation to call out the next time. There is what I call a poor-in-spirit lifestyle. Each time I face a problem or take on a project, I pray this prayer: God, I have some resources of my own to use to face this challenge, but I'm sure they aren't enough, so here at the beginning, I give them to you and ask you for your help along the way, for I know this will go far better with you than without you. I prayed for God's help as I was coming here tonight.

"The second thing is this: Unless we understand what Jesus said about the poor in spirit, we will be unable to do anything else Jesus asked of us from this point on. His teachings will seem incredibly difficult and his standards far too high. The life Jesus asked us to live is a life that we can only live with God's help. We can't live this life on our own. It's beyond us, but it's not beyond God beacuse these are the values God builds in us as we give more and more of our lives to him and allow his kingdom to reign in our hearts. These values are the values the kingdom of heaven produces in us as it moves into our lives.

"Are you ready for the second Beatitude?" Matt asked. Joe took a sip of his coffee and nodded that he was.

"'Blessed are those who mourn, for they will be comforted'" (Matthew 5:4).

"That's nice for funerals," Joe said, "but it doesn't seem to have anything to offer the rest of us. Personally, that's a Beatitude I don't ever want to need. I hate funerals, and I hate losing people."

"It's about far more than funerals, Joe, but funerals are a good way to help us understand what Jesus was talking about. I remember when Ray, my mentor at work, died. I didn't think I could go on without him. He had taught me so much. He was always there when I had a problem. It seemed no work situation I faced was beyond him. I leaned on him a lot. When he died, I didn't know how I was going to go on. Management had just unrolled a new product initiative that was dumped in my department. They wanted everything accomplished in half the time we normally invested in a project that size. Without Ray there to guide me through it, I didn't know how I was going to make it.

"When we lose someone, we go through a transition from having them with us to living life without them. That is a huge transition to make. That transition is called mourning. Its stages are denial, anger, bargaining, depression, and acceptance. It's not until we accept the loss that we can begin to go forward again. It wasn't until I accepted Ray's death that I was able to figure out how to go on without him. It was hard getting to that point. There were times I didn't think I was going to make it, times when I was overwhelmed by grief, times when I was so angry I couldn't see straight, times when I was so depressed I didn't care if I lived or died or if the project made any progress, times when I couldn't imagine the future without Ray even though he had been gone for months."

"I hear you," said Joe. "I've been there too. It hurts. I know some people who have never recovered from that kind of thing. It's sad. So where's the blessing in this?"

"Loss and transition are a part of life," Matt replied. "People die, jobs change, we move, friends leave us, children grow, and sometimes life requires that we change. Sometimes, in order for us to go forward, we must let go of old patterns of behavior or old stories we have told ourselves and learn new stories and new behaviors. The blessing in all of this is if I can mourn, if I can make the transition, my life can go forward in a new way, a different way. If I can mourn, I can walk into the new future God has for me. Those who mourn grow, change, adapt, and thrive no matter what life throws at them."

"I never thought of it that way," Joe said thoughtfully. "But this mourning business is hard to do."

"Yes, it is," Matt replied. "Because it's so hard, some people don't do it. They get part way through the mourning process and quit. They bail on the mourning process because they don't have the strength to get through it. They fear being swallowed by the emotions of anger and depression. They lack the imagination to see a new tomorrow. Sometimes, they just plain refuse to enter the new world that is waiting for them, choosing to try to live in the memories, and clinging to every shadow that looks the way it used to be. They can't go forward, and they can't go back; so they're stuck in anger, depression, or denial and often become bitter or just lose touch with reality. What does Jesus offer, in the Beatitude, for those who are mourning?"

Joe responded slowly, "Comfort is what Jesus offers, but does that really help? A hand on the shoulder or an encouraging word is nice, but it doesn't seem to do much."

Matt nodded and said, "Those are the things we think of when we think of comfort, but Jesus had more in mind than that. *Comfort* means *with strength*. For those who will do the work of mourning and call out to God for help, Jesus brings the strength, the courage, the fortitude, and the guts to go through the mourning and make the transition to the new day that is waiting. In the dark days following Ray's passing, I remember calling out to God for help. I remember saying, 'I can't make it on my own. I need help. I don't know what to do at work, and I don't have the strength to do it.' I don't know exactly what happened, but a couple of days after praying that prayer things didn't seem so dark. I began to remember some things Ray had told me. I started thinking about things differently. I began to have hope that I would get through, and things would get better. They did. We got the project accomplished, with lots of struggle, but we got it done. Pulling it off without Ray being there was miraculous, but the really incredible thing was the confidence we all gained from getting through the project without Ray. That confidence launched a bunch of us, including myself, into more responsible roles in the company. I just wish Ray had been there to see us do it.

"While I still don't like to mourn, I have the confidence that Jesus will see me through whatever changes I need to make or whatever changes come my way."

"That's good stuff," Joe said. "I had no idea, from just reading the Beatitudes, how much help is there. In fact, the help I could have, just from the first two Beatitudes, would change a whole lot of the way I live and respond to people. What's in the third one, about meekness? 'Blessed are the meek, for they will inherit the earth' (Matthew 5:5). I think the meek probably will get what is left after everyone is done. I'm not anxious to inherit acres of desert sand, so I'd like to hear how you turn milk toast and being walked on into a strong character trait. While you get ready to do that, let me refill your coffee cup and get you a chocolate chip cookie."

When Joe got back with the coffee and cookies, Matt took a sip, broke off a piece of the cookie, and said, "I can't turn milk toast and being walked on into a strong character trait, but what I can do is help with the definition of *meek*. In the days in which Jesus lived, *meek* didn't mean being walked on, being bullied, or hiding in a corner hoping no one would notice you. The definition of the word *meek* Jesus used is *power under control*. If you could have looked in a dictionary in Jesus' day, next to the definition of meek would have been a picture of a Roman war horse."

"As meek as a war horse?" Joe questioned. "You've got to help me with that."

"Remember," Matt continued, "the word *meek* means *power under control*. A war horse is a horse that has been trained and drilled to put all of its power under the rider's control. The war horse puts all its power, athletic ability, and even its emotions under the control of the rider. The war horse trusts in the rider and awaits the rider's instruction, responding to even the smallest of cues. It is this horse's ability to put its power under the rider's control that gets them safely through battle. The rider jumps the horse through fire. The horse is scared to death of fire but jumps because he trusts the rider. On the other side of the fire, the horse is surprised to find safety. If the horse balks or fights with the rider, both will die in the battle."

"I understand the war horse, but what does that have to do with what Jesus said about the meek inheriting the earth?" Joe wanted to know.

"Remember," Matt repeated himself as he watched Joe take a bite of cookie, "meekness is power under control. As we put ourselves—our power, our talent, our money, our emotions, our fears, our hopes and dreams, our hurts and wounds—under the control of Jesus, the way a war horse puts itself under the control of the rider, we will inherit the earth. That is to say, we will make the most of each opportunity, each day, each encounter, and each relationship."

"How?" Joe asked.

"Imagine," Matt continued, "never flying off the handle with anger again, or being able to focus your sexual energy to improve your marriage, or being able to say the right thing at the right time to the right people in the right place, or being able to step through your fear, or being able to use your deepest wound to rescue someone going down for the last time, or being able to control impulse spending, so there is money to do something significant. Meekness is about having your life—your heart, your mind, your emotions, and your perceptions—so controlled by Jesus that you can say or do the right thing, in the right way, at the right time, the majority of the time. Meekness is about putting ourselves under the control of Jesus, so he can control the things in our lives we can't, and so he can fix the things in our lives that are broken, that we can't fix."

"So," Joe said, "if I become meek, put myself under Jesus' control, I'll lose my temper less often, not put my foot in my mouth as much, and have fewer embarrassing moments when I think to myself, 'You idiot. Why did you do that?'"

"That's right," Matt replied, "but there is more to meekness than that. Imagine that as we put ourselves under the control of Jesus, he uses our power, our emotions, our hopes and fears, our talents and ambitions, and our money and resources to bring good news to the poor, to set the captives free, to release the oppressed, and to give sight to the blind; he uses our words and actions to declare that now is the time God has drawn near to make things right. Jesus wants to use us to heal hurts, repair relationships, free addicts, give a future and a hope, change systems that enslave, and offer a connection to the Living God. Jesus will use us to expand his kingdom.

"Now if I put my resources under Jesus' control, and if he uses me to do things like this, my life, my influence, and my place in this world will grow. I will not squander my life, but rather, I will become established and create blessing that will extend through generations."

"Whoa, slow down, Matt," Joe said. "If you aren't careful, you're going to start preaching. So let me see if I have this. If I put my life under the control of Jesus the way a warhorse puts his life under the control of a soldier, there is this grand adventure waiting to happen where Jesus wants to use me to make a huge difference in people's lives?"

"That's right."

"I thought this Jesus stuff was just a way to get my life straightened out and maybe get me a place in heaven. I had no idea he would want to actually use me to help someone else. He might want to use me to help someone the way you have been helping me. I mean, can he use someone like me?"

"That's the whole point, Joe," Matt replied. "Jesus puts us back together, so he can use us to go back out into the hells from which we came and rescue our friends. As we do that, Jesus furthers his work in our lives and establishes us."

"I had no idea," Joe said.

Matt paused for a moment to take a bite of his chocolate chip cookie. "Are you ready for the next one?" he asked.

Joe replied, "I'm still taking that one in. That meekness thing can change the direction of my life. I need to think on that for awhile, but go ahead. It says here the next one is, 'Blessed are those who hunger and thirst for righteousness, for they will be filled' (Matthew 5:6). I've been so far off on what I thought the first three Beatitudes were about, I'm not even going to take a shot at this one, so tell me, what was Jesus saying here?"

"Jesus was talking about righteousness," Matt began. "We often think of righteousness as good things we do. Particularly, we think of righteousness as good religious things we do in an attempt to gain God's favor. Often, we think of a checklist having to do with praying and reading the Bible, going to church, helping the poor, and feeding the hungry; but that is not what Jesus meant by righteousness. Jesus was not talking about a religious checklist. In verse 20, Jesus told us our righteousness must exceed the righteousness of the Pharisees and teachers of the law. Those people were masters of the religious checklist. I can't imagine people hungering and thirsting for a religious check list.

"I'll tell you what I hunger and thirst for: I hunger and thirst to be right with God—I want to be able to be with God without apology, to feel loved and welcomed by God, to feel that all is right between us, to have God glad to see me, and I want to be glad to see God. I want to be right with myself—I want to be able to look in the mirror without shame and guilt, to feel good about what I have done and what I'm thinking, to feel good, solid and strong, deep in my heart. I want to be right with the people around me—I want to be in good relationships with them. I don't want things between us like misunderstandings, offenses, and hurts that can cause relationships to break down. I want to have relationships where we love and forgive each other and allow each other room to grow. When all my relationships are right, and I'm in good standing with everyone, it doesn't get any better than that. Psalm 133:1 says, 'How good and pleasant it is when brothers live together in unity!'"

"I can't remember the last time I felt like that," Joe said. "I'm always fighting with someone or in someone's dog house. I'm always working hard to try to make up for something I said or did. I hate being in that position. There is just something about being at odds with someone that eats away at my soul. The more people I'm at odds with, the tougher it is to get through the day. It feels like I'm carrying a big weight on my shoulders. I hate it when I unexpectedly bump into someone I'm at odds with. It's so awkward because we both know what's wrong, we haven't done anything to fix it, and we aren't about to do anything anytime soon. I want to be nice, but often I say or do something that makes things worse, and we both leave the encounter not wanting to ever see each other again. I don't like spending my days trying to avoid people because things aren't right. When it's my wife I'm at odds with, and that's the case more often than I care to admit, it's just devastating. Here's this woman I love, who I'm making my life with, and half the time I think she's a jerk, and the other half the time I think I'm the jerk. Most of the time, I have no clue how to make the marriage, or any of this, any better. I just live for those days when two or three of my most significant relationships happen to be right. I love it when it happens, but I have no idea how to get it to happen more often. It's like when I'm on the golf course, and I hit a really good shot—I have no idea how it happened or how to repeat it. I just enjoy the moment and hope the next swing doesn't slice into the next fairway. So if Jesus was talking about relationships here, I agree with him. There would be nothing that would satisfy my soul more, feel sweeter, or cause me to love life more than to have all my relationships line up at the same time. That would be better than winning a $213 million lottery jackpot. I often feel I have more of a chance of hitting the lottery big than I do of getting my relationships in order. If it's possible for relationships to be in order, how does it happen?"

"Yes, it's possible, and you're right—nothing satisfies like having all our relationships line up. Jesus helps us with how to do it later on," Matt replied, "but his point here is, in his kingdom, relationships that are in order are valued. Further, he wants us to know that when we hunger and thirst, when we long for those relationships to be right—like a man without a canteen coming out of the desert longs for water—when we're desperate for our relationships to be right, there is hope. But I will let you know now this is not something we can pull off on our own."

Hungry and thirsty, both Matt and Joe ate some more of their chocolate chip cookies and drank some more of their coffee, seemingly unaware that their actions were related to what they were talking about.

Returning to the Beatitudes, Matt read the next one, "'Blessed are the merciful, for they will be shown mercy'" (Matthew 5:7).

"I like mercy," Joe said. "So tell me about this one."

"The merciful," Matt replied, "are those who forgo judgment and punishment of those in the wrong and offer forgiveness and pardon instead. The merciful are able to offer forgiveness and pardon because they are not looking to make the other party pay for the wrong that was done. The merciful are able to trust God to make provision for the payment for the wrong. The merciful offer mercy with the hope of helping to change the heart of the one in the wrong. Then there can be reconciliation and rightness all around. The merciful are able to offer mercy because this is precisely the treatment they have received from God in the kingdom of heaven."

"Let's slow down just a little and see if I get this," Joe said. "The merciful aren't interested in justice?"

"That's not so," Matt responded. "The merciful are interested in justice. They want things to be made right as much as the next person. It's just that the merciful know that the party in the wrong *can't* pay the price to make things right. It's like when an employee shows up with the owner to make a presentation to a prospective client and hasn't prepared for his part of the presentation. This causes the presentation to flop and the client to take his business elsewhere. The owner would certainly like the employee to pay for the lost account and the damage done to the reputation of the small business as well as extract a piece of the employee's hide for the sheer stress the owner went through watching the presentation go south, but the owner is one of these merciful types. He knows the employee can't pay the price of the amount of business that was lost that day. He also knows the employee can't restore the reputation of the small business or even make up the owner's stress. However, this merciful owner lives in the kingdom, and he knows that somehow, someway, God will make this right. So rather than blowing up in anger at the employee, docking his pay, or firing him on the spot, the owner trusts God to work out the damages, which frees the owner to focus on developing his employee. The owner is able to focus the energy of his anger on this question: What can I do to help this employee to be prepared the next time? Because the merciful owner can forgive and offer pardon, his focus can go from, How can I make this person pay? to, How can I help this person behave differently?"

"Wow! How is the owner able to do that?" Joe asked.

Matt replied, "The owner's ability to be merciful comes from the owner having received mercy from God in the kingdom of heaven. Apart from having received mercy and having experienced this dynamic in his relationship with God, the owner would be unable to be merciful."

"Won't this merciful owner be taken advantage of by his employee?" Joe wondered.

"No," Matt said. "The owner's focus is to make changes so that this kind of thing doesn't happen again. If the owner just offered forgiveness and pardon and stopped there, without working for a change in the employee's behavior, then he might be taken advantage of again and again. But because the owner is focusing on changing the behavior, both the employee's and his own behavior if necessary, he won't be taken advantage of."

"That's really a much better way to deal with things than the way I handle them," Joe said. "If I had been that owner, I would have blasted that employee for his incompetence, and then I would have fired him. However, even as I say that, it occurs to me there could have been all kinds of reasons why the employee was unprepared, and with a little help, he could become very valuable to the owner. Very interesting..."

Matt picked up the conversation again by beginning with the next Beatitude, "'Blessed are the pure in heart, for they will see God'" (Matthew 5:8).

"I'd like to see God," Joe said, "or at least I think I would. How does being pure in heart help us to see God? Does that mean if we're good all the time we can see God?"

"Being pure in heart is not about being good," Matt replied. "Being pure in heart is about integrity. It's like the soap commercial from years ago. The bar of soap was 99 percent pure. That meant it was soap all the way through. No matter where you cut into the bar of soap, or how deep you dug into the bar of soap, it was soap all the way. It was pure. It had integrity. A banana is 100 percent pure. Under the skin of that banana, you have a banana, 100 percent. It doesn't matter which end you open it from, it doesn't matter whether you open it in the city or the country, at home or at the mall, with friends or by yourself, the banana is 100 percent banana. It's pure. It has integrity. Being pure in heart is having integrity. Are we the same on the outside as on the inside? Are we different at work from who we are at home? Do we respond differently with different people? Are we able to live out our values when people are watching and when we are alone? Are we the same in our unguarded moments as when we are on stage? Are we able to keep our promises and do what we say we will do? In Psalm 27:4, David showed us a pure heart: 'One thing I ask of the Lord, this is what I seek: that I may dwell in the house of the Lord all the days of my life, to gaze upon the beauty of the Lord and to seek him in his temple.' David desired only one thing. David desired to be with God. David didn't want fame and fortune. David didn't want acceptance and affirmation. David just wanted God. One thing. One thing only. David desired God on the battlefield and at home. David desired God when he was with his friends and with his family. David was able to shape everything in his life to desire God, and that which didn't, he left behind. David lived this desire. Integrity, purity, and singleness of intent and purpose all add up to being pure in heart. As David desired and sought God with all of his being, he found God. Those who seek God see God."

"If being pure in heart is desiring one thing and having integrity inside and out all the time, I have a long way to go. I'm often messed up on the inside. I mean there are so many directions I want to go at the same time, all driven by competing desires. I want to be a good husband, and I want to be a good father, and I want to be a good employee, and I want to have a new muscle car, and sometimes I want this woman at work. It's hard to get my heart desires to line up and to want one thing, but it's hard having so many desires too. They are always fighting with each other. To be a good employee and a good father often come in conflict with each other. Being a good husband is in direct conflict with the feelings I sometimes have about this woman at work. When I'm putting in that extra time on the job to get the promotion, to get the raise, to get the stuff we all want to have as a family, I feel like I'm slipping in the father area, and my children are growing up without me. If I spend the time with the children, then I don't have the money to buy them the things they want. Most of the time the desires of my heart have little to do with God, and I'm not even sure how he enters into all this. Maybe that's why I feel like God is distant most of the time. My heart is a long way from pure."

"The blessing that comes with being pure in heart is peace," Matt said. "All the warring that goes on in our hearts is silenced as we have the clarity and strength to say no and silence some desires and have the ability to bend other desires to our primary purpose. Being pure in heart is having that primary purpose nailed down like David and bending everything else to it. The trouble is, as you described, there are so many primary purposes to choose from. In the kingdom Jesus brings, he was telling us, if we will make God the primary purpose of our lives, 100 percent, the rest will line up, and we will see God. There is something about seeing God, about being near God, that makes the rest of these things come into line. When, like David, we want God more than anything else, we feel the blessing of this Beatitude."

Joe leaned back, took another sip of coffee, and stared across the room at something that wasn't there. In a while he said, "I'm a long way from this kingdom Jesus is talking about. I'm a long way from the values and the blessing he upholds. Is it possible for a guy like me to actually experience all this?"

"Yes," Matt replied, "it is. That's why Jesus came to tell us about the kingdom. He's not dangling something out there that's beyond us or rather beyond our ability to receive. I'll talk some more about this in a few minutes. Are you up for the next Beatitude?"

"That depends, "Joe responded, "on whether I'm going to feel better or worse after you take me through it."

"I think you'll feel better," Matt said.

"Then let's go for it," Joe said.

"Okay," Matt replied. "'Blessed are the peacemakers, for they will be called sons of God' (Matthew 5:9). Let me begin by saying that peace is not the absence of conflict. Peace doesn't occur in my house when I send my two fighting children to their rooms. There is no yelling and screaming, no rolling on the floor, no punches being thrown, no furniture broken, and no holes put in the walls. It's quiet. However, each child in his own room is still at war with the child in the other room. Peace won't occur until there is a change in the heart of each child. It's the same thing with any conflict. There won't be any peace until there is a change of heart. That's true with friends, marriages, companies, communities, and countries. What do you suppose the change agent is that causes people to move from conflict, seeking the destruction of each other, to peace, seeking the best for each other?"

"Let me take a wild guess—the kingdom of heaven that Jesus came to bring," Joe said.

"That's absolutely correct," Matt continued. "It is the kingdom of heaven that puts in people's hearts the desire to forgive, to work out conflict, to live in harmony with another, and to seek the other's highest good. It is the kingdom of heaven that provides the resources and the strength to live out those desires."

"So to be a peacemaker is to be a kingdom bringer?" Joe asked.

"I think you've got it," Matt responded. "Peacemakers, kingdom bringers, are called 'sons of God.' In the days in which Jesus was teaching, a son imitated his father, so to be called 'sons of God' means we're about the same business, the same goals, and the same activities as God. God's business is bringing the kingdom of heaven to us. When the kingdom comes near, we experience help from God. All the resources of heaven are made available to us through God's great love and mercy for us. As you remember, the principle sign of the kingdom is God's totally out-of-proportion love for us. He loves us far more than we think we're worth. The kingdom wins in the end, regardless of what we do, so we can relax. Our response to this incredible kingdom is to rejoice, for it has what our hearts long for, and God is giving it away. As we experience the kingdom, we discover incredible resources for life change, and we begin to change because many of the ways we were living just don't make sense anymore if this message about the kingdom is true. As we speak and act in ways that bring the kingdom of heaven to the people and the world around us, we're acting like 'sons of God.'"

"Then you should feel very much like a 'son of God,' Matt," Joe said, "because the last few weeks you have been very helpful in bringing the kingdom to me and helping me enter it. I know I have a long way to go, but with you as my guide, I look forward to getting further into the kingdom and getting a whole lot more of the kingdom in me."

This time it was Matt who stared off in reflection at a ceiling tile several feet away. Finally he said, "I hope so."

Joe said, "Let's tackle the last one. It bothers me. 'Blessed are those who are persecuted because of righteousness, for theirs is the kingdom of heaven' (Matthew 5:10). Then right after that, Jesus said something about being blessed when we're abused because of him. What's that about? I'm not sure I need any persecution."

"Believe it or not, this Beatitude is one of high honor," Matt replied.

"How in the world is losing your job, or being thrown in jail, or being eaten by lions because you follow Jesus a high honor?" Joe wanted to know.

"It's a high honor for two reasons. One, you took a hit for the kingdom. Who is honored on Memorial Day? It's the veterans, but some veterans are honored more than others. It's not the veteran who served his time in a supply office far from combat who suffered no pain, who took no hits, who gave nothing to advance the cause who is highly honored. It's the veterans who gave their lives, the ones who took the ultimate hit for the cause, who are honored most. Taking a hit for the kingdom means you value it over your comfort, your reputation, your career, your financial well being, your health, and your life. In America, we read this Beatitude and give thanks we aren't taking hits for the kingdom and feel bad for those around the world who are. Further, we hope we never have to take any hits for the kingdom. When kingdom honors are passed out, we won't make the list.

"The second reason taking a hit for the kingdom is a high honor is that it means we're living kingdom values and doing kingdom work. If we live out these kingdom values—if we're poor in spirit, mourning, meek, hungering and thirsting for righteousness, pure in heart, merciful, and peacemaking—we're going to tick some people off. People who are full of themselves don't like people who are full of God, and those who are out of control aren't happy with those who have control, and those who hunger and thirst for that which is not righteousness and who have impure hearts will be angry and feel threatened by those with pure hearts who hunger and thirst for righteousness. Those who are gaining much from the current injustices and conflicts in families, communities, and the world will do all they can to crush the peacemakers. When we begin taking hits for the kingdom, it's a sign that we're beginning to fully live these kingdom values. If we're taking no hits for the kingdom, then we have to ask how much of these kingdom values are being lived, how much kingdom work is being done, and how much kingdom advancement is occurring.

"Jesus told us when we take a hit for the kingdom, the kingdom of heaven is ours. All the resources of the kingdom help us absorb the hit and get us back up to keep going. The promise of the kingdom to those who are taking hits takes us back to the first Beatitude, 'Blessed are the poor in spirit.' I know I don't have the strength to stand up to a solid hit, but if I call out for help, the kingdom and all its resources are there to help me."

"So the payoff for living out these Beatitudes is that I will be persecuted? I'm not sure that's a good deal," Joe said.

"Maybe not," Matt replied, "but I've taken grief for nearly everything I've done. When my wife was pregnant with our fourth child, I shared that news with the guys I play basketball with, and one of them verbally attacked me for being irresponsible, for contributing to overpopulation, worldwide starvation, and adding an additional drain on the already stretched and limited resources of the world. He and his wife had two children, a boy and a girl. The children were given birth to replace the parents when they were gone. Replacement was enough and any more was irresponsible. He was really angry with me. Even though this guy and others who believe like him oppose my action, I wouldn't trade my fourth child to make them happy. We live in a world of conflicting values. If I try to live my life to avoid persecution, I will be miserable and not have anything of worth or value in my life. Now, if these values of Jesus take up residence in my life, and the kingdom of heaven becomes mine, and I receive strength when I mourn, the ability to inherit the earth, soul satisfaction, mercy, the ability to see God and be claimed as one of God's sons, I have gained much. Would I be willing to give up that gain so that some people who disagree with me would be happy? I don't think so."

"When you say it that way, it makes sense," Joe said. "I do want these things even if it means I will be persecuted, so how do I get this stuff in my life?"

"Let me tell you first how you don't get them," Matt said. "You don't get them by trying harder. You can't try harder to be poor in spirit and become poor in spirit. You can't try harder to be meek and become meek."

"If trying harder doesn't make this happen, then what does?" Joe asked.

"These values are created in your life by the presence of the kingdom of heaven," Matt answered. "The more kingdom there is in your life, the more the values of the kingdom will be present in your life. These values are created in your life by the presence of the kingdom of heaven."

"So how do I get more of the kingdom of heaven in my life, so these values will be more present?" Joe wanted to know.

"The first Beatitude is the key to the whole thing," Matt replied. "Being poor in spirit is what gets you in the door and what grows you in the kingdom and grows the kingdom in you. Do you remember poor in spirit?"

"Sure," Joe said. "Poor in spirit is knowing I need help and asking for it. Does that mean the way to get these values in my life is to pray, 'Jesus, I don't have these values in my life. I would like them to be more present. I need more of your kingdom in my life. I can't do it myself. Would you please give me more of your kingdom and cause it take up residence more completely in my life?'"

"I think you've got it," Matt said. "That's enough for tonight. What do you say we go home?"

"Only if we come back next week and do some more," Joe responded.

Matt and Joe picked up their coffee cups and napkins, put them in the trash, and walked out the door. As they left, Joe wondered what kind of changes these values would bring in his life if he actually asked for more of the kingdom in his heart. On his way home in his car, he asked for just that. Little did Joe know where that prayer would lead.

CHAPTER 3

SALT & LIGHT

"Matt!" Joe yelled across the parking lot. "Hey, Matt! Over here! You won't believe what happened this week!"

"Let's go inside, and you can tell me all about it," Matt said.

Once they were seated, with cups of steaming hot coffee firmly in hand, Matt said, "Okay, what unbelievable thing happened this week?"

Joe said, "I actually talked with my wife about money!"

"Why is that unbelievable?" Matt asked.

"We don't talk about money," Joe said. "We fight about money."

"So what happened this time?" Matt asked.

"The credit card bill came last week. As usual, it was way too high. In addition, I hadn't had a good day at work. The boss chewed me out pretty good. Needless to say, I wasn't in the best of moods when I opened the bill. So I went off about how Sue spends money like it's water coming out of the tap. Then, Sue started yelling back at me about how little time I spend with her, how little I talk with her, how I don't understand her, and how I have no idea what it costs to run a household. I was about to blast back with, 'You don't know how hard I work to earn this money, and why can't you stick to a budget,' but I didn't."

"Why not?" Matt asked.

"Something stopped me," Joe said. "I think it was God. In that moment, I didn't blast back at Sue. It was like the fight flashed before my eyes, this fight and all the other ones we've had about money.

I saw that they were all the same. We each yell about how neither understands the other, we hurt each other, we go to opposite ends of the house to nurse our wounds, and we never deal with the problem. I was struck by the utter futility of what we were about to do, and at the same time, my inability to do anything different. Then I remembered the first Beatitude we were talking about, where Jesus said, 'Blessed are the poor in spirit, for theirs is the kingdom of heaven.' So I said a quick poor-in-spirit prayer, which was basically, 'I don't want to do this again, and I don't know how to do anything different. Help me do something different.'"

"What happened next? Were you able to do something different?" Matt asked.

"Amazingly enough, I did do something different. I asked a question. The question was: What is the connection between how much time I spend with you and how much money is on the credit card? I have no idea where that question came from. To me, those are two different issues. Yet, every time we fight about money, the amount of time I spend with Sue comes up. Well, I guess I do know where the question came from. God sent me that question out of his kingdom resources. Even though the question didn't make any sense to me, I asked it because it was better than yelling at Sue for the next half hour. Then I did something even more amazing than ask the question."

"Something more amazing than asking that question? What could that possibly be?" Matt asked.

"I listened," Joe said. "I actually listened to what she had to say. I listened like I might learn something. I listened like I wanted to know what she had to say, not so that I could shout something back at her. And in my listening, I learned a lot. I learned that at our house there is a one-to-one correlation between how much time I spend with Sue and how much is on the credit card bill. Sue pulled out the last six month's credit card bills and her calendar. Four of the bills were too high, two of the bills were about where they needed to be, and one of those two was even a little under. I wanted to yell at her all over again for those four months that were too high, but from somewhere, I received the grace to keep my mouth shut and listen.

"Then she pulled out her calendar. She showed me I wasn't home two of the months the credit card bill was high. During those two months, she showed me I was working six and seven days a week, twelve to fourteen hours a day. I told her the company put the heat on to finish up a project early, and everyone was working like that. I started to tell her how important those hours were to my job, to our lives. She stopped me, and to my surprise, I let her stop me. She said, 'I'm not blaming you or scolding you about those hours. I'm just telling you what happened.' Then she showed me the third month, the month after I had worked all those hours. I spent the extra hours I had been working either on the computer, watching baseball, or golfing with the guys. I started to tell her it took me a month to recover from that big push for the job. The way I recover is time with the guys, sports, and the computer. She told me I didn't need to be defensive, she was just telling me about the hours. The fourth month Sue showed me I had spent a lot of time with her. We went on walks, we had some long talks, and I was home for supper with the family. I even took her on a trip in the country and out to dinner at an old inn. Then Sue showed me the fifth month. Her calendar recorded that I was out again most of the month. This time she said I was spending most of my time putting together a fund-raiser for the kids' soccer league. I started to tell her how important that was, but she put up her hand. I said her sentence for her, 'I'm not blaming you or yelling at you, I'm just telling you what happened.' The last month Sue showed me I was around again, hanging out at the house, playing with the kids. She showed me I had taken her to a couple of movies, we went out for dinner a few times, and I went to one of the concerts in the city park with her.

"I'm pretty dense because I still didn't know where she was going with this. Then she put the credit card bills next to the calendar and asked me what I saw."

"What did you see?" Matt asked with a smile.

"You know what I saw," Joe said. "The four months with the high credit card bills were the four months I didn't spend any time with Sue. When I saw that, my temperature started to rise again. I wanted to yell at her to stop punishing me for living my life. But again, something stopped me. Rather, I asked, 'What are you trying to tell me?' With tears in her eyes, Sue said, 'Joe I need you. I can't do my life by myself. I can't run the kids around, manage the household, and work part time without you. I need to have you around. I need to know you care about me. I need to hear your voice. I need to feel we're in this thing together. When you aren't around, I feel unloved and lonely, and I get depressed. When I'm feeling low, I shop. I can't help it. I buy a dress, jewelry, or something for the house. During the shopping and the purchase, I feel special and wonderful, but when I get home, I feel low again. Then I get angry with myself for blowing the budget. It's a cycle that I don't like. I don't like the fighting we do over the money either. I'm just saying, Joe, I need more from you than you're giving to me. I don't know what to do about it except to tell you.'"

"Wow," Matt said. "She said all that? So what did you say?"

"I was completely blindsided. I had no idea, no idea at all she felt that way. I didn't know my absence had that kind of effect on her. I thought that earning a living, paying the bills, and keeping food on the table was what being a husband was about. All I could say to her was, 'I didn't know.' Then I just held her for a long time. The exchange wiped out both of us. I kept waiting for something profound to say to come to my mind but nothing did. We both agreed we need to talk some more about this. Neither of us know what we should do next, but we both agreed we need to do something. That is how we left it.

"Sue is fine with me being here tonight though. She said something good is going on for all of us as a result of what you and I are doing here over coffee. I guess she's right. If we hadn't talked about the Beatitudes last week, I wouldn't have prayed for more of the kingdom to come into my life. If I hadn't prayed for more of these values of Jesus to be active in my life, then I wouldn't have asked that question, and I certainly wouldn't have listened to her answer. So what do we have cooking tonight?"

"We've got more of the same coming tonight," Matt said.

"Well then," Joe said, "bring it on."

"Let's reflect a little about these Beatitudes that Jesus gave us. What do we learn about God from them?" Matt asked.

"I don't know, let me think a minute." Joe took a sip of his coffee. "I guess one thing is that God thinks a lot differently than we do. These Beatitudes sure don't reflect what having it made looks like here in America."

"That's certainly so," Matt replied. "What else do we learn about God from these Beatitudes?"

"Well, let me look at them (Matthew 5:3-10):

> "Blessed are the poor in spirit,
>   for theirs is the kingdom of heaven.
> Blessed are those who mourn,
>   for they will be comforted.
> Blessed are the meek,
>   for they will inherit the earth.
> Blessed are those who hunger and thirst for righteousness,
>   for they will be filled.
> Blessed are the merciful,
>   for they will be shown mercy.
> Blessed are the pure in heart,
>   for they will see God.
> Blessed are the peacemakers,
>   for they will be called sons of God.
> Blessed are those who are persecuted because of righteousness,
>   for theirs is the kingdom of heaven.

"It looks like God likes to give. He is giving away the kingdom of heaven, comfort, the earth, satisfaction, and mercy. It looks like God wants us to be satisfied. It appears God wants to share his work with us and involve us in what he's doing. God wants to extend mercy. God is honored when we take a hit for him. I guess I'd say from the Beatitudes we learn God is a loving God. He is looking to give away his kingdom along with the stuff we long for in our hearts. He would like us to be his partners in his work, in this incredible universe he has made. Also, it seems like God would rather extend mercy than judgment. I'd say this is the type of God I'd like to know better."

"Okay, good," Matt responded. "What do we learn about the kingdom of God from the Beatitudes?"

"I suppose," Joe replied, "the kingdom would be wherever these values are lived out. That would be a wonderful place, wouldn't it? I think it would be great to live with people who have the resources of God functioning in their lives, who know that without God they are nothing, and who know that with God they have all they need. These people wouldn't fear or fight change. Rather, they would thrive in the midst of it. They would, more often than not, say and do the right things. They would care far more about people than things, and they would have integrity. They would extend mercy, work for the expansion of the kingdom, and go the limit for God. It would be a wonderful place to be. So when can I move?"

"You're in the process," Matt replied. "Now what do these Beatitudes tell us about humans?"

"Ouch! That one hurts," Joe said. "It seems that humans want very much the second phrase of each Beatitude. We work very hard to get the things God is giving away. The second thing I see is that the first phrase of each Beatitude is very far from us. These things just aren't what we're concerned about. These values don't reflect how we act, nor would we consider them the gateway to the very things we desire. In some cases, we actually fight against these values; but I also see hope for us because the things we long for do exist, and while they may seem beyond our grasp, they can be received."

"You're doing well," Matt said. "Maybe someday you could become a theologian. Next question: What do we learn about the relationship between God and humans from the Beatitudes?"

"Is this a test? All these questions," Joe whined.

"No," Matt replied, "It's just some reflection to allow the implications of the content to sink in. We want to do more than just know the material. We also want to know how to use it and apply it."

"Okay, the relationship between God and humans, as I see it, from the Beatitudes," Joe said, "is that God wants to give us what our hearts long for, and we want what God has to offer, but we can't see this. We can't see that God has what satisfies our hearts. And even if we could, we wouldn't think the way God says to receive what our hearts long for is actually the way to get it in our lives. So I guess that means we're messed up."

"It sounds that way, doesn't it?" Matt responded. "You mentioned it looks like God is standing on the street corner saying he has the desires of our hearts, and he is telling us how to get them. We all walk by God saying, 'No, the desires of my heart are over there. I need to hurry because I have to work hard for them, and someone else might get them before I do.' At the end of the long day, God is still standing on the street corner trying to give us the desires of our hearts. We walk home past God saying, 'I didn't get my desires today, but just wait until tomorrow.' Maybe God pursues us, but we send God away saying, 'You wouldn't understand what I'm looking for, and even if you did, you couldn't possibly have it or know how to get it.' I guess you're right. It's messed up.

"Here's another question: What would your life look like if the Beatitudes were firmly anchored in your heart and controlled your actions, words, and attitudes?"

"If the Beatitudes were firmly anchored in my heart, controlled my actions, words, and attitudes, what would my life look like? It would look a whole lot different," Joe said. "Not just different but better. Just take my marriage, for instance. I would have known what to say to Sue after she told me how she felt, and I would have known what the next move was. Well, more than that, we wouldn't have been in the situation to start with.

"If I were living out the Beatitudes, I wouldn't worry because I would have confidence that as I ask God for help, he would come through for me. I would face life with confidence that God is in my corner, knowing the two of us can tackle whatever comes along. I would be learning and growing from change, and be able to leave the past behind. I would be able to do and say the right thing, at the right time, in the right way, and with the right people. My relational world would be in far better shape than it is now. I would draw joy, satisfaction, and support from my relationships with other people and with God. I would develop more integrity, and I would see God at work in the world around me more and more. When things go wrong, I would be able to offer pardon and forgiveness rather than blasting, blaming, and shaming, like I often do now. I would be a full and active partner with God in helping to spread his kingdom, and thereby, create peace. I would be so focused on God and what he thinks and desires of me I would be willing to take a hit for him without caring about what others think of me.

"If all the Beatitudes were firmly anchored in my heart and controlled my life, my life would be a lot different and a lot better. Just for the record, I'm a long way from being there, but I would certainly like to get there."

"Your description reminds me a lot of a couple of E. Stanley Jones quotes," Matt said. "Stanley was a United Methodist missionary to India a generation ago. At eighty-seven years of age, after living in the kingdom for most of his life, he wrote, 'There is more joy to the square inch in being a Christian than there is to the square mile outside.'[i] Somewhere else, he wrote, 'I never woke up in the morning and said to myself, "Stanley, you were a Christian last night. Why did you do it?"'"

"I like those quotes," Joe said, "so since I'm such a long way from there, how do I get there?"

Hey," Matt said, "that was my next question."

"I asked it first," Joe replied.

"Okay, first let me tell you what doesn't work," Matt said. "These values do not become firmly anchored in our hearts and control our lives through human effort. Trying hard to be pure in spirit just doesn't make it happen. Lots can be accomplished by human effort, but it's just not how kingdom values from Jesus take root in our lives.

"The place to begin is where you started last week. You asked God to put them into place in your life. The first place to start with anything Jesus has for us is the first Beatitude. We can't pull it off by ourselves. We need God's help, and we need to ask for that help.

"The second thing to do is develop your relationship with God. We will talk a lot more about that in the coming weeks, but let me share just a couple of things now. Daily prayer and Bible reading time are a must. Worship is mandatory. Obedience, actually doing the things we learn or hear from God, is vital. Participation in a small group provides the help and the encouragement to do what we need to do to develop our relationship with God.

"The third thing to do to get the Beatitudes firmly anchored in our hearts and controlling our lives is to keep them in front of us. Post the Beatitudes somewhere in your office where you see them often. Put them on the bathroom mirror or the refrigerator or in the garage where your tools are. Our attention and thought life often follow what we see, so we need to see the Beatitudes.

"A fourth thing to do may be to keep a Beatitude log. Get a spiral notebook or journal, and at the end of the day, ask yourself how your actions during day align with the Beatitudes. Write down the things that did line up with the Beatitudes, and celebrate with God. Then ask yourself where your actions were not in alignment with the Beatitudes, and write those things down too. Don't beat yourself up about the shortcomings though. Just ask God to continue his work to anchor these values in your heart.

"These four things will get you started, and like I said, there is more to come on these lines."

"It looks like I need to make some changes if I want to get the Beatitudes firmly anchored in my heart. I need to get a daily time to spend alone with God and read the Bible. I pray here and there, and I read the Bible in worship and here with you, but I'm not very intentional or systematic with either, so I think I'll try to carve out thirty minutes a day to spend with God, alone. I'll get those Beatitudes posted at my office and in my garage. I'll try the log. I've never been very good at that kind of thing, but I'll give it a shot."

"Joe, are you ready to move on?" Matt asked.

"Sure, what's next?" Joe responded.

"Let's look at the next words of Jesus," Matt replied. "They're found in Matthew 5:13-16 where Jesus says:

> "You are the salt of the earth. But if the salt loses its saltiness, how can it be made salty again? It is no longer good for anything, except to be thrown out and trampled by men.
>
> "You are the light of the world. A city on a hill cannot be hidden. Neither do people light a lamp and put it under a bowl. Instead they put it on its stand, and it gives light to

everyone in the house. In the same way, let your light shine before men, that they may see your good deeds and praise your Father in heaven.

"If we're the salt of the earth, what is Jesus trying to tell us? What does salt do?"

"Salt adds flavor to food. It makes us thirsty. It preserves," Joe said.

"It does all that," Matt replied. "Plus, we use it to melt ice. So what is Jesus trying to tell us about the kingdom in our lives?"

"I'm not sure, but I think if we're salt, we're to make people thirsty for God. Maybe we add flavor to life. Maybe we help preserve life, and we melt cold hearts," Joe said.

"Yes," Matt responded. "As the values of the kingdom play out in our lives, all that happens. Your description of what you thought your life would be like if the Beatitudes were firmly anchored in your heart is a life that makes people thirsty for what you have. It would be a life that would help hold things together because the values found in the Beatitudes keep everything from unraveling. For instance, it is the poor in spirit, who keep asking for help, who get the help they need. This keeps things together for those who think they can handle life on their own. It would be a life that makes things go better for others. The kindness and goodness found in a Beatitude-anchored life melts hearts that are hard toward God and others."

"What about the light part? What does light do?"

"Light does two things," said Joe. "It helps us see. You can't see in the dark. Also, light gives clarity. In the light, you can see a thing for what it is."

"Bill Hybels, in his book, *Becoming a Contagious Christian*, talks about light as clear communication," Matt said. "Bill claims that the salt qualities attract people to us. However, those qualities don't explain what is attractive about us, where it came from, or how they can become salty too.[ii] I think he's right. When someone notices us living out a Beatitude lifestyle, and they comment or ask a question, we have to be ready to talk about this new life we have found in Jesus. People will not figure this stuff out on their own. They need someone to explain it for them."

"Like you did for me, Matt," Joe responded. "If you hadn't taken the time to answer my questions, I never would have figured out Jesus had what I was looking for. I never would have known how to connect to him."

"Let's put this together," Matt said. "A little review will help us. The good news of the kingdom is:

1. Our lives can change because of the nearness of the kingdom.
2. The day of salvation has dawned. God has drawn near with all his resources to help, heal, and save.
3. The principle sign of the kingdom is God's incredible love for us.
4. The kingdom will triumph.
5. In light of this, we rejoice.[iii]

"The Beatitudes are the values of the kingdom. If were are able to live as though the kingdom message is true and have the Beatitudes firmly anchored in our hearts and actions, what kind of impact and influence would we have on the people and the world around us?"

"It would be huge," Joe said.

"What kind of huge?" Matt asked.

"Huge, huge," Joe said. "To live the kingdom message and the values of the Beatitudes would be like you said before, to be in the zone with God. We would have peace and confidence that what is needed will show up when it is needed. We would have good relational skills and have our hearts in order. We would have the freedom to mess up and know it would be alright. We would know everything is going to be alright in the end and wouldn't be anxious. A person like that would have a huge influence and effect everywhere she or he went. Everyone is looking for that stuff, and anyone that remotely has those characteristics leads, calms, and heals. People would constantly be seeking them out, wanting what they have, and wanting to know how to get it themselves."

"Kind of like salt and light," Matt replied. "I think Jesus has called us to be salt and light in two settings. The first setting is the everydayness of our personal lives. We live with family, spend the day with co-workers, and see other people after work. In just that everydayness, the kingdom news and kingdom values of the Beatitudes have a huge impact, like you said.

"The other setting is bringing the kingdom news and kingdom values to a specific set of people or a particular need. For instance, I want to bring the kingdom message and values to guys who like vintage custom cars. To do that takes me beyond my everyday life. Or maybe I want to bring the kingdom news and values to those who have cancer. Once again, that takes me beyond the everydayness of my life and out into the larger world. The rest of the Sermon on the Mount, Matthew 5, 6, and 7, prepare us for the relational, personal, everyday world. Jesus prepares us to take this kingdom news and values beyond our everyday worlds in chapter 10. Before we get into the Sermon on the Mount, which is one of the most amazing addresses in all of history, I want us to take a quick look at chapter 10. This chapter shows the sending instructions Jesus gave his disciples for mission. We're going to go out in mission just like those first twelve disciples. I want us to begin to prepare for that, so go home, and read chapter 10."

"Matt, I'm not sure what all this mission stuff is about, but I'm up for it. It would be cool if Jesus could use me to help someone just like you've been helping me," Joe said.

"Okay, let's go," Matt said.

"Alright," Joe responded, and they got up to leave. As they were leaving, Joe wondered where this 'go' might take him. He wasn't at all sure, but he was excited about the prospects of being used by God.

Suggested resources:
E. Stanley Jones, *The Unshakeable Kingdom and the Unchanging Person*, Abingdon Press, 1972.
Bill Hybels, *Becoming a Contagious Christian*, Zondervan, 1994.

CHAPTER 4

JESUS' SENDING INSTRUCTIONS

When Matt found Joe at the table with the coffee, Joe was agitated.

"Hey," Joe blurted out, "have you read the stuff in chapter 10? Jesus wants me to cast out demons, heal the sick, and the raise the dead? Is Jesus crazy? I can't do that stuff. This is me. Just plain Joe. I live in suburbia. I'm not even sure there are demons, and I wouldn't know what do if I found one. I can't competently dispense children's pain medication to my kids. Raise the dead? Most mornings, it's all I can do just to get out of bed."

"Hello, Joe," Matt replied. "It's good to see you, too. How are the wife and kids?"

"Alright," Joe said. "I'm sorry. How are you? It's just that I've been reading chapter 10 all week, and Jesus is trying to drive me crazy. There's no way I can do what he's asking here."

"That's why I wanted to hit this early. We need time to look at this and get ready," Matt replied. "But I must say, you do sound like you're ready."

"Are you as crazy as Jesus?' Joe asked.

"Do you remember the first Beatitude?" Matt asked.

"Let me see. I think it was 'blessed are the poor in spirit, for theirs is the kingdom of heaven,'" Joe replied.

"What did we say that meant?" Matt asked.

"The poor in spirit are those who know they need help, those who can't make it on their own, and those who are desperate enough

Coffee with Matt & Joe

to ask God for help. When they ask, all the resources of the kingdom come their way," Joe said.

"Very good. You have remembered well. It sounds like you just might be poor enough in spirit to pull this off," Matt replied.

"Very funny," Joe said. "I'm serious here. There's no way I can do any of this stuff."

"I'm serious too," Matt responded. "It's only when we come to the realization that on our own we can't do any of this stuff Jesus asks us to do that we can receive his help to do it."

"You mean Jesus is really serious about sending me to cast out demons, raise the dead, and cleanse the lepers?" Joe asked.

"Maybe," Matt replied. "Let's take a closer look. How did Jesus go about doing ministry? What was his pattern? What did he do?"

"I have no idea," Joe said. "Not only do I have no idea, I don't even know where to look to get ideas."

"We'll look together then," Matt said. "What does Matthew 4:23 to the end of the chapter say?"

"Let me look," Joe responded. "It says, 'Jesus went through Galilee, teaching in the synagogues, preaching the good news of the kingdom, and healing every disease and sickness among the people.' It seemed like one healing led to another. Soon, everybody from everywhere was bringing their hopelessly sick to Jesus, and he healed them. Then there were these huge crowds around him. It seemed that when the crowd got large enough, he taught the people."

"Good. Now, what do we learn about the activity of Jesus from Matthew 8-9:35?" Matt asked.

"It looks like more of the same," Joe said. "There were more healings, more crowds, and more teachings. Large crowds followed him from the Sermon on the Mount. A leper came to him, and Jesus healed the leper. Then Jesus healed a centurion's servant, then Peter's mother-in-law, then everyone in town, and it just kept going."

"So what was Jesus doing with these healings?" Matt asked.

"I don't know," Joe said. "Maybe he was just helping people who were in trouble. It does seem the more he helped, the more crowds gathered."

"I think you're getting it," Matt replied. "There was something else going on here too. Jesus was the only one doing ministry at this point. He was the only one healing. He was the only one teaching. In your words, he was the only one helping those people who were in trouble. At the end of chapter 9, we see Jesus was looking at the crowds, was seeing all the people in trouble, was realizing there were only so many people he could touch, so he sent out the disciples. What did Jesus tell the disciples to do?"

"They were to preach the message, 'the kingdom of heaven is near' (Matthew 10:7), then they were to heal the sick, raise the dead, cleanse those who have leprosy, and drive out demons, all for free," Joe answered.

"Tell me, just what is the message, 'the kingdom of heaven is near?'" Matt asked.

"It's what we've been talking about the last three weeks. God and all the resources of heaven have drawn near. There is help available from God here, now, today. God loves us far more than we think we're worth. The kingdom wins in the end. Rejoice. Things can be different. I can be different. Life can be different," Joe said.

"What the disciples were asked to do," Matt replied, "was to go act like this is true. If the kingdom of heaven is near, then the sick can be healed, the lepers can be cleansed, the demons can be driven out, and even the dead can be raised. The disciples went out, proclaimed the kingdom is near, people got healed, and demons got driven out. What would it have been like to have two of these disciples come to your town?"

"It would have been like having Jesus there," Joe responded. "People would have been helped and healed. There would have been a lot of excitement. There would have been some confusion and probably some misunderstanding as people tried to figure out what was going on."

"What do you think Jesus was trying to accomplish by sending these twelve disciples out?" Matt asked.

"I think Jesus was trying to spread the kingdom and trying to reach more people," Joe said.

"In addition to that, I think Jesus was trying to grow the disciples," Matt added. "As the disciples spread the news that the kingdom is near, and as they saw the people they prayed for were healed, stuff was happening in the lives of the disciples. This message was no longer just something they had heard and hoped was true. As the disciples were engaged in spreading the message and living it out, they discovered that this message is reality. They discovered they could be partners with God. They experienced the thrill of being used by God. Their faith in God grew like an acorn becoming an oak tree. They found significance. They experienced the joy of the one who is healed or helped. I think it was a huge growing and learning experience for the disciples.

"Further, I think Jesus was working on creating a multiplier. At this point, Jesus was the only one doing ministry. He was the only one telling people the kingdom of heaven has drawn near. He was the only one acting like this message is true. Jesus was the only one healing and helping those in trouble. If Jesus could get the message into the disciples, get them to act like it's true, and get them to heal and help people, then it would become possible for the disciples to help other people get the message, act like it's true, and heal and help other people. Then those people can help others, and so on. At that point, it begins to take off. Suddenly, there are all kinds of people spreading the message, healing, and helping."

"I get all of that," Joe responded, "but there's just one problem. I can't do it. In Matthew 10:1, Jesus gave those twelve disciples the authority to drive out demons and heal disease. I don't see that he gives me the ability to do that."

"You're right—it's not there," Matt said. "It's somewhere else. In John 14:12, Jesus said, 'I tell you the truth, anyone who has faith in me will do what I have been doing. He will do even greater things than these, because I am going to the Father.' Then in his last words to the disciples, in Acts 1:8, Jesus said, 'But you will receive power when the Holy Spirit comes upon you; and you will be my witnesses.' You're right—you can't do it. Jesus does it through us.

"Let's try this. If two of the disciples came to town actually healing the sick, raising the dead, cleansing those who have leprosy, and driving out demons, who would be left helpless?"

"I don't know anyone who has leprosy," Joe said, "so that would be totally wasted here. I don't know a whole lot about demons, so I don't know who that would help. There are a lot of sick people around though, so they would be helped. Those who have addictions of various kinds wouldn't be helped. Those without jobs wouldn't be helped. Those who are abused wouldn't be helped. Those who are deep in debt wouldn't be helped. Those with bad marriages or dysfunctional families wouldn't be helped either."

"Why do you suppose Jesus sent the twelve disciples to deal with sickness, leprosy, demon possession, and death?" Matt asked.

"I think maybe those were the biggest problems of the day," Joe responded.

"So what are the biggest problems of our day? What would Jesus send disciples out to do today?" Matt asked.

"It would be great if someone could show up and heal cancer," Joe said. "It seems like someone in every family gets cancer. It would be good if someone could heal AIDS. Those things I mentioned before need attention. It seems like everybody working for corporate America could use help figuring out how to do more with less and deal with the stress that comes from trying to meet high expectations on limited resources. In some parts of the city, it seems life is just broken. Marriages don't happen. Family units don't form. Children are being raised by single parents or grandparents. Schools can't teach, and government can't provide security and order. Jobs are in short supply, and there is very little money. I have no idea how to solve these problems, but if someone could address them, that would be huge."

"Now, let me ask," Matt said, "can you picture yourself praying for someone who has cancer and supporting a family with a loved one who is dying of cancer; or helping someone deal with debt, finances, and the choices that got them into financial trouble; or helping someone in a recovery program get freed from an addiction; or helping someone in a dysfunctional family figure out the family dynamics, get freed from them, and help the family?"

"I'm starting to get the picture," Joe replied. "I could see myself being a part of one those kinds of activities. In fact, I could benefit from some of them myself. I don't know if anyone would get healed if I pray about their cancer; they might die if I pray for them. But I suppose you're right—if the message about the kingdom of heaven is true, and if I act like it's true, then I might end up doing something like this.

"Maybe Jesus isn't as crazy as I thought. I'm a long way from being ready to be sent out, and I have no confidence at all that I could a make a difference at the moment, but I'm starting to feel much better about these sending instructions. I must say, it would be cool if Jesus could actually use me to make a kingdom difference in someone's life."

"Jesus wants you to make a kingdom difference in the lives of lots of people," Matt replied, "and he's beginning to prepare you. You're just getting started, and Jesus has lots of work to do in your life to get you ready.

"I want you to start thinking and praying about who you could help and how Jesus might call you to make a kingdom difference. When we get through the Sermon on the Mount, and after we go through these sending instructions with a fine-toothed comb, you and I are going to do a mission project.

"As we think about that, let me say a couple of things. The project will last eight weeks. It will be local. It will be something we will spend a couple of hours on once or twice a week. As we continue on, ideas for our mission project will surface. Let me say though, the more desperate people are, the more receptive they are. Here are some questions to ask: Who are the desperate people in town? Who is desperately sick? Who is desperately in pain? Who is desperate financially? Who is desperate in a family or marriage? Who is desperate in a job? Who is desperate about God or for God? Who is desperately alone? Sometimes we look at the affluence of suburbia, and we think the nice house, new cars, expensive clothes, and trips mean there is no desperation. We couldn't be more wrong. It's a different desperation than in the inner city, but people in suburbia are just as desperate. So who are the desperate people?"

"You're right," Joe said. "I was desperate until about a month ago. It wasn't until I was desperate that I was open to God. It wasn't until I was desperate that I was willing to consider that my actions, choices, and beliefs were contributing to the circumstances causing my desperation. It wasn't until I was desperate that I was ready to seriously consider making changes of some kind. Now I'm not desperate. I'm hopeful. God has started to help me. He's starting to change me. As a result, I can see life beginning to get better."

"The second thing I want to say about the mission project," Matt said, "is that, whatever mission we get involved in, we have to be able to talk about the message of Jesus, 'the kingdom of heaven is near.' Only when we get people connected with the resources of the kingdom is there help.

"A few years ago, I was involved in helping a family in the inner city. They were on welfare. The dad was disabled and the mom had some handicaps. There were some children. They lived in the projects. I was part of a group of families that took them back-to-school shopping and bought birthday and Christmas presents for the kids. We helped the mom with the legal system. We also helped them move a couple of times. Even though we gave them lots of financial support and help with the legal system, things kept getting worse. Their son got arrested and was released. As we talked about the family in that crisis and what we could do to help, we realized we had shared everything with them except our faith, so we decided to ask the family if we could pray for them. One of our group members did a Bible study for the family about the good news Jesus brought. A couple of the neighbors came too. It wasn't until we started the Bible study and began to pray with them that we discovered a cycle of abuse and drug addiction wreaking havoc within the family. A couple of the family members came to Christ. Over the course of a couple of years, they were able to make decisions to get out of the drugs and abuse. Some of the other family members looked the choice right in the eye and chose the drugs and abuse over the freedom in Jesus. It hurt to watch those family members continue to self-destruct, but we rejoiced with the ones who chose life in Jesus.

"Whatever we do, we have to have a way to pray with people, talk about Jesus, and share how he can help."

"I'm okay with that," Joe said. "You know, if it weren't for Jesus, I'd still be desperate. I'm not exactly sure how to do what we're talking about, but count me in. Maybe Jesus can use me to help some desperate person find help and hope, like you did for me."

"Speaking of help and hope," Matt replied, "how are things going for you and Sue? Last time we talked you shared that you actually listened to Sue and discovered a relationship between your time with Sue, or lack of time, and her spending patterns. I've been praying for you guys this week. How's it going?"

"Thanks for asking," Joe said. "I need to spend more time with Sue, but I haven't figured out how to do that. I went to a soccer association meeting last week. I found myself volunteering to organize the golf outing. I was so pumped. Then I got home, and as I was telling Sue about the meeting and what I volunteered to do, I saw her face fall. Then it hit me. I just did it again. I just scheduled myself right out of her life. I have no idea why I did that or what I was thinking. I tried to apologize, but she wasn't buying it, so I'm in the doghouse right now. I guess I need to figure out why I schedule her out of my life. I've never thought of it that way before. I always thought about what I was scheduling in. I may need some help to get this worked out. I sure hope Jesus is good at marriage counseling, or schedule control, or both. Maybe I'll get a brownie to take home to Sue.

"What do we have next week?"

"Next week," Matt said, "we'll look at the rest of the Sermon on the Mount. As we get into it, we'll discover it's the most amazing sermon ever delivered. It touches on everything we face in life. Jesus is brilliant—incredibly, amazingly brilliant. I'm excited about unpacking this sermon with you. It will take several weeks. Are you up for it?"

"I can't wait to get started," Joe said. "What has happened to me so far, as I have gotten into Jesus, is the best stuff that has happened to me in a long time, maybe ever. I'm thinking if a little Jesus has helped this much, then more Jesus would help a whole lot more."

Then Matt and Joe prayed about Joe's marriage and what their mission project might be.

As they left, Joe had absolutely no idea how much more help he was going to need.

Suggested resource:
Matthew, Chapter 10, *The Message*, by Eugene Peterson, Navpress.

CHAPTER 5

ANGER

This time Joe was surprised to find Matt already seated at the table, mindlessly stirring his coffee with a stir stick and just staring out the window.

"Hi, Matt," Joe said.

"Hi," Matt responded listlessly.

"Hey, are you alright?" Joe asked.

"To quote my dad, 'I'm in pretty good shape for the shape I'm in,'" Matt replied. "I lost my job this past week."

"You what?" Joe asked, not believing what he was hearing. "How did that happen?"

"I think it had been coming for awhile," Matt said. "A new CEO was hired eighteen months ago from outside the industry to shake things up and to get the stock moving upward again. He has been gradually replacing a lot of upper management people, who know the industry inside and out, with MBA types from other industries. It seems like the accumulated knowledge gained over the years in the business isn't worth much anymore. Now that they have replaced enough upper management people, they're starting to work on the next layer down. Even though my department and I have always hit our numbers or better, I've been in the industry too long for their comfort level, so Thursday morning they called me in and explained there wasn't a place here for me anymore. They gave me a nice severance package, said they would give me a good reference, gave me the number of a job placement place, and wished me well. What hurt, though, was the way they had the guy from security take me to my desk, watch me pack my desk into some boxes they had ready for me, and then escort me off the property."

"You've been there a long time haven't you?" Joe wanted to know.

"Twenty-two years," Matt replied.

"How are you feeling?" asked Joe.

"I think I'm just numb right now," Matt said. "Friday was weird. It was time to get up and go to work, and there was nowhere to go. I came over here for awhile, hung out, and drank some coffee. Then I went home and buried myself in some lawn and landscaping work I've been meaning to get to."

"I'd be really angry. So what are you going to do?" Joe asked.

"I don't know. I have some time," Matt responded. "The severance package was really good. I think the job placement people will want to do some inventories on me—interests, talent, experience—that kind of thing. I want to do some thinking and praying about it too. I'm sure God has some ideas on what he would like me to do next."

"How will you know which ideas come from God and which ones don't?" Joe asked.

"God has his ways of letting me know. I'll tell you about them as we go along," Matt said.

"How's Mary taking it?" Joe asked.

"She's pretty shaken up," Matt responded, "but she'll be alright."

"Hey, are you sure you want to be here with me tonight helping me understand Jesus and how to follow him? I mean, I can wait. We can meet some other time. I don't want to intrude," Joe said.

"Yes, I want to be here," Matt replied. "I've been looking forward to it. It's one position I still have, so let's get started. In Matthew 5:15-20, Jesus talked about the law, the Pharisees, and righteousness."

"Yes, he did," Joe said. "I have no idea what he was talking about. What's a Pharisee?"

"A Pharisee," Matt began, "was a Jewish male who took a special vow to keep, uphold, promote, and honor the law. They believed that when you kept the law, God did good things to you, and if you ignored the law or disobeyed it, then God punished you. Up to this point, there were two key events in Israel's history. The first was the Exodus, with Moses leading the people out of Egypt. The second, centuries later, was the exile. Samaria, the northern kingdom of Israel, was attacked by Assyria, and its people were carried off into exile, never to return. They melded into the cultures where they were sent. Judea, the southern kingdom of Israel, a century or two later, was conquered by the Babylonians. There was a terrible siege of Jerusalem with intense suffering. The city fell, and the survivors were shipped to Babylon and other parts of the empire. These people didn't meld into the cultures. They adapted in order to live, but they maintained their Jewish culture, particularly their worship of God. Seventy years later, a ruler, named Cyrus, decreed all the Jews could return home. Many did, but many more stayed in their surroundings.

"For those who returned, there were some critical questions: Where was God in all this? What was God doing? How could God allow this tragedy to happen? They quickly rejected the notion that the gods of other nations were stronger than their God. They reviewed their history, they reread the laws of Moses, and they looked again at the words of warning the prophets had issued in the centuries and decades before the exile occurred. Their conclusion was that God used the exile to punish them for not keeping the Law; so now that they were back home and rebuilding, they began to pay close attention to keeping the law, every last line and nuance of it. They didn't want something like the exile to occur again. They kept the law for personal well-being and for national security purposes.

"The people who most vigorously supported this point of view were the Pharisees. They worked hard to keep the law and tried by whatever means possible to get everyone else to keep the law as they were doing. They also looked down their long noses at anyone who was not as committed to keeping the law as they were. The people of the day both respected and resented the Pharisees."

"Let me see if I have this," Joe said. "The Pharisees believed that keeping the law made them right with God, got them God's favor, and kept bad things from happening to them. That's basically how it works, isn't it? Didn't Jesus come to offer us forgiveness for breaking the law and to help us keep the law so that we could now be loved by God?"

"You're right about the Pharisees," Matt replied, "however, we need to work on the rest of it. Hang with me here for a few minutes. Jesus and the Pharisees had radically different ideas about the law. The Pharisees believed that keeping the law made you right with God. The Pharisees believed if you just tried hard enough, you could keep the law. Further, the Pharisees focused on the part of the law that you could do. To honor the Sabbath and keep it holy meant doing no work on the Sabbath. That is what the commandment said. What the Pharisees did with that commandment was to define work. You could walk a quarter of a mile and that wouldn't be work, but a quarter of a mile and one step was work. Now if I followed the Pharisees' guidelines, and I didn't work on the Sabbath but was worried about work all Sabbath to the point of distraction, or if I filled the time I wasn't working with pursuits that would take me far from God, have I honored the Sabbath? The Pharisees would say I have honored the Sabbath because I didn't work. Jesus would say the Pharisees have missed the point. Jesus would say honoring the Sabbath and keeping it holy is about what's in my heart. On the Sabbath, Jesus would have me set aside both the work and worries of the week and rest in God—be with God—so that I can be renewed, refocused, and energized for the coming week. Further, Jesus would say the Pharisees' understanding of the exile was flawed. Yes, the people didn't keep the law, Jesus would agree, but Jesus would go further. Jesus would say the reason they didn't keep the law was because their hearts were far from God. The problem at the exile was not a law problem, it was a heart problem. Two passages from the prophets deal with this. The first one is Jeremiah 31:31-33:

> "The time is coming," declares the Lord,
>   "when I will make a new covenant
> with the house of Israel
>   and with the house of Judah.
> It will not be like the covenant
>   I made with their forefathers

when I took them by the hand
> to lead them out of Egypt,
because they broke my covenant,
> though I was a husband to them,"
>> declares the Lord.
"This is the covenant I will make with the house of Israel
> after that time," declares the Lord.
"I will put my law in their minds
> and write it on their hearts.
I will be their God,
> and they will be my people."

"A new covenant, one that is different from the covenant God gave to Moses and the people, is what the prophet talked about—a new covenant where God would change both the hearts and the minds of the people. The prophet heard God identify the people of Israel as having a heart problem.

"The second passage is Ezekiel 36:26-28:

"I will give you a new heart and put a new spirit in you; I will remove from you your heart of stone and give you a heart of flesh. And I will put my Spirit in you and move you to follow my decrees and be careful to keep my laws. You will live in the land I gave your forefathers; you will be my people, and I will be your God."

"Once again a prophet heard God promise to give the people a new heart, a heart that could keep the law.

"Notice one other thing in these passages. God is the one who gives the new heart. We humans are not able to change our hearts. We humans can recognize we need different hearts and ask God to give us new hearts, but we can't make the change ourselves. Jesus, in his preaching, 'Repent for the kingdom of heaven is near' (Matthew 4:17), talked about the need we have for a heart change. To repent is to change the basic structures of your life—your heart. In the coming of the kingdom of heaven, heart change becomes possible. In the first Beatitude, 'Blessed are the poor in spirit, for theirs is the kingdom of heaven,' Jesus showed that the way to a new heart is to recognize the inadequacy of my current heart, my own ineffectiveness and futility in trying to change my heart myself, and to call out to God to change my heart. The change God brings is a kingdom heart whose desire is to love God and to love my neighbor. When your heart is full of this love, then keeping the law is the least of your concerns. Using the Sabbath for an example, your heart would be so full of love for God that you would welcome a day free from work to love and be with the God you love. A kingdom heart, the new heart God gives, is motivated by love, not by keeping the law.

"For Jesus, the purpose of the law was diagnostic. The law is a diagnostic tool. The law shows if I'm good or righteous, or not. The law is like an x-ray, it shows what is inside of me.

"If I consistently work on the Sabbath, setting aside no time for God or renewal, I have a heart problem. As I recognize that heart problem, illuminated by the law, I call out to God to change my heart. God then begins to change my heart so that I'm able not only to keep the commandment but to exceed it.

"When Jesus said our righteousness must exceed the Pharisees and teachers of the law to enter the kingdom of heaven, this is what he meant. The Pharisees were attempting to keep the law under their own power. Jesus knew that simply wasn't possible. Jesus knew keeping the law was not the way to God. Jesus was offering us the opportunity to have God change our hearts so that we could have hearts full of love for God and our neighbor. Jesus knew the way to God was to humbly ask for a new heart.

"I just laid a lot on you. Let's see what you got. Tell me the difference between the Pharisees' approach to God and Jesus' approach to God."

"I'm glad you didn't ask me something hard!" Joe laughed. "I'll give it a shot. The Pharisees believed the way to be right with God was to work hard to keep the law by their own effort. Jesus believed the way to be right with God was to recognize I'm not right with God and to ask God to make me right by giving me a new heart. The Pharisees believed the law could save—if I just keep enough law, then I can become right with God. Jesus believed the law was a diagnostic tool for the heart—that is, the law shows me where my heart needs to be changed, so I can call out to God for help. Is that it?"

"That's it exactly," Matt replied.

"Even though I know that's it, even though that's my experience of coming to Christ, and I see that new heart being formed in me, the Pharisees' way is hard to shake," Joe said. "It seems like the Pharisees' way has been ingrained in me all my life. Do the law. Keep the law. Do more good things than bad. God likes people who do good things. When you've done enough good things, maybe God will let you in heaven. Even though that has been ingrained in me, it leaves me frustrated. I never felt like I could do enough good things to make up for the mistakes I've made or to get God to accept me. I never felt like I knew where I stood. Sometimes I resented God and these good things I was supposed to do because they weren't nearly as fun as the stuff I wanted to do. I would even get mad at the people who were doing what I wasn't supposed to be doing. Sometimes, I wouldn't stop at the bar when I wanted to. I wanted to go in and have some drinks, flirt with the women, and laugh at the dirty jokes. They were having fun, and I wasn't. It wasn't fair.

"With Jesus, though, it's entirely different. With Jesus, I have discovered that God's love, acceptance, and approval aren't something I have to earn. Jesus has showed me that God already loves me. I feel at peace with God, and I'm confident that when I die, God will welcome me into heaven's gate. Now I have no trouble not stopping at the bar. I recognize that the drinks and the flirting were messing up my marriage. With this new heart God has given me, I have hope that my marriage can improve. With that hope, I now value what my marriage can become more than I do stopping in the bar. I now sometimes wonder about the other people in the bar. I wonder what areas of their lives they have given up on and what could be changed with new hearts. I wonder what would happen if instead of putting energy into drinking and flirting and carrying on, they used energy in positive ways."

"You've got it," Matt said. "Let's move on. In the rest of the Sermon on the Mount, Jesus showed us what life with a kingdom heart looks like. As we get into it, I want to say a few things. The first is that Jesus is absolutely brilliant. In the next 2½ chapters,

Jesus dealt with every situation we face and every facet of the human heart. It's amazing how well Jesus knows us. The second is that Jesus' response to our situations and our hearts is very different from the ways we usually respond. Sometimes Jesus' responses seem brilliant, and other times, it's hard to even imagine how his ideas work. The third is that while most of the concepts are relatively simple, they're impossible for us to apply under our own power. You'll most likely become frustrated with Jesus at some point and want to throw your hands up in the air and say, 'You've got to be kidding—I can't do this.' You'll be right—you can't do this. The only way to do this is by asking Jesus for heart help. The fourth is that the material in the whole sermon is laid out in order. It's not just random sayings that Matthew strung together as an example of what Jesus taught. Rather, Jesus laid out a different way to live, with different values, and with different resources from what we've ever used before. In order to live in this way, we need to deal with the material in the order in which Jesus laid it out. This will become clear as we go along. Are you ready to look at the first area?"

"After that introduction," Joe said, "I can't wait. Let's get started, after I get some more coffee."

When they were seated again, Matt began to talk.

"Jesus began to show us what a kingdom heart looks like by addressing anger, found in Matthew 5:21-26," Matt began. "But first let me say a word about anger. Anger is a good thing. It's an emotional response in the face of danger, wrong, or harm that tells us something is not right. Anger brings energy to do something about what isn't right."

"Let me guess," Joe said, "the problem we have with anger is that we don't use it right."

"You sound like you could be an expert," Matt replied.

"You have no idea," Joe countered, "but please continue. I want to find out exactly how I'm messing up anger."

"Let's talk for a minute about some ways we express anger," Matt said. "There are the hit-and-run expressions of anger. These include behaviors like verbal outbursts, sarcasm, gossip, blame, poisonous talk, complaints, stubbornness, intimidation, criticism, and cynicism. Then there are the silent-but-deadly expressions of anger.

These are behaviors like the silent treatment, half-hearted efforts, compliance, procrastination, depression, forgetfulness, preoccupation, hypochondria, and laziness.

"I have a tendency to employ the silent-but-deadly forms of anger more than the hit-and-run forms of anger. When I get angry, I get quiet. I don't want to talk about it. I don't want to talk to the person I'm angry with. If I don't deal with the anger, I find myself acting in passive aggressive ways. The anger sneaks out even though I'm trying not to express it directly. How about you Joe? How do you tend to express your anger?"

"I'm a hit-and-run guy," Joe responded. "I'll yell. I'll scream. I'll carry on. I'll say things I'll regret. I'm very expressive with my anger, but often I have to go back and clean up the mess I've made with my verbal outbursts."

"Those are just ways we express the anger," Matt said. "There are ways we misuse the anger too. Some of those ways are manipulation, intimidation, punishment, control, blaming, shaming, avoiding, procrastination, failure, and not trying.

"Just for fun let's take this sixty-question test about how angry we are. Just circle t or f, and then total the number of ts."

A few minutes later, and with a fresh cup of coffee, Joe said, "I'm ready. I have thirty-seven ts. How many do you have, and what is a good score?"

"I have twenty-four ts," Matt replied. "What does it mean? Fifteen to thirty ts means that you have a normal range of anger going in your life, that you're aware of it, and that you're working on keeping it under control. Thirty-one to forty means you have probably had a lot of dissatisfaction with life, that you often find yourself responding to life out of anger, and that it's on the verge of becoming a problem if you don't give it some attention. Forty plus means head to the nearest psychologist, anger is boiling out of control.

"Right now I'm in the normal range. I suppose as I begin to deal with losing my job, my number of ts could begin to increase."

"I see I'm on the high side," Joe responded. "I suppose that's accurate. No, to be honest, if you were to ask Sue, she would say there is no supposing about it. She would say I'm often an angry person. So how do I lower my t count?"

"You're getting ahead of me, Joe," Matt said. "Let's take a look at what Jesus said and see if we can get to how you lower your t count.

"Jesus upped the ante on the whole righteousness thing. He equated being angry with your brother to murder. He invoked the same sentence on both acts. Now before you respond, let me say that the word Jesus used for *anger* is *intense anger*. This is not just the normal kind of anger that flares in up in a typical relationship. This is anger that has been fueled so that it's intense. All of us deal with anger. It comes in the course of events, but we have to choose how we'll respond to our feelings of anger. Let me say just a little side note here: Others don't make us angry. We choose to become angry in response to some situation, so how much anger we have and what we do with it is a choice we make."

"Wait," Joe interrupted. "We choose to be angry?" What about the idiot who cuts me off in traffic, so I have to slam on my brakes not to hit him and hope the guy behind me can slam on his brakes quick enough not to hit me? He made me angry by his bad driving. Somebody needs to pull him over, make him see the consequences of his bad driving, take his license, send him to remedial driving school, and fine him hundreds of dollars. How in the world you can you say he didn't make me angry?"

"If he made you angry," Matt replied, "then everyone would react the same way to being cut off in traffic. Sometimes when I get cut off in traffic, rather than thinking the driver is an idiot, I wonder what's going on in his life that he would act that way. I don't always react in anger, which means the angry reaction and the not angry reaction is a choice on my part."

"Well maybe you have a point," Joe admitted, "but I still think the guy is an idiot."

"That is an excellent place to pick up what Jesus had to say about anger. I get cut off in traffic. I have an angry response. With the angry response, I have a choice: I can let it go, in which case Jesus isn't talking about me with his words about intense anger, or I can hang on to the anger at the driver and his actions, nurse it some, and fuel it. At that point, it becomes intense anger. To get this kind of anger going and to maintain our anger at others, we have to have a sense of self-righteousness, a sense of being mistreated, a sense of fighting against an unbearable wrong that only my anger can right; we have to nurse a wounded ego to keep anger going.[i]

"One of the reasons Jesus takes a hard stand against intense anger is that it leads to contempt. Jesus spoke against contempt with his words about anyone saying *Raca* to his brother. *Raca* was a term of contempt in Jesus' day. In our day, this contempt is expressed as we scream epithets through the windshield questioning the driver's parentage, heritage, character, and future resting place. All of this is degrading to the driver. After we're done with downgrading the driver's heritage, character, and future, we usually wrap the driver in filth—human and animal—suggesting that there is no place for him and his kind in polite society. This is contempt. We degrade and devalue the person to the place where he doesn't deserve to live among the rest of us or like the rest of us. We cut him off.

"This leads to Jesus' third item in the anger cycle. '"But anyone who says, 'you fool!' will be in danger of the fire of hell."' *Fool*, in Jesus' day, was a term that meant one was stupidly perverse and was rebelling against God and all that was good and right with the world. At this point, violence becomes a preferred option. They shouldn't be allowed to live. This combines anger and contempt.[ii] When we reach this point with the driver in the car, what do we have?"

"Road rage," Joe answered. "I get angry. I get worked up with my anger. I scream through the windshield at the driver all the things you said and then some. I decide someone needs to teach him a lesson (who better than I?) so that he doesn't continue acting in ways that endanger all of us. He deserves whatever is coming to him because he's such an idiot, so I run him off the road or take a shot at him. I suppose you're going to tell me this happens in all kinds of ways?"

"Yes," Matt said, "I am. This is where murder comes from. Very few cases of murder do not follow this pattern. This is where abuse comes from—physical, sexual, emotional, and verbal. We all suffer to some extent from the anger in the lives of the people around us, and we, with our anger, cause suffering in their lives."

"Does Jesus have a better way for us to use our anger?" Joe asked.

"Yes, he does," Matt responded. "Jesus wants us to use the energy from our anger to promote reconciliation. Jesus gave us two examples:

> "Therefore, if you are offering your gift at the altar and there remember that your brother has something against you, leave your gift there in front of the altar. First go and be reconciled to your brother; then come and offer your gift." (Matthew 5:23-24)

"Reconciliation is so important it affects your relationship with God and must be tended to before approaching God. In the second example (Matthew 5:25-26), Jesus said if you're on your way to court, be reconciled with your adversary before you get to court. In the kingdom of heaven, the purpose of anger is to give us the energy to address something that isn't right. The response in the kingdom of heaven to anger is to use the energy from the anger to seek reconciliation. Also, notice that Jesus points out that reconciliation is needed both when I have the problem and when the other person has the problem. I'm responsible for working to achieve reconciliation no matter where the problem is in the relationship or how it began. I need to ask, 'In what ways do I need to change? What do I need to do differently? How can I help this person who is desperately loved by God?' So then, a kingdom of heaven response to being cut off in traffic might be to ask the question, 'What is going on with that guy?' I wonder if he's alright. I wonder if there's anything I can do to help him. I might pray, 'God, please help that guy get safely where he's going. Help him get his mind back to the road. Help him deal with whatever is distracting, bothering, or troubling him. Bless him and keep him in your peace.'"

"That's a long way from 'you idiot,'" Joe said. "I can follow how you got there, but I have no idea how in the world to begin to live this out. I'm a long way from there."

"Let me ask," Matt replied, "what kind of change does the kingdom of heaven bring to our hearts to help us live this way?"

"I have no idea," Joe said.

"Let's see if we can help you get one," Matt said. "What is the good news of the kingdom?"

"The good news of the kingdom," Joe answered, "is that the kingdom of heaven has drawn near. That means the day of salvation is now — help is available from God here, now, today. It also means the principle sign of the kingdom is the incredible, out of proportion, hard to believe love God has for me. Further, in the end, the kingdom wins, so I can rejoice. In addition, all this means there are incredible resources available for life change, so I can be different. I suppose that also means I can use my anger differently."

"If this is true," Matt said, "that means the kingdom engulfs us in the outlandish love of God that loves us regardless of who we are or what we have done. God loves us with a love that cannot be taken away. It is a love that brings with it all the resources, possibilities, and opportunities of the kingdom to protect, secure, and heal us in the course of this life. It is a love that fills us and overflows into the lives of those who are around us. It is a love that values those who annoy us and those whom we would count as enemies as much as it values us.

"This reality affects our anger in a number of ways. First, the less secure, the more fragile a person is, the more easily one is harmed, the greater the threats seem, and hence, the greater the anger. The love of God, experienced in the kingdom along with all the kingdom resources, removes the insecurity that causes much of our anger."

"I never thought of it that way," Joe said, "but you're right. In the past, I was so insecure that everyone had to do everything just right so that things would go well for me. Just one slip up was a threat to undo my whole life. I don't feel that way anymore. I feel that this kingdom stuff is real, and it's becoming more a part of my life everyday. Maybe that's why I could listen to Sue during that last money talk instead of getting angry with her and trying to force her to do what I want, so my life would be smooth."

"Second," Matt continued, "when we're injured by another person, the kingdom brings the resources needed to heal us. It's not just us and them. God and his kingdom are involved in every relationship and every relational transaction, so another person is not able to destroy me because God is with me to help me.

"Third, when we need someone to change, the kingdom gives us the resources to change ourselves, which brings change in the relationship, and then change in the other person.

"Fourth, the love expressed in the kingdom plants within us the value of other people and gives us the desire to free them from the ill effects our anger would cause them.

"Finally, the kingdom gives us the resources to use the energy of our anger for reconciliation and gives us the courage to face the anger of others."

"I guess," Joe said, "the kingdom brings some significant changes to my heart that affect how I use anger. I'm beginning to experience this a little, but not very much yet. How do I get this more fully in my life so that I can use my anger to create reconciliation?"

"Once again, there are a number of things you can do, Joe," Matt replied. "First, participate daily in activities that build kingdom awareness in your life. Some examples are writing in a gratitude journal, reading the scripture, listening to and singing along with praise music, or spending some time outside in the beauty of God's creation.

"Second, remember the first Beatitude, 'Blessed are the poor in spirit.' Ask God to make the changes needed in your heart, so you can use anger in a kingdom way.

"Third, identify some relationships where anger is a problem. Ask God to show you what changes you need to make to improve the relationship. Then ask God to make those changes and to help you do what He has shown you.

"Fourth, identify some situations where you get in trouble with anger, like driving, and once again, ask God to show you what changes you need to make to improve the relationship. Then, ask God to make those changes and to help you do what He has shown you."

"That sounds easy enough," Joe said.

"Easy enough until you start to do it," Matt said. "Then it gets tough because sometimes God shows you things you don't want to change. Sometimes God points to hurts that haven't healed yet.

Sometimes God shows us that our plans aren't his plans. But the struggle through all that is worth it because I have yet to be disappointed in the outcomes the kingdom has produced in my life.

"Now, with my job situation, I have the opportunity to practice what we've been talking about more than I want, but I know that somehow, someway, it will be alright in the end."

Joe prayed for Matt's job situation, and Matt prayed for Joe's marriage. As Joe walked across the parking lot, he wondered what kinds of changes this new approach to anger would bring in his marriage, with his children, and in his job.

Suggested resources:
Dallas Willard, *The Divine Conspiracy*, HarperCollins, 1998.
Dan B. Allender & Tremper Longman III, *Bold Love*, NavPress, 1992.
Les Carter, *Getting the Best of Your Anger*, Fleming H. Revell Company (a division of Baker Publishing Group), 1983. Chapter 2, pages 21-25, *Mirror, Mirror on the Wall*, provides a 60-question true/false anger survey.

CHAPTER 6

SEXUALTIY

After they were seated with coffee and armed with chocolate chip cookies, Joe said to Matt, "I've been trying to work on what you said about anger last week. I've been learning a lot this week."

"I've been dealing with anger this week too. Tell me what happened with you," Matt said.

"As we were wrapping up last week," Joe replied, "you suggested that one way to begin accessing Jesus' kingdom approach to anger would be to identify a situation where I get angry often. I prayed some about that and asked Jesus to show me such a situation in my life. Almost before I could finish the prayer, driving popped into my head. We talked some about that last week. I get angry. No, let me tell the truth. I get very angry when someone does something stupid in traffic. It seems like every time I go out, some idiot makes a boneheaded maneuver that endangers everyone else on the road. I definitely get angry every time I go out in traffic. I asked how I could get Jesus' approach to anger to work for me out there. As I thought about it, an idea came. Instead of yelling demeaning phrases through the windshield, I can use the energy to pray for the idiot—I mean, person—who makes the boneheaded move—I mean, uses poor judgment in driving. As you can see, I'm still a work in progress."

"How did you do in traffic? Did you actually pray for people instead of cuss them out?" Matt asked.

"Some of the time I did, and some of the time I didn't," Joe said. "I learned my anger in driving was as much about myself as the other driver's poor judgment. During the drives that I had plenty of time, I was actually able to pray for the drivers who did dumb things. I asked God to help them, bless them, and get them safely to where they were going. During the drives that I was in a hurry, because I was running late or just didn't allow enough time for the trip, I lost my temper when someone made a driving mistake and ended up cussing them out. God showed me my poor planning was far more instrumental in causing me to lose my temper than what the other drivers were doing. I have been asking God to help me plan my trips better. This second half of the week, I've been doing a much better job allowing adequate time to get where I need to go. I'm becoming a blessing machine out there on the highway, praying for all those people exercising poor judgment. One of the side benefits of this is I feel a lot better about myself and about life when I get to the end of my trip."

"Good for you," Matt replied. "You're learning, and you're starting to get it."

"How about you?" Joe asked. "You said you were dealing with some anger this week. Was it about being let go by your company?"

"Yes, it was," Matt said. "About Tuesday, the numbness of the shock wore off, and I was really ticked at the company. I have given them the last twenty-two years of my life. I moved when they said move. I took all the difficult assignments they gave me without complaining. I accomplished all the company asked and more. I lived and died for them. I bled for them. I loved working for that company. How could they let me go like that? As I began thinking those thoughts and feeling those feelings, I knew I would begin heading down a treacherous slope. I knew I would find myself going from intense anger to contempt to believing those in charge of the company shouldn't be allowed to live. I asked God to help me rechannel my thoughts and my anger with kingdom priorities. God helped me calm down. Then, in the silence, I heard God whisper to me, 'Is it possible you gave too much of yourself to them and not enough to me?' I was shocked by the question. I began to argue with God. I should realize by now that arguing with God is a futile exercise. The argument ended as all the seventy- and eighty-hour weeks flashed through my mind. I saw all the time with Mary I had missed, the time with the children I had missed, the worship services I had missed, and the ministry opportunities I had missed. I had missed the time with God those twenty-two years. It began to occur to me that the company had granted me an excellent opportunity to examine my life and my priorities and to make adjustments for the next season of my life. As that thought came, another followed it. Maybe the company had not granted me that opportunity—maybe it was God. I wrote a letter to the CEO, the Board Chair, and the Board, thanking them for the opportunity to work for them the last twenty-two years, hoping their steps in leading the company would cause it to enter into a new golden age. It still hurts that I'm not there. It still hurts that they asked me to leave. It still hurts that I don't know what I'm going to do next or where I'm going to go. But I know God will help me through the hurt and has a more sane life for me down the road somewhere. I have no idea where or when. I suspect there are some issues God wants me to work through before the next steps become apparent."

"That's some pretty heavy duty stuff," Joe said. "I'm sure I wouldn't be able to respond as gracefully."

"Speaking of heavy duty stuff, did you read what Jesus has for us this week?" Matt asked.

"Yes," Joe replied. "Adultery, lust, sex, divorce, and marriage seem to be his agenda this week. After what Jesus had to say about anger last week, I'm not sure it's safe to dive into what Jesus has to say about sex."

"Maybe, but we're going to dive in just the same," Matt said. "Go ahead and read Matthew 5:27-32."

"Do I have to?" Joe replied. "Okay already, I will.

"You have heard that it was said, 'Do not commit adultery.' But I tell you that anyone who looks at a woman lustfully has already committed adultery with her in his heart. If your right eye causes you to sin, gouge it out and throw it away. It is better for you to lose one part of your body than for your whole body to be thrown into hell. And if your right hand causes you to sin, cut it off and throw it away. It is better for you to lose one part of your body than for your whole body to go into hell.

"It has been said, 'Anyone who divorces his wife must give her a certificate of divorce.' But I tell you that anyone who divorces his wife, except for marital unfaithfulness, causes her to commit adultery, and anyone who marries a woman so divorced commits adultery."

"I read this and think there's no way I can do this, even if I want to. I'm a guy, a red-blooded, American male. What Jesus says here just isn't possible. I thought the old saying 'do not commit adultery' was difficult enough. Now Jesus says I can't even look at a woman, and divorce is out of the question. I love my wife, but this is too much. It makes me feel stuck and trapped. I need some help here. I'm going to be a miserable guy trying to follow Jesus, or I'll be following Jesus in lots of other areas, but not this one."

"You're right—we can't pull this one off on our own anymore than we could handle anger on our own," Matt said.

"Okay, I know the first Beatitude—ask for help. But I'm not even sure I want to ask for the help," Joe responded.

"Let's take a good look at what Jesus said and see if we can't change your mind," Matt said. "To get started, let me say that sexuality is a good gift from God. It provides the attraction that leads to marriage. It provides a way of entering into another and knowing another. It provides a way of reproducing. It provides the bonding and glue that helps hold a marriage together. It's a metaphor of the intense love that God has for us in his longing to have an intimate relationship with us.

"Sexuality is also very powerful. When harnessed positively, it contributes to intimacy, companionship, home, family, health, prosperity, security, and a legacy of love and blessing. When sexuality is unharnessed and allowed to roam free, it becomes destructive, destroying intimacy, companionship, home, family, career, health, and security and leaves a legacy of brokenness, shattered relationships, and damage that can't be overcome by human effort. Out of control sexuality will create the dynamics that will destroy a family line in three to four generations. Controlled, positively harnessed sexuality produces dynamics that provide blessing in a family line for generation after generation. Harnessed sexuality is a blessing. Unharnessed sexuality is a curse."

"That's some pretty heavy stuff," Joe interrupted. "Sexuality is a part of all that? I've never really thought about it like that."

"Let's unpack what Jesus said," Matt continued. "Jesus said, 'You have heard it said, "Do not commit adultery."' But Jesus didn't stop there. As Dallas Willard, in his book, *The Divine Conspiracy*, points out, just because I haven't committed adultery doesn't mean my relationships are sexually healthy or that I'm right with my own sexuality."[i]

"What do sexually healthy relationships look like?" Joe asked. "What does it look like to be right with my own sexuality? I'm not sure I know."

"As we continue looking at what Jesus said, I think we'll find that out," Matt replied. "'But I tell you,' Jesus said, 'that anyone who looks at a woman lustfully...' Let's stop there for a minute. Let's talk about what looking at a woman lustfully is. I'm at the gym working out, minding my own business, dying a slow and cruel death on the cardio machine. A beautiful woman, wearing spandex in a way that pushes the legal limits for wearing spandex, walks past me. After I regain what's left of my breath and put my eyes back in their sockets, I'm confronted with a choice. The choice is: Do I use her or bless her?"

"I think I can describe the use her choice," Joe said. "That would be continuing to look at her, imagining what she would look like without any spandex at all, and then imagining what could happen next if such a scenario occurred. I could go into a lot more detail, but I'll stop. Tell me what the bless her choice would look like."

"The bless her choice," Matt said, "is to acknowledge her beauty, her wow power, and then also recognize the rest of her. She's a person. What can I do for this person? I can pray that God would bless her and at the same time pray that God would keep me out of trouble. I can strike up a conversation and start a relationship with her, looking for a way to do good to her. I can become an influence for God in her life. At my stage of life, that's what the bless her choice would look like. Now, if I were younger and single and started the relationship, I might discover that she's single too. At that point, there's another set of options available, but available from the perspective of doing what's good for both of us. When she walks by, the bless her choice has me using the disruption of my slow death on the cardio machine for kingdom purposes."

"How in the world do you do that?" Joe asked.

"We'll get there," Matt replied "but there's one more scenario here that's darker than the other two. That scenario is that I go to the gym only to see beautiful women in spandex, for the purpose of imagining what they would look like without the spandex, and then imagining what could happen next. My working out is just an excuse to be there. I suppose we could call that the abuse her choice, because that choice is premeditated. When Jesus talks about looking at a woman lustfully, which scenario is he talking about?"

"Certainly the abuse her scenario and the use her scenario," Joe answered. "I guess the bless her scenario is something completely different. If I understand, what you're saying is that if this mostly naked, pretty, young thing walks by, and my eyes pop out of my head, I'm alright."

"Yes, if your eyes didn't pop out of your head, then I'd be worried. That's how we're wired," Matt replied. "It's not the first look that gets us in trouble. It's what we do after the first look. The struggle is that often the decision about what happens next occurs nearly instantaneously, seemingly without any conscious input from us. Are we ready to move on?"

Joe nodded.

"Let's look at the next words of Jesus," Matt went on. "'Anyone who looks at a woman lustfully has already committed adultery with her in his heart.' I find Dallas Willard to be helpful here. He says a thief would steal, given the opportunity, if he or she wouldn't get caught. In the same way, an adulterer would have wrongful sex if the circumstances were right so that he or she wouldn't get caught. Since I have been lusting after this woman, the only thing preventing the actual adultery from occurring is opportunity. If the opportunity were to occur, I would act on it. Willard says a good question to check our hearts with is: 'What would you do if you could?'"[ii]

"Are you telling me that Jesus says if I look at a woman lustfully, it's the same as if I actually had the affair with her?" Joe asked.

"Yes," Matt replied.

"That seems kind of harsh to me. Isn't that an overreaction on the part of Jesus?" Joe asked.

"It's the same logic Jesus used with anger," Matt said. "Intense anger toward someone receives the same penalty as murder. That is, Jesus was saying intense anger is the same as murder. The point is that the murder is in my heart. The adultery, the affair, is in my heart. The only thing that separates the lustful look from the adulterous act is opportunity. If the adultery, the affair, is in my heart, the opportunity will present itself, and I will do the deed.

"I know it looks impossible, but Jesus is very serious about this. Look at what he says next, 'If your right eye causes you to sin, gouge it out and throw it away.' If your right eye is the eye that's looking at a woman lustfully, get rid of it. If your right hand is the hand that's going to reach out and touch the woman, get rid of it. 'It is better,' said Jesus, 'for you to lose one part of your body than for your whole body to go to hell.'"

"That wouldn't help," Joe said. "If I plucked out my right eye, my left eye would look. If I plucked out both eyes, my ears would hear her voice, the sound of her shoes, or the movement of her clothes as she walked by. If I cut off my ears, my mind would still remember and imagine. I don't think I could remove enough body parts to save myself. As you said, the problem is with my heart. So why does Jesus say to gouge out my eye or cut off my hand?"

"I think Jesus does that for two reasons," Matt replied. "First, I think Jesus is using some exaggeration to get across the point that this is serious business. This not something Jesus wants us to wink at and say, 'Everyone is doing it, maybe we shouldn't, but we will all go on doing it just the same.' He wants to get our attention. The second reason is that Jesus wants us to see the total futility of trying to deal with a heart issue by doing something to our bodies. The body is merely carrying out the desires of the heart, and if we deal with the body and leave the heart unchecked, the heart still has the same issue."

"I think maybe I'm in trouble," Joe said. "But why did Jesus make such a big deal out of this?"

"Because," Matt replied, "Jesus cares about our marriages. Marriage is hard work. The phrase *the honeymoon is over* refers to that. At some point, I discover that this woman, who I think is the most wonderful woman ever to have walked the face of the planet, is human. She's flawed. She makes mistakes. She's limited. She has a mind and a life of her own, which don't always mesh well with what I think or what I want to do. At about the same time, she discovers that I, the most wonderful man ever to have walked the face of the planet, am human too. In order for us to have a marriage that is loving, satisfying, and fun, there is work that has to be done. I have to make some changes. She has to make some changes. I have to forgive. She has to forgive. We both have to grow. The work that marriage requires of us is some of the most difficult work humans have to do. There is tremendous temptation to bail when faced with that work."

"You mean, like, walk out and leave?" Joe said.

"Yes, but there are all kinds of ways of leaving," Matt continued. "I can stay in the marriage, but still leave. I can get angry with my wife because I think she has somehow broken an agreement we had about how our life was going to be. I can refuse to forgive her. I can stay angry with her, enter into the anger cycle that Jesus described, and just shut my heart to her. I can pour myself into work, forgetting she's there. I can become emotionally distant, buried in ball games and the internet. You could probably add some more ways to this list.

"One of the purposes of the sex drive is to bring us back to our spouses when we try to check out. That's why it's so powerful. Now, if my sexual energy becomes directed to lustfully looking at spandex-clad women at the gym, visiting the internet porn sites, engaging in sexually charged internet conversations, going to strip clubs and topless bars, flirting with some woman at work, or engaging in the poor me, my wife doesn't understand me routine, then we're beginning to destroy the bridge back into the marriage. It's the sex drive that helps us to do the hard work that allows the marriage to be a joy again.

"Further, if my sexual energy becomes diverted from my wife, I begin to resent her for not responding to me like I imagine all these other women would respond. I also begin to resent her for not looking like I imagine all these other women would look. If I actually do have an affair and continue the adultery, it's because my wife doesn't respond to me the way this woman does, and my wife doesn't understand me the way this woman does. Now my sexuality is starting to rip apart and destroy what remains of my marriage.

"An additional complication is that there are lots of people attempting to seduce our sexuality away from our marriages. There's a ton of money made from both men and women whose sexuality is about to stray or has already strayed. I suspect that a third to a half of a typical bookstore's revenue comes from the more socially accepted outlets for strayed sexuality. I could go on here.

"There's one final factor complicating all this. That factor is a spiritual factor. Dan Allender, in his book, *Bold Love*, views lust as an attempt to fill emptiness and find satisfaction. He says lustful fantasies come in two varieties—to capture or to be captured. He argues that we want to overwhelm or to be overwhelmed in such a way as to be transported to another plane of existence. We live for an experience of worship that fills our being with a joy so deeply in awe of the other we are barely aware of ourselves.[iii] There is a fullness and satisfaction we long for that comes only in a relationship with God. If we expect our spouses or sex with anyone, in any variety, to fill that spot, we'll be disappointed with our spouses and with sex our whole lives."

"I can follow all you said, except for one thing," Joe said. "Why does Jesus consider my marriage so important that he doesn't want me to bail? What's the big deal? If she's not happy with me, or if I'm not happy with her, or if I don't love her anymore, or if I fall in love with someone else, why can't we just leave? Or what if I discover that I married the wrong the person? I mean, it's better to leave than to be stuck in a loveless marriage, isn't it? Jesus wouldn't want me to suffer out the rest of my days in a miserable marriage, would he?"

"No, Jesus doesn't want you to spend the rest of your days in a miserable marriage," Matt replied. "He wants you and your spouse to do the work that would transform your marriage into a wonderful, loving relationship. The purpose of marriage, stated way back in Genesis 2:24, is that a man and woman join together, and the two become one. This process requires much growth on the part of anyone entering into marriage. If we don't do this work in the marriage, it will plague us until we deal with the growth and the change necessary for a healthy marriage.

"Let's imagine for a minute that we give up on the marriage, and we follow our sexuality outside the marriage to find sexual fulfillment. I trade my wife in for internet porn sites, skin magazines, and x-rated movies. Will that satisfy me?"

"I guess not," Joe answered. "That stuff isn't real. The women aren't real. No one really looks like those women do after the photos are all touched up. The porn stuff is an enticing place to visit, but it leaves me empty and feeling dirty. I wouldn't want to live there. I have a couple of buddies who have their computers filled with this stuff. It's like once they get started, they can't stop."

"Porn is addictive,' Matt said. "It's only been in the last few years that people have begun to talk about that. There are now sites on the internet to help people get off porn. Let's imagine I trade my wife in, and instead, I lustfully look at women at the gym who are barely clad in spandex. Will that satisfy me?"

"Probably not," Joe said. "That might even get you in trouble. I'm not sure the women working out would want to be looked at lustfully. I think they dress that way because they want to be noticed, but I don't think they want to be leered at. I suspect that if a woman thought a guy was leering at her and drooling over what he imagines he could do with her, she might get angry with him. If it became apparent that the guy was leering at all the women every time he went to work out, he might be asked by the management to leave."

"Let's imagine, for a moment, that the flirtation option grows into an affair, and I leave my wife for the other woman," Matt proposed. "How do you think that will work?"

"I don't know," Joe responded. "Maybe it would work out, or maybe it wouldn't."

"Often it doesn't," Matt replied. "The dynamic there is that both the man and the woman are trying to escape something. They find a brief solace with one another during the affair. But sooner or later, there comes a time when the honeymoon or the affair moon is over. At that point, each discovers in the other precisely the traits and the dynamics they were trying to escape. Sometimes, what they discover are different traits and dynamics that are just as discouraging as the traits and dynamics from the previous marriage.

"If we allow our sexuality to become detached from our marriages because we think we will find something better, we always overlook three items. The first is the huge amount of pain that comes with divorce. For most people, the pain is as intense as a death. In some ways, it's worse because you can't close the casket. Along with the pain, there is a sense of failure and a feeling of being devalued as a person. That pain is usually felt by both sides. This says nothing of the pain felt by the children involved or the extended families and friends.

"The second is the belief that when the divorce occurs, we won't have to deal with the ex or the surrounding issues anymore. If there are children, we have to continually deal with the ex, and so the ex and the issues from the marriage remain. Unless the issues get dealt with after the marriage ends, they will always be there in the dealings with the ex.

"The third item that is omitted is a nasty little statistic. Most second marriages don't last as long as the first marriage. Most third marriages don't last as long as the second marriage. The reason for this is that unless I deal with the issues that caused the first marriage to come apart, I will marry a woman similar to my first wife and face the same issues all over again. If I do manage to marry a woman different from my first wife, the areas of growth and change that I ignored before will come back and wreck this marriage too. The people who make the second marriage last are those who, between marriages, do the work demanded by the first marriage."

"It certainly sounds like the cards are stacked against me if I bail out of my marriage," Joe said. "But how in the world do I make my marriage better? That seems to be the option Jesus would have me pursue."

"Given what we have learned from Jesus thus far, what kingdom resources does Jesus offer us to draw upon for our marriages?" Matt asked.

"Let me think about that while we get another cup of coffee, as I try to behave myself walking past the women in here," Joe said.

After Matt and Joe were back at their table again, hot coffee steaming from their cups, Joe observed, "When you're trying not to look at women, it seems like there are more of them, and they're more attractive. Before we talk about the kingdom resources for marriage, let me ask a question. It has just been us guys talking here. Do women have the same struggles with their sexuality?"

Matt laughed. "They sure do," he said. "They struggle with sexuality, using it in healthy ways, and channeling its energy into marriage. The particulars are different for them. Women, so some of them have told me, struggle with being in love with being in love. They like the emotional high. Their desire is often more emotional than physical. They like the attention. They also like to catch a man. Different things cause them to be frustrated with a marriage. When the sexuality begins to stray outside the marriage, it looks different for women too. Yet, the results are the same. If not harnessed and focused in the right direction, a woman's sexuality will trash a marriage just as thoroughly as a man's sexuality."

"Thanks. Let me get back to kingdom resources for marriage," Joe said. "I think one of the resources might be the first Beatitude: God help, I don't know what to do with my marriage. I don't know how to make it any better or even if it can be any better. Maybe the second Beatitude would be helpful too: Help me to face and make the changes I need to make to improve the marriage, although I'm sure she needs to change more! It's possible the third one might help too: Jesus, please put my power under your control in my marriage. Maybe even the fourth one: Jesus, let me hunger and thirst for a good marriage. That's what I can think of. Is there more?"

"Yes," Matt said. "Jesus' teaching last time, about anger, is a big resource. Often our reactions to each other pose a bigger problem than the issues within the marriage. When we misuse our anger in our marriage, using it to punish, blame, and shame our spouse, we become a bigger problem than whatever it was we got angry about.

When we use the energy from our anger to work toward reconciliation, we take big steps forward.

"What you said about the Beatitudes is good. If I pursue those in relation to my marriage, then help will come, maybe from a counselor, a book, a friend, a group, or even from my wife. I'll be shown the changes I need to make. Sometimes we're without a clue as to what needs to be changed. We're just blind to it. Jesus will show us later that the way to bring about change in a relationship is for me to change. As I change, the other person is free to change too. I might be challenged to learn to speak my wife's language, to enter more fully into her world, to learn what she thinks and feels about the marriage, and to learn how she wants to be treated.

"Earlier, you asked what healthy sexuality looks like. Do you have an answer for that question now?"

Joe played with his coffee some. Thoughtfully he began, "A healthy sexuality in a marriage might be where both the husband and the wife channel their sexual energy into the marriage rather than letting it be bled off into sexual distractions. The sexual energy combined with the properly applied energy from anger could give them the impetus and the courage to face the challenges and make the changes. When everything is going well, it would really be going well. When I notice other women because of their sexuality, I could thank God for their attractiveness and then ask the right questions: How can I bless them? How can I help them? Or in business language, how can I add value to their lives? How does it work for single people?"

"That's a good answer to my question and a good question. It has been a long time since I was single," Matt said. "But I think if I'm single and would like to be married, I would need to use my sexuality to drive me to make the changes I need to make to become the kind of man a woman would love to have for a husband. I think I would need to use my sexuality to drive me to make the kinds of changes I would need to make to get myself into the places and situations where I can meet the kind of woman I would want to marry. If I'm single and like being single, then I could focus my sexuality on growing the relationships I have, causing them to become richer and deeper."

"I have one question left," Joe said. "What if I try all this, and I'm so dense I still can't get the marriage to work? What if I do everything right, and she doesn't want any part of it? Is divorce an option then?"

"Jesus talked about divorce here and in chapter 19:1-12," Matt said. "Here, in Matthew 5:32, Jesus said, 'But I tell you that anyone who divorces his wife, except for marital unfaithfulness...' Let's stop there for a moment. In Jesus' day, there was a widely accepted school of thought that let a man divorce his wife for nearly any reason at all. If he didn't like the way she looked anymore, if she burnt his toast, or whatever, all the man had to do was go to the priest, fill out a divorce certificate, and send her out.

"Let me give you a little side note here. In that culture, a woman couldn't divorce a man. So in a divorce, it was always the woman's fault. Dallas Willard argues that, in Jesus' day, a divorce put a woman in the category of damaged goods.[iv] There must be something wrong with her that she was asked to leave. Also, in Jesus' day, a divorced woman had three options: She could be taken in by kind relatives, she could remarry, or she could become a prostitute. The option of being a single woman and getting a job to pay the bills didn't exist in that day outside the sex industry.

"In Matthew 19:8, Jesus said the reason divorce occurs is hardness of heart. Sometimes it's the man's heart that's hard, sometimes it's the woman's heart that's hard, and sometimes it's both hearts that are hard. A hard heart won't change, won't grow, won't forgive, and won't be merciful. Dallas Willard says the cause of all divorce is hardness of heart.[v] When hardness of heart occurs and is not dealt with, the harm is done whether the marriage continues or not. A marriage is never the same after uncured hardness of heart enters it.

"Here, Jesus said divorce is permissible if there is marital unfaithfulness. I think marital unfaithfulness is the point where the marriage has been violated, and enough is enough. Maybe the steps a person goes through to become unfaithful wreck the marriage. I don't know, but Jesus says at that point divorce is permissible. Jesus doesn't mandate divorce at this point, he just permits it.

"The rest of what Jesus was doing here was sharing the responsibility of the wrecked marriage, for whatever reason the woman was divorced. No longer is the woman solely responsible. Now the man has responsibility for the well-being of the marriage. Further, the man is now responsible for what his actions will cause her to become.

"As I read Jesus, I see divorce happens because our hearts become hard. This isn't the way God intended marriage to work. Let me say one more thing here. Divorce is not the unforgivable sin. God does not hate divorced people. God's heart goes out to divorced people. God hates to see people in that pain and in that position. God wants to help. If someone who is divorced works the first Beatitude, there is help, healing, recovery, and a new future available from God."

Joe swirled his coffee in his cup and said, "I guess I have a lot of work to do in my marriage and in getting my sexuality fully focused back on my marriage. I have no idea what the work is I need to do or how I get my sexuality back on track with Sue. But I think I know what the starting points are."

"What," Matt asked, "are the starting points?"

"I think," Joe said, "it's the same process you gave me to use for anger: Pray the first Beatitude about my marriage and sexuality — ask for help. Ask God to show me where lust is a problem and where my sexuality is off track. Ask God to show me what changes I need to make in the marriage, and ask for the help to make them. Ask God to show me if I have any relationships that aren't sexually in line with the kingdom."

"That," Matt replied, "would be an excellent place to start."

"I thought," Joe responded, "you would say that. Like I said back at the beginning, I'm not sure this would be safe, but I guess it's hopeful and potentially more satisfying."

As Matt and Joe walked across the parking lot, Joe began to pray for help with his marriage and his sexuality. He had no idea what the answers to those prayers would look like, but that didn't stop him from looking forward to the answers.

Suggested resources:
Dallas Willard, *The Divine Conspiracy*, HarperCollins, 1998.
Dan B. Allender and Tremper Longman III, *Bold Love*, NavPress, 1992.

CHAPTER 7

YES & NO

It was cold and raining hard when Matt reached the coffee shop that night. When he got out of the car, he stepped in a deep puddle and got his foot wet. By the time he got in the shop, all of him was wet and miserable. He found Joe huddled over a cup of hot coffee looking like a drowned rat. Matt looked at Joe, laughed and said, "What a miserable looking pair we are."

"I hope," Joe replied, "that your misery is only skin deep, because my misery goes considerably deeper than that."

"Let me hang up my coat and get some coffee," Matt said. "Then, I want to hear all about it." Soon Matt returned to the table with a cup of coffee warming his soggy hands. "Okay, let's hear it."

"It's cold. It's raining. The game went badly," Joe began. "Sue and I had this monster fight. During the fight, I probably violated every kingdom principle we've talked about. It was weird. It was like I was watching the fight from the outside. I saw myself yelling and not listening and not wanting to hear her point of view. I saw myself wanting to hurt her, not physically, but emotionally and verbally. I was watching all this like I was in a bad movie saying, 'Don't do it,' but I couldn't stop what was happening."

"What was the fight about?" Matt asked.

"I've been in the doghouse the last couple of weeks. We had that breakthrough about her spending money correlating to the time I spend with her, but we haven't been able to build on it. By that I mean, we haven't been able to make any changes. Sue thought changes were going to be happening right away. I would like to see changes too, but we haven't figured out how to make any changes or even what the changes are that need to be made. Not only haven't we figured that out, we haven't even really talked about changes at all. I made matters worse by agreeing to organize the soccer league's golf outing. She has been upset with me since.

"I came home last night and decided to focus my sexuality on my marriage. As you can imagine, with Sue upset with me like she is, there hasn't been much happening sexually. There's this woman at work I flirt with pretty heavily. At times, when Sue is upset with me, I imagine what it would be like to be with this woman. After our talk last week, I decided I wouldn't flirt with the woman this week, and I would try to focus on Sue. I came from a golf outing meeting late on Thursday night. Sue was watching a chick flick on some women's network starring some blonde actress. I should have known then I might be in trouble. I sat down on the couch next to her and put my arm around her. The next thing I knew, she exploded, 'How dare you come in here and put your arm around me after you have been out all evening.' I had no idea where that came from, so I yelled back at her, 'I thought that was what married people did.' She yelled at me, 'Do you call this a marriage?' It got ugly after that.

"As best I can remember, we fought about how I never spend any time with her and my telling her that I have other responsibilities—to our children, to my employer, to the community. I wasn't kind at all, and neither was she. That round of the fight ended with Sue storming out of the room yelling back over her shoulder, 'You go put your arm around those people then!' Then the bedroom door slammed.

"Since then, we haven't spoken except about who's picking up who after which practice. It's driving me crazy. I've been thinking if I go back to flirting with the woman at work, this would be easier to take. If I had kept flirting with her, maybe I wouldn't have put my arm around Sue on the couch, and we wouldn't have gotten into this fight. Now that I'm in it, I don't know how to get out."

"It's not surprising you're in this mess," Matt said.

"It's not? How can you say that?" Joe asked.

"You received the insight about how much she needs to spend time with you," Matt replied, "and you haven't changed anything to have more time to spend with her. It was only a matter of time before this happened. Your decision to stop flirting with the woman at work was a good one. It contributed to this fight, but issues were already brewing. If you hadn't gotten in the fight this past week, it would have happened soon. The longer something brews before it comes out, the nastier it is when it does come out. It's like shaking a pop can and then opening it. So as bad as the fight was, it would have been that much worse in another week or two.

"It seems to me the words of Jesus we're going to look at tonight are going to be particularly helpful to you and Sue."

"How?" Joe asked. "All Jesus talked about in this week's reading was to make sure your yes is yes and your no is no. How is that going to get me out of the doghouse and back in the bedroom?"

"It looks to me," Matt said, "like you're having trouble with your yes and no. It sounds like you're saying yes when you should say no and you're saying no when you should say yes."

"I'm all confused," Joe said.

"I can see that," Matt replied. "How about reading Matthew 5:33-37?"

"Alright," Joe said. "Here goes:

> "Again, you have heard that it was said to the people long ago, 'Do not break your oath, but keep the oaths you have made to the Lord.' But I tell you, Do not swear at all: either by heaven, for it is God's throne; or by the earth, for it is his footstool; or by Jerusalem, for it is the city of the Great King. And do not swear by your head, for you cannot make even one hair white or black. Simply let your 'Yes' be 'Yes,' and your 'No,' 'No'; anything beyond this comes from the evil one.

"Jesus got into the subject of yes and no," Matt said, "by talking about making oaths, which are ways to convince or persuade people that our yes is yes and our no is no when people aren't sure about our yes and no. Dallas Willard, in *The Divine Conspiracy*, takes oath making a step further by claiming, 'It is simply a device of manipulation, designed to override the judgment and will of the ones they are focusing upon, to push them aside, rather than respecting them and leaving their decision and action strictly up to them.'[i]

"This reminds me of the salesman who swears on his mother's grave that his product will not only outperform the other products on the market, but his product is so superior you would gladly pay twice the outrageous asking price if you only knew what it would do in your home."

"I know what you're saying," responded Joe. "Any time someone starts a sentence with 'I swear on a stack of Bibles,' I figure he's lying. I guess Jesus was saying we need to respect people, let them make up their own minds, and not try to manipulate them. So how does that help me with Sue?"

"Patience, we're getting there. Jesus was certainly saying that someone with a kingdom heart will not be into manipulation, but there is more here than that," Matt said. "What is it that prevents our yes from being yes and our no from being no? What would cause us to want to manipulate someone?"

"Let me think about that for a minute," Joe replied. Joe took a sip of coffee while he did his thinking. "Maybe," Joe began, "I don't trust the other person to make the decision I want. I want things to go my way badly enough that I have to make sure the person makes the decision I want. Maybe I want people to like me, and I don't think I'm very likeable on my own merits, so I have to con people into liking me. Maybe I refuse to accept my own limitations and continue living in the illusion that I need others to do certain things. Maybe my life is so out of control that if others don't respond in the way I want, everything will come apart."

"Those are some good maybes Joe," Matt said. "Sometimes our yes isn't yes because we couldn't figure out how to say no, and then we don't follow through on our yes. Henry Cloud, in *Boundaries*, has a chart that depicts this.[ii] Let me draw it on the napkin:

	CAN'T SAY		CAN'T HEAR
NO	The Compliant Feels guilty and or controlled by others; can't set boundaries	NO	The Controller Aggressively or manipulatively violates boundaries of others
YES	The Nonresponsive Sets boundaries against responsibilities to love	YES	The Avoidant Sets boundaries against receiving care of others

"That's a nice looking napkin chart Matt," Joe replied. "Can you explain it to me and tell what any of this has to do with Sue and me?"

"As we go through the chart," Matt said, "I think you will begin to see what it has to do with you and Sue. The first category is the man or woman who can't say no. Cloud calls this type of person Compliant. This person tries to do everything he or she is asked to do. It doesn't matter if the request overloads them, or if it's something they have no ability to do, or if it's a task they hate, or if it's something that's destructive. They can't say no. They can't say no because they are afraid they will hurt the feelings of the person asking them, or the person asking them won't like them if they say no. They can't say no because they are trying to get the people who make requests of them to like them. They can't say no because they don't value their own desires and self. A person who can't say no ends up with a life out of control, not doing the things they want to do, and full of anger and resentment hidden behind a sweet public persona.[iii] Do you know anyone like that?"

"Bill is like that," Joe answered. "He'll do anything in the world for you. Anytime I'm organizing an event, I call Bill when I can't find anyone else to do a particular job. He always accepts the assignment. Whenever I talk with Bill, I always hear about all the things other people are asking him to do. Once I heard him complain about something they asked him to do at work that was going to require a ton of extra time for no extra compensation. I said, 'Why don't you say no.' He said, 'I couldn't do that.' As you talked about this kind of person, it occurred to me that Bill has no life. I never see him with his kids or his wife. I see him with other people's kids and doing lots of good stuff out in the community, but I never see him doing anything I would consider just Bill stuff.

"What happens to this kind of person?"

"When they get overloaded on time," Matt replied, "and can't do anymore, yet take more on, they get sick. They can't say no, so their body shuts down because it can't keep up. Others use a family member or a boss to say no for them. They respond, 'I'd like to do that, but my wife won't let me. I can't believe how mean and unfeeling she is sometimes.' Sometimes they suffer a meltdown of some type because they can't do it all. Usually there is a lot of anger just below the surface.

"Sometimes people like this can say no in some areas but not in others. I know some moms who can't say no to their kids even though the time, attention, and financial demands are outrageous. I know some men who can't say no to work no matter how damaging all the long weeks are to their family and to themselves.

"The next box on the chart is the people who can't say yes. These people are called Nonresponsive. The people who can't say no always say yes to every request, good or bad, right or wrong. The Nonresponsive people don't say yes to any request, whether it's a good request or not. These people ignore the healthy responsibilities we have for each other. They say things like: 'Get over it'; 'That's a problem isn't it'; 'You caused the problem, so get yourself out of it'; 'Pull yourself up by your own bootstraps'; 'Just deal with it'; or 'I hope you find someone who can help.' Or sometimes they might respond, 'Let's not talk about you—let's talk about me,' or they might act like they didn't even hear the request.

"There are two types of Nonresponsives. The first type is critical toward others. The faults and failings in the other person trigger feelings about the Nonresponsive's own faults and failings, which he is trying to deny. To help someone else, he is required to face his own weakness. Because a Nonresponsive won't face his weakness, he won't help others. The second type of Nonresponsive is so self-absorbed he doesn't know anyone else is out there. As the first group couldn't say no because of fear of rejection, the second group can't say yes because they're afraid of facing the truth about themselves. If they face the truth about themselves, others will also see the imperfections and shortcomings, and this could lead others to reject them. Both groups operate out of a fear of rejection by other people.[iv]

"Do you know anyone who is a Nonresponsive?"

"The mother of one of the kids on my boy's soccer team is that way, I think," Joe said. "I think her name is Robin. She seems to have little patience with her son's soccer failings. The other women don't talk with her much because they say she's cold, which I think means she has no time or patience with anyone's troubles. She never brings snacks or helps with any of the team's family gatherings. I sometimes think I'm glad I married Sue because this woman would be impossible to live with.

"What happens to this kind of person?"

"They end up alone," Matt said, "and resented by their families and any friends they pick up on the way because they don't help anyone.

"The third group can't hear no. They're called Controllers. These people never take no for an answer. This is the boss who keeps calling his employees about work issues when they're at home. This is the relative who never calls before coming but just pops in and completely changes everyone's plans for the day. Often their lives are out of control. Controllers believe that it's the job of the people around them to deal with their out of control areas on a moment's notice. Further, Controllers doesn't ask. Controllers manipulate or steamroll the people around them into doing whatever they want. Some Controllers, like Nonresponsives, are so self-absorbed they don't even know they are crossing the boundary lines of other people. Like the other types, Controllers are driven by a fear of rejection. Controllers need to accept responsibility for their load in life and need help to do that. But rather than getting the help to deal with the cause, they use others to deal with the symptoms because they fear if anyone knew the cause, they would be rejected.[v]

"Do you know people like this Joe?"

"Do I ever," Joe replied. "My boss is a classic steamroller. He never takes no for an answer. He'll call me anytime, day or night, to bail him out of something. He'll make impossible demands at work in regard to deadlines and budgets. If he can't bully us with threats into doing what he wants, then he uses guilt to get us to act.

"I know what happens to guys like that. Someone finally snaps and shoots him."

"Is that what you want to do to your boss, Joe?" Matt asked.

"Sometimes. I hope I'm not the one who snaps," Joe said. "I suppose a more peaceful end is that people will fear and dislike this person as long as he has any kind of power. Then once the power is gone, I bet everyone leaves him alone. But tell me, how to do you deal with a guy like this?"

"We'll get to that," Matt said. "Let's look at the fourth type. These people can't hear yes. They're Avoidants. These people can't accept help. When someone reaches out to them, they decline the help saying: 'There are others so much more needy and deserving than I am. My problems are so minor compared to others.' Or they might say, 'I don't want to bother you, what you're doing is so much more important.' If they pray, they never ask God for help because they don't want to bother him with their insignificant problems when God has so many other important things to deal with. They will help others, but when the time comes, they'll be unable to accept the very same help they give. Like the other groups, the Avoidants suffer from fear of rejection. They fear that if they accept help and someone really gets to know them, that person will reject what they find.[vi]

"Do you know anyone like this?"

"My mother is like this," Joe responded. "I can never remember her asking for anything. When we were growing up, she was always the one with the help, the answers, and the strength to help us and anyone else for that matter. But I never remember anyone helping her. It's hard to buy a gift for her because she doesn't need anything. Now that she could use some help, she keeps declining the offers to assist her. She's constantly telling us she's getting by alright, that we have so many more important things to do, and that she doesn't want to be a burden to us.

"I know how these people will end up. Like Mom, they'll begin to have struggles they need help with, and there will be no end of people to help; but they'll continue to refuse until something overwhelms them, and they have no choice in the matter. Then help will come, but they'll be nervous and uncomfortable the whole time they're being helped.

"This has been very interesting, but what does it have to with Sue and me?"

"Patience, we aren't there yet. Let me say one other thing about these four types of people. Often, one person suffers from two of these boundary issues at the same time. The Compliant, who can't say no, often also is an Avoidant, who can't hear yes. These people are able to give hours of time helping others, but it's impossible for them to ask for even ten minutes worth of someone else's time, even when they desperately need it. The Nonresponsive, who can't say yes, is often at the same time a Controller who can't hear no. These people do very little, if anything, to help another person, but yet expect everybody to pitch in on a moment's notice to help them. A lot of unhealthy marriages feature a Compliant Avoidant married to a Nonresponsive Controller.

"These relational boundary issues often have no bearing on a person's competence to accomplish their tasks at work or in the community. This is why it's often possible to find a successful business person whose relational life is a wreck. They wonder why work goes well and their relationships stink.

"Getting back to Jesus, all these people have problems with saying yes and no. They often say yes when they should say no, and they say no when they should say yes. Their yes and no is consistently given to the wrong things. This makes it very hard for them to honor each yes and no because their yes and no rub across the grain of human nature. When yes and no are consistently given to the wrong things, the door to addiction is opened. The addictive agent, at first, eases the pain of yes and no given to the wrong thing and gives courage to face the fear that drives yes and no to the wrong thing. However, the addictive agent is a yes given to a wrong thing, and soon, the addictive agent strips a person of the ability to say no to it.

"When all of this is factored in, Jesus' straightforward statement about letting your yes be yes and your no be no becomes very difficult and complicated for us.

"Joe, which section of the chart are you most like?"

"I'm afraid to tell you, Matt, because if I do, you won't want to have coffee with me anymore." Joe laughed. "Seriously though, I think I have Compliant tendencies. I have a hard time saying no."

"From what you've told me the last few weeks," Matt responded, "I think you're understating the case. I also think you regularly say no to what is most important, and you regularly say yes to unimportant or trivial things, so you don't have to deal with what's really important. Further, and not surprisingly, you have a steamroller, controlling boss to whom you have no idea how to say no, so you put in far more work hours than you would like. Is that accurate, or have I missed something?"

"Ouch!" Joe said, "You nailed me, and it hurts."

"Now, do you want to know what this has to do with you and Sue?" Matt asked.

"Yes, I do" Joe said.

"You won't like it. Are you sure you want me to continue?" Matt asked.

"Even if it hurts, I want to know because I want to get out of the doghouse and back into the bedroom," Joe said.

"Here goes," Matt continued. "Your compliant behavior has you consistently saying no to Sue, who should be holding down the number two priority in your life, just behind God, who should be number one. The way you say no to Sue is by saying yes to all kinds of secondary things like organizing and running every community or athletic event in town. Another way you say no to Sue is by not getting help in dealing with your steamrolling boss so that you spend far too many hours at work. I'll bet your boss calls you regularly at dinnertime, other family times, and especially during those precious few times you give to being with Sue. When he calls during those times, you can't let the answering machine pick up the call, you answer it yourself, and drop what you're doing immediately to satisfy your boss, except your boss is never satisfied."

"How did you know that?" Joe asked amazed.

"Isn't this exactly why Sue threw you in the doghouse?" Matt asked. "Your compliant behavior, your fear of rejection by these people who are of secondary importance in your life, has you saying yes to whatever they send your way. That same fear of rejection has you saying no to Sue, who has gotten too close for comfort. The fear is that if she gets any closer, she'll find something not to like and leave you. If it weren't that she loves you so much and wants so much to be with you and be a part of your life, she would have left you long ago.

"You're right—I don't like it, and it hurts," Joe said.

"Is that what's going on?" Matt asked.

"When you lay it out that way, I have to say yes," Joe answered. "Before you started, I didn't see it. Now I can't understand how I missed it all these years. No wonder Sue's upset with me. Every time we got close, I found a way to take a couple of steps back, and I never knew why. You're right—I'm scared to death she'll find out I'm not the wonderful guy she thinks I am. I have no idea why she married me. How could someone as beautiful and wonderful as Sue want to spend her life with a slob like me? The only way I can figure is that she thinks I'm something I'm not. I don't want to ruin her illusion and lose her, so I keep her just far enough away so she can't see past the illusion, whatever it is."

"What if," Matt responded gently, "Sue is under no illusion? What if she sees more in you than you do? What if Sue sees the stuff you think is horrible about yourself and to her it's no big deal? What if that stuff is only important to you, and Sue isn't even concerned by it? What if Sue knows you far better than you think she does and still loves you? What if Sue wants to know more of you, so her love for you can grow even greater?"

"I wish I could believe that," Joe said as his eyes glistened with something that could be tears. "Do you really think that could be true?"

"Yes, I do," Matt answered.

"How do I believe it?" Joe asked. "How do I change my behavior to say yes to the high priority people in my life and no to the low priority people? How do I deal with my boss? I can't afford to lose my job."

"What kingdom resources does Jesus offer to deal with this?" Matt asked.

"This one's too close. I can't see it. I have no idea," Joe said.

"Let's start with the incredible, amazing love God has for us," Matt began. "The principle sign of the kingdom of heaven is this love of God for us. As Jesus told us, God loves us too much. God loves us way out of proportion to what we find appropriate or what we think we deserve. God loves us far more than our capacity to be loved. I have a friend who says there's nothing I can do to cause God to love me more than he does right now, and there's nothing I can do to cause God to love me any less than he does right now. This friend also says God doesn't love us because he's supposed to or because that's what God does best. Rather, God loves us because there's something about us, each of us, that flat out turns God on. To quote another friend, 'God's bananas about us.' This love of God for us is not for humans in general. Rather, it's for specific, individual people. Which is to say, Joe, God loves you far more than you can ever imagine. God loves you this way not from afar, but from up close and personal. God made you. God knows you inside and out. God knows you better than you know yourself. God doesn't carry the baggage about being you that you do. God even knows what it is about you that you think is unlovable. In spite of what you think about yourself, God knows all that, and it doesn't matter. He still loves you.

"Second, all the resources of God are available in the kingdom. That includes healing. Ask God to touch that part of your heart that's convinced you're unlovable. Ask God to heal that hurt and remove the fear of rejection.

"Third, there is the first Beatitude. Admit to God your issues with yes and no and ask for the resources to help you say yes to the good and the high priority items in your life and to say no to the bad and to the lesser priorities in life.

"Fourth, ask God to show you particular yes and no areas he wants you to work on.

"Fifth, draw on the wisdom of other Godly people who have dealt with these issues. I have a couple of lists I've found helpful. I'll get you a copy of them. The first list is from Henry Cloud, in *Boundaries*.[vii] He offers the following steps for growing toward mature boundaries, which is what we have meant when we have been talking about yes and no:

1. Use resentment as an early warning signal that you have entered boundary trouble—Be aware of anger, frustration, and resentment as feelings that are telling you that you're saying no when you should be saying yes and saying yes when you should be saying no.
2. Become drawn to boundary-loving people—Seek out and spend time with people who know when to say yes and when to say no. Observing their examples helps us know what changes we need to make.
3. Treasure our treasures—This is Cloud's way of saying that we weren't treasured as children, and we have learned to not value or treasure ourselves. As we begin to grow toward healthy boundaries, we have to begin to treasure ourselves. We have to see ourselves as lovable, valuable, and worthwhile. Until we believe that, we will not be able to consistently get our yes and no correct.
4. Practice baby no steps—Ask the boundary-loving people you have begun to spend time with to help you. Practice appropriate yes and no with them. They know how to handle yes and no. When you get it right, they will praise you. When you need work, they will help you.
5. Be aware that when you begin setting boundaries, you will experience guilt—This unhealthy guilt comes out of the old mind-set of saying yes and no to the wrong things. As you begin to say yes and no to the right things, it won't feel right. That guilt or those feelings that something isn't right lets you know you're changing. Ask one of your boundary-loving friends to help you deal with this guilt.

6. Practice grown up no—At this point, begin to develop a strategy for dealing with your biggest boundary busters. Work out what the limits are, and specifically, what you will say when your boundary buster tries to steamroll you. Sometimes it's helpful to role-play this interaction with some of your boundary loving friends.
7. Rejoice in the absence of guilty feelings—As you get more comfortable with healthy yes and no, the feelings of guilt will disappear.
8. Love the boundaries of others—As you grow, you will begin to help others with yes and no. Specifically, you'll become aware of people with messed up yes and no, and you will not take advantage of them. You'll work to help protect them from themselves until they get help with this too.
9. Free our yes and no—Cloud mentions 2 Corinthians 9:7, about giving with a cheerful heart, as a guide to yes and no. If you can accept and do the request gladly and with a cheerful heart, and it won't overload and cause resentment down the road, do it. If your heart is not glad, but feels obligated or burdened by the request, say no or at least ask for time to consider the request until you work through your feelings. Then after you have considered, if you still don't feel right, say no.
10. Set mature boundaries—Use your yes and no as a way to live out your values and help you achieve your goals. If saying yes takes you where you want to go and helps you become the kind of person you want to be, then go for it. Otherwise, say no.

"The second list is from Helmfelt, Minirth, and Meier, in *We Are Driven, the Compulsive Behaviors America Applauds*.[viii] It's a list of questions:

1. Do I adhere to a strong set of moral, spiritual, and human values?
2. Do I nurture a healthy balance between security and spontaneity?

3. Do I have adequate recreation in my life?
4. Do I have a way of expressing myself artistically?
5. Do I have high quality love relationships in my life?
6. Am I an equal partner in several give and take relationships?
7. Am I part of a spiritual body?
8. Am I maintaining an ongoing relationship with God?
9. Am I willing to admit my weaknesses?
10. Have I made peace with the fact that life is limited?

"Those lists sound helpful," Joe said. "Get me a copy of them, so I can look at them and think about them. The one thing that stood out to me was the question about give-and-take relationships. Most of the relationships I have are ones where I do all the giving and no taking. The relationship I have with you, Matt, is one of the few I can take from, and hopefully, I can give some to you too.

"This has been both helpful and painful tonight. I have a lot of work to do here. It seems to me if more of us had our anger, sexuality, and yes and no under control, the world would be a whole lot better place. Jesus certainly knows his stuff.

"I think I know what I need to do to deal with my boss. I need to stand up and say no to him. That won't be easy, and I'll need help getting there, but at least I know what to do.

"What do I do with Sue?"

"I would suggest," Matt said, "that when you get home tonight, you spill your guts. Tell her she's right to be angry with you. Tell her you're sorry. Tell her what you learned about yourself tonight—full confession. Then ask her to help you with the changes you need to make."

"But," Joe hesitated, "what if I spill my guts, and she throws me out?"

"I guarantee," Matt replied, "if you *don't* spill your guts, she'll throw you out."

"Can you pray with me?" Joe asked. "Can you pray that I get a better sense of God's love and feel more of it and more confident in it? Can you pray that I get the courage to face Sue? Can you pray that Sue would still want me after I spill my guts?"

"Sure I can," Matt said.

Matt prayed with Joe about all that and more. As they were leaving, Joe felt somewhat better about God's love for him, but he was still not at all sure how Sue would respond. He just hoped that as he drove home, he would somehow find the courage to ask Sue's forgiveness and confess his messed up world of yes and no. As he left the parking lot, he had no idea where the courage would come from. As Joe pulled out into traffic, he wondered if Matt would take him if Sue threw him out.

Suggested resources:
Dallas Willard, *The Divine Conspiracy*, HarperCollins, 1998.
Henry Cloud, *Boundaries*, Zondervan, 1992.
Robert Hemfelt, Frank Minirth, Paul Meier, *We are Driven: The Compulsive Behaviors America Applauds*, Thomas Nelson Publishers, 1991.

CHAPTER 8

TURN THE OTHER CHEEK

As Matt entered the coffee shop, he saw Joe, his back towards the door, seated at their usual table. Before Matt hung up his coat or got any coffee, he went over to the table and asked Joe, "How did it go?"

"Go hang up your coat and get some coffee, and I'll tell you," Joe said without giving Matt a hint at what had happened.

Matt quickly returned and sat down. He looked at Joe and said, "So???"

"It was hard," Joe said. "I didn't drive straight home. I didn't have the courage. I went through the park. It started raining again. Hard. I could barely see where I was going. Even though I still lacked the courage to talk to Sue, I pointed the car towards home. As I pulled in the driveway, I asked God to give me the courage to talk to Sue. I was hoping to feel different inside—stronger, or encouraged, or less afraid, or something. Instead, a lightning bolt struck nearby, and a crack of thunder rattled the windows in the car. I ended my prayer with 'alright, I'm going.'

"I walked in the house and found Sue sitting in the family room watching another chick flick, this one starring a redheaded actress. I hoped the redhead was going to be better to me than the blonde. I didn't sit down next to Sue. I sat across the room where I felt much safer. I started with, 'Hello,' and when she responded with, 'Hello,' I felt encouraged. I asked her to turn the TV off so we could talk. She picked up the remote, pointed it at the TV and clicked. As the picture faded, I hoped Sue wouldn't be pointing the remote at me in a few minutes.

"I told her that as you and I talked, you helped me see I was going through life saying no to important things and yes to unimportant things. At that point Sue made a sarcastic comment about my lack of insight. I decided to keep going and told her you helped me understand that I was trying to gain everyone's acceptance by saying yes to all these things. Then I quickly said the reason I was saying no to her by saying yes to everyone else was that I had already gained her acceptance, but I was afraid if she got too close she would find out things about me that were repulsive and wouldn't love me anymore.

"As I said that, Sue's expression began to soften, and her arms unfolded. 'Really?' she asked. Then she started talking about how she thought I didn't love her anymore, that I was tired of her, that maybe she didn't look as good as she once did, that I didn't find her interesting anymore, that maybe there was somebody else, and that those were the reasons I spent so little time with her. I told her that wasn't it at all. I told her there was no one else like her, and I didn't want anyone else. I was just afraid she wouldn't want me. She started laughing and crying at the same time. We found ourselves in each other's arms, and she whispered in my ear that we should take this upstairs.

"Later, after we got the kids to bed, Sue said we needed to talk some more. She asked me what I thought she'd find out about me that she wouldn't like. I decided to take a risk and mentioned something. Her response was, 'Is that what you're worried about? That's no big deal — I've known that for years.' I couldn't believe it. I mentioned a couple of other things, and her response was, 'You're kind of cute when you're neurotic.' I still find it hard to believe she didn't want to throw me out of the house after those confessions.

"Then Sue said that since my boundaries were porous, we had to work on rebuilding them. She told me at the next golf outing meeting I had to delegate everything I was doing for the golf outing except run the meetings. I agreed. Then she told me I was not allowed to accept any new positions or volunteer for any new jobs without her okay first. So what I will do now is tell people I'm interested, I'll talk it over with my wife, and I'll get back to them.

"Then we spent a long time, a couple of days, talking about my boss and my job. We decided I would turn my cell phone off during dinner and anytime I was spending with her. We also decided we would let the answering machine pick up any other calls that came in during those times too. We have more work to do concerning my boss, but we both seem to be happy with this new arrangement.

"When we finished, Sue told me whatever phantom fears I have, they were not hers. There wasn't anything floating around in my head or my heart that would cause her to turn away from me. Then, in no uncertain terms, she said the way to lose her is to ignore her, leave her home, and leave her out of my life. 'I want in,' she said, 'and I want to stay in. When that becomes a problem,' she said, 'then we have problems.'

"I still can't believe it," Joe said. "She loves me more than I thought possible. The other thing I can't believe is how you knew that all along."

"Just a little divine insight," Matt replied. "How are you doing on Sue's new boundary plan?"

"So far," Joe said, "so good. I really haven't had time to mess it up yet. I had a golf outing meeting, and I did what Sue asked. I managed to delegate everything out. It wasn't too hard, and nobody got upset with me. Sue was waiting for me when I came home. When I told her I had actually delegated, she was ecstatic. We've started turning the phones off and letting the answering machines pick up. My boss has been quiet recently, but I'm sure he'll start steamrolling again. We'll see what happens then. Speaking of jobs, how are you doing with the job hunt?"

"I'm still getting used to being unemployed," Matt said. "I've been to the job placement place and have taken the surveys, the assessments, and reworked my resume. I've sent it out several places, but no word yet. I don't expect to hear anything for awhile. From the way they talk, finding a job seems to be a full time job by itself. The severance package is good, so I've got some time. A couple of times a week I have to pray self-pity and anger away. One of the things I've begun to do is pray once a week for the top management people. That seems to help. I've picked up a couple little jobs around the church helping out. Rev. Jim gave me the names of two guys who have recently come to Christ that he wants me to follow up with like I'm doing with you, so I have plenty to do and enjoy what I'm doing, but at night I miss having the job and the paycheck."

"Sounds like you're keeping busy," Joe responded. "Maybe I can help you with those two guys you're following up, but before I'm ready to do that, I need a better understanding of Jesus. Just when I feel like I might be beginning to understand, he says some stuff, and I'm just clueless. Like this stuff we read for today, Matthew 5:38-42, don't resist an evil person, and turn the other cheek. I don't get it. How is this stuff helpful? Doesn't it make us doormats?"

"The concepts Jesus was talking about in this passage," Matt said, "are some of the most difficult for us to understand. In addition, our reading of Jesus' words here is somewhat blurred by a translation difficulty."

"Really? I thought I was just dense. It's nice to know I'm not alone," Joe replied. "You are going to help me make sense of this, aren't you?"

"That's what I'm here to try to do," Matt continued. "Let me read the passage (Matthew 5:38-42):

> "You have heard that it was said, 'Eye for eye, and tooth for tooth.' But I tell you, do not resist an evil person. If someone strikes you on the right cheek, turn to him the other also. And if someone wants to sue you and take your tunic, let him have your cloak as well. If someone forces you to go one mile, go with him two miles. Give to the one who asks you, and do not turn away from the one who wants to borrow from you.

"First, verse 38 is an upgrade. The 'Eye for eye, and tooth for tooth' comes from the law given through Moses. Before that, the standard was if you harm me, I'll take you out and your whole family too. This dates back from early in our history. In Genesis 4, right after Cain killed Abel, a man named Lamech is quoted, in verses 23-24, saying to his wives that he killed a man for wounding him and that if Cain is avenged seven times, then Lamech seventy-seven times. 'Eye for eye' was meant to limit the vengeance. But we all know places where blood feuds still exist."

"You mean," Joe jumped in, "like the Hatfields and the McCoys, and the gang wars? I suppose some wars start this way too.

"That's correct," Matt said. "Jesus, in verse 39, brought us an upgrade for an 'eye for an eye.'"

"I'm not sure it's much of an upgrade," Joe replied. "It looks like I just stand there and take it—I give whoever wants me an opportunity to take another pound of flesh, and then I let them just walk away."

"That's not what Jesus was saying," Matt responded. "Jesus was talking about how to live a kingdom life, with a kingdom heart, using kingdom resources, in a way that exceeds the law. Here, Jesus talked about a kingdom response to evil and violence. We trip here because many of the biblical translations aren't helpful. Most translations render the beginning of verse 39 as, 'Do not resist an evil person.' Walter Wink, in his book, *The Powers That Be*, argues that the words of Jesus recorded there say this, 'Do not resist an evil person with evil.'[i] The Contemporary English Version translates this phrase this way, 'But I tell you not to try to get even with a person who has done something to you.' We see this same thought in the writings of Paul and Peter. Romans 12:17 says, 'Do not repay anyone evil for evil.' Romans 12:21 says, 'Do not be overcome by evil, but overcome evil with good.' 1 Thessalonians 5:15 says, 'Make sure that nobody pays back wrong for wrong.' 1 Peter 3:9 says, 'Do not repay evil with evil or insult with insult, but with blessing.'"

"All this talk about translations," Joe said, "is too technical for me, but from the other verses I get the idea. Jesus was saying not to resist evil with evil. It sounds like splitting hairs to me. What's the difference between not resisting evil with evil and not resisting at all? Either way it sounds to me like you're going to get your butt kicked."

"That's the other part of the problem," Matt continued. "We misunderstand Jesus because we can't imagine what he was talking about. We think there are only two responses to evil. The first response is to fight fire with fire. If someone strikes me, I'll strike him back. Sometimes we strike back to destroy, and sometimes we strike back just enough to get the other person to stop. The second response is to just take it. Let the person who is striking me continue to strike me until he gets tired of striking or gets bored that I'm not striking back. But Jesus said there is a third option."

"What third option?" Joe asked. "All there is is kick butt or get your butt kicked."

"Thank you for making my point so eloquently," Matt said. "In the verses that follow, Jesus gives us three examples of a third option."

"I don't see any third option in those three examples," Joe replied. "Turn the other cheek is getting my butt kicked twice. Giving up my tunic and cloak is getting naked before I get my butt kicked. Walking two miles instead of one is getting my butt kicked for a whole mile more."

Matt just shook his head. He took a sip of coffee and tried again. "Let's look at the background of those examples and see if we can find the third way Jesus advocated. Example one, as you pointed out, is to turn the other cheek. Jesus said, 'If someone strikes you on the right cheek, turn to him the other also.' We need to act this out to understand what Jesus was telling us here."

"Only if I get to be the one doing the striking," Joe said.

"If that will make you happy," Matt replied. "Let's stand up. Wind up to take a swing at me. Hit me on the right cheek."

Joe curled the fingers of his right hand into a fist and began to swing, then stopped and looked puzzled.

"That's correct," Matt said. "You can't hit my right cheek with your right hand. My nose is in the way, and I'm not about to remove it. So to hit my right cheek, you have to use your left hand. Wait a minute. You can't hit me with your left hand. The left hand may only be used for unclean tasks. If you were to hit me with your left fist in Jesus' day, you would have been excluded from the community and would have had to do penance for ten days. You would have had to go back to your right hand. That's right. How are you going to hit me now?"

Joe made a gesture with his right hand.

"You're pretty clever," Matt said. "The only way to hit my right cheek with your right hand is to use a backhand blow. In Jesus' day, a backhand blow was delivered by a superior to a subordinate. It was delivered to insult, humiliate, degrade, and put back in line. A backhand blow was never given to an equal, only to an inferior. It was given by Masters to slaves, husbands to wives, parents to children, Roman to Jew.

"Now watch this: You have backhanded my right cheek, and I turn to you my other cheek, my left cheek. Can you, with your right hand, backhand my left cheek? No, my nose is in the way again. The only way for you to hit my left cheek is with your fist in a forehand blow. But wait before you strike me, you must know this: A forehand blow is delivered only among equals. I can't stop you from striking me, but I can define who it is you strike. I will not be struck as your inferior. I will not be struck as an insult or in humiliation, and you can beat me, but I will never be put back in line again. In the moment you strike, you're forced to recognize my equality. I'm on the same footing as you. We're both human beings created in the image of God.[ii] Having fun yet?"

"You took all the fun out of it," Joe said. "Acting like that can land you in serious trouble, or even worse, seriously dead."

"That's right," Matt replied. "But what would have happened if a significant number of Jews refused to accept the humiliating behavior of the Romans? What would have happened if a significant number of slaves on a plantation refused to accept the humiliating behavior of the plantation owner?"

"You can't make someone do something they don't want to do," Joe answered. "You can beat them, imprison them, or execute them. Those are the options. If a significant amount of the population refuses to accept the treatment and is willing to be beaten, imprisoned, or executed, then everyone is in jail. The soldiers or police have a full-time and unsuccessful job of trying to make people do what they aren't about to do. If everyone gets thrown into prison, there's no one left to work the crops and pay the taxes. Isn't this what a labor union strike is about? All the workers agree they won't work under conditions they deem to be unfair, and they bring the powerful companies to their knees."

"In this turn-the-other-cheek situation," Matt asked, "is there a way to resist evil without resorting to butt kicking or violence of any type? Would you say the cheek turner was just standing there and taking a butt kicking? Or is there a third alternative at work here?"

"Okay, I'll give you that one," Joe said. "There appears to be a third way here, which looks like just not cooperating; but there's not a chance that anything like that is going on in the other two examples, and no, I'm not going to act out getting naked here in the coffee shop. There's no way you can convince me there's some third alternative to butt kicking going on there. I'll put a chocolate chip cookie on it. I can taste it already."

"We'll see about that," Matt said. "The second example, which you call 'getting naked,' is where Jesus said, 'if someone wants to sue you and take your tunic, let him have your cloak as well.' The background of this example is the economic system of the day. The Romans heavily taxed the wealthy to fund their wars. The wealthy began to seek nonliquid assets in which to hide their wealth. The best nonliquid asset was land, however, land was ancestrally owned. It was passed from generation to generation. No peasant would sell his land. To pry the peasant from his land, the wealthy created high interest rates, 25 percent to 250 percent. The peasant, because of the high taxes, would eventually be forced to borrow money to stay afloat. Then the wealthy just waited until the peasant couldn't make his payments and used the courts to evict him from the land. This process was well progressed by the time Jesus was teaching, so Jesus was telling the people that when the creditors take them to court to take their land and all their possessions, give up the cloak as well as the tunic. Give them both the outer garments and the undergarments and walk out naked."

"What good does that do?" asked Joe. "You're working hard, but I'm tasting that chocolate chip cookie."

"What good does it do?" Matt replied. "Here's what happened. Nakedness was taboo in Judaism. The shame of being naked fell not on the naked person, but on the person who caused him to be naked. The creditor may win the court case, but in so doing, he is shamed in front of the community, and his greed is revealed for what it is. He is no longer able to hide his greed behind the law, but now he is fully exposed for what he is. What kind of person would take the shirt off someone's back in a court of law? Perhaps, for the first time, the creditor is brought face to face with his own greed, and in so doing, he has the opportunity to change. The debtor, though now naked, has not been humiliated or put in his place. Rather, he has exposed the whole system, and now no one can claim to be a good, upright person and continue to support and profit from such a system. Everyone is called to account and to choose how they will live. Such an act has the power to bring the whole system down on itself, by using the system against itself. Jesus was saying that if you have some creativity, you can push an unjust system to its outer limits and there expose it for what it is. This is done without violence and is far beyond just passive acceptance of the evil at hand."[iii]

"I'm not giving up my cookie yet," Joe said. "Show me how something like that could work today."

"Walter Wink, in *The Powers that Be*, tells a story from South Africa," Matt answered. "Just before apartheid fell, the police went to a squatters camp they had long wanted to destroy. The police were in their legal rights to wipe out the camp. They brought bulldozers and told the women in the camp they had five minutes to assemble their things and move out before the camp would be demolished. The women, sensing that the police were squeamish with nakedness, went out of the camp and stripped naked in front of the bulldozers. The police fled, and the camp still stands to this day. They overcame the police without any violence."[iv]

"Either your theory works," Joe said, "or those were some of the ugliest women to walk the planet!"

"Either way, no one's butt was kicked. Joe, I love chocolate chip cookies," Matt said. "I want that one just to the right of the center of the display case."

"Let's go double or nothing," Joe responded, "on the two-mile walk example."

"I wouldn't mind it at all if you bought two cookies for me, Joe," Matt said. "In this instance, Jesus said, 'If someone forces you to walk one mile, go with him two miles.' Today there is a lot of talk about going the extra mile, but little of it has to do with what Jesus was talking about. When Jesus talked about being forced to go a mile, his listeners minds went to the Roman soldiers who were occupying their country. A Roman soldier carried a pack weighing sixty to eighty-five pounds plus his weapons. Those soldiers who had a high enough rank had donkeys or slaves to carry their packs. The low ranking soldiers were allowed to impose a civilian to carry the pack for a mile, but no more. If a civilian was forced to carry the pack for more than a mile, the centurion would reprimand the soldier. The problem was the reprimand was entirely up to the centurion. There were no guidelines—it was determined by what the centurion felt like that day. The soldier could be flogged or issued a mild warning, or anything in between. The problem was that the soldier didn't know what would happen.

"Let's play that out. A Jewish man has been taken off his job in the field and been forced to carry the soldier's pack, even though it wasn't convenient, it was hot, and the soldier was rude. The mile comes to an end, and the soldier says, 'You can put down the pack and go.' The Jewish man says: 'No, I don't think so. I like carrying the pack. I'll keep it for another mile or two.' Then the Jewish man starts walking the second mile. The soldier is now at the mercy of the civilian. The soldier is worried that the centurion might see or someone might turn him in. The tables have completely turned. The powerless has become the powerful.[v] Notice that this happened without the civilian kicking the soldier's butt.

"I'll take my two cookies now, but since I'm a kind, compassionate, non-butt kicking kind of guy, pick the second cookie for yourself."

"Alright wise guy, you win," Joe muttered. "But when I get back, I want you to show me how that kind of thing works today."

When Joe returned, Matt thoroughly enjoyed his chocolate chip cookie. As he was finishing the cookie, Matt said, "Let me share some principles, then tell you some stories, and then give you a scenario to script out.

"In situations of conflict and situations where power is abused, Jesus is not about winning and losing. Jesus is not about giving his followers weapons or strategies of conquest. Jesus is about reconciliation. Jesus is about win-win situations. Jesus gave these examples of a third way and then commanded us to love our enemies. Jesus wants us to pray for the transformation of our enemies, and in so doing, both of us will be transformed. We'll talk more about that next week.

"The prohibition of responding to evil with evil, or violence with violence, is based on two principles. First, if we answer a violent attacker with violence, then we become as violent as the attacker. We become what we oppose if we oppose our opponents with their own weapons. World history of the last fifty years is enough to show us that a violent regime is often overthrown by violent revolutionaries appalled at the cruelty of the violent regime. It isn't long after the overthrow that the violent revolutionaries become as violent as the regime they overthrew.

"Second, if we respond to violence with violence, or evil with evil, we have let the attacker chose both the battle and the terms of the attack. The attacker has chosen the battle and the terms because to that he has the advantage. Most criminals attack with superior weapons and surprise to give them an advantage. Most of us, when confronted with a violent attack, respond with fear, uncertainty, and confusion, if only for a moment. That moment is enough to give the attacker the advantage, and we don't stand a chance. If we refuse to respond in kind, the attacker becomes the one who is uncertain and confused. I'm reminded of a story from the life of Abraham Lincoln that may or may not be true. As a young man, he was a lawyer. He was goaded into a duel. The opponent in the duel was an excellent marksman. Lincoln was allowed to choose the weapons of the duel. Rather than the traditional dueling pistols, the much taller Lincoln chose long-handled shovels. Lincoln did not get to choose the battle, but in choosing the terms of the attack, he gained the advantage.

"Jesus' third way demands as much courage as responding with violence. It takes courage to return good for evil. It takes courage to give blessing for insult. We cannot be cowards and live Jesus' third way.

"This leads to another point. The third way leads to suffering but so do the other ways. There is suffering with violence. There is suffering with passivity.

"Finally, let me say that Jesus' way of nonviolent resistance will work where violence is effective. Sometimes nonviolent resistance will work where violence does not. Sometimes neither violence nor nonviolent resistance works, but consider this: Violence always fails at least half the time. Wherever violence is used, there is always a loser. When Jesus' third way of nonviolent resistance and reconciliation is used and works, there is no loser."

"I hear the principles," Joe said, "although I'm not sure I understand them. I've never really thought this stuff through. I've seen enough westerns, gangster movies, detective stories, and spy movies to know that you have to fight fire with fire. In order to survive, you have to be bigger, stronger, faster, and better equipped. Smarts help, but it's always violence that saves the day. With the possible exception of Gandhi and Martin Luther King, Jr., I can't think of anytime, or any movie or TV program, or any person where it wasn't violence that ultimately saved the day. The best way to be is to be like Teddy Roosevelt, 'Speak softly and carry a big stick.' Do these principles work? Can you live this way? Has anyone actually tried to do this stuff?"

"Believe it or not, these principles overcame Nazi Germany," Matt replied. "Wink claims every time nonviolence was practiced against Nazi Germany it worked. Bulgaria saved all its Jewish citizens from death camps by national campaigns of civil disobedience. People laid down in front of trains on railroad tracks, marched in the streets, flooded Berlin authorities with letters of protest, and clergy made converts of Jews with nonbinding vows just to save them from the Nazis. Finland saved all but six of its Jewish citizens through similar means. Norway, Italy, and Holland also saved a large percentage of their Jewish citizens in the same way. In Germany, German wives of Jewish men demonstrated in Berlin and won the release of their husbands.[vi]

"Wink also references the fall of the Iron curtain in 1989-1990. The Soviet empire collapsed without a shot being fired except in Romania and some of the southern U.S.S.R. It was all nonviolent resistance and prayer that brought it down. Wink says that in 1989 alone, 1.7 billion people in 13 nations comprising 32 percent of humanity experienced nonviolent revolution. Wink goes on to say that in the twentieth century, nearly 3 billion people were touched by major nonviolent actions. That is about 64 percent of humanity.[vii] It works. It's just that Hollywood doesn't make many movies about nonviolent heroes."

"I remember the Iron Curtain falling," Joe said. "I remember being completely surprised by what happened. It seemed like it went down like dominoes, but the press coverage I remember seemed confusing. It almost was like the press didn't know how to report it, so I don't ever remember getting the full picture."

"Chuck Colson, in his book, *The Body*, writes about what happened and gives references where you can get more information about what happened,"[viii] Matt responded.

"Does this stuff work for everyday ordinary people like you and me?" Joe asked.

"In 2005, the Akron Beacon Journal, along with a lot of other newspapers, carried a story about Ashley Smith, who was out buying cigarettes at the wrong time.[ix] Brian Nichols had killed three people, including a judge in an Atlanta courthouse and a federal agent. Nichols, who had a machine gun, barged into the home of a former girlfriend, tied her up with duct tape, sexually assaulted her for three days, and began to look for a place to hide. He grabbed Ashley Smith and forced her to take him back to her apartment. She became his hostage. Later she told reporters she thought Nichols was going to strangle her. Even so, Ashley believed God brought this man to her doorstep so that no one else would get hurt. She treated him like a wounded human being, and through the course of events, which included reading to him from Rick Warren's book, *The Purpose Driven Life*, she was unharmed, and the police were able to arrest him without harming him.[x]

"A year or two before that article was written, I read a story in a newspaper. A man with an automatic weapon shot up a neighborhood. A family in the next development, having dinner in their garage, saw this dazed man coming toward them. They invited him into the garage for some dinner. He ate with them and left without harming them. This allowed the police time to catch the man. The police were amazed at what happened but said if the family hadn't invited him in to dinner, he would have shot them too.

"At about the same time, I saw another story in the news, but I don't remember which community it was. On a cold day, a man broke into a house. He was surprised to find two elderly women there. He was going to rob the house and use the money to buy drugs. The elderly women invited him to sit down, and they served him hot chocolate and cookies. The combination of the hot chocolate and the warm house had an effect on the cold man, causing him to fall asleep in the chair as the women talked. When he was asleep, one of the women called the police. The man was arrested, and the women were unharmed.

"These stories are around. They show up in the metro sections of the newspaper on the second or third page. They are oddities, or so it seems. They are reported without any fanfare. If we look for people practicing the principles of Jesus, we can find them.

"Let me share two stories that Wink tells in his book. The first is about Angie O'Gorman, a nonviolence theorist. Angie describes being awakened one night by a man kicking open the door to her bedroom. He was verbally abusive as he walked towards her bed. The thoughts that went through her mind were: If she screamed, there was no one around to hear, and if she had a gun under her pillow, this man wouldn't wait for her to find it and aim it. A third thought came, and Angie believed it saved her life. She realized with clarity that either they made it through this night together unharmed, or they both would be damaged. She would be raped, or worse, and he would go to prison. Their safety was connected. That thought freed her from her desire to lash out and from her paralysis. She was still very much afraid, but she began to talk. She asked him what time it was. His watch was fifteen minutes different from the clock on her nightstand. She told him she hoped his watch wasn't broken. The tension began to ease. She asked him how he got into the house. He told her he broke the glass in the back door. She said that was a problem because she didn't have the money to fix it. He talked about financial problems of his own. She kept him talking until they weren't strangers anymore. Then she asked him to leave. He said he had nowhere to go. She told him firmly, equal to equal, she would give him a set of clean sheets, and he could make his own bed downstairs. He went downstairs, and Angie sat up in bed shaking the rest of the night. The next morning, they ate breakfast together, and he left."[xi]

"That really happened?" Joe asked amazed.

"That's what Wink says," Matt replied. "He quotes Angie's book, so I think you could read it from Angie herself.[xii] Wink says Angie treated the intruder as a human being, which caught the man off guard. Second, she engaged the man in conversation, which defused his violence.

"Another story that Wink quotes is about a woman walking home from a supermarket on a deserted street carrying heavy packages. She hears footsteps behind her. She realizes she's being followed. The footsteps draw closer, closer, closer. Just before the footsteps overtake her, the woman suddenly turns, smiles at the stranger, hands him her packages and says: 'Thank God you showed up! I hate to walk alone on these streets, and these packages are so heavy.' The man carried her packages, and escorted her safely home."[xiii]

"Stop," Joe said. "My head is spinning. All this stuff turns the world upside down for me. I can't imagine thinking like this, let alone being able to actually do it. If I wanted to do this, I'm not saying I do, but if I wanted to, how would I even start?"

"There are kingdom resources available to help you," Matt responded. "In the kingdom, all the resources of God have drawn near to help, heal, and save. This means that any hurt we suffer or that is inflicted on us is not our whole life. There is nothing that can be done to me that is fatal. God can bring healing to any injury. God has healed and continues to heal all kinds of harm humans have done. What did we learn about anger?"

"Jesus calls us not use our anger to blast, blame, or shame," said Joe. "He wants us to use our anger to bring about reconciliation. He also talked about going down the slippery slope of intense anger to contempt and then to identifying a person as a fool, where the person ceases to be human."

"Good," Matt replied. "Add that to what we heard tonight from Jesus' teaching about playing by different rules. We're not to return evil for evil, but to return good for evil. If you put all those things together, how does that change us?"

"You gotta help me," Joe said, "My head hasn't stopped spinning yet. I don't know."

"If I continue to develop kingdom awareness," Matt said, "my sense of security increases, and I become less fearful because I'm convinced God can see me through anything that happens. I approach life differently. I begin to look for opportunities to see God working in the world around me and to look for ways to allow God to work through me. Further, as I let the kingdom continue to change my heart, my approach to anger begins to change. I'm becoming better at seeing everyone as a human being with hurts and hopes. People are no longer obstacles or threats or means to an end, so I approach people differently. Each encounter becomes an opportunity to see God at work or to be used by God to touch the other person. Since I want to touch the other person for God in some way, I'm going to find ways to bless people who want to harm me.

"It's helpful to script out some scenarios of what this might look like because our imaginations are barren here, and our life experience is equally as empty. We probably don't have role models we can look to either. So Joe, since your head is spinning, let me give you two scenarios to work on that you can bring back next week. The first one is this: You're driving on the expressway early in the morning. You see a woman on the side of the road with her car's trunk open, and the jack is out. Your first thought is your cell phone, but since it's Saturday, you forgot it. Your second thought, which you act on, is to pull over to help. You're glad your wife isn't with you, because she'd tell you not to take stupid risks like this. The lady is glad you stopped. She tells you the flat tire is on the passenger side of the car. You go around to look and with your back to her, you hear her say, 'Turn around slowly,' and as you do, you notice the pistol in her hand. What do you do?

"The second scenario happens at work. You have been assigned a new boss. He attends a meeting at which you're reporting on a project you have been working on for some time. The previous reports have been well received. The new boss, who is hearing about this project for the first time, tears you, your work, and your character to shreds in the meeting in front of everyone else there. Then his parting shot is, 'I want to see you in my office right after lunch.'

When you arrive at his office, he takes some more shots at you, like this: 'I don't like you. I have never liked you. I don't know who you fooled to get this position. If I have my way, you will be terminated by year's end. Dust off your resume, and don't expect a good reference.' What do you do?

"Apply what we've learned from Jesus about the kingdom of heaven and what a kingdom lifestyle looks like. Maybe something from the Beatitudes might be helpful too. I'll be eagerly waiting to hear what you come up with next week."

"Me too," Joe replied, "because right now, I have no clue."

Before they left, Matt and Joe prayed with each other. They thanked God for his work with Joe and Sue and the upturn the marriage had taken, and they prayed for a job for Matt. Joe drove out of the parking lot this week feeling much better about life but without a clue as to how he would complete his assignment.

Suggested resources:
Walter Wink, *The Powers That Be*, Augsburg Fortress, 1998.
Chuck Colson, *The Body: Being Light in Darkness*, Thomas Nelson, Inc., 1992.
Terry Pluto, "God Speaks to Hostage, Her Captor," *The Akron Beacon Journal*, March 15, 2005.
Rick Warren, *The Purpose Driven Life*, Zondervan, 2002.

CHAPTER 9

LOVE YOUR ENEMIES

Joe got to the coffee shop at the usual time. He looked around and didn't see Matt. He bought his coffee and turned to go to his usual table, but some giggly high school girls had taken it while he was waiting for his coffee. He looked at them for a moment, then smiled and took another table.

Minutes passed. Joe checked his watch against the clock on the wall. They agreed with each other. It wasn't like Matt to be late. Joe pulled out his cell phone. It was dead. He forgot to charge his battery again. Joe wondered how long he should wait. He looked at his cup of coffee and watched the steam rise off it, and then he thought maybe he should pray for Matt. As he started praying, Joe began to reflect on how much his life had changed over the past several weeks. Just sitting down at a different table with a smile on his face and amusement at the high school girls was something that wouldn't have happened a few weeks ago. He would have been angry, his evening would have been ruined, and he would have made everyone else's evening miserable too; but now things were different. For the first time in his life, he felt like some part that had been missing had fallen into place. He felt forgiven, free of the guilt, and clean of the dirt that comes with living. He felt loved by God. He didn't feel alone anymore. He didn't feel desperate anymore. He was beginning to feel that God really was sending resources to help him. His outlook on life had turned from gloomy to mildly optimistic. His marriage had improved drastically. His relationships with his children were better. He felt that in the teachings of Jesus he had found a compass to guide him. He admitted he couldn't remember anything challenging him as much and pushing him as hard as these words of Jesus. Yet, the challenge and the push were without menace. Every time he tried something Jesus was pushing him on, it worked out. He found some of it very hard to understand and even harder to do. Yet, every time he actually tried to put the words of Jesus into practice, it always worked out in ways he had not been able to imagine. Joe found his mind filled with two words he kept uttering to God again and again—*thank you*.

His reflection was interrupted in mid thank-you by a harried Matt. "I'm sorry I'm late," Matt said. "We got held up at the soccer field. There was a fender-bender in the parking lot that blocked the exit. I tried to call you, but all I got was your cell's answering service."

"Don't worry about it," Joe replied. "I've been putting the time to such good use I'm almost sorry you showed up."

"I can leave," Matt said.

"No, that's not what I meant." Joe laughed. "Go get some coffee and catch up to yourself."

When Matt returned, he looked calmer. "Tell me," Matt said, "what were you doing while you were waiting?"

"I was thanking God for all the changes he has brought into my life," Joe replied. "I could spend all night talking about that, but you gave me some homework, and the words of Jesus this week seem to be among the most challenging things he has said yet."

"You're right," Matt responded, "But first, tell me about the homework. How did you work out the scenarios?"

"The one where the woman on the side of the road had the gun turned out to be easier to script than the one with the psycho boss," Joe said. "I didn't like imagining looking down the barrel of the woman's gun, but it seemed less threatening somehow. I just didn't believe she'd really pull the trigger. I also imagined on a Saturday morning I wasn't carrying much cash, and any credit cards she took would be quickly traced. I didn't think she would get far with my car if she took it. I purposely don't speed through that part of the expressway because the local police use it to boost their pension fund. I looked at the gun. I looked at the woman holding the gun.

I said to the woman, 'You look scarier than the gun.' She was surprised by that and said, 'What do you mean?' I told her that her hair was a mess, her eyes were bloodshot and there were dark circles under them, she had a bruise on the part of her arm I could see, and she looked like she had slept in her clothes. Then I asked her if she was alright. When I asked her that, she bit her lip to try to stop from crying. I told her she wasn't very good at this. I said, 'Why don't you tell me what's wrong, and let's see if I can do something to help that won't get me hurt or you in jail?' She started to cry and slumped over the back fender of the car letting go of the gun. Then she looked up at me and told me her very sad story."

"That's good," Matt said. "You engaged her in conversation. You saw her as a person in trouble and offered to help. Imagining that kind of thing begins to create a script we can follow if we ever find ourselves in those kinds of situations. How did you do with the boss?"

"I didn't," Joe replied. "I couldn't work that one through. All I could imagine was getting into a yelling match with him or reporting him to Human Resources or staring him down and saying, 'Just try it.' How would you handle it?"

"It's a tough one," Matt agreed. "Let's review what Jesus said for a minute, 'Do not resist evil with evil.' The passage from Romans 12 we looked at said to return good for evil. Jesus wants a win-win situation, and his examples included leveling the playing field, so I might respond to the boss by saying, 'I'm sorry you feel that way about me. Whether you like me or not, I would appreciate the courtesy of having you talk with me about something you don't like before bringing it up at a meeting. That way, I have an opportunity to work on it before the meeting, so everyone has a chance to look good. Before I go, I want to know if there is anything I can do for you to help you get settled into your new position.' After I left, I would begin to work on some things I could do that would benefit the boss and help him out. I might call his former department and talk with someone about what makes this boss feel comfortable, what he likes, and how he operates, so I can begin to add value to his work life. Then I would look for something specific to do each day to add value to him. I would use the energy from my anger to do good to this man. I wouldn't expect him to notice, but I would watch to see what Jesus' concept of returning good for evil would do. At that point, I have nothing to lose. He has said I'm as good as gone anyway. If I follow Jesus here, something might happen. It sure couldn't make things worse."

"That," said Joe, "is much more difficult than looking down the barrel of a gun. I can't imagine at the moment being able to do that. I see how it's a way to live out what Jesus said. I guess in such a setting I would need lots of help from Jesus to actually pull that off."

"It's difficult," Matt agreed again. "What Jesus had to say in the passage we're looking at today is just as difficult. 'Love your enemies,' he said."

"I know, I read it. I see the words on the page," Joe said, "but I just can't get there. Love your enemies, but I don't even like these people. How can I feel warm and fuzzy toward them? I liked the old way better, 'Love your neighbor and hate your enemy' (Matthew 5:43). I'm not sure Jesus had any understanding of my situation or had any appreciation for the people who are my enemies, or the people I hate, and what they've done to me. If Jesus truly knew, then he would understand and approve my feelings toward these people. I just don't understand how Jesus could tell us to love our enemies. What Jesus should have said to us is, 'Say the word, and I'll wipe them off the face of the earth.' If he did, this world would be a whole lot better place to live in, and my life would have a lot more peace and a lot less stress."

"Let me start by saying this," Matt replied, "Love is a choice, not a feeling. Love is a choice to seek the highest good for a person. Love is wanting the best for a person and doing what I can to contribute to the best happening toward the person. I may feel warm and fuzzy about doing this, or I may grit my teeth while doing it. There are some things I do because I love Mary that I enjoy doing and feel good about doing, like taking her out to dinner. There are other things I do for Mary, like adding an errand she asks me to do as I'm heading out the door, but I don't have enough time to do what I already had planned. I add her task to the list, not because I feel wonderful about doing it, but because I know it will help her."

"So you're telling me love is not a feeling but a choice and a set of actions that follow that choice, and there may or may not be emotions that accompany that decision," Joe said. "I need to think about that. But even if that's the case, why in the world would Jesus want us to love our enemies instead of wiping them out? If somehow you can convince me tonight that Jesus is serious about this, then how in the world do I ever love them?"

"Remember, Jesus was talking about life in the kingdom of heaven," Matt began. "The kingdom of heaven is the place where God reigns. The kingdom of heaven is the place where what God wants is done. The kingdom of heaven is the place where God's values are lived out. The kingdom of heaven is where God makes available his resources to live out his values. When Jesus told us to love our enemies, he was telling us to act like God acts. God loves his enemies. Jesus said, 'Love your enemies and pray for those who persecute you, that you may be sons of your Father in heaven.' If you remember from the Beatitudes, we learned that a son is someone who does what his father does. Jesus wants us to love our enemies because that is what God does.

"Walter Wink, in *The Powers That Be*, has three excellent paragraphs about God loving his enemies. Let me share them with you:

> Much of what passes for religion denies the existence of such a God. Is not God precisely that moral force in the universe that rewards the good and punishes the evil? This had been the message of John the Baptist, and it would later be the message of the church. In John's preaching, God is depicted as verging on a massive and final counteroffensive against evil in which all evil will be exterminated. One whole side of reality will be wiped out. Ostensibly John has chaffy people in mind. God will obliterate them by fire.
>
> Jesus by contrast, understood judgment not as an end but as a beginning. The penitential river of fire was not to consume but purify, not annihilate but redeem (Luke 15:1-32, 18:9-14). Divine judgment is intended not to destroy but to awaken people to the devastating truth about their lives. Jesus seizes the apocalyptic vision of impending doom and

hurls it into present time, into the present encounter with God's unexpected and unaccountable forgiveness. Judgment no longer is the last crushing word on a failed life, but the first word of a new creation.

Jesus lived this new creation out in his table fellowship with those whom the religious establishment had branded outcasts, sinners, renegades: the enemies of God. He did not wait for them to repent, become respectable, and do works of restitution in hope of gaining divine forgiveness and human restoration. Instead he audaciously burst upon these sinners with the declaration that their sins had been forgiven, prior to their repentance, prior to their having done any acts of restitution or reconciliation. Everything is reversed: You are forgiven; now you can repent! God loves you; now you can lift your eyes to God! The enmity is over. You were enemies and yet God accepts you! There is nothing you must do to earn this. You need only accept it.[i]

"Because God loves his enemies, because God loved us—you and me—when we were enemies of God, we're called to love our enemies just as God loves us."

"Slow down a minute," Joe said. "Let me read over those paragraphs a couple more times. There were a couple of words in there I didn't get. I think I get the basic idea, but let me go through it some more. You can get us some chocolate chip cookies while I sort through this."

As Joe read and pondered, Matt purchased two of the largest chocolate chip cookies he had ever seen, which caused him to reflect on just how good God is. As Matt returned with the cookies, Joe looked up and said, "I think I've got it. This is just what Jesus had been saying about the kingdom of heaven. God has drawn near to love us, and God has drawn near because he loves us. I guess that means God loves my enemies as much as he loves me. That's what Jesus meant by saying, 'He causes his sun to rise on the evil and the good, and sends rain on the righteous and the unrighteous.' I'm not exactly sure I'm going to like the implications of that."

"Let's play them out and see," Matt responded. "Wink has insights into enemies that I find helpful. He says we have two things in common with our enemies.[ii] The first is that God created us both. God created my enemy with as much love and wonder as he used to create me.

"The second is that I, like my enemy, am evil. I know that is a hard thing to say. We have people we consider to be our enemies, and some of those people think the same thing of us—we're their enemies. If we would ask them why they're our enemies, they would name a list of our offenses and proclaim us evil as a result of these actions. Of course, our initial response would be they misunderstood our actions or they had it coming. Further, we would claim to be on the side of right, which means our actions were justified and theirs weren't."

"Wait a minute," Joe interrupted. "Are you saying there is no difference between me and a terrorist? Are you saying that I could murder innocent women and children and hide behind sacred places and hospitals to escape?"

"If you were to ask a terrorist to describe us, what would he say?" Matt asked, "Would he say the United States in on the side of right and never makes a mistake? Would he say that when the United States makes a mistake it's alright because they mean well? Or would he be as threatened by us as we are of them? Doesn't he think the world would be a much better place without us? Aren't we, with our weapons and ways of warfare, killing them in greater numbers and with more efficiency than they killed our people?

"I'm not saying I agree with the terrorist actions or agenda. I'm just pointing out they think the same things of us that we think of them. I also want to say that I don't have to do the exact deed my enemy has done—the potential for dark deeds lurks in me. It's out of the human heart that all this comes. The darkness that causes terrorists to do their atrocities is the same darkness that causes the United States to be the world's largest exporter of child pornography and pornography period. The terrorists, fighting for their cause, wreck lives with suicide bombers. The pornographers, turning a profit, wreck lives with a river of sewage. I, in my own way, am as evil as my enemy is in his way."

"Is that true?" Joe asked. "Is the U.S. the world's largest exporter of pornography?" As Matt nodded, Joe continued, "That's disgusting. I think I'm starting to see what you mean. If God answered my prayer to wipe my evil enemy off the face of the earth, then he would have to answer my enemy's prayer to wipe his evil enemy off the face of the earth—which would be me."

"That's right," Matt replied, "let me say it this way: If I believe God hates my enemies, then I must, at some point, face the idea that God hates me too.

"What we do with this is try to hide our evil. We read Jesus' words, talking about being perfect like God, and we think he's talking about never making a mistake or doing anything wrong. This further compels us to hide our evil, our shadow, and our flaws. The problem is that those parts of our lives refuse to be hidden. They sneak out around the edges. The place where the evil, the shadow, and the flaws sneak out is our enemy. We project on our enemy all the evil within us.

"Wink has a wonderfully uncomfortable exercise to help us see this. He invites us to get out a piece of paper and write down the name of one of our enemies. The second step is to list all that we dislike about our enemy. The third step is to examine the list and put a check mark next to the traits we have in common with our enemy.[iii]

"As we identify these traits, we're able to shed light on our shadow, learning things about ourselves that we would never have been able to learn otherwise. In this sense, Wink says our enemy is a gift to us. Part of the enemy's job is to illuminate our darkness so that we might see it, bring it to God, and have it transformed.

"The way it works is that we have a role in transforming our enemies, and they have a role in transforming us. As we become aware of our projections on our enemies, we're freed from the fear that we'll overreact murderously toward them. Wink says, 'We are able to develop an objective rage at the injustices they have perpetrated while still seeing them as children of God. The energy we squandered nursing hatred then becomes available to God for confronting the wrong or transforming the relationship.'"[iv]

"Matt, all this looks good in theory, but it doesn't really work that way, does it?" Joe asked.

"Doesn't it?" Matt responded. "I once had a problem with one of my direct reports. There were some behaviors he needed to change. I worked with him toward those changes, HR worked with him toward those changes, but he resisted. Finally, HR and I talked with him and told him we would like him to continue with us, but if he didn't make the changes we were requesting, then there was no future for him. He responded that if that was the case, he didn't want to work for us anymore. So together we plotted an exit strategy. That was on a Friday. I left feeling pretty good going into the weekend, but something happened over the weekend. When we came back on Monday, the place was abuzz with rumors of how I had fired this guy, and on and on. At that point, the exit strategy went out the window, and HR had the security guard escort him to his desk to clean it out and then escort him to his car and off the property. I got called on the carpet by the company brass who didn't know the whole story. In addition, I had a lot of damage control to do in my own department.

"I forgave him as soon as it happened. I knew he couldn't clean up the mess he made or in any way pay for the damage his actions caused. I asked God to give me the strength and the resources to clean up after this man. Then all I wanted was for this man to go away. I bore this man no ill will. I just didn't want to be anywhere near him so that I wouldn't have to go through this again. I even gave him a good reference for a job a few months later.

"That was fine until I bumped into these words of Jesus and the accompanying material from Wink. I became convinced that I was supposed to reconcile with this man, to see how he was doing and if there was anything I could do for him. I did Wink's enemy exercise. I wrote down the man's name, made the list, and then went through it to identify any traits we shared. I was surprised to find that the fourth trait I had listed next to his name was one I had trouble with myself. I began to work on that trait.

"But even though I had done that work, it was still nearly six months before I called him. I wasn't afraid of him, I was afraid of me. I was afraid of something I might say or do. I was indeed afraid that I might murderously overreact towards him. I was afraid that if he said something out of line or made light of what I went through with him, I might kill him. Like I say, I dealt with this for several months before I called him.

"We had lunch. It was a good lunch. I got a better understanding of him and what he went through. I also saw for the first time the struggles he was going through around the issues we dealt with and how he was trying to grow through them. I no longer was afraid that I might kill him. I now genuinely was rooting for him and offered to assist him in any way he might ask. We left the lunch agreeing to get together again and maybe even play some golf.

"Part of what happened for me was that in having lunch with him, I was able to see this man as a human being again and not as a problem. As he became human, I began to care about what happened to him again. I began to understand that faith in God means believing that God can transform anyone. If God could make changes in me, he certainly could make changes in this man whom I had written off. I saw once again that what is impossible for me is very possible for God."

As Matt finished his story, Joe stared off into space. Matt sipped some coffee and nibbled on his cookie, waiting for Joe to speak. Finally Joe spoke, "I don't mean to make light of your experience, but with me it's different. My enemy is my dad. You don't know, you don't understand the beatings, the taunting, the steamrolling, the never being good enough, fast enough, strong enough, smart enough. There's no pleasing that man. It took me until I was twenty-five to be able to break away from him. I haven't spoken to him since. If he were to get back in my life, he would continue the destruction that I barely survived those first twenty-five years of my life. Maybe God was able to do something with your direct report, but my dad is beyond that.

"I can get the concepts of what you've been saying tonight in my head, but my heart just can't go there."

"It sounds to me," Matt said, "like you're still an eight-year-old boy, unable to do anything to protect himself from his dad's actions. You've grown a lot stronger than an eight-year-old boy, and you're both stronger and wiser now than you were at twenty-five. Your dad must be in his late sixties or early seventies. You're bigger and stronger than he is now. In addition, Jesus doesn't ask you to face your dad alone. He will go with you."

"I don't know," Joe replied. "It's just beyond me. I'm not even sure where he is. When I was in my early thirties, he left my mom. It was one of the happiest days in my life. I got my mom back, but I don't ask about him, and the family knows not to mention him to me."

"I'm not going to push you, but at least try the enemy exercise using your dad," Matt said.

"I think I can do that," Joe said.

"There's another book that can help us as we go about the task of trying to love our enemies." Matt said. "Dan Allender, in his book, *Bold Love*, talks about how to love the enemy while God is in the process of transforming the enemy. Allender identifies three types of people and strategies for dealing with each type. I think it might be helpful to talk about these three types of people. Maybe you can identify which one your dad is and hear the strategies for dealing with that type of person. Would it be okay if we talked about that?"

"I think that might be interesting. I'm not sure I can do anything with the information right now, but I'd like to hear it," Joe responded.

"These personality profile types," Matt said, "and how to deal with each, are drawn by Allender, largely from the book of Proverbs. The first kind of person is what Allender calls the *normal sinner*. Three characteristics of the normal sinner are:

1. Envy—they long for what they don't have and envy those who have it.
2. Naïve—they are gullible; they deny what the world is like and how it works.
3. Poor Judgment—they wander into danger, have relational troubles, and are unwilling to accept how the world works and get in trouble.[v]

"In item three, they're like the story of the snake and the boy. A boy has climbed to the top of a mountain. It's cold, and he's ready to descend the mountain. As he starts to begin his descent, he sees a snake. The snake talks to the startled boy. The snake tells the boy, 'I'm cold. Please put me in your shirt and carry me down the mountain.' The boy replies, 'You're a snake. If I put you inside my shirt, you'll bite me, and I'll die.' The snake says, 'I will not bite you if you carry me down the mountain.' After a time the snake convinces the boy. The boy picks up the snake, puts it inside his shirt, and carries him down the mountain. Just when they reach the bottom of the mountain, the snake bites the boy. As the boy is dying of the snake's bite, he asks the snake, 'Why did you bite me after promising not to?' The snake replied, 'Because I am a snake. You knew I was a snake when you picked me up.'

"Jesus said we are to love these people. We can do that by asking two questions: How do we work for their best interest? What good gifts can we give them? Allender offers four good gifts to give the normal sinner. They are:

1. Cover over the sin—let the sin go unpunished and unchallenged until you have more data.
2. Find the pattern and context of the behavior—after you observe the behavior over a period of time, you will discover the patterns and contexts.
3. Talk with them at the right time, usually in private and shortly after an episode.
4. Be aware of how simple I can be.[vi]

"For instance, on some Mondays, my Administrative Assistant used to be short tempered with me and everyone else too. Some Mondays she wasn't. I didn't appreciate her short temper. After a couple of month's behavior, I had a pattern, but no context for the pattern, so I talked with her. I asked her to come into my office on a Monday when she was being short tempered. I asked her if everything was alright. She said, 'No.' I asked what the problem was. She told me she had a college-age son who was home over the weekend. He brought a huge pile of laundry that he expected her to do, ate all the food in the house, spent the weekend with high school friends, and then went back to school with his clean laundry without even a thank you. As she shared her feelings about this, I asked how often he came home. She told me, and I discovered his visits coincided with her short-tempered Mondays. She had no idea that her emotional distress was affecting her coworkers. I asked her if she knew anyone she could talk with about how to deal with her son. She said she did. She talked with that person. She made some changes, and now Mondays aren't a problem even if her son does come home from college.

"Do you deal with anyone like this?"

"Yes," Joe replied. "I work with some guys who live and die with their favorite college football teams. This year has been pretty good, but if their teams lose, things are pretty ugly on Monday. I'm sure there are others, but that's what immediately comes to mind."

"The second type of person Allender identifies is the *fool*," Matt continued. "A fool has these three characteristics:

1. Hot anger—The anger is used to avoid responsibility, to gain compliance or control. The anger is disproportionate to the situation. They want to be adored and obeyed.
2. Self-centered—They are self-centered and arrogant. They are fragile and have empty hearts. God is not important. Stuff is used to fill the heart and to keep life under control.
3. Hate discipline and wisdom—They despise the cost of growth and want quick relief. They rant and rave. They seek pleasure, not redemptive pain. They hate anything that exposes their hearts.[vii]

"Allender offers three good gifts to give a fool. They are:

1. Expose their folly—Help them to see their foolishness. Find a way to give them a mirror and then get out of the way. They will be angry.
2. Enforce consequences—Pain must be involved for the consequences to be real.
3. Be willing to talk—Talk only after they show signs of desiring to change.[viii]

"Author Pat Conroy was raised by an abusive father who fit this profile. Pat wrote a book, *The Great Santini*, about a man who raised his son the way Pat was raised by his father. In the book, the father undergoes a major character change and becomes a father who learns how to love and value his son and becomes the son's best friend before dying. Pat was afraid his father would the read the book and become abusive. To Pat's surprise, his dad read the book but did not become abusive. Rather, he changed like the character in the book, and today Pat and his dad are best friends. Pat's dad saw himself in the book and changed.[ix]

"The third type of person Allender identifies is what he calls an *evil person*. An evil person is driven by a self-interest that is so heartless that he/she consciously and cruelly delights in stealing life blood from the soul of another. Three characteristics of an evil person are:

1. Cold and unfeeling—They commit harm without sorrow or openness for feedback. They have no empathy.
2. Hard—They have no shame or morals beyond self. They are arrogant and use mockery, heartless accusations, to wound and control. They are unaffected by having their actions exposed.
3. Destructive—As a result of being around this type of person, one feels a loss of self, vitality, strength, desire, hope, direction, and purpose.[x]

"Allender says the evil person is committed to winning. They are committed to getting their own way whatever the cost, so a good gift to give them is to not let them control you. By not allowing them to win, it causes them to second guess their strategy. Allender offers three good gifts to give an evil person. They are:

1. Catch him in the act, and limit his ability to do damage—When an evil person acts in evil ways, call him on his behavior immediately. Name what he is doing. 'You are trying to shame me into going along with you.' To do this, however, one must have nothing to lose, because the evil

person will attack with more shame, anger, guilt, or whatever they think will cause you to give in. One must be able to set and enforce boundaries. 'You can shame me all you want, but I will not be shamed into acting.'
2. Offer of repentance—Such an offer sounds like, 'Your actions of shaming me are damaging both to me and to our relationship. I love you and myself too much to allow this type of behavior to continue. If you would like to simply ask me to go along with you and are willing to accept my yes or my no, I will continue this conversation with you. If not, I must go. Even if you do not choose to deal with me honestly, I will continue to love you and will look forward to the day when we can have a relationship where you respect me as much as I do you.'
3. Excommunication—If the evil person is unwilling to respond to the offer to change, one must have the courage to cut off the relationship for a time. Give the evil person a relational time-out and then try again days, weeks, or months later.[xi]

"It takes a great deal of courage to do this because the evil person believes that this evil behavior is the key to getting what they want out of life. If we resist the evil person, he/she simply increases the evil behavior. It's only after a period of time and several failed attempts to get us to do what the evil person wants that the evil person can begin to consider that maybe their evil ways don't work here. It will be difficult to get them to that point. If we don't though, they'll continue treating us and everyone else in these evil ways because they get the results they want with this behavior.

"To be honest, I've not had much experience in dealing with this kind of person. I've dealt with plenty of the normal sinners and the fools that Allender has described, and from time to time, I've been there myself. But in my life anyway, I've not really had dealings with evil people.

"Which kind of person is your dad, Joe?"

"From your descriptions, I'd say he's most like the fool," Joe said. "He was very hot tempered, and it all came from how I didn't measure up to what he wanted. He never acted like I had any feelings or desires of my own. It was all about him. I couldn't breathe around him because there was no space or air for me to be me. Like your man Conroy, I could write a book. Then I'd like to have him eat every word and choke on them."

"Sounds like you're still pretty angry, and the wounds have never healed," Matt observed.

"Yes, I'm still angry, and no, the wounds have never healed," Joe said. "I still feel some of what he did to me as if it were yesterday. I was having a pretty good day. While I was waiting for you to show up, I was just reflecting on all the changes God has brought into my life since I started following Jesus. I've received a lot of help and lots of things have improved in big ways. For the first time, I feel my life has an upward possibility, or least I did until we started talking about Jesus asking us to love our enemies."

"Let me ask you a couple of questions, Joe," Matt replied. "Since you started following Jesus, has life gotten better?"

"Yes," Joe answered. "That's what I've been saying."

"Has Jesus asked you to do some things you didn't understand and didn't think you had the strength to do?" Matt asked.

"Yes," Joe answered. "My marriage has taken a giant step forward because I did what Jesus asked, although I didn't understand and didn't think I could do it."

"Do you think it will be any different with your dad?" Matt asked.

"No. Maybe. I don't know," Joe answered. "All I know is that it hurts too much to contemplate anything but keeping him out of my life."

"Does Jesus offer any kingdom resources to help you deal with this hurt that's keeping you from moving forward?" Matt asked.

"Kingdom resources?" Joe pondered. "I hadn't thought about kingdom resources in relation with my dad. I had been just as alone in dealing with the wounds and the feelings as I was when dad inflicted the damage and the pain. But with Jesus in my life and my following Jesus, I'm not alone with this anymore, am I? Now, Jesus is here to help me. I suppose the first Beatitude, 'Jesus, help me,' is the place to start. 'Please heal the hurts in my heart my dad inflicted.' Do you suppose Jesus would heal my heart that way?"

"I think Jesus would love to do that," Matt replied. "But let me warn you, if you pray that prayer, it might get worse before it gets better. You might have to face some things you've buried. You might need someone's help to process it.

"Let me also tell you what's down the road if you ask Jesus for help with your dad. Jesus will ask you to forgive him. Jesus will ask you to pray for him. Jesus will ask you to plot and implement a strategy to be reconciled with him. Jesus will use you as a chief change agent in your dad's life. Right now he's like a live hand grenade waiting to go off in someone else's life. Jesus will ask you to defuse that bomb. Jesus will ask you to learn from him. Jesus will ask you to use what you learn to help others go through the same thing. With all that Jesus asks, he will be with you and will provide the resources to pull it off."

"Jesus doesn't ask much, does he?" Joe responded. "All I know right now is that if there's a chance Jesus can heal this wound, I'll take it and deal with the rest later. Sue has been after me for years to deal with my dad. Would it be alright if we prayed now about that healing?"

Matt and Joe both prayed that Jesus would bring healing to Joe's heart. As they prayed, Joe felt something happening in his heart. He didn't know what it was, but when they finished praying, Joe felt both a sense of peace and expectancy that God was going to do something. Joe had no idea what, but he was starting to get used to the unexpectedness of God.

Suggested resources:
Walter Wink, *The Powers That Be*, Augsburg Fortress, 1998.
Dan B. Allender and Tremper Longman III, *Bold Love*, NavPress, 1992.
Pat Conroy, *The Great Santini*, Houghton Mifflin, 1976.

CHAPTER 10

PRAYER & WORSHIP

Still embarrassed by showing up late last week, Matt arrived at the coffee shop fifteen minutes early. He didn't want to be late two weeks in a row. When Joe walked in at the usual time, he saw Matt and laughed, knowing exactly what Matt had done.

"I see you aren't late this week," Joe said to Matt as he walked by to get some coffee. When Joe returned with his cup of steaming hot coffee, he said, "You really messed with me last week. I didn't get to sleep at all last Sunday night."

"Why?" Matt asked with a smile.

"All of that 'love your enemies' stuff. You got me thinking about my dad again. I swore to myself I would never talk to that man again the rest of my life. I don't even plan to attend his funeral.

"Every time I closed my eyes Sunday to go to sleep, I saw my dad. Sometimes what I saw was a child being yelled at and beaten. Those old tapes have a way of coming back and haunting me. But I saw some other things, too, that were much more shocking. Somewhere between waking and sleeping, I saw a younger man beating an older man without mercy. The old man was trying to shield himself from the blows delivered by the young man. The blows just kept coming. The old man couldn't protect himself or withstand the force of the blows, and he fell to the ground. The old man writhed in pain as the young man just kicked and kicked and kicked. The kicking and beating continued long after the old man had stopped moving. I was horrified to see that I was the younger man and my father was the older man. Another time I closed my eyes, and I saw my dad, weak, alone, and afraid. He had the same look in his eyes as I did when I was a young boy.

"Then I saw some really weird stuff. I saw the old familiar tape with my dad beating me, but this time I saw something else. I saw Jesus take hold of my dad's arm in mid blow and stop the beating. Then I saw the younger man beating the older man again. This time I saw Jesus step between the younger man and the older man and stop the kicking.

"The last thing I saw was the weirdest of all. I saw Jesus take the hand of the weak, alone, and afraid young boy. Then I saw Jesus with his other hand take the hand of the weak, alone, and afraid old man. Jesus wanted to put the hand of the old man into the hand of the young boy, but he was asking the young boy for permission to do so. Evidently the old man was agreeable."

"Wow," Matt said, "No wonder you didn't sleep. I wouldn't have slept either. What do you think it means?"

"I'm not sure," Joe replied, "but I think maybe Jesus was with that frightened little boy all the time and kept the beatings from being far worse than what they were. I think Jesus was showing me that having cut my dad out of my life is a beating far worse than anything he did to me. I saw that my anger at my dad is as out of control as his anger at me. Maybe I'm no better or no different than my father. I think Jesus was telling me to stop the beating. With that last image, it looks like my dad wants to be reconciled, and certainly Jesus wants us to be reconciled, but I have yet to make up my mind."

"That is heavy," Matt said. "What are you going to do?"

"I don't know," Joe replied. "I know I need some sleep. It wasn't only Sunday night I didn't sleep. I didn't sleep well the rest of the week. The whole thing is disturbing. I find it hard to believe I'm mercilessly beating my father and inflicting as much pain on him as he did to me. I'm just trying to live my life, but I can't escape the eyes of the old man as Jesus had a hold of his hand. Those eyes are pleading with me for another chance."

"Do you remember how we defined mercy?" Matt asked.

"I think we said," Joe answered, "mercy is forgoing judgment and punishment to those in the wrong and offering forgiveness and pardon instead. I think we said something about the merciful not demanding the offending party to pay but trusting God to make payment so that the merciful could work on resolution and reconciliation. But I'm not sure that applies here. I'm not so much trying to make him pay as I am trying to live safely beyond his reach."

"I may get in trouble here," Matt said, "but I'm going to go ahead anyway. If safety, and not punishment, was your only concern, haven't there been opportunities in the last twenty-some years for you to learn to use your power as an adult to form a safe relationship with him? You said earlier you don't even plan to attend his funeral. That sounds to me like something more than being safe is at stake."

"I don't know," Joe said thoughtfully. "Maybe you're right. Maybe Sue's right. Maybe I do need to talk to someone about this. Maybe it's possible to have a safe relationship with him using some of what we talked about last week. Maybe I just don't want to. Maybe I'm going to be haunted by those dreams until I work this out. Is that something God does? Will he just leave those pictures in my head until I do what he wants?"

"God works in mysterious ways," Matt replied. "God may have put those pictures in your head, but there's something in you that won't let go of them, so I think you're haunting yourself. I also think the healing we prayed for last week has definitely started. Did you do the enemy exercise?"

"Yes," Joe said. "I hate it when you're right. I made a list of the traits my dad had that I didn't like. Then I compared myself to that list. I have three or four of those traits myself. I'm not usually aware of those traits, but they stood out to me on the list. I don't really think I acted in those ways, or at least not often, so I called Sue, showed her what I had done with the list, and asked what she thought. She made me promise not to respond in any of the ways on the list before she answered me. Then carefully and patiently, she helped me see that I act in those ways far more often than I realize. I have a lot to work on.

"Do you really think the healing has begun?"

"I do," Matt answered. "That's what those dreams are about. Why don't you talk with Rev. Jim about all this? He has good insight and can steer you to someone to talk with."

"Maybe I will," Joe said. "A good night's sleep would be a wonderful thing. Are we going to talk more about this? It looks like Jesus changed gears as we head into chapter 6 of Matthew."

"He did," Matt replied. "Jesus was still talking about what life with a kingdom heart looks like, but he turned his focus away from anger, sexuality, yes and no, and dealing with conflict and our enemies. He moved from talking about how we relate to one another to how we relate to God."

"When Jesus talked about 'acts of righteousness,' in verse one, what was he talking about?" Joe asked.

"Jesus gave us three examples of 'acts of righteousness' following verse one," Matt said. "They are giving, praying, and fasting. Through the centuries, since the time of Jesus, these kinds of activities have been called *spiritual disciplines*. There are fifteen to twenty of them. These are activities that open our hearts to God, make us more receptive to God's leading and guidance, draw us closer to God, and help us build a strong relationship with God. We'll look at most of the spiritual disciplines next week and talk about how they work, and we'll begin to use them. Before we get into each of them specifically, let's look at what Jesus had to say about them in general.

"Dallas Willard, in *The Divine Conspiracy*, claims there are two main things that will prevent or block a life constantly interactive with God and our growth in the kingdom. These two things are:

1. Desire for the approval of others
2. Desire to secure ourselves by means of wealth[i]

"Do you struggle with these things in your own life, and how do they affect your relationship with God?"

"Both of those are big deals," Joe answered. "That's why we spent all that time talking about yes and no. I was messing up my marriage because I was saying yes and no to the wrong things. We all want to be liked, and we all fear being rejected. To be honest, I hadn't thought about how wanting approval affects my relationship with God. If I think about it for a minute, I might say there are times I have to choose whose approval I'm trying gain. Just like I have to choose between spending time with Sue and organizing the golf outing, there are times I have to choose between pleasing God and pleasing people. If I choose people over God, I'm probably headed for trouble. However, the choices don't always seem clear at the time.

"Security is big a deal. I mean, how much money, how many investments, how much insurance is enough to provide both the standard of living Sue and I want and to ensure that we can maintain that standard no matter what happens? My best answer to that question always seems to be more than what we have now. It all could be gone in an instant. That's a major concern. For the moment, we have Sue's credit card binging under control. But one over-the-top binge, or a downturn in the economy, or one of us starts having health problems, or I lose my job, and our security very quickly disappears. I haven't figured out how God factors into all of this yet. I know the kingdom wins in the end and that everything will be alright. I think that means that somehow, someway, God is involved in security."

"I have come to experience in my own life," Matt said, "the impossibility of seeking both the approval of people and the approval of God at the same time. Likewise, I have experienced the impossibility of serving God and at the same time trying to make enough money to be secure. It's not that God has anything against people or money or security, it's just that we can't do both at the same time. We'll be unpacking all that in the next two or three weeks. But for now, let's ask a question: What does Jesus' main point seem to be in Matthew 6:1-18. Will you read the passage, Joe?"

"Sure," Joe replied.

> "Be careful not to do your 'acts of righteousness' before men, to be seen by them. If you do, you will have no reward from your Father in heaven.
> "So when you give to the needy, do not announce it with trumpets, as the hypocrites do in the synagogues and on the

streets, to be honored by men. I tell you the truth they have received their reward in full. But when you give to the needy, do not let your left hand know what your right hand is doing, so that your giving may be in secret. Then your Father, who sees what is done in secret, will reward you.

"But when you pray, do not be like the hypocrites, for they love to pray standing in the synagogues and on the street corners to be seen by men. I tell you the truth, they have received their reward in full. When you pray, go into your room, close the door and pray to your Father, who is unseen. Then your Father, who sees what is done in secret, will reward you. And when you pray, do not keep on babbling like pagans, for they think they will be heard because of their many words. Do not be like them, for your Father knows what you need before you ask him.

"This, then, is how you should pray:

>"'Our Father in heaven,
>hallowed be your name,
>your kingdom come,
>your will be done
>on earth as it is in heaven.
>Give us today our daily bread.
>Forgive us our debts,
>as we also have forgiven our debtors.
>And lead us not into temptation,
>but deliver us from the evil one.'

For if you forgive men when they sin against you, your heavenly Father will also forgive you. But if you do not forgive men their sins, your Father will not forgive your sins.

"When you fast, do not look somber as the hypocrites do, for they disfigure their faces to show men they are fasting. I tell you the truth, they have received their reward in full. But when you fast, put oil on your head and wash your face, so that it will not be obvious to men that you are fasting, but only to your Father, who is unseen; and your Father, who sees what is done in secret, will reward you.

"I didn't know the Lord's Prayer was in here."

"Yes," Matt said. "This is where it is. We aren't going to look at the Lord's Prayer here. We're going to pick it up several weeks down the road. What, do you suppose, was Jesus' main point in this passage?"

"Jesus talked about a lot of things in these verses," Joe replied, "but he kept coming back to one thing. He seemed to be saying that if you're going to be doing God stuff, then do it for God and not for others."

"That's right," Matt said. "Willard says it this way: We are to live our life for an 'audience of one.'[ii] To live for an audience of one is to live for that one's approval, applause, acceptance, and love. The struggle we have is that we're surrounded by audiences."

"Tell me about it," Joe responded. "Sue wants one thing, each kid wants something different. The guys at work want something else. The neighbors are watching with a still different focus. My extended family has expectations. You know about my dad. And then there's my boss, who, most of the time, wants everything. There's no way possible for me to live my life in a way that pleases everybody. I can't get everyone's applause at the same time for the same actions. They all want me to act in different ways. Now Jesus is telling me God has expectations too."

"Let's take a look at audiences from an internal perspective rather than an external perspective," Matt said.

"What do you mean by that?" Joe asked.

"Everyone," Matt continued, "has an internal audience. The external audience is all the people who are watching with their various expectations. The internal audience is the person or group we want to watch us. The internal audience is the person or the group whose approval, applause, acceptance, and love we want most. For a lot of us, that internal audience is mom or dad, a sibling, or maybe a grandparent. For some of us, that internal audience is our spouse or one of our children. We want them to approve us, applaud us, accept us, and love us. We do everything with the hope that this action or this award will gain their approval. Sometimes, if we can't convince that internal audience to applaud us, we work hard to get lots of applause from everyone else so we can say, 'Look, everyone else is applauding me, so why can't you?' Sometimes we get so frustrated from trying to gain the applause from the internal audience we give up. We just mark time because no matter what we do, it doesn't matter. At other times, we choose destructive behavior as if to say, 'If you're not happy with me, I'll really give you something to be unhappy about.' Or sometimes we choose the destructive behavior because while boos aren't applause, it's better than being ignored.

"This internal audience is a very powerful force in our lives because in nearly everything we do, we do it looking over our shoulders to see how that audience is responding to us. As you look around your life, Joe, who is that internal audience you're seeking to please?"

"I'm glad we don't talk about anything personal here," Joe said. "I guess for a lot of years, it was my dad. You have no idea how hard I worked to get his approval, to get his applause, but nothing was ever good enough. I don't ever remember a time when I got anything that even remotely resembled applause. As you pointed out last week, this left me with audience issues. Since he never applauded, I've worked hard to get others to applaud me because I think their default view of me is negative, but somehow, their applause doesn't quite make up for his lack of applause. As you know, I have Sue's applause, but because my dad never applauded, I don't quite believe her applause. I keep thinking she's going to turn on me and treat me like my dad did, which is why, at the same time, I want both to hear her applause and keep her at a safe distance.

"After listening to myself talk, it sounds like my dad is still my internal audience. I've written off the chance of ever getting his applause. Maybe that's why I haven't wanted to see him all these years. I don't want more disapproval to deal with. So what did Jesus say to do with audience issues?"

"Jesus said to change audiences," Matt responded.

"Change audiences? Is it that easy?" Joe asked. "How in the world do I do that? If I changed audiences, who would the audience be that would treat me better than my dad? What audience could applaud so loudly, so warmly, so enthusiastically that it would make up for all the years dad didn't applaud? Do you know how many curtain calls it would take for me to recover from just one time my dad didn't applaud, let alone the beatings I took for trying to impress him? I don't think that kind of audience exists. What audience would Jesus have me adopt?"

"Jesus would have you adopt your Father as your new audience," Matt said, "The one who is in heaven, the one who is unseen, the one who sees what you do in secret, the one who rewards you. Jesus tells us about the incredible, lavish, abundant, out-of-proportion-to-anything-we-know kind of love that God the Father has for us. God wants us to hear his applause. God wants us to receive his approval. God wants us to accept his acceptance of us. God wants us to adopt him as our audience of one.

"One of the descriptions Moses gave us of God in the Old Testament was that the Lord your God is a jealous god. We usually shy away from that description because it makes us uncomfortable. We don't see jealously as a positive trait. People do all kinds of crazy things when they're jealous, but here it is—God is jealous. He wants to be our audience of one.

"Why does he want to be our audience of one? Because he loves us so much. When God is our audience of One, we receive approval and applause that touches the depth of our soul. God's love for us is so great we don't even have to perform to get approval and applause. He loves us the same way people love infants. A baby doesn't have to do anything to get lots of approval and applause. The baby can just lie there asleep, and people 'oh' and 'ah.' The love, the approval, the acceptance, and the applause are already there. Now, if the baby opens her eyes and smiles, the crowd goes wild. It's the same with God and us.

"I'm going to let you in on a little secret. We were made for God's applause. Our hearts long for God's applause. The applause we get or don't get from the human audiences around us is designed to make us hunger even more for God's applause. Those who get applauded by their audience, other than God, find it isn't enough. Those who don't get applauded by that audience, wonder if there is an audience somewhere that can applaud them.

The truth is we're applause addicts. The applause that satisfies our souls comes from God. He wants to give us that applause as much we want to receive it.

"The problem is that we have a hard time letting go of human applause, so we find ourselves trying to use God to get human applause. I give so people will applaud me. I pray so people will think I'm wonderful. I fast so people will be impressed. When we use God to get human applause, all we get is that fleeting five-second, half-hearted applause from the audience. Then it's over, and we go looking for another applause fix. God says if that's what you want, that's what you'll get.

"However, if we genuinely desire God's applause, we give for God, we pray to God, and we fast for his cause, Jesus says God, who sees what we do in secret, will reward us. What kinds of rewards do we receive from our Father who sees in secret?"

"What kinds of rewards?" Joe echoed. "Based on what we've been talking about, maybe the reward is a longer, more deeply satisfying, soul affirming applause from God himself."

"I think that's certainly part of it," Matt replied. "I think part of the reward is the realization that God is present and actively attentive to us, tuned in to us so intently that he doesn't miss anything of what we do or say. I think another part of the reward is that God is an audience who is rooting for us even before we act and is just waiting for an opportunity to applaud. Like you said, God offers an applause that satisfies more deeply than human applause. I think God's applause comes with a lasting peace, contentment, and affirmation. Further, I think God not only applauds us, I think he acts on our behalf. Problems get solved, people get healed, resources appear, obstacles melt away, and gifts are given. I think we feel loved to the core of our being."

"Here's my question," Joe said, "How do I get the applause of God? How do I experience this love and affirmation that comes from God that you have been talking about? I have felt fleeting touches of it, so I know it's there. How do I get more of that going on in my life?"

"First," Matt answered, "you have to make God your audience of one. We do that by deciding we're going to live for him. We get up in the morning and ask God to help us live for him. We ask God to change our hearts so that we have him as our internal audience. Then for the rest of the day, we ask what God thinks about what we're thinking, feeling, and doing. Would this make God happy? Is God pleased about this? In all we do, we keep checking in with God.

"Second, we must be honest with ourselves and with God. God wants to applaud us in relationship with him. God doesn't want to applaud from the balcony. He wants to be up close and personal. He wants to connect with us. Part of what Jesus said about prayer is not to keep on babbling like the pagans. For the pagans, prayer was about quantity, not quality. They thought the more words they said and the more times they said them the more effective their prayers would be. They thought words were magic, and the right number—a lot—would cause God to act on their behalf. Jesus told us God is interested in quality far more than quantity. God wants a relationship.

"To have a relationship requires honesty. In Psalm 51:6, the Bible tells us that God desires truth in our inner parts. He wants us to be honest with him. If you have issues, say so. If you're ashamed of something, say so. If you need something, say so. If you're afraid of something, say so. There's nothing in us or about us that's off limits in our relationship with God. He wants to us be honest. God already knows all about it anyway. Our talking to God about it opens our hearts to God.

"To be honest with God means we have to be honest with God about who God is. We're coming before the one who made all that is and who holds life and death in his hands. We have to be honest with God about God's character. We find God's character in the pages of the Bible, especially in the person and words of Jesus. Many of us have old tapes, playing in our minds, about God as angry, hateful, and vengeful. Some of us have tapes about God as far off, uninterested and uninteresting. Some of us have tapes about God as having no personality or preferences and condoning of anything anyone happens to do. Some of us have tapes of God as a stingy taskmaster. If we approach God out of these mind-sets, we haven't connected with him at all because that is not who he is. As we make the effort to learn who God is and what God is like, we connect with him better, which enables us to receive the applause from God more easily. We will be forever growing in our knowledge and understanding of who God is.

"To be honest with God, we have to be honest about who we are. Right now, I'm not talking about what I have done or not done, but rather I want to talk about how I'm wired. Many of us try to approach God based on someone else's wiring, from an image we have of what's correct or pleasing, and when we do that, we don't connect. When we approach God based on how we're wired, it's much easier to hear and feel God's applause.

"Gary Thomas, in his book, *Sacred Pathways*, explores eight different ways people respond to God. Gary talks about the various things or activities we engage in that cause us to feel close to God, to feel God's presence or love. What may really cause me to feel close to God may be boring to you, and what connects you with God's love may drive me crazy. Would you like to take a look at these eight pathways?"

"Yes," Joe immediately answered. "I'm very curious."

Matt gave Joe a copy of the descriptions. "Let's walk through them. I'll give a brief, sentence or two, description of each pathway followed by six statements describing the pathway. Next to each statement, write a number from 1 to 5, with 5 being very true of me and 1 being not true of me at all. When we're done, we'll total the numbers and see which pathways fit us.

"The first pathway Thomas explores," Matt started, "is the Naturalist. A naturalist feels close to God in nature. A naturalist would make the following statements:

1. I feel closest to God when I'm surrounded by what he has made—the mountains, the forests, the sea.
2. I feel cut off if I have to spend too much time indoors, just listening to speakers or singing songs. Nothing makes me feel closer to God than being outside.
3. I would prefer to worship God by spending an hour beside a small brook than by participating in a group service.

4. If I could escape to a garden to pray on a cold day, walk through a meadow on a warm day, and take a trip by myself to the mountains on another day, I would be very happy.
5. A book called *Nature's Sanctuaries: A Picture Book* would be appealing to me.
6. Seeing God's beauty in nature is more moving to me than understanding new concepts, participating in a formal religious service, or participating in social causes.[iii]

"The second pathway is the Sensate. This person feels close to God when all the senses are stimulated. They love beauty and color. A sensate would make the following statements:

1. I feel closest to God when I'm in a church that allows my senses to come alive — I can see, smell, hear, and almost taste his majesty.
2. I enjoy attending a "high church" service with incense and formal Communion or Eucharist.
3. I'd have a difficult time worshiping in a church building that is plain and lacks a sense of awe or majesty. Beauty is very important to me, and I have a difficult time worshiping through second-rate Christian art or music.
4. The words *sensuous*, *colorful*, and *aromatic* are very appealing to me.
5. A book called *The Beauty of Worship* would be appealing to me.
6. I would really enjoy using drawing exercises or art to improve my prayer life.[iv]

"The third pathway is the Traditionalist. This person feels close to God through rituals and traditions that have been around for generations. Corporate worship is very important to them. A traditionalist would make the following statements:

1. I feel closest to God when I'm participating in a familiar form of worship that has memories dating back to my childhood. Rituals and traditions move me more than anything else.

2. Individualism within the church is a real danger. Christianity is a corporate faith, and most of our worship should have a corporate expression.
3. The words *tradition* and *history* are very appealing to me.
4. Participating in a formal liturgy or prayer-book service, developing symbols that I could place in my car, home, or office, and developing a Christian calendar for our family to follow are activities that I would enjoy.
5. A book titled *Symbolism and Liturgy in Personal Worship* would be appealing to me.
6. I would really enjoy developing a personal rule (or ritual) of prayer.[v]

"The fourth pathway is the Ascetic. This person feels close to God when they are alone and away from things that distract one from God. An ascetic would feel at home in a monastery. An ascetic would make the following statements:

1. I feel closest to God when I am alone and there is nothing to distract me from focusing on his presence.
2. I would describe my faith as more "internal" than "external."
3. The words *silence*, *solitude*, and *discipline* are very appealing to me.
4. Taking an overnight retreat by myself at a monastery where I could spend large amounts of time alone in a small room, praying to God and studying his word, and fasting for one or more days are all activities I would enjoy.
5. I would enjoy reading the book *A Place Apart: Monastic Prayer and Practice for Everyone*.
6. I would really enjoy spending time on a night watch, taking a short vow of silence, simplifying my life.[vi]

"The fifth pathway is the Activist. Activists feel close to God when they are righting some wrong or fighting some injustice. Activity is very important to them. An activist would make the following statements:

1. I feel closest to God when I'm cooperating with him standing up for his justice: writing letters to government officials and newspaper editors, picketing at an abortion clinic, urging people to vote, or becoming familiar with current issues.
2. I get very frustrated if I see apathetic Christians who don't become active. I want to drop everything else I'm doing and help the church overcome its apathy.
3. The words *courageous confrontation* and *social activism* are very appealing to me.
4. Activities like confronting a social evil, attending a meeting to challenge the new curriculum before the local school board, and volunteering on a political campaign are important to me.
5. The book, written by Francis Schaeffer, *A Time for Anger*, would be an important book for me to read.
6. I would like to awaken the church from its apathy.[vii]

"The sixth pathway is the Caregiver. Caregivers feel close to God when they are helping others and taking care of them. Often for them the most important part of the worship service is the prayer requests. A caregiver would make the following statements:

1. I feel closest to God when I see him in the needy, the poor, the sick, and the imprisoned. I feel God's presence most strongly when I am sitting quietly beside the bed of someone who is lonely or ill or taking a meal to someone in need. You can count on me to offer a ride or volunteer for helping activities.
2. I grow weary of Christians who spend their time singing songs while a sick neighbor goes without a hot meal or a family in need doesn't get help fixing their car.
3. The words *service* and *compassion* are very appealing to me.
4. I sense God's power when I am counseling a friend who has lost a job, preparing meals for or fixing the car of a family in need, or spending a week at an orphanage in Mexico.

5. A book entitled *99 Ways to Help Your Neighbor* would be very appealing to me.
6. I would rather nurse someone to health or help someone repair their house than teach an adult Sunday school class, go on a prayer and fasting retreat, or take a lonely walk in the woods.[viii]

"The seventh pathway is the Enthusiast. The enthusiast feels close to God when his emotions soar. Music is very important to them. An enthusiast would make the following statements:

1. I feel closest to God when my heart is sent soaring, and I feel like I want to burst, worship God all day long, and shout out his name. Celebrating God and his love is my favorite from of worship.
2. God is an exciting God, and we should be excited about worshiping him. I don't understand how some Christians can say they love God, and then act like they're going to a funeral whenever they walk into church.
3. The words *celebration* and *joy* are very appealing to me.
4. I would enjoy attending a workshop on learning to worship through dance or attending several worship sessions with contemporary music. I expect that God is going to move in some unexpected ways.
5. I would enjoy reading the book *The Mystery and Excitement of Walking with God*.
6. I spend more money on music and worship tapes than on books.[ix]

The eighth pathway is the Contemplative. A contemplative likes to be alone with God and feel his presence. They like to be with God. A contemplative would make the following statements:

1. I feel closest to God when my emotions are awakened, when God quietly touches my heart, tells me that he loves me, and makes me feel like I'm his closest friend. I would rather be

alone with God, contemplating his love, than participating in a formal liturgy or being distracted by a walk outside.
2. The most difficult times in my faith are when I can't feel God's presence within me.
3. The words *lover*, *intimacy*, and *heart* are very appealing to me.
4. I really enjoy having thirty minutes of uninterrupted time a day to sit in quiet prayer and "hold hands" with God, writing love letters to him, and enjoying his presence.
5. I really enjoy reading *The Transforming Friendship*.
6. When I think of God, I think of love, friendship, and adoration more than anything else.[x]

The ninth pathway is the Intellectual. An intellectual feels close to God when their minds are stimulated with new thoughts and ideas. They love theology books. An intellectual would make the following statements:

1. I feel closest to God when I learn something new about him that I didn't understand before. My mind needs to be stimulated. It's very important to me that I know exactly what I believe.
2. I get frustrated when the church focuses too much on feelings and spiritual experience. Of far more importance is the need to understand the Christian faith and have proper doctrine.
3. The words *concept* and *truth* are very appealing to me.
4. I feel close to God when I participate in several hours of uninterrupted study time—reading God's word or good Christian books and then perhaps having an opportunity to teach (or participate in a discussion with) a small group.
5. A book on church dogmatics would be appealing to me.
6. I spend more money on books than music tapes.[xi]

"Which ones do you relate to?"

"I think," Joe said, "I might be a naturalist. I know a lot of guys joke about going to church on the golf course, but when I'm out in nature I feel close to God, whether it be on a golf course, or a hiking trial, or just working in my back yard. I have some caregiver tendencies too. I like helping people. I feel like I'm partnering with God, and he's smiling at me all the time I'm helping someone. How about you? Which ones fit you?"

"The enthusiast and the contemplative are the two I scored the highest on," Matt said. "I just love the contemporary praise music, and I like being alone with God in his presence, spending time with him. The thing to remember is that no pathway is more sacred than the others. One is not more spiritual or better connected to God. It doesn't matter whether you're a traditionalist or an enthusiast or an activist. What matters is that you spend time with God in the way that causes you to feel the closest to him. As you do, you begin to feel God's applause.

"Let me summarize some. To have God as our audience of one, we must choose God for the audience and let go of the other audiences. Second, we have to be honest with God. We have to be honest about who God is, and we have to be honest about who we are. When we're honest, we connect with God. A third thing to add is that when you get direction or an instruction from God, act on it as soon as you can. If God is your audience, you want to do what you can to please him. When you act on something, God gives you the ovation roar from the audience box."

"I know," Joe said, "that I would much rather have God as my audience of one than my dad. I'm going to try and make that change, so I'm going to spend some extra time outside this week and find someone to help. Even though I feel very uncomfortable about this right now, I'll go talk to Rev. Jim about my dad and hear what he has to say. I should get a major ovation from the audience box for that. Can we pray about that?"

They did. They also prayed for Matt's job search and for the two other men Matt was beginning to disciple.

As Joe walked out to the car, he thought, "I've been here before: The night I asked Jesus to come into my heart, I left here not knowing what to expect but hoping something good would happen even though I had no idea how; the night I left knowing I had to talk with Sue and not having the courage, I had no idea something good could come out of it; now I'm leaving to deal with my issues about my dad, and I don't think anything good can come of that either. I wonder if this is what it means to follow Jesus—to get some marching orders, have no idea how it will work out, but go ahead anyway and see what God will do. I suspect this is what I have to look forward to the rest of my life. If God always shows up and does something unexpected, it's an exciting way to live." Joe certainly had not been bored the last nine weeks. As Joe pulled out into traffic, he thought he heard some applause in the distance. He just shook his head and smiled.

Suggested resources:
Dallas Willard, *The Divine Conspiracy*, HarperCollins, 1998.
Gary Thomas, *Sacred Pathways*, Zondervan, 2000.
Terry Teykl, "The Prismatic Movement," *How to Pray After You've Kicked the Dog*, Prayer Point Press, 1998.

CHAPTER 11

FASTING & OTHER SPIRITUAL DISCIPLINES

It was a beautiful evening as Matt walked across the parking lot toward the coffee shop. He was amazed this evening at the goodness of God. He had seen such major changes in Joe. Now Matt wondered what Joe had done this week about his dad. He was very curious to see if Joe had actually followed through on what they talked about last week.

Matt walked into the coffee shop, saw Joe getting settled, said a quick 'hello,' and got in the short line for some coffee. Along with the coffee, he purchased a couple of chocolate chip cookies. As Matt sat down, Joe greeted him and asked, "How goes the job search?"

"I've found some temporary relief," Matt replied. "A former boss of mine, Peter, from the old company, has been running a consulting firm. He knew I needed some work, and he was short a consultant. He called me, and I'm doing some work for him at a company on the south end of the city. I put in three days last week. It was okay. I think I can help the company. Consulting will put some bread on the table, but I don't want to do it long term. Pete sounded like he could keep me busy in the area for six, maybe nine months."

"Do you have any ideas about what you're going to do long term?" Joe asked.

"No," Matt said. "The only thing I know right now is the thought about getting another job in the same industry isn't appealing. The things I've been looking forward to are what I've been doing with you and the other two guys I've been working with, but I don't see a paycheck connected with that kind of thing. So I'm praying, and dialing, and waiting.

"How about you? Did you take any steps in dealing with your dad?"

"The weather was great this week," Joe answered. "I was able to spend time outside three days. On one of those days, I was able to hike along the river. It was beautiful. While I was hiking, I felt close to God. I was aware of his presence. I felt his love. When I got back, I felt strengthened somehow. I don't think I could lift any more weight, but I just felt stronger on the inside, so in that moment of strength, I dialed the church phone number and asked for an appointment to see Rev. Jim. I have one for next week. I'm glad it's next week and not this week because when I hung up the phone I got cold feet. I guess I used up all that strength, so I'll see if I can get two walks by the river before I actually go to the appointment."

"You sound like a kid at school who got a major project postponed," Matt replied.

"I guess I do," Joe responded. "I'm still trying to get used to the idea. All these years Dad has been cut out of my life and now to think about working to include him again is really pushing me. Sue thinks it's a great idea. I told her it wasn't anything I needed to rush into doing. She told me dragging my feet wouldn't make it any easier. She's right, but I'm still glad the appointment isn't until next week. What do we have going tonight?"

"We're going to dive into spiritual disciplines tonight," Matt said. "Do you remember what we said last week were the two things that prevent or block a life interactive with God and growth in the kingdom?"

"Yes, I do," Joe answered. "One of them is what got me in all this trouble in the first place. Those two things are desire for approval of others—having the wrong audience of one—and the desire to get security through the use of wealth."

"You're on it," Matt said. "Last week we started Matthew 6, where Jesus talked about acts of righteousness or what we call spiritual disciplines. Jesus' discussion was about the spirit in which to practice them. He assumed his listeners in that day knew all about them. They may have, but not many today know all that much about them or how they work.

A spiritual discipline is a practice that enables me to receive power from God to live a kingdom life, a transformed life, a life like Jesus lived. Spiritual disciplines are the method for transferring God's kingdom resources into our hearts and lives.[i]

"Spiritual growth doesn't come from right beliefs, although it's hard to grow without right beliefs. Spiritual growth doesn't come from knowing the Bible, although it helps. Spiritual growth doesn't come from spiritual experiences, although they're nice to have. Nor does spiritual growth come from trying harder, even though effort is needed."

"I thought that was what spiritual growth was all about," Joe said.

"No, it's not," Matt continued. "It's like weight lifting. I would like to bench press two hundred pounds. I go to the gym and walk into the 'big boy' where the free weights are. I put two hundred pounds of weight on the bar. I slip beneath the bar, get a grip on the bar, and lift. The bar doesn't budge.

"I leave the gym and go work on my weight lifting beliefs. I come back shored up in my weight lifting beliefs. I believe weight lifting will make me stronger, healthier, and more attractive to chicks. I put two hundred pounds on the bar. I slip beneath the bar, get a grip on the bar while telling myself over and over I do believe weight lifting will make me stronger, healthier, and more attractive to chicks. I lift. The bar doesn't budge.

"I leave the gym, go home, and read all the back issues of weight lifting magazines I can find. I learn a ton of stuff. I have great new techniques for gripping the bar and lifting. I have a bunch of inspirational and motivational stories from guys just like Charles Atlas, who went from ninety-eight-pound weaklings to buff and ripped. I even have the workout routines that actors use to get bulked up for their hunk roles. I go back to the gym. I put two hundred pounds on the bar. I slip beneath the bar, get a grip on the bar while telling myself over and over I do believe weight lifting will make me stronger, healthier, and more attractive to chicks. This time I use all the latest grip techniques and know I'm on my way to becoming buff. Convinced that I will bench press two hundred pounds, I lift. The bar doesn't budge.

"I leave the gym, go back home, and start watching the weight lifting channel to have weight lifting experiences. It's incredible! On TV, some of the lifters are benching six hundred pounds, and that's just the women! I go back to the gym and watch some of the big boys there bench press. Right in front of my eyes I watch one of them load four hundred pounds on the bar, slide under the bar, grip, and lift. As he lifts, his muscles tense, the veins pop on his arms and neck, sweat beads appear on his forehead, and he makes a grunting noise. Slowly the four hundred pounds move up and up until he has his arms straightened out. Then he lets it slowly back down. He does this ten times. It's amazing. I'm pumped. When he's done, he says to me, 'If I can lift four hundred, you can lift two hundred.' The experience of it all touches something deep within me. I go over to my bench. I put two hundred pounds on the bar. I slip beneath the bar, get a grip on the bar while telling myself over and over I do believe weight lifting will make me stronger, healthier, and more attractive to chicks. This time I use all the latest grip techniques and know I'm on my way to becoming buff. With that deeply moving weight lifting experience still fresh in my soul, I know the bar will move this time. I lift. The bar doesn't budge.

"I leave the gym, and I go back home. I review and reload. My beliefs about weight lifting are correct. My knowledge about weight lifting is superb. I have experienced some awesome weight lifting. I'm missing effort. I just need to try harder. I need to be The Little Engine That Could: 'I think I can! I think I can! I think I can!'[ii] I go back to the gym. I put two hundred pounds on the bar. I slip beneath the bar, get a grip on the bar while telling myself over and over I do believe weight lifting will make me stronger, healthier, and more attractive to chicks. This time I use all the latest grip techniques and know I'm on my way to becoming buff. I still have those deeply moving weight lifting experiences lodged deep within my soul. But this time I will succeed in lifting the bar because I'm going to try harder. I'm going to give it 120 percent. I lift. I give 130 percent.

My face turns red, my muscles bulge, my veins pop out. The bar doesn't budge.

"I'm at a loss. Is there anything I can do to lift the two hundred pounds?"

"Sure there is," Joe answered. "I used to lift a lot in high school and college. All those things you talked about are helpful, but they aren't the main ingredients in lifting. The way it works is you start with what you can lift. I started at eighty pounds in high school. After I was able to lift eighty pounds for ten repetitions three days a week, I added ten more pounds. Then when I could do ninety, I moved to one hundred. Over the course of about four years, I got to three hundred pounds. As you increase the weight a little at a time, you grow stronger and can lift more. What does this have to do with spiritual growth?"

"Our hearts," Matt answered, "grow and become stronger just like the muscles in our body. We grow spiritually, we grow our hearts, by exercising. Spiritual disciplines are spiritual exercises designed to grow our hearts. As we do spiritual disciplines on a daily routine basis, our hearts begin to grow. Sometimes we experience growth spurts, and sometimes we grow so slowly we hardly notice it happening.

"Dallas Willard, in his book, *The Spirit of the Disciplines*, says it this way: 'When through spiritual disciplines I become able to heartily bless those who curse me, pray without ceasing, to be at peace when not given credit for good deeds I've done, or to master the evil that comes my way, it is because my disciplinary activities have inwardly poised me for more and more interaction with the powers of the living God and his kingdom.'[iii]

"Spiritual disciplines open us to God—they're not ways to impress God. If we do the spiritual disciplines to impress God or to impress others, we're wasting our time. God is not impressed if we pray two hours a day. However, if we do the spiritual disciplines to God and for God to become open to God's work in our lives, then they work wonders. If we pray two hours a day to genuinely talk to God and hear from God, then amazing things begin to happen in us, for us, and through us.

"Spiritual disciplines are not the Christian life—they're the preparation for living the Christian life. Once again, the Christian life is not praying, but rather, time spent in prayer prepares us to live as Jesus lived. Time spent in prayer helps me to do the kingdom thing, at the kingdom time, in the kingdom way, with the people the kingdom puts me in contact with.

"Once again, spiritual disciplines create spiritual openness and receptivity to God. Much of our struggle with God happens because we aren't open or receptive to him. People ask, 'Where is God?' or say, 'I can't hear God,' or, 'God doesn't speak to me.' The truth is that God is here among us and is speaking to us all the time. We just aren't able to hear. We aren't receptive. We don't have our radios tuned to WGOD. Spiritual disciplines tune our hearts to WGOD, so we can hear, see, feel, and respond to God."

"I understand weight lifting," Joe said. "I think I'm beginning to understand what you're saying about spiritual disciplines, but what are they? I know the exercises you use to prepare for basketball or football or how to train for a marathon, but what, specifically, are the spiritual exercises? If I were to put together a workout of spiritual disciplines to grow my heart and my openness to God, what would it look like?"

"There are two types of spiritual disciplines," Matt replied. "The first type is called *disciplines of abstinence*. These disciplines are about abstaining from, or not doing, certain activities for a period of time. Abstaining from these activities creates space in our lives for God. There's nothing wrong with any of these activities—it's just that sometimes our lives are so full there's no room for God. The disciplines of abstinence are:

>solitude
>silence
>fasting
>frugality
>chastity
>secrecy
>sacrifice[iv]

"In a moment, we'll talk more about of each one. Dallas Willard, in his book, *The Spirit of the Disciplines*, says,

> If the places in our blood cells designed to carry oxygen are occupied by carbon monoxide, we die for lack of oxygen. If the places in our souls that are to be indwelt by God and his service are occupied by food, sex, and society, we die or languish for lack of God and right relation to his creatures. A proper abstinence actually breaks the hold of improper engagements so that the soul can be properly engaged in and by God.[v]

"The second type of spiritual disciplines is ***disciplines of engagement***. These disciplines are about filling the space we have cleared for God with God. The disciplines of engagement are:

> study
> worship
> celebration
> service
> prayer
> fellowship
> confession
> submission[vi]

"Dallas Willard, in *The Spirit of the Disciplines*, says,

> Abstinence and engagement are the outbreathing and inbreathing of our spiritual lives, and we require disciplines for both movements. Roughly speaking, the disciplines of abstinence counteract tendencies to sins of commission, and the disciplines of engagement counteract tendencies to sins of omission.[vii]

"Are you ready to look at them individually?" When Matt saw Joe nod his head, he continued. "The first one is solitude. ***Solitude*** is purposefully abstaining from interaction with other people. It frees us from our interactions with others and the dynamics and the patterns of thought that go with those interactions. As we get apart from others, the distance does two things. The first thing it does is bring us face to face with ourselves. We have nowhere to hide from ourselves. This gives us the opportunity to face what's in our souls—those things we're proud of and those things we're ashamed of. The first attempt at this can be terrifying or comforting, or both.

"The second thing it does is give us clarity about our relationships. We're able to see the dysfunctions more clearly and what our role is in them. Willard claims that solitude is the most fundamental discipline as we begin the spiritual life.[viii] Solitude gives us strength in our relationships. Once we get comfortable with solitude, we don't fear being alone. This helps us shake the fear of rejection. We're able, then, to re-examine our relationships and re-enter them without fear of what would happen if we were left alone.

"In solitude, we're not so much alone with ourselves as we're alone with God. This alone time with God begins laying the foundation for allowing God to work change in our lives.

"Solitude can be practiced by taking a trip to a monastery or a retreat center where everyone has his space in which to practice solitude, or solitude can be practiced in smaller doses by getting up before anyone else in the house or staying up later than everyone else. Spending time in a park or outdoors by ourselves is another option. I think mothers with small children have a difficult time being able to practice solitude, but empty nesters or single people have lots of opportunity.

"*Silence* adds to solitude. Solitude is being alone. Silence is cutting ourselves off from sound. Most of us live in noise. TV, radio, computers, traffic, office equipment, the hum of the refrigerator, and the ringing of the phone are the soundtracks of our lives. Silence is about turning the soundtrack off. Willard says that 'silence is frightening because it strips us as nothing else does, throwing us upon the stark realities of our life.'[ix]

"For me, silence allows the soul to settle. Life and all the noise swirl us like a glass of water. When the glass of water is put down, the water stops swirling, all the dirt sinks to the bottom, and the water becomes clear. Silence allows all the turmoil of my soul to settle. It clears my head. If I'm silent long enough, I discover the lies I'm telling myself.

"In order for that to happen, I have to shut off the external soundtrack and the internal soundtrack. The internal soundtrack is my never-ending to-do list, my anxieties with all their 'what ifs,' the tapes from the past with their destructive messages, and the call of addictions and temptations that always seem to be on the outer edges of my consciousness. I find this soundtrack harder to shut off than the external soundtrack. Sometimes, in order to shut it off, I have to literally write down the to-do list, the anxieties, the destructive tapes, and the siren calls. There's something about writing down the soundtrack that robs it of its power.

"In the solitude and the silence, my soul finally settles. There is amazing clarity there and rest. When my soul settles, I'm able to hear the still small voice of God. I have found if I spend time in the silence listening for God, even if I don't hear God then, I have prepared myself to hear him when he does speak. It's often after the silence that I hear God.

"I've found that silence does something else. Silence is practice in not speaking. If I refrain from speaking in the silence, I find myself not having to speak when I'm with people. I find my foot in my mouth far less often if I've been practicing silence. I find I just don't blurt things out. I have the ability to not talk. I have the ability to control what I say and when I say it."

"I think I know what you're saying," said Joe. "I like being alone and quiet in the woods. Whenever I have time to be out in the woods by myself, it calms me somehow. When I return, I feel better and find myself better able to deal with life for awhile. Sometimes, Sue will prompt me to take a walk in the woods. I guess it's an attitude adjustment for me. I think all that stuff you talked about goes on with me. I just hadn't put it all together that way before."

"As we eat our chocolate chip cookies and sip our coffee," Matt said, "let's talk about fasting. ***Fasting*** is going without food for a predetermined amount of time. As I've experienced fasting, I've seen four things that happen.

"First, fasting allows us to take control over our appetites. I tell my body when I will eat and when I will not eat. My body tells me if I don't eat lunch, it will die. That's ludicrous—an ample body like this dying by missing a meal? I tell my body, 'You won't die,' and to its surprise and mine, it doesn't. I begin to take control over my body.

"Second, fasting gives my body a rest and a chance to clean itself out. I usually feel pretty good after a fast and sometimes even during a fast. As I have fasted, I get to know the hunger, when it will come, and how long those feelings will last. I welcome the hunger pains now because I know they won't last and are just part of the process.

"Third, fasting creates an openness, an awareness of our spirituality. It makes us more aware of God. I don't how it does that. Maybe, since we aren't so full of food, we become aware of our souls. Maybe, since we aren't using our energy digesting, that energy is redirected to focus on God. Maybe, as I turn off the food cravings, I become aware of my God cravings.

"Fourth, I discover that when I fast, God usually does something. Sometimes God sends people with messages for me. Sometimes an answer to a prayer I've been waiting for comes. Sometimes God gives me a new insight. The amazing thing about this is that God's actions, in response to my fast, aren't all internal. Some of them are very external. For whatever reason, when I fast, God's action in and around my life intensifies."

"Do you do much fasting?" Joe asked. "And when you do, how long do you fast?"

Matt replied, "For a while, I was fasting a day each week. I would eat supper one evening and not have any food until the next evening. I would drink water and juice, no coffee or soft drinks. The first couple of times I would get headaches around meal times and feel very hungry. A couple of times the appetite got nasty and said it had to be fed now. I just said no and held my ground. I didn't die, and the appetite came under control. I've found fasting helps me to say no to other appetites too."

"I've never fasted," Joe said. "I don't think missing breakfast because I didn't get up early enough counts. I doubt that missing a lunch or dinner because I worked through them counts either."

"You're right, Joe, that's not fasting." Matt laughed. "That's having your schedule so out of control you didn't leave time to eat. Let's talk about frugality next.

"***Frugality*** is refraining from using money to buy status, luxury, and entertainment, yet frugality goes further than that. There is a God-shaped hole in each heart. We have a hunger, a yearning to fill that hole. We attempt to fill that hole with other people, family, food, sex, alcohol, drugs, escapist entertainment, and stuff. While each of those items brings a momentary buzz, they don't satisfy. The hole is still there. Frugality is the choice to not spend money, which, in turn, causes us to become aware of how much we use our purchasing power to fill that hole.

"My practice of frugality involves setting aside some days when I do not enter any stores, do not visit shopping sites on the computer, do not read the car or hardware ads, and do not spend any money. I may also turn off the radio, the tv, and the internet because they are advertisement driven, trying to get me to purchase something. Sometimes I find it very difficult to do. Today, for instance, I couldn't do it. I'm here with you drinking coffee and eating chocolate chip cookies, but I find it refreshing when I can do it. When I'm able to practice frugality, I remember that happiness and satisfaction are not things that can be purchased. I remember that popularity and acceptance aren't dependent on my having the latest stuff. I remember that self-esteem is not purchase based.

"Frugality helps me to say no to impulse purchases. Frugality makes it possible for me to resist the urge to keep up with the neighbors. I don't have to add a deck or an addition or expand my garage or buy a new car just because someone else on the block did. Frugality helps me understand my worth is not connected to what I own or what I buy. The practice of frugality helps create the ability to make the hard lifestyle choices necessary to get spending under control so that we can spend less than we make and free ourselves from debt. I was amazed when we got our finances under control how much less Mary and I fought. When we got our finances under control, there was less tension, less anger, less pressure, and less frustration with life. We began to experience peace, and we had the energy to love one another and our children again. It was amazing.

"Further, frugality helps me say yes to significant uses for money. Frugality helps me remember that the one who dies with the most toys doesn't win. I don't want people at my funeral saying, 'Matt always had the neatest toys.' Frugality helps us to live simply so that others may simply live. It helps me use my purchasing power to benefit others. When I die, I want people at my funeral to say, 'Matt helped fund houses for the homeless, there were fewer hungry people in the world because he lived, and the money he gave to the church helped fund ministry that brought people to Jesus and changed their lives and the lives of their families and their neighborhoods.'

"Frugality and fasting reveal addictive behaviors that may be going on in my life that I have been denying. When I take control of the appetites to eat and to spend, even if only for a time, I become aware of other appetites that are out of control. When I first started practicing fasting and frugality, I was amazed at how much I was addicted to caffeine, sugar, and adrenaline. It was not pretty coming down off those things, but I'm much better off without using them to prop me up.

"Finally, frugality, along with fasting, helps me remember those who live on the planet with me who are poor and hungry. The going without, even for a short time, raises my awareness of those who go without all the time. It softens my heart and helps compassion to grow within me."

"Fasting and frugality do all that?" Joe asked in amazement. "Can you tell me how to put Sue on a frugality regimen? Once I get Sue's spending under control, then there will be plenty to purchase the things I want. It doesn't work that way? I was afraid of that. What's the next one?"

"You'll love this one, Joe," Matt said with a wry grin. "**Chastity** is refraining from the practice and use of our sexuality both inside and outside of marriage. Like eating and spending, sex is an appetite that needs to be controlled. Our culture tells us if it feels good, do it, and if we experience attraction or chemistry with someone, we should act on it. However, acting on any and every sexual impulse, we will quickly destroy our lives.

"Chastity gives us the practice to say no to our sexual drive. Like the hunger drive and the spending drive, the sex drive will tell us unless we act, we will damage ourselves, we will miss golden opportunities we will regret for the rest of our lives, and we will diminish our masculinity or our femininity. It will tell us we must act now. Chastity puts us in touch with the protests the sex drive makes when we don't act, and it shows us we can live lives of love and satisfaction without acting on every impulse. Once again, sex and sexual relationships are something that attempt to fill the God-shaped hole in our souls, and sexuality is also a place where addictions get a hold of us. Saying no to our sexuality, for a time, puts us in touch with all this.

"Chastity can be practiced by making arrangements with your spouse that on this particular day you will not engage in intercourse or other sexual or sexually stimulating activity. To do so, you need your spouse's agreement. If the spouse doesn't agree, don't force this or make it an issue. In addition to whatever arrangement can be made with a spouse, chastity involves limiting our exposure to sexually charged situations or material. So on a day I'm practicing chastity, I would choose to turn off the tv, the radio, and the internet because of the sexually charged content. I would avoid the checkout stands at the grocery store and the magazine racks at bookstores and convenience stores. If there is someone at work, or some other place I frequent, with whom I feel chemistry or an attraction, I will keep her at arm's length that day. Maybe I will not go work out because of the women barely clad in spandex.

"Like fasting and frugality, chastity takes some effort to do. Chastity puts us in touch with just how sexually charged our culture is and just how much sexuality drives us. In addition, chastity begins to teach us how to control ourselves and how to have relationships with others without sexual entanglements. Chastity helps us live out Paul's admonition that we find in 1 Thessalonians 4:3-7:

> It is God's will that you should be holy; that you should avoid sexual immorality; that each of you should learn to control his own body in a way that is holy and honorable, not in passionate lust like the heathen, who do not know God; and that in this matter no one should wrong his brother or take advantage of him. The Lord will punish men for all such

sins, as we have already told you and warned you. For God did not call us to be impure, but to live a holy life.

"You're right Matt," Joe said. "It would take effort to practice chastity. Sexuality is everywhere. I've never thought about trying something like that. Is five minutes a long enough time period?"

"A day would be a good way to start." Matt smiled. "There are only two more on the abstinence list. The next one is secrecy.

"***Secrecy*** is doing good things anonymously. This helps us to control our hunger for recognition and acceptance. This puts us in touch with how much of what we do is done to gain the approval of other people and the attempt to control what they think of us. Secrecy can help free us from being bound to our desire to have others like us. Willard says that secrecy 'enables us to place our public relations department entirely in the hands of God.'[x]

"Secrecy is practiced by determining for a day or a week that I will do a certain number of good or helpful actions for other people without them knowing I have done the actions. I realize that by sharing some of my experience with you, I risk diminishing the effects of the actions. In the winter, when I'm in a parking lot cleaning the snow and ice off my windshield, I'll clean another car or two. At home, if there is no one around, I might do dishes or some other household chore that is usually done by another family member. At work, I might put some chocolate chip cookies in the lunch room or empty a wastebasket. I would do small simple things, and no one would know but me.

"It's kind of fun. In most of these cases, not only do I not get recognition for doing the deed, I often don't know how the deed was received. I don't get to see the gratitude on the face of the person whose windshield I cleaned or the smile of someone finding an empty wastebasket. Since I'm getting no feedback, I have the opportunity to look at my motives. God knows and I know. Is that enough? If it isn't, maybe I have a problem. If it is, then that helps give me the strength to act when I know my action will not gain me approval.

"The last act of abstinence is sacrifice. ***Sacrifice*** is using my resources to help someone else, and I go without. Sacrifice is using my resources for a greater cause, and I do without. Sacrifice forces me to rely on God. It shows my inability to provide for my life on my own. It gives me the ability to practice trust and dependence on God. If I have been practicing sacrifice, then having to trust God to help is far less scary because I have seen the supply turn up when I need it time and again.

"To practice sacrifice would be to choose on a particular day to give someone my lunch or lunch money, and I go without. It might be that instead of taking the trip or making the purchase, I give the money to something the church is doing. It might be that instead of watching the big game, I'm volunteering at the homeless shelter.

"My experience has always been that when I go without for someone else, God always supplies and always repays me, and I end up with more than I had if I had not sacrificed at all. Many of us hold our resources so tightly because we believe we worked so hard to get them, the resources are limited, and we may not have resources like this again anytime soon. Many of us hold tightly to our resources because we worry that something will happen, and we'll need the resources. Sacrifice helps me see that all I have comes from God. God made it possible for me to have the resource to begin with. Sacrifice helps me see that God is not limited, and his ability to supply me with resources isn't limited. Sacrifice helps me experience God's supply so that I can be generous with all that God has given me."

"Is that really true?" Joe asked. "If we sacrifice, if we give, God repays us?"

"Yes, it is," Matt replied, "but the only way to really know that is to take the risk, give, be without, and see what God does. Once you risk and God supplies, you will never be the same. We discover the truth that if we give to God and use the resources we have for God—if we open our hands and let go of what we have—God puts more in our hands than what we had to start with.

"Let me say two things about these disciplines of abstinence before we move on to the engagement disciplines. Most of us have heard stories of people who have misused these disciplines, and so we have a tendency to shy away from them. We hear of the guy who fasts for 120 days and looks like he has starved himself, or of the guy who tries to swear off sexuality totally and wants all women to wear extra large burlap feed sacks, or of the guys who nail themselves to crosses and sleep on beds of nails. Those are extreme people doing extreme things. They are not healthy. It would be like going to the gym every day for a week and doing every exercise machine at the most possible weight until our bodies gave out. Rather than building ourselves up, we would be destroying ourselves."

"I understand," Joe said. "Maybe those people need a discipline or an exercise in rest. You're talking about using these disciplines like a workout, one or two a day, or a week, to build our hearts, and as our hearts increase, adding more disciplines/exercises more often for more growth. But just like working out, there is an outer limit."

"Right," Matt agreed. "The other thing to know is this list of disciplines of abstinence is not all-inclusive. If you have a habit or behavior you're trying to stop, make your own spiritual discipline. If coffee is a problem, give up coffee for a week, and see what happens. Sometimes just breaking the habit for that amount of time is long enough for us to regain power over the habit.

"Speaking of coffee, let's get some more to help us through the disciplines of engagement. It looks like we might go a little longer tonight to lay out all of these."

After Matt and Joe returned to the table with cups of steaming hot coffee, Matt started the disciplines of engagement.

"These," Matt said, "are more fun to do. Let's start with study. **Study** is about filling ourselves with the words of God found in the Bible. Even as solitude is the beginning discipline of abstinence, so study is the beginning discipline of engagement. By study I do not mean just reading the Bible and getting familiar with its content. I mean digging into what it means, and then doing the extra work to ask what it means for me. As I do that work, then I ask: How do I apply this? How do I put it into action? What do I need to do differently? As I get answers to those questions, then I need to act. Study of the Bible without acting on what I learn is to be the foolish man Jesus talked about who built his house on the sand.

"The work between understanding and action is called *meditation*. Meditating is thinking about what this looks like, feels like, what it means for my life, and what God is trying to tell me. Meditation is about getting the stories, images, and thoughts of the Bible into my imagination so that the Bible is able to shape my future, guide my present, and recast my past.

"This discipline of study of the Bible provides us with the hard data, the facts, the black and white, the objective information about who God is, how God acts, what God expects of us, how God has wired the world, what we can become, and how God feels about us. It is this information that sets our compass for navigating through life. Without this information, we have no better chance of survival in life than a pilot, flying on a cloudy night without instruments, has of safely reaching his destination.

"There are all kinds of aids to help us study, such as Bibles with notes, commentaries, books by scholars and pastors about specific passages, Bible study groups, teaching tapes and videos, and sermons, just to mention a few. It doesn't matter so much which aids you use as it does that you put in the time and the effort to do the work. There is one other major help for our study of the Bible, the Holy Spirit. Jesus told us, in John 14:26, one of the main jobs of the Holy Spirit is to teach us."

"It sounds like this one is really important," Joe commented.

"I can't overstate its importance," Matt replied. Let's turn now to worship. **Worship** is declaring the worth of God. It's telling God how much God is worth to us, how much he means to us, and how much we love him. Willard says we do this as 'we engage ourselves with, dwell upon, express the greatness, beauty, and goodness of God through the use of words, rituals, and symbols. We do this alone as well as in union with [others].'[xi] Sunday morning worship is not a passive activity where we sit and watch others sing, pray, and preach. Rather, Sunday morning worship is active as we follow the worship leaders using the songs, prayers, and message as ways to express the feelings we have about the worth of God.

"Worship is a bit of a paradox. The more I engage in expressing God's worth to him, the more refreshed, energized, focused, loved, forgiven, helped, reconciled, and strengthened I feel. The Psalmist tells us God inhabits the praises of his people. As I praise God in worship, God draws near, and when God draws near, all that I described and more happens."

"I've been wondering how that works," Joe said. "When I get caught up in focusing on God and worshiping him like you describe, all that happens. When I start to pay more attention to the musicians or the preacher, I always walk away from worship feeling empty. I often think about what the musicians or the preacher need to do better to fill me and feed me. But what you say is that it's not so much about what they do as it is about what I do."

"You got it," Matt replied. "Let's move on. **Celebration** is throwing a party as a result of the goodness of God's actions on our behalf. Christmas, Easter, and Thanksgiving are holidays the whole culture celebrates, but we don't have to limit our celebrations to those days. The Old Testament is full of God's instruction to the people to celebrate the goodness and greatness of his actions. Many of the parables Jesus told involve a party to celebrate the kingdom. One of the primary images of the end of time is a wedding feast.

"It's important to celebrate because celebrations tell us what is important. Celebrations help us to remember. Celebrations break up the mundaneness of life. Besides, what else can we do? When God answers a prayer, when God works a circumstance on our behalf, when God brings a loved one to Christ, when God uses us to make a difference in someone else's life, how can we not celebrate? Even if the celebration is as mild as telling a friend, 'Guess what God has just done,' we need to celebrate. There are plenty of downturns and disappointments in life, and if we don't celebrate when we have the chance, we can turn sour."

"**Service** is using our actions to promote God's kingdom in the lives of other people. It's following the example of Jesus to put a towel over our arm and go serve. It's loving others and working for their good. Jesus told us, in Matthew 20:25-28, that those who are great in the kingdom are those who serve. Service trains us in how to use power in the kingdom. In the kingdom, power is used to serve others, not to get others to serve me. Further, there is something transforming about service to others. It takes the focus off me, my troubles, and my agenda. While I'm focusing on others, working on God's agenda, he slips by me and blesses me while I'm not looking. Joy can be found in serving others. As we continue to progress through the teachings of Jesus in Matthew, we will have more to say about service.

"***Prayer*** is conversation with God. It's talking with God and listening to God as God talks to us. It's a dialogue and not a monologue. Prayer as a discipline is not prayer on the run. Rather, it's prayer as an appointment with God. It's scheduling time—thirty to sixty minutes—to be with God. It's scheduling a place to meet with God. It might even be scheduling certain items to discuss with God. Prayer is the heart of our relationship with God. Even as our relationships with our spouses or our friends would deteriorate if we rarely spoke with them, so our relationship with God deteriorates if we never speak with him. I believe it's the Chinese who pray that God would increase their capacity to pray. As with service, as we continue with Jesus, we will have much more to say about prayer.

"***Fellowship*** is having spiritual conversations with fellow believers about how God is working and moving in our lives. Fellowship is having conversations with fellow believers about what we experience in any of the disciplines we've been talking about. Fellowship is accepting and feeling accepted, affirming and being affirmed. It's how we become family. Out of those conversations, deep bonds form among us as we support one another. Further, fellowship prepares us for spiritual conversations with our friends and neighbors who have not yet come to Christ."

"So fellowship is what we're doing here?" Joe asked.

"Yes, fellowship is part of it," Matt replied. "The final two engagement disciplines are not as fun as the others. Let's talk about confession first. ***Confession*** is sharing with others with whom we trust our weaknesses and failures. I'm not talking about something as formal as the Roman Catholic practice of confession but something that occurs within the bonds of deep fellowship. Confession is about being open, honest, and transparent.

"Confession is about using the resources of those with whom I am in fellowship to grow beyond my failures and find strength for my weaknesses. Willard illustrates this with two scripture passages. The first is in James 5:16 where we're told confession is part of healing. Evidently, keeping failures and weaknesses a secret is a burden that weighs on us. In addition, sometimes a sinful pattern in our lives directly contributes to our need for healing, and healing will not happen until the sinful cycle is addressed. Confessing frees me from carrying the burden, brings assurance of forgiveness, reinforces my acceptance by the community, and adds resources to my life to help me deal with the problem. The other passage is in Proverbs 28:13 where confession is linked to forsaking the sin. As I share my shortcoming, I know I have others rooting for me. I don't want to fall in the same way again and have to tell them I have failed. Their knowledge of me, coupled with their acceptance of me, keeps me from giving in and giving up. Their strength helps provide the resources to see me through the heart change God is working in me until I have conquered the problem.[xii]

"Further, confession is necessary if the community, created by the bonds of fellowship, is to continue and grow. The closer we are to a group of people, the more opportunity we have to cross each other's lines. It's only a matter of time until someone hurts someone else. The only way to get through that is confession and forgiveness. The discipline of confession is practice for the times when we actually have to confess because we just blew it in some way."

"Is confession what I've been doing in talking about the struggles I've had with Sue and with my dad?" Joe asked.

"Yes, that's one part of confession," Matt replied.

"Then I can say 'ditto' to what you're saying," Joe said. "Confession is a big help because if I hadn't talked with you about those things, Sue would have thrown me out of the house by now, and I wouldn't even be considering doing anything about my dad."

"Last one—here we go," Matt began again. "This one is downright un-American. **Submission** is voluntarily yielding to another. It's putting aside what I want to do, to do what someone else wants. It's giving honor and respect to those in authority even though I disagree with their actions. It's following the wisdom of a spiritual leader or mentor when I think I know best. It's yielding to my spouse. It's un-American because Americans are working for the time when I can have what I want, when I want it, because I want it. Here's the secret about submission: 1 John 4:20 says that if we don't love our brother whom we do see, we can't love God whom we don't see. I have a paraphrase: If we don't submit to our brother whom we do see, we won't submit to God whom we don't see. We'll talk later about how to practice submission.

"Let me say a closing word about disciplines of engagement. Most of them are fun. After we empty ourselves with abstinence, it's good to refill on the goodness of God. As we get the disciplines into our schedule, we'll find ourselves filled more with God and his kingdom. One of the purposes of these disciplines is to fill us so full of God and his kingdom that when someone bumps into us, they get God and his kingdom spilled all over them.

"From here on out, we'll do a discipline a week to see how they work in our lives. If it's all right with you, let's try fasting to begin with. Let's eat supper Tuesday evening and then not eat anything again until Wednesday evening."

"That works for me," Joe said. "Those are a lot of spiritual disciplines we covered tonight, but I'm looking forward to the spiritual workouts that will follow."

As they left, Joe wondered what it would be like to be buff spiritually. He hoped he would get a chance to find out.

Suggested resources:
Dallas Willard, *The Spirit of the Disciplines*, HarperCollins, 1989.

CHAPTER 12

JESUS & TREASURES

As Matt came in the coffee shop, he saw Joe already seated at their customary table with a cup of steaming hot coffee and a chocolate chip cookie.

"Hi, Matt," Joe called out. "I got the chocolate chip cookie because I figured we weren't fasting tonight. I thought maybe I would celebrate that I made it through the fast."

"Celebrating your ability to survive a one day fast," Matt responded, "is like a football player spiking the ball and celebrating because he made a five-yard gain. Since you have a chocolate chip cookie to go with your coffee, I need one too."

"You don't fool me," Joe said, "I know you're getting that chocolate chip cookie to make up for the cookies you didn't eat on Wednesday."

When the trash talking was concluded, Matt got some coffee and a chocolate chip cookie and came back to the table. "How was your fast?" Matt asked.

"It didn't seem fast," Joe replied. "I thought the day was never going to end. I felt hungry at breakfast time. I felt hungry again at lunch. In the middle of the afternoon I got a little shaky from not having any caffeine. I felt empty. Not just my stomach was empty, but I felt an emptiness in my heart too. It felt strange, and I wanted to eat so it would go away, but I didn't because it wasn't time yet.

"After work, I had my talk with Rev. Jim about my dad. The emptiness followed me into his office. The longer we talked the more intense the emptiness felt. I had never thought of emptiness as intense before. I basically told Rev. Jim my story about how my dad beat me and yelled at me, and how I never measured up, wasn't good enough, fast enough, strong enough, or smart enough. I told him about how I finally broke away from my dad at age twenty five and haven't had contact with him since. I told him about our conversation, the dreams I had, and the feeling of being pushed by God to reconcile with my dad. I told him I knew God was in it, but I wasn't sure I was, and I have no idea how to reconcile. Rev. Jim smiled at me and said it certainly sounded like it was time for me to deal with this stuff. He referred me to a family systems counselor not far from here and told me although it would be difficult, the rewards of doing the work would far outweigh the pain. I told him I hope so. Then he prayed with me before he left.

"That was weird. As Rev. Jim prayed, I felt the emptiness leave and something else take its place. The only way I can describe it is that it was a pleasant fullness. It felt like I had just finished a steak dinner with a baked potato and had topped it off with cheesecake for dessert. I felt so good I didn't have dinner that night even though I hadn't eaten all day. Breakfast tasted really good in the morning. Do you think this means anything, and did it have anything to do with my fast?"

"Maybe. Is it possible," Matt asked, "that God was using the emptiness to help you see how empty your life is as a result of having cut off your dad? Is it possible the fullness is a promise of what awaits you as you do the work to reconcile with your dad?"

"I was wondering the same thing," Joe said. "How was the fast for you?"

"I didn't have anything as spectacular happen as you did," Matt replied. "But that afternoon I got not one, but two phone calls for job interviews."

"Nothing as spectacular? Right," Joe said. "Are they interviews with good companies?"

"One," Matt said, "is with a company we have competed with for years. I had to turn them down during the phone call because of the non-compete agreement I signed before I left the other company. I can't do anything in direct competition with them for twelve months. I'm not sure I would have liked working for that company anyway, so it was alright to turn them down. The other call came through a headhunter agency I've been working with. It's for a company not in the industry but who wants my leadership and management skills to help move them in their new efforts to increase their market share. It sounds interesting, but I have a lot of homework to do before I go to the interview or even know if I want the job. We'll see."

"Fasting is powerful stuff," Joe replied. "If this kind of thing happens with just a one-day fast, I may never eat again!"

"Right!" Matt laughed. "Let's get to what we're looking at tonight. Do you remember what the two items are that Dallas Willard said would mess up our life with God and our ability to live and grow in the kingdom?"

"I think my notes say," Joe answered, "one was the desire for the approval of others or having the wrong audience. We talked about that. The second was the desire to secure ourselves by means of wealth which I suspect has something to do with money. We haven't talked about that yet. Is tonight a money talk?"

"Kind of," Matt said, "but not in the way you think. Let's take a look at what Jesus says in Matthew 6:19-21:

> "Do not store up for yourselves treasures on earth, where moth and rust destroy, and where thieves break in and steal. But store up for yourselves treasures in heaven, where moth and rust do not destroy, and where thieves do not break in and steal. For where your treasure is, there your heart will be also.

"Treasure is that which we value, collect, and protect. Treasure, in and of itself, has no value. The value of any treasure is determined by the person or the culture that treasures it. Treasure is a matter of the heart. Show me a person's treasure, and I can tell you a whole lot about that person's life.

"What do you suppose Jesus treasured?"

"I don't know," Joe answered. "I've never thought about that. Using the process of elimination, I don't think Jesus treasured gold, money, or stocks. I don't think he valued houses, cars, or boats. He didn't seem to value clothes or antiques. He lived a nomadic type of life going from place to place, finding places to stay as he went. It seemed like he traveled light. I don't picture him traveling around with a donkey, pulling a trailer. I can't picture him as a baseball season ticket holder either. I suppose he could have valued chocolate chip cookies, but I don't think he ever talks about them. I guess I can tell you what he didn't value, but I'm not sure what he did value."

"I think," Matt said, "Jesus valued the kingdom of heaven. He talked a lot about it. In Matthew 13:44-46, Jesus even described the kingdom as treasure. Listen to what he said:

> "The kingdom of heaven is like treasure hidden in a field. When a man found it, he hid it again, and then in his joy went and sold all he had and bought that field.
> "Again, the kingdom of heaven is like a merchant looking for fine pearls. When he found one of great value, he went away and sold everything he had and bought it.

"If the kingdom of heaven is as valuable as a treasure hidden in a field or a pearl of great price, or in today's terms, having the winning Super Lotto jackpot ticket, just what is it? How would you describe this kingdom that Jesus treasures?"

"Based on what we've talked about and what I've experienced thus far," Joe replied, "the kingdom of heaven is near. It's not out there somewhere. The kingdom of heaven is God drawing near to us with all the resources of heaven. The kingdom of heaven is God drawing near not to blame, judge, condemn, or punish. The kingdom of heaven is God drawing near with all the resources of heaven to save, heal, restore, reconcile, prosper, deliver, forgive, redeem, strengthen, encourage, help, and love. The kingdom of heaven is God drawing near with that outrageous and insane love that you say God has for each of us. The kingdom of heaven is God triumphant, which means love and hope win, and everything will be alright in the end. The kingdom of heaven is full of resources that make it possible for our lives to change in ways we have wanted and in ways we haven't yet imagined."

"In the kingdom of heaven," said Matt, "there is a treasure that outshines the kingdom itself. The treasure in the midst of the kingdom is God. It is God who is at the center of the kingdom, and it is God who causes the kingdom to be, and it is God who brings the kingdom near. To put it rather crudely is to say that the kingdom is the golden egg, but God is the goose that lays the golden egg. Not only does Jesus value the kingdom, but he treasures God, the king of the kingdom.

"Now let me ask this: What would life look like if we had Jesus' treasure in our lives?"

"We've talked about that too," Joe answered. "We said it would be like being in the zone with God. We would live in the fullness of his love and grace that are without measure. We would be living out the blessedness of the Beatitudes—having the resources and comfort of the kingdom, inheriting the earth, finding satisfaction, seeing God, receiving mercy, and being the sons of God. We would be embracing the values of the kingdom—poor in heart, mourning, meekness, hungering for righteousness, purity, mercy, peacemaking, and being persecuted. There's more. Help me out here."

"Okay," Matt responded. "We would live a life exceeding the law by using our anger for reconciliation, using our sexuality for blessing, having soft hearts in our marriages, having the wisdom to know when to say yes and no and the strength to say them, being able to return good for evil, loving the people who are out to get us and who hurt us, living for an audience of one, and having significance through being part of the kingdom business. We would have hearts filled with love, joy, peace, patience, kindness, goodness, gentleness, faithfulness, and self-control. We would be people of influence. We would have security. We would be people who would be about the kingdom business of bringing God's love, resources, and kingdom to other people. We would also be laughed at, misunderstood, mistreated, excluded, and even persecuted.

"How do we get this kingdom Jesus treasures into our lives?"

"Commit myself to doing whatever it takes to get it into my life," Joe said. "I think that looks like the first Beatitude—ask for the treasure of the kingdom. Use spiritual disciplines to create openness to the kingdom and to create the capacity for the kingdom in our lives. Live out the values of the kingdom."

"If the kingdom Jesus treasured is my treasure, what will I do with my stuff, my time, and my talents?" Matt asked.

"That's easy," Joe replied. "I would use my house, my car, my golf clubs, my tools, and my clothes for kingdom purposes. I would find ways to invest my money in kingdom activity or kingdom causes. I would use my time and my talents to advance kingdom purposes, to work in the kingdom, and to spend time in the kingdom."

"Can you give me an example of what this might look like?" Matt prodded.

"Let's see," Joe said. "I might use my tools, my talents, and my time to join a group that's building houses for the homeless. I might use my car and my time to pick up my neighbor's kid while his car is in the shop. I might host a neighborhood get-together to strengthen relationships in the neighborhood and find someone who is struggling with something. I could follow up after the party and find a way to help or pray for that person somehow. I might give money to support kingdom causes like missionaries, new churches, or disaster relief.

"If we treasure the kingdom," Matt added, "we would use all of our resources to value, collect, and protect the kingdom.

"This kingdom that Jesus treasures is not the only thing people treasure. People treasure everything from cars to championships to family to china to dolls to nature to money. In addition to all that, there seems to be a cultural treasure that a lot of people have. It's a version of the American Dream that Tom Sine, in his book, *Mustard Seed Versus McWorld*, calls McWorld.

"I hope as I play out the McWorld version of the American Dream you will recognize it. Let me describe McWorld. It's about getting ahead—specifically, it's about getting ahead in the suburbs. It's about having a house—a nicer house than our neighbors, certainly nicer than the last one we lived in, and nicer than any house our parents had—in a safe neighborhood with good schools.

"It's about getting ahead on the job. It's about moving up the career ladder and getting on the fast track. It's about salaries, promotions, and perks and having a better job than the next guy and getting it much sooner than the last guy.

"It's about getting our children ahead in their activities. They need to be at the head of the class, the best player on the best team, and dressed head to toe in the best logo-marked clothes and accessories. They need to have the latest video games on the latest game systems while listening to the latest tunes on the latest portable digital music gadget while communicating with their friends on flat-screen monitors driven by huge amounts of ram and megahertz. They need to have access to every opportunity available.

"McWorld is about economic upscaling. Doing well in McWorld means having more stuff, newer stuff, and better stuff than last year's stuff. Last year's car must be traded for next year's model, and it must have all the latest techno gadgets. But it's not enough to do this with one car, there must be several cars. Last year's clothes must be upgraded in quality and quantity. Everything must be bigger and better than what was done previously.

"McWorld is about the freedom to pursue individual material happiness. Life is about how much stuff we have. The more stuff we have the happier we are. Money may not buy happiness, but it buys the stuff that makes us happy. This part of McWorld is well summarized by a bumper sticker, 'the one who dies with the most toys wins.'

"McWorld is about being accountable to no one but me. It's getting into the position where I can do what I want when I want. It's being able to buy what I want when I want. It's being able to go where I want when I want."[i]

"Hey," Joe said, "I've been working hard to do that all my adult life. Doesn't everyone?"

"If," Matt asked, "I were able to achieve McWorld, what would my life be like?"

"It's not hard to answer that question," Joe replied. "I'd have lots of neat stuff. I'd get to upgrade the neat stuff every time something new came on the market. I'd live in the best house in the best neighborhood, drive the best car, send my kids to the best schools, and have them on the best athletic teams with the best coaches and trainers. No one would be telling me what to do. We would have more than our neighbors and more than we had last year.

"But there's a dark side to McWorld too. During my time in McWorld, I've felt empty, lonely, anxious, nervous, and afraid. I've had messed up relationships. I've fought a battle or two with alcohol. I've found that purchasing power doesn't give me the power to change my life in any meaningful way.

"Sometimes it feels like I'm on a treadmill. Who am I trying to get ahead of and why? What do I gain when I get ahead? How far ahead do I have to be and for how long? Whenever those questions arise, it seems like there's something new to buy or some new promotion to distract me. I find myself resentful towards those who have more. The only way they can have more than I do is that they cheated somewhere along the line."

"It sounds like you've been a citizen of McWorld for quite some time," Matt said. "How do we get McWorld?"

"Once again," Joe replied, "that's an easy question. To get ahead you have to work hard and work long. You have to have persistence. You have to be self-reliant. You have to be good at getting a strong grip on those bootstraps and pulling hard. You have to have diplomas."

"If McWorld is what I treasure," Matt asked, "how will I use my money, my time, and my talents?"

"In McWorld, I use my time and my money to hone my talents," Joe said, "so that I can make more money. I use the money I make to buy all the stuff for my family and myself.

"So can you give me an example of what this looks like?" Matt asked.

"It looks like putting in the extra hours the boss wants," Joe responded, "so I can make the money to buy the latest video game system for my son. It looks like making some stock trades to increase my portfolio, so I can take Sue on the cruise she wants to go on. It looks like buying the most recent techno driver so that the next time we play golf I can out-drive you or, at the very least, have you envious of my equipment.

"It looks like these two different kinds of treasures lead to different kinds of systems producing two very different kinds of lifestyles."

"Yes," Matt replied. "Two very different kinds of lifestyles. Which one looks better to you?"

"When you put them right next to each other like this," Joe said, "I don't see much of a contest. The kingdom offers me a full heart with the resources to face life and a chance to do something significant with my life. McWorld offers me a house full of stuff. It's nice stuff, but still it's only stuff. The problem is that stuff offers some instant gratification. It's exciting to be on the hunt and buy something. There's something within me that responds to the ads, the packaging, and all the bells and whistles. It's only after the excitement of the new thing wears off that I notice my heart is still empty.

"Is there a way to do both? Is there a way to have both the kingdom treasure and the McWorld treasure?"

"That's a good question," Matt said. "The McWorld answer is yes. McWorld says you can do both, but you do McWorld first and use what time, energy, and money you have left for the kingdom stuff. Sine says what happens when we do that is we make our commitment to follow Jesus, but

> Everyone knows that getting ahead in the job comes first. Getting ahead in the suburbs comes first. Getting the kids off to their activities comes first. And we tend to make decisions in these areas pretty much like everyone else does, based on our income, our professions, and our social status.
>
> Essentially, most Western Christians unquestioningly allow modern culture to arrange the furniture of our lives: forty- to eighty-hour work-weeks, single-family detached housing, congested time schedules for our lives and children. Over the last fifteen years, I have seen Christians becoming busier and busier, which means they have less time left over for prayer, church, ministry, or even family. As we have seen, we are racing into a future in which McWorld wants an even

larger chunk of our time and money, which means having even less time for the things of faith.

...Following Christ is too often trivialized to little more than a devotional lubricant to keep us from stripping our gears as we charge up the mountain, trying to get ahead in our careers, the suburbs, and our kids' activities...Following Christ is for too many of us reduced to little more than fifteen minutes in the morning and two hours on Sunday. In this model, we wind up with a highly privatized and spiritualized piety that is often largely disconnected from the rest of our lives.[ii]

"When I first read this, I felt like Sine had really nailed me. That was exactly how I was living. I was going to church and spending fifteen minutes a day in prayer. The rest of my life looked no different from anyone else in McWorld. When it was time to make major decisions, I made them based on economics, career path, and how my children would fare with the decision. That was basically the order of priorities. Then after making the decision, if I thought about it, I might ask God to bless my choice.

"I would hear people talking about knowing God, hearing God, and doing what God wanted in some very specific ways and not be able to relate to them. I never heard God or knew God in those ways. Doing what God wanted was reduced to going to church and being nice to everyone. I would wonder how they could speak so confidently about God. I would wonder why they would risk for God. I thought they gave foolish amounts of money to God.

"In fact, I would usually get upset when the minister would talk about money because I needed it to fuel my McWorld lifestyle. I thought they were trying to get my money, so they could do in their lives what I was trying to do in mine. Talk about God providing and God blessing us when we give were just words without any meaning to me because McWorld doesn't work that way. I would occasionally hear stories about someone giving and some windfall coming their way, but I always thought it was coincidence or the exception that proved the rule.

"My experience had been that I was so into McWorld that when I needed something from God, all I could do was pray 911 prayers. I had little idea of how God worked, how God answered prayer, or how to hear God. When the crisis would pass, I had no idea whether God had done something or things had just worked out. Like Sine said, I was using what little faith I had to try to get God to help me do the McWorld thing.

"So even though McWorld says you can do both, it's lying. If we follow McWorld, it will slowly and systematically starve our faith until we have none at all.

"I learned this the hard way. Several years ago I was happily chasing McWorld when it seemed like the bottom fell out of my life. I had just been promoted. I wasn't doing well with my new position. To be honest, I was failing miserably at it. I was doing so poorly there was talk of my being transferred to the company's back forty in Malaysia somewhere. This affected how I related to Mary and the kids. Those relationships went south. I didn't like work, I didn't like home, and I didn't like myself. As Malaysia looked more and more like a possibility, Mary informed me if I transferred there, she wasn't going and neither were the kids. She didn't say the rest, but I saw it in her eyes. That led to many sleepless nights.

"On one of those sleepless nights, I got out of bed and wandered around our new 2,400-square-foot house we had custom built. I sat down on the new leather sofa, sinking deep into its comforting cushions, but I wasn't comforted. I got up, went out to the garage, and sat down in my new car. It was new enough that I could still smell a trace of that wonderful new car aroma, but the beauty, power, and technology of that car did nothing for me that night. I went inside to my home office and sat down in the high back leather chair and surveyed my state of the art laptop and all the goodies that went with it, but none of the calculations on any of the excel spread sheets had the formula to make me feel any better.

"I felt like my heart was about to fall out, and none of this stuff was able to help me. Sometime before dawn, I prayed. I told God, 'I don't care about all this stuff, whether I get to keep it or lose it. I just want to feel better. I want help with my job. I want my family back. I don't want to go to Malaysia. I feel like my life is a mess, and I don't know how to fix it. I just want to get back on track with you and feel again the peace and love that you bring.' Shortly after praying that, I drifted off to sleep in the desk chair with the assurance everything was going to be alright.

"The next day I called Rev. Jim and told him what I was going through. I told him I didn't want his help to get out of the fix. I told him I wanted his help to do a better job of following Jesus. He began to take me through the same process I'm now taking you through, but my life was so thoroughly McWorld, it took me six weeks to be able to clear the time to meet with Rev. Jim to start that journey with Jesus. It took me another three years of working hard on the debt I incurred while living in McWorld, so I didn't have to continue to work as hard, and so I could have money to give.

"That's a long way to say you can't treasure both McWorld and the kingdom. It doesn't work. Jesus said, in Matthew 6: 24: 'No one can serve two masters. Either he will hate the one and love the other, or he will be devoted to the one and despise the other. You cannot serve both God and money.'

"One of the reasons I haven't been too excited about getting another job is there's more McWorld in me than I like. That's one of the things God showed me during the first couple of weeks off the job. I don't want to slide back into it.

"Jesus said, in verses 22-23, 'The eye is the lamp of the body. If your eyes are good, your whole body will be full of light. But if your eyes are bad, your whole body will be full of darkness. If then the light within you is darkness, how great is that darkness!' I think Jesus is still talking about treasure in these verses. If the treasure our eyes desire is dark, that darkness covers our entire life."

"I hear you," Joe replied, "and I know the feeling. But help me some with just how this works in the kingdom. McWorld is so stuff oriented that it has no heart. The kingdom is very heart oriented. Is it okay to have stuff in the kingdom? Is it okay to have money in the kingdom?"

"It's okay to have stuff and money in the kingdom. The trick is in not allowing them to be the treasure. If we make the kingdom the treasure, then we'll use our stuff and money for kingdom purposes. Mary and I still live in that house, but it's not our house anymore.

It's God's house. Occasionally the church has people in. We always offer to host them. We host a couple of cul-de-sac gatherings each year to mix our neighbors with each other and some of our church friends. We try to have it open for the kids and their friends. God has made it possible for us to have this house, so we try to use it for him.

"It's the same with the rest of what we have. It's not ours—it belongs to God. We try to look for ways to use it for God's purposes. We feel the same way about the money—it's God's money. We take more pleasure now in using money for kingdom purposes than buying stuff for ourselves. I know a couple who are working toward arranging their income and their lifestyle so they can live on 10 percent of what they earn and give 90 percent of what they earn to kingdom purposes. They love funding kingdom stuff. They figure the more they earn the more they can give.

"I try to do the same with the job. It's not my job—it's God's job. I try to be God's man at work. How can I accomplish kingdom purposes during my time at work? One of those ways is to do my job well, so I gain the respect of the people I work with. Another way is to care about all the people I work with and especially care for those it's difficult for me to work with. Through the caring, I look for ways to build and strengthen relationships, so when the time comes when someone is open to hearing a kingdom word or has life questions, I'm present for those conversations.

"Our job is to treasure the kingdom and use our other small 't' treasures in service of the large 'T' Treasure, the kingdom. I like what Jesus said in verses 25-34:

> "Therefore I tell you, do not worry about your life, what you will eat or drink; or about your body, what you will wear. Is not life more important than food, and the body more important than clothes? Look at the birds of the air; they do not sow or reap or store away in barns, and yet your heavenly Father feeds them. Are you not much more valuable than they? Who of you by worrying can add a single hour to his life?

"And why do you worry about clothes? See how the lilies of the field grow. They do not labor or spin. Yet I tell you that not even Solomon in all his splendor was dressed like one of these. If that is how God clothes the grass of the field, which is here today and tomorrow is thrown into the fire, will he not much more clothe you, O you of little faith? So do not worry, saying, 'What shall we eat?' or 'What shall we drink?' or 'What shall we wear?' For the pagans run after all these things, and your heavenly Father knows that you need them. But seek first his kingdom and his righteousness, and all these things will be given to you as well. Therefore do not worry about tomorrow, for tomorrow will worry about itself. Each day has enough trouble of its own.

"Jesus told us if we will make the kingdom our treasure, then God will take care of all the stuff McWorld wants us to accumulate and worry about. God knows that we need food, clothing, shelter, and all the rest. God knows that. Jesus told us if God takes care of the birds, he will take care of us because we're worth far more to God than birds. God did not draw near with all his kingdom resources to watch us starve. God provides.

"God's provision is not a stingy provision. King Solomon was at the top of the McWorld food chain. He was known for his great wealth. Yet Jesus said, as wealthy as Solomon was, he was not able to dress in a way that would outshine a lily of the field. If God adorns the lily in beauty and splendor for its brief life, won't God adorn us the same way?

"Our job is to seek the kingdom. As we seek the kingdom first and foremost, as we treasure the kingdom, God will provide the stuff. It almost seems like God is just giving it away. All the stuff we work so hard and worry about God will provide. All we have to do is put the same effort toward the kingdom that we were putting toward getting stuff.

"As we seek the kingdom and grow kingdom hearts, our feelings about stuff change. It's no longer the measure of our worth, the trophy of our success, or what makes us happy. With the kingdom, we find contentment and peace, and stuff is just icing on the cake.

Coffee with Matt & Joe

"How do I get started?" Joe asked. "With the way Sue is with her spending, we have more trouble about money and stuff than anything else."

"I seem to remember," Matt said, "that Sue's out-of-control spending is directly related to your lack of attention toward her. I think the first step is making sure you're spending the time with Sue that she needs. The second step would be to talk with Sue about the stuff we've talked about tonight, so the two of you can be on the same page. The third step is to commit to giving 10 percent of your income for the next 6 months."

"Ten percent? Are you crazy? I can't do that." Joe protested.

"Why can't you do that?" Matt asked.

"We're still recovering from Sue's last couple of credit card binges," Joe said.

"If you commit to making no new purchases so that you can pay off the credit card, how long will it take before you could give 10 percent?" Matt asked.

"It's not that easy," Joe said.

"Why not?" Matt persisted.

"Ten percent is quite a chunk of change," Joe replied. "I'm just not sure we could do it. I mean, I'm not sure we could afford it. I can't imagine just lopping off 10 percent of what we spend. Plus, we have college for the kids coming up, and we need to save for retirement. I haven't been able to do that saving, how can I give away 10 percent? What if something happened? What if I lost my job?"

"My experience," said Matt, "is that there is never a good time to start. There will always be something to buy and something to save for. The kids will always need something. The house will always need repairs, and the cars will always need to be replaced.

"The way Mary and I did it was we just started. Someone told us we wouldn't miss that 10 percent. We heard someone else say they figured they wasted 10 percent of their income on junk food and impulse buying. They thought giving that money to God would be a much better use of it.

"I remember writing that first check. It was very difficult. As I was trying to write the check, I was flooded with fear. Ten thousand what ifs descended on me. I almost didn't write the check because of all the what ifs. I decided to step through the fear and write the check anyway. As I began to sign my name, the what ifs all disappeared. The thing that was really amazing me to me was that we had more money left over that month than we usually did. Since then, I've been giving God a good bit more than 10 percent.

"I discovered that I like giving. I like giving to support the church and what it's doing in the lives of the people in the community and around the world. That's one of the ways in which I feel I'm helping to spread God's kingdom.

"Something else has happened. Since I've been giving, I have far more peace about my checkbook. We've had some tight times along the way, but we've never cut our giving percentage to make ends meet. A couple of times we were staring not having enough money in the face, but God came through with what we needed when we needed it. Now we have more than we ever thought we would have. Even though I've been living off the severance package, we've still been giving. That's one of the reasons I'm not worried about the financial side of this. God will provide for us as we go along."

"Where did this 10 percent number come from?" Joe asked.

"Do you remember the Pharisees, the list makers and the law keepers?" Matt asked. When he saw Joe nod, he continued. "They saw that the law talked about giving 10 percent of their income. They meticulously gave away 10 percent of their income right down to whatever profit they made from their gardens. They did this because that is what the law said to do. It was on the list, and they were going to be checking it off. Didn't Jesus say the kingdom was about having a new heart that was able to exceed the law? Didn't we talk about the way to exceed the law was to love? Don't we give or spend our money on what we love, what we treasure? This is one of the ways we can see our hearts."

"I've been in McWorld so long," Joe said, "that my first reaction is a McWorld reaction. I'll talk to Sue and see if we can come to some agreement on this. I hope we can get to that 10 percent soon. I'd like to see what God would do in our checkbook and in our hearts if we gave that way. I'd also like to see how his provision works. It would be nice to feel we're doing something significant with our money. Stuff is nice, but I think maybe I have enough stuff.

I'm feeling a little short on significance. Maybe this will help that. That's my plan."

"Sounds like a good plan to me," Matt said. "I'll look forward to hearing what you've come up with next week. Let's pick a spiritual discipline to do for next week."

"Okay, let's do worship," Joe responded. "Following my worship style, I'll take another long walk in the woods, spend some time there in God's presence, and see what happens to this heart of mine."

They prayed for each other and went out into the parking lot. Joe's head was reeling some at all they had done over the past twelve weeks—his marriage, his job, his dad, and now his money. "Don't you ever quit?" Joe asked Jesus as he started the car. Joe just hoped he could keep up, because he didn't ever want to go back to the way it used to be.

Suggested resource:
Tom Sine, *Mustard Seed Versus McWorld*, Baker Books, 2002.

CHAPTER 13

DYNAMICS OF CHANGE

Since the time change, it had been getting darker and darker outside, week by week, as Matt came to the coffee shop to see Joe. This night it looked like a few small flakes of snow were scurrying around the parking lot like small children looking for their parents. Matt smiled at the memory of when his children were small enough to scurry. Inside the coffee shop, he welcomed the warmth as he looked around for Joe. Joe wasn't there yet, but that was alright. Matt wanted some time to catch his breath and warm his hands on a cup of steaming hot coffee. He had been doing a lot of thinking, and it would be good to just sit a few minutes and be still.

Joe wandered in some minutes later. He waved at Matt and got his coffee.

"What's going on?" Joe asked Matt.

"All kinds of things," Matt responded.

"Like what?" Joe asked.

"I've been thinking about this job thing," Matt said. "I have an interview next week with that company I was telling you about. I've done some research. They look like a good company. They have some problems, but over the last two years they've been addressing the problems and making some changes. I can see that I certainly could help them. It could be a nice fit."

"But..." Joe hopped in. "Tell me the rest of it."

"I bumped into someone this week who is a life coach,' Matt replied.

"What's a life coach?" Joe asked.

"It's someone who helps you reach your goals," Matt answered, "by walking with you through a series of assessments, questions, and goal-setting exercises. A life coach, like an athletic coach, is able to help with the fundamentals and translate strategy and plans into action to move someone forward. I'm going to have lunch next week with the life coach I met. I want to find out what kind of training is required, how to get started, and what it's like being a life coach. It's intriguing to me."

"And…" Joe added.

"And," Matt continued, "Rev. Jim was talking with me about how it's going with you and the other two guys I'm working with. I told him if I thought there was a way to make a living doing this kind of thing, I'd be very interested. He told me there might be a way. He's going to pray about it for a few days and get back with me. Lots of things are going on. How about you? Did you talk to Sue? Did you call the family systems counselor Rev. Jim told you about?"

"I guess I have a lot going on too," Joe said. "I called the family systems counselor last week. They gave me an appointment for next week. I hope I don't back out. Some days I want to deal with this and get it behind me. Other days I don't want to go anywhere near the issues of my dad. I told one of my younger brothers about this. In words and tone only a brother can use, he told me it was about time. I thanked him for his encouragement and then told him to get a life.

"Sue and I had a long talk about the treasures in the kingdom of heaven and McWorld. Sue said she likes to spend money. She doesn't really care what she spends it on, she just likes to spend it. The concept of spending money on something that could help someone and provide peace for our checkbook and significance for our lives was as new a concept to her as it was to me. We looked at our finances and figured if I spend quality time with Sue, and if Sue doesn't binge, we could have our credit card payment back down to a reasonable level in six months. We could give the extra we were paying on credit cards and work towards giving 10 percent or more. Sue was alright with that as long as she got to do the shopping to find out what we would give where. I was surprised at first.

But as I thought about it, this was typical Sue behavior. She likes to spend, and I have to figure out how to balance the books. Sue gets to explore a whole new world of spending. Then Sue pushed me and asked, 'Couldn't we do something before six months?' I told her we could if we traded something off. She said one of the boys needs new basketball shoes. Instead of paying $150 for shoes, she'll get him shoes for $50. I agreed. So Sue is going shopping next week to decide where to give the $100. Maybe something will happen in her life as she starts to explore where to 'spend' our giving."

"I must admit that's an interesting take on giving," Matt replied. "If it works in your house, go for it."

"Jesus seems to have a lot going on tonight too," Joe said. "He's talking about judging, and then he has all these metaphors using planks and specks, pigs and pearls, dogs and the sacred. I think I get some of it, but I look forward to what you have to say about it."

"Yes," Matt responded, "there's a lot going on here. Let's get the passage in front of us, Matthew 7:1-6. Will you read it?"

Joe read:

> "Do not judge, or you too will be judged. For in the same way you judge others, you will be judged, and with the measure you use, it will be measured to you.
>
> "Why do you look at the speck of sawdust in your brother's eye and pay no attention to the plank in your own eye? How can you say to your brother, 'Let me take the speck out of your eye,' when all the time there is a plank in your own eye? You hypocrite, first take the plank out of your own eye, and then you will see clearly to remove the speck from your brother's eye.
>
> "Do not give dogs what is sacred; do not throw your pearls to pigs. If you do, they may trample them under their feet, and then turn and tear you to pieces.

"I think those first words of Jesus, about not judging, are known and used by just about everybody."

"Yes," Matt replied. "It seems like everyone quotes those words. However, few of the people who quote them actually understand what Jesus meant by them. Those who quote them use them to make the case that since we're not to judge, that means all behavior is condoned. Since we're not to judge, everything I say and do is to be accepted by everyone else. If anything is wrong, it's to be ignored because to deal with it would be judging.

"But that's not what Jesus was about here. Just a few verses later, in verse 15, Jesus told us to watch out for false prophets. We're able to identify false prophets by their fruit. Jesus asked us to distinguish between good fruit and bad fruit. That sounds like a judgment call to me.

"Dallas Willard, in *The Divine Conspiracy*, talks about the difference between making a distinction and condemning. A dentist, Willard says, may say, 'I see you have not been brushing regularly. Your gums are receding, and there is a cavity over on this right lower side.'[i] The dentist has made a distinction, a judgment, an observation about the patient's teeth. There's no value judgment of the patient's life involved in that. The dentist doesn't say, 'Your teeth are in bad shape, therefore, you are a bad person.' The dentist does say, 'If you will brush regularly, and let me fix the cavity, we can make some improvements in your teeth.' The dentist might also add, 'If we don't do something about the condition of your teeth, they will get worse and cause you lots of pain.'

"Condemning is using the observation to deduce that the whole of a person's life is bad, wrong, or morally inferior. This deduction is usually followed by another one which is that the reason the person is this way is that they like being this way. The only way to get this kind of person to change, if change is possible at all, is some type of severe punishment. Further, this person's existence is a threat to all of society, and action needs to be taken now before we're all contaminated."

"This sounds a lot like what we were talking about when we were dealing with anger," Joe observed. "What you just described sounds like contempt. Let me play this out to make sure I have it. An observation, a distinction, a judgment of behavior is like noticing Tom is having an affair. Condemning would be to say, 'That lying weasel, Tom, is cheating on his wife.'"

"That's right," Matt said. "The observation deals with acts of behavior. Tom has a problem. Condemning is about degrading a person's entire existence. As you said, this is contempt. Tom no longer has a problem; Tom is a problem, and because of that, Tom is now less than human. He's a lying weasel.

"Jesus said that when we condemn others, they will return the favor by condemning us. So once that lying weasel, Tom, knows what I think of him, he'll return the attack by saying, 'At least I'm not a hypocrite pretending not to be interested in other women.' Or Tom may find one of my many character flaws and call me a dirty dog. Dirty dogs and lying weasels go to war with each other."

"So what are we to do instead?" Joe asked.

"Let me back up and go at this from another direction," Matt began again. "Jesus was talking about the dynamics of change and how to go about getting change to happen. The change may be in a relationship or in a situation. The dynamics are the same.

"We're all involved in dysfunctional dances. The dysfunctional dance looks like the old saying:

You do it to me once—shame on you
You do it to me twice—shame on me
You do it to me a third time—shame on both of us

We keep doing the dance because we don't know how to stop it. When someone does something to us we don't like, how do we try to stop it?"

"The first thing I do," Joe answered, "is tell them to stop it."

"Does that work?" Matt asked.

"Occasionally, but not very often," Joe replied.

"What do you do next?" Matt asked.

"Increase the volume," Joe said. "If I say it louder or even with some anger in my voice, I think they'll see I'm serious and back off."

"What if that doesn't work?" Matt asked again.

"Then I try force," Joe answered. "I look for some kind of leverage to force them to change."

"What if that doesn't work?" Matt asked yet again.

"Then I find myself falling into the condemnation cycle you talked about," Joe answered. "I try to blame and shame them into changing."

"Dallas Willard calls that 'condemnation engineering,'"[ii] Matt replied. Then he asked, "What if that doesn't work?"

"Then obviously there's something wrong with them," Joe answered. "Fortunately for them, I happen to have the antidote, and I'm going to give it to them whether they want to hear it or not because it's for their own good."

"I call that *pearl pushing*.[iii] What if that doesn't work?" Matt asked still again.

"There's always guilt, shame, intimidation, belittling, and just plain cutting them off," Joe answered. "I know. What if those don't work? Then, I'm completely frustrated."

"How often do any of those things work to stop the dance?" Matt asked.

"I thought you'd never ask a different question," Joe replied. "When my children were small, those tactics were effective. If the change I want someone to make is small, and if they can see immediate benefits from the change, it works. But 97 percent of the time these tactics don't help. In fact, often they make them worse. People get hurt, the dance continues, condemnation runs rampant, and pearls are flung everywhere."[iv]

"So why do we persist in doing these things?" Matt asked.

"We do them because they come naturally and because I have no idea what else to do," a flustered Joe responded. "Now, it's my turn to ask the questions. How do we stop the dance, and what can I do differently?"

"I think you might be ready for the key insight Jesus brings to the dysfunctional dance," Matt said. "We focus our efforts on stopping the dysfunctional dance by trying to get the other person to change. The other person doesn't change because either there is some benefit to them to do the dance that way, or they would like to change but don't know how. No matter how hard we push, we can't change them.

"But we don't have to despair. Jesus brings a different option. Rather than trying to change the other person, Jesus says to change yourself. That's what he meant in verse 3 when he said, 'Why do you look at the speck of sawdust in your brother's eye and pay no attention to the plank in your own eye?' Jesus followed that, in verse 5, by saying we're to take the plank out of our own eye, and then we'll see clearly to work on the speck in our brother's eye."

"Why should I change when they're the ones with the problem?" Joe asked.

"Yes, they have the problem, but they aren't going to change," Matt replied. "That makes it my problem. Let's look at this from a basketball perspective. How do you stop the other team from pressing? Do you ask them, yell at them, or threaten them? No. Your team has to break the press. When your team breaks the press, the other team stops pressing because then the press is a liability rather than an asset. When my children were younger and one would pick on the other, I would tell the one being picked on to ignore the behavior rather than being upset. Once the aggressor was ignored and saw this wasn't fun anymore, he would stop.

"In order to stop the dance, I have to stop dancing. I have to change. I have to act differently. Often, this means I have to deal with my own stuff. I have to answer the questions: Why do these actions bother me? What buttons do they push? In Jesus' terms, I have to do the work of board removal. I have a friend who reminds me that the purpose of removing the board is not to use it to hit the other person with it.

"Robert Quinn, in *Deep Change*, says the process of board removal that Jesus talked about is difficult because it means I have to face all the things for which I deserve blame and condemnation. I, too, deserve to be discarded.[v]

"At this point, we have kingdom assistance. In the kingdom, how are things dealt with for which I deserve blame and condemnation?"

"Forgiveness," Joe responded. "Jesus paid the price for all the stuff I've messed up. He got me off the hook. I'm free. I'm no longer blamed. I'm no longer condemned. I don't have to hide stuff anymore. I don't have to be controlled by my past mistakes or by my fears, and I can grow beyond my character flaws."

"That's right," Matt continued. "I can face my issues and see where change needs to be made. I think the change Jesus asks us to make is difficult on another level. Often, I don't know what I need to change. I can see clearly what the other person needs to change, but I have a much more difficult time seeing what I need to change.

"Kerry Patterson, along with a host of other authors, in *Crucial Conversations*, helps us see more clearly the changes we can make to stop the dysfunctional dances in which we find ourselves.

"One of Patterson's key concepts is that we need to master our stories. Part of the human condition is that we're meaning freaks. Everything has to have a meaning. We're unable to let anything happen without meaning. To get meaning, we tell stories. Emotions then follow the stories we tell about what happens.[vi]

"I had a coworker who always came late to the meetings I ran at work. His lateness always disrupted the meetings and added about thirty minutes to their length. It was a problem. It was a dysfunctional dance. The first time he was late I didn't think anything about it. Unexpected things happen to everyone. It was no big deal. The second time he was late, which was the next meeting, I began to wonder what was going on. The third time he was late, I began to suspect it was because he didn't like meetings and didn't care about the work we had to do there. The fourth time he was late, I was sure it was personal. I was running the meeting, and he was disrespecting me by not showing up on time. The fifth time he was late not only was he disrespecting me, he was disrespecting all his other coworkers by wasting their time and not giving his input on the projects on which they were working. The sixth time he was late, I was convinced that he was an antisocial, self-centered, self-absorbed little man who took great joy in upsetting the routines and working rhythms of other people.

"What are the facts in what happened? What are the stories? What are the emotions? What actions do you think these emotions caused?"

"The fact is," Joe answered, "this coworker was consistently late for the meetings you were running. I think you told a number of stories: Something unexpected happened; he was disrespectful; he enjoyed upsetting people. The emotions that followed the 'something unexpected' story would have been mercy or compassion or something like that. I'm a guy. I'm not good with emotions. The later stories would have generated emotions of anger, rejection, and hurt. The actions that followed probably were something like you told him not to be late again. Then you yelled at him not to be late again. Then you yelled louder and threatened to take action that could cost him his job."

"You sound like you were there," Matt said. "That's exactly what happened. I got no results. I wasn't able to change him. I kept getting more and more angry and frustrated with the situation. Since I couldn't change him, I needed to change myself. Patterson would have had me change the story I was telling myself. Patterson says there are lots of stories that fit every set of facts. If we tell different stories, we have different emotions, and we can act differently."

"What different stories could be told here?" Joe asked. "It seems cut and dried to me. If he keeps coming late for the meetings, he's disrespecting you and the rest of the team."

"At first," Matt said, "that's what I thought too. That was the only story that fit the facts, but I was encouraged by my supervisor to look for other stories that fit the facts. It took me a little time to let go of my story, so I could explore other stories, but my supervisor helped me with that. He gave me a question that Patterson uses: 'Why would a reasonable, rational, and decent person do what this person is doing?'[vii]

"That question helped me walk away from what Patterson calls 'three clever stories' that keep us from changing. The first story is the **victim** story. In the victim story, I'm a victim. The coworker who comes late to the meeting has all the power, and I have none. My meetings are trashed, and I'm powerless to change what's going on. I'm just an innocent sufferer. What has happened is not my fault—I'm an innocent victim who was just minding my own business. The victim story ignores the role I play in the problem. It lets me off the hook from having any responsibility in this situation at all.[viii]

"The second story is the **villain** story. The villain story says it's all your fault. In my case, it was all my coworker's fault. The villain story portrays my coworker as evil with no socially redeeming qualities. We assume the worse about the person's motives and character. We degrade them. We expect them to act poorly, and when they do, we're not disappointed. Everyone knows it's impossible to do anything with a villain. The villain story overstates the role of the other person in the problem. It also assumes I'm pure. It lets me off the hook from having any responsibility in this situation at all.[ix]

"The third story is the **helpless** story. The helpless story says the other person's actions are responsible for my own poor behavior, so when I threatened to take action to have my coworker removed from the job, I was justified. There was nothing else I could do based on his refusal to show up on time. Victim and villain stories look backward to explain why the situation exists. Helpless stories look forward to explain why we can't make any changes to go forward. Helpless stories, once again, let me off the hook from having any responsibility in this situation at all.[x]

"As I applied the question, 'Why would a reasonable, rational, and decent person do what this person is doing?' with the three clever stories, a different picture began to emerge. When I set the time for those meetings, I didn't ask anybody if the time was good. I just said, 'This is when the meeting is—be there.' After my coworker was late for the first meeting, I didn't ask him why he was late. In fact, during the whole situation, I never asked him why he was late. I just told villain stories about him. When I asked the 'reasonable, rational, and decent person' question, one of the stories I told was that I know he reports to a couple of different people. Maybe someone else's meeting overlaps with mine. He should have told me if that was the case, but I didn't really give him a chance.

"Now I have a problem. I have acted poorly. If I want to change the dysfunctional dance, I have to apologize for my poor behavior. In order to get my coworker on board, I have to share my story. To do that, I have to start with the facts. I have to go back to why I'm having the meetings. I have to explain how important they are to me in getting the department to move forward with everyone on the same page to not just accomplish the goals we have, but to go beyond them. I have to explain how this impacts my career path and compensation and how it impacts everyone else's too. I have to share with him I'm feeling pressured this quarter and my fears about our inability to meet the goals. I have to share with him about how his lateness to the meetings and the disruption he caused were perceived by me as a threat that would keep us from accomplishing our goals. Then I have to tell him the stories I told myself about his behavior and the emotions that followed. I have to apologize for those stories, my emotions, and actions that came from them.

"To do this, I have to take my coworker on the same journey I took. I have to start with the facts. He was late for important meetings. Then I have to share my story about those facts, which was a villain story. Next, I have to show the emotion that followed and the actions that came afterward.

"To keep my coworker on board, I have to make sure the conversation is safe. If my coworker becomes silent or starts accusing me at some point along the way, I need to back up to the facts again and make it safe. I need to affirm my coworker by telling him how valuable and necessary he is to the department and what goes on in those meetings.

"After I have done all that, then I need to ask my coworker for his story. Chances are his story about what happened paints as bad a picture of me as my story painted of him. I think Jesus said something about this: 'Do not judge, or you too will be judged.' My coworker's story will be hard for me to hear. As I find myself getting silent or starting to accuse my coworker, I need to get him to share the journey he took, starting with the facts, moving to story, to emotion, to action.

"When we both have the facts on the table in front of us and each of us owns up to his story, then we'll have a chance to change the dysfunctional dance.[xi]

"This process that I needed to go through in order to talk with my coworker is what Jesus was referring to when he said we need to get the plank out of our own eye in order to deal with the speck in our brother's eye."

"That's hard work," Joe said. "If I do all that work, I have to face all kinds of things about myself that I would rather not face. It's just much easier to say the guy's a jerk and go on. That's what Quinn was talking about. But if I do the work with the help of kingdom resources, I can grow and change. It seems much of what Jesus has been asking us to do is this process of board removal. It looks like if I want to follow Jesus, I have to be honest with him, myself, and others about what's going on in me. It appears, thus far, if I'm honest with myself—if I get my story straight—about anger, sex, yes and no, enemies, an audience of one, treasure, and now this dysfunctional dance, I find I am my biggest problem. When I change the stuff that's in me, then others become much easier to deal with.

"But getting my story straight is the hardest part. You talked about fact, story, emotion, and action. They all happen so fast that most of the time I don't even know the story I'm telling, and so I have no idea why I feel the way I do or act the way I do. I haven't looked at this, but I suspect I have three or four main stories that run on autopilot. Because I've told myself these stories for years, I don't recognize them as stories. It seems to me they're simply the way the world works. I've told myself the same story about my dad's actions for so long, I can't imagine a different story. I suppose that will be some of the work I need to do. I suppose that's why those dreams about my dad were so startling. They were telling me a different story.

"How do you get the story straight? How do you identify the stories, so you can act differently?"

"What kingdom resources are available?" Matt asked.

"The first Beatitude," Joe said. "I could pray like this: 'God, I have messed up stories. Please help me see them. I can't change them. Give me different stories to tell.' Probably the second Beatitude could help as I mourn the passing of the old stories and get ready for new stories. Certainly the meek Beatitude would be a resource as I get myself under the Spirit's control to tell different stories."

"That's right," Matt replied. "I don't just want different stories to tell. I want kingdom stories to tell. I ask God to give me kingdom stories to tell to replace my old stories.

"Another thing that helps us identify the stories is to journal. I slow myself down by journaling and ask the following questions: Was there a time yesterday when I acted badly and don't know why? Was there a situation that bothered me or felt very awkward? Did my emotions spike? Those are clues to faulty stories at work. As I journal, I can replay the scene in slow motion and find the story. Sometimes because we have told the same faulty story for decades, we have to search the crime scene hard to find it because at first we don't recognize it.

"I've found the book, *Crucial Conversations*, is very helpful with this whole process. The writers understand the stories, how they work, where they hide, and the damage they do. Having their understanding of the stories has helped me immensely. I imagine there are other books that deal with this, but I don't know them."

"I think I'll pick up a copy. So what happened with your coworker?" Joe asked.

"As it turned out, the poor guy was stuck with overlapping meetings. It was difficult for him to hear my story, and it was hard for me to hear his story. The guy running the other meeting was just as hard nosed about his meeting as I was about mine. Neither one of us gave the guy a chance to explain that he was caught between the two of us. Since the guy running the first meeting had more power in the company than I did, my coworker stayed for all of that meeting and got to mine as soon as he could. He told a helpless story and villain stories about both of us. He apologized for not coming to see me. I felt like an idiot. If either one of us had just talked with the other, the whole thing could have been worked out. We could have avoided months of pain.

"I ended up rearranging some things so we could hold the meeting an hour later. That way, he could finish the other meeting and have some time to catch his breath before he came to my meeting. Once we changed the meeting times, he was on time, the department began to work better, he became a key contributor, and we developed a good friendship."

"What happens," Joe asked, "if I do all the board removal work, have the conversation with the person, and discover the problem is that other person has a character flaw that is producing the problem?"

"For instance," Matt said, "I do the board removal work, have the conversation with my coworker, and my coworker says, 'Don't sweat it. I've never been on time for a meeting in my life. I'm always late for meetings, and yours is the meeting I'm the least late to.'"

"That's what I mean," Joe replied. "What do you do then?"

"Shoot him!" Matt laughed. "No, seriously, Willard refers us to Galatians 6:1, which reads: 'Brothers, if someone is caught in a sin, you who are spiritual should restore him gently. But watch yourself, or you also may be tempted.'

"Willard sees a four-step process here.[xii]

"Step one: Be sure of the sin. Do you remember what we talked about when we looked at dealing with a normal sinner? Establish the pattern. In this case, we have my own experience with the coworker being late. I would check with leaders of other meetings this coworker attends to verify his tardiness. I would come back and have another conversation with him, looking for him to share more of his story. I might suggest three or four stories, such as his life is out of control, or he has no sense of time, or he doesn't like meetings, or he's completely self-centered, or he doesn't care about the trouble he causes others by being consistently late. Trying to keep the conversation safe, I would ask him if one of these stories is true for him or if there is another story that explains his constant lateness. I need to be able to get his story so we can work together on it.

"Step two: The one doing the restoring must be spiritual. Two things are going on here. First, the board removal work must be done. Second, the person doing the restoring must be meek—the person must have his power under the control of the Holy Spirit. The person must be open to leadings and nudges from the Holy Spirit and be courageous enough to act on them. So I have to be in tune with the Holy Spirit.

"Step three: Restoration, not correction. Correction is about straightening someone out. It's about telling them what their problem is and then telling them how to fix it. Correction is rarely well received. It gets the same response as judging. The one being corrected begins looking for ways to correct the one doing the correcting. (Pause.) You got that, right?

"Offering correction in this manner is what I call *pearl pushing*. Jesus said, 'Do not throw your pearls to pigs. If you do, they may trample them under their feet, and then turn and tear you to pieces.' Jesus was not calling the people with whom we have problems 'pigs.' The dynamic here is that pigs do not value pearls.[xiii] In addition, I'm throwing the pearls at the pigs. The pig thinks it's being pelted with something and charges at what it perceives to be a threat. If I start dispensing what I think is valuable advice to someone who I think needs it, I will not be thanked. The person I'm straightening out didn't ask to be straightened out. He doesn't see the value in my advice. He feels like he's being attacked, and maybe he is. 'It's for his own good,' I say, and so I justify my actions; but he still feels attacked, and so he attacks back. My telling this coworker about how to manage his life better using someone's time management system is not received. No one is helped. The relationship begins to unravel some more.

"Restoration is about restoring relationships, not correcting someone. In order to restore the relationship that has been damaged by the coworker's tardiness to meetings, we need to work together on restoring the relationship and changing the behavior. In order to do this, I must do the board removal work and keep the conversation safe, like we talked about. After I get his story about why he's always late, I ask what we can do to get him to the meeting on time so we can all work well together. That question indicates this is not his problem—it's our problem. It identifies the fact that he's late, and I'm bothered that he's late. That question also indicates that we're going to work together to arrive at a solution. The solution will not be dictated to him. Finally, that question indicates that I have some work to do and so does he. We're in this together. We're going to get out of this together. Together, we're going to go on to a better future.

"Restoration is about dealing with the issue as both people define it, finding a mutual solution, and working together on it. This means that help is requested, help is given, and help is received by both parties. Restoration is about the relationship.

"Step four: Be careful I'm not tempted also. The temptation may be about the behavior the restoration is about, but I also need to be careful I don't get tempted to be a pearl pusher, to tell faulty stories, or to bail on the work I need to do.

"In this whole process of board removal and restoration, I need to heed Jesus' admonition, found in Matthew 10:16, to 'be as shrewd as snakes and as innocent as doves.' The innocent dove has no ulterior motive. We need to check and recheck our motives. We need to check and recheck our stories. If we have ulterior motives and have told a faulty story, it will come out in the process, and the other person will run from us or attack us.

"To be as shrewd as snakes is about timing.[xiv] I have never seen a snake chasing after its prey. It waits and waits until the right time and then springs. The timing here is about how I have the crucial conversation. I never start with my conclusion. In order to get the other person to take the journey with me, I have to start with the facts, then share my story, then the emotions, and then my actions. I have to get the other person's story, emotions, and actions. Only then can we work together toward a solution. Often I have worked the whole thing out in my head with my own stories to the point where the solution or the conclusion is obvious. Because it's obvious to me, I think it's obvious, or should be obvious, to the other person, or at least it will be once I tell them. So I start with the conclusion or the solution, and if I get a funny look from the other person, I work backwards through the emotion to the story to the fact. The other person can't hear all that because the conclusion or solution made the conversation unsafe. In the unsafe conversation, the trail can't be followed backwards, everything gets messed up, the situations get worse, and relationships become even more difficult.

"One final thing: If we don't do the board removal work, the other person can't change, because he doesn't know how. As I do the board removal work in sharing our actions from fact to action, the other person receives a model of how to change. As we work together on what needs to happen, he gets support in working the change model and can begin to learn to do it himself."

"There's a lot there," said Joe. "When I first looked at this, I had no idea. I must confess, I'm not very good with board removal skills. I can see how my relationships would improve if I got better with them all. I think I'm beginning to get to know Jesus. I suspect that very soon he will give me the opportunity to hone those skills. I just hope it doesn't hurt too much."

"You're right, we all get in situations fairly often where we need to use these skills, but you'll have kingdom resources to help you this time, and the spiritual disciplines you've been practicing have created some open space in your heart where God can work. Did you get to spend some time in worship this week?" Matt asked.

"Yes," Joe replied. "It's always good to get out in the woods alone with God. I felt more peaceful the rest of the week."

"Which one shall we do next week?" Matt asked.

"Let me look at the list," Joe said. A couple of minutes later Joe suggested, "Let's try silence."

"Works for me," Matt replied. "Let's be silent on the outside by being somewhere as noise free as possible. Let's be silent on the inside too. We'll do that by listening for God. Let's try three ten-minute sessions during the week."

Joe agreed. They prayed for each other, being careful not to use the prayer to push pearls. As Joe drove away, he wondered what, if anything, he would hear in the silence.

Suggested resources:
Dallas Willard, *The Divine Conspiracy*, HarperCollins, 1998.
Robert Quinn, *Deep Change*, Jossey-Bass Inc., 1996.
Kerry Patterson, Joseph Brenny, Ron McMillan, Al Switzler, *Crucial Conversations*, McGraw-Hill, 2002.

CHAPTER 14

THE RULE OF THE KINGDOM: ASK

"It seems like a long time since last week," Joe thought as he entered the coffee shop. So much had happened. As Joe looked around, Matt came in behind him. They exchanged greetings as they got some coffee and headed towards their usual table.

"I've been dying to ask," Matt said. "What happened with your first counseling session?"

"We covered a lot of ground," Joe said. "He asked me all sorts of questions about family. He wasn't interested in my dad. He wanted to know about my mom, brothers and sisters, and extended family. He wanted to know about my kids, my wife, and her extended family. He asked about my job, how well I get along with my boss, and how many jobs I've had. He did some kind of personality test, which I think I flunked. Then he asked me what I wanted to accomplish with our time and why I was doing this now instead of ten years ago or ten years from now."

"What did you tell him?" Matt asked.

"I told him it was all your fault," Joe said. "I told him I was just trying to follow Jesus, minding my own business, when we came across the 'love your enemy' passage in Matthew 5. I told him about the dreams I've been having. I told him the dreams certainly seem to indicate that things between my dad and me need to change. I told him how you talked about reconciliation, but I wasn't sure what that would look like. He told me that I was in the right place, and we would get to work on it next week.

"It wasn't nearly as scary as I thought it was going to be. The counselor seemed like a nice guy, so I guess I'm ready for next week. I thought going to the counselor was going to be the big deal this week, but it wasn't. Sue really surprised me."

"What did Sue do?" Matt asked.

"Sue is becoming a one woman crusade about AIDS. She read a short article in the newspaper about AIDS deaths in Africa. She got curious and did some research on the internet and picked up a little book, *The Skeptics Guide to the Global AIDS Crisis*, by Dale Bourke. I brought it with me because I wanted to show it to you. This paragraph, from the first chapter, jumped out and hit me in the face:

> AIDS is the biggest public health problem the world has ever faced. It has already surpassed the bubonic plague, which wiped out twenty-five million people—one quarter of Europe's population at the time. An estimated three million people die each year from AIDS, a death tool that has been compared to twenty fully loaded 747s crashing every single day for a year...Each day nearly 8,500 people die due to AIDS.[i]

"Sue says all those deaths have huge consequences. Perhaps the biggest consequence is that a large percentage of those who die of AIDS have children. In 2010, the number of AIDS orphans in the world is expected to reach 25 million. Sue asked if we could send the $100 we had earmarked for donations to an orphanage in Africa that cares for AIDS orphans. She didn't know which orphanage. She has some research to do.

"Each day, Sue is learning more about the AIDS crisis. Each day, she becomes a little more passionate. She has begun to talk about changing how we live so that we could have some money to help fight the AIDS crisis. I suspect sometime soon she'll want to go to an AIDS conference somewhere. I wouldn't be surprised if a trip to Africa is in our future.

"Right now, I'm not into this as much as she is, but that's okay. I'm amazed at the change in her. It's good to see her pouring her energy into more than driving kids to and from practices and games. It's good to see Sue work toward something beyond her next trip to the mall. I have no idea where this will take us, but I think I might like the ride."

"That is a big deal," Matt agreed. "I had no idea the AIDS crisis in Africa was so bad. I don't see it in the papers or hear about it on the news. I would think if AIDS is worse than the bubonic plague, we would hear about it. We get the constant body count from Iraq. Yet the 4,424 US soldiers who have died in Iraq since 2003[ii] pale in comparison to that number you showed me—8,500 people a day dying of AIDS. That boggles the mind. Why don't we hear more about it?"

"I asked Sue the same question," Joe replied. "Sue didn't have a good answer except to say there is a lot of political fighting between countries, health agencies, and drug companies. She says it looks like it's very complicated.

"What about you? You were checking out some employment options. What has been happening?"

"I'm still consulting," Matt said. "I talked with the life coach. I liked what I heard. I talked with Rev. Jim about the options he had in mind, and they sound intriguing. I have the interview with the company next week."

"Do you know what you're going to do?" Joe asked.

"This surprises me, but I think I'm going back to corporate America," Matt answered. "As I have prayed about what to do, I seem to be hearing a couple of things from God. One is that God invested in me by giving me leadership gifts, training, and management abilities. God has honed these areas in my life in the corporate world. A second thing I've been hearing is that God loves the people and the companies that make up the corporate world. God shows his love by sending people into the corporate world who carry kingdom values to help guide corporations. God also uses the people with kingdom values as salt and light as they build relationships with people at work and influence them with kingdom values. A third thing occurred to me: With salary and stock options, I have

Coffee with Matt & Joe

the opportunity to make more money in the corporate world than with those other options."

"Don't tell me, after that discussion we had about McWorld, you're going for the money?" Joe asked, incredulous.

"Yes, I'm going for the money, but not like you think," Matt replied. "I've been talking with Mary about what to do. One of the things we want to do is invest more money in the kingdom, so we agreed that if I go corporate, we're going to downsize our lifestyle. We would like to live on 50 percent of my income and invest the other 50 percent in kingdom business. We could help fund a new church, fund some missionaries, help our church extend its kingdom reach, or fund people who are fighting AIDS or...We haven't figured that out yet, but I'm excited about the possibilities.

"I want to go back into the corporate world, but this time it's not to chase after a career. I want to be Jesus' agent in the company for which I will work. I want to bless that company, I want to lead some of its people to Jesus and help disciple them, and I want to help that company become a blessing to its customers, employees, and stockholders."

"That sounds good," Joe said. "That sounds a lot like what you've been talking about with me these past weeks. But can I ask you a question? You talked about hearing from God. How does that work for you? I pray, and I see God do stuff in my life. I talk with you, and the things Jesus said become alive. I go to worship and feel inspired and sometimes nudged to do something. Is that what you're talking about, or is it something more?"

"It's all that and more," Matt replied. "God talks to me in the ways you mentioned. In addition, I hear from God through the counsel of Christian friends and the small group I'm in. Sometimes God gives me an insight that's bigger than I am. Sometimes, not often, I have a dream that comes from God. Sometimes I feel God's presence in conjunction with a thought or an idea. Sometimes I get excited about something. God talks in lots of ways. When I receive the same message from several of these sources, I'm convinced God is telling me something.

"In this case, the message—God investing in me to be one of his people in the corporate world—came from an insight bigger than I am, from my small group talking about God in the work place, from things Jesus said that we've been talking about here, through Mary's input, and from a sense of peace and expectancy about what the future will bring as I go in the direction God is leading me."

"So hearing from God is not so much hearing an audible voice from heaven calling my name," Joe clarified, "as it is being in God's presence, being open to God, and putting myself in the situations to receive a message from God. Worship, prayer, small groups, reading the Bible, and conversations with Christian friends are some of the ways God communicates with us, and we just go with the flow of the communication that comes in from those sources. Is that what you're saying?"

"Yes, you could say that," Matt replied. "The spiritual disciplines we talked about open us to hearing from God in whatever method he chooses to communicate. So how did the time in silence go?"

"Quietly," Joe said. "It was hard. It was hard to turn off the internal soundtrack. It wasn't until the third time I tried that I was able to do it. When I finally got quiet and listened to the silence, I was amazed at how much noise there is in the silence. There was the humming of the refrigerator and the furnace, the ticking of the grandfather clock, the whooshing of cars, and the roaring of an airplane overhead. I don't know if I heard God any better this week, but I was more at ease with myself. How did it go for you?"

"I always find it difficult," Matt answered. "I can get quiet, but I get bored with the silence. I want to think something, pray something, or something something. But I think the silence helped me to hear God answer my questions about what kind of job to get. Where are we with Jesus?"

"We're with Jesus at Matthew 7:7-12," Joe prompted. "Let me read it:

> "Ask and it will be given to you; seek and you will find; knock and the door will be opened to you. For everyone who asks receives; he who seeks finds; and to him who knocks, the door will be opened.
> "Which of you, if his son asks for bread, will give him a stone? Or if he asks for a fish, will give him a snake? If you,

then, though you are evil, know how to give good gifts to your children, how much more will your Father in heaven give good gifts to those who ask him! In everything, do to others what you would have them do to you, for this sums up the Law and the Prophets."

"Yes, it's coming back to me now," Matt said. "Last week, we talked about board removal. We saw how telling, yelling, and forcing don't bring about change. We saw the need to examine our own issues and to make changes before trying to get someone else to make a change. Once we've done this work, Jesus told us how to seek change from other people. He said we're to ask. We put the asking in context by sharing our story with the other person. That leads to the asking. If we don't share the story, which is part of the board removal, we won't get very far."

"Does this work?" Joe asked. "It sounds like Jesus has us working from weakness, not strength. Further, asking puts a lot on me, the asker. When asking, I feel powerless. Asking makes me feel that v word, vulnerable, which is not a comfortable feeling. Asking puts the risk on me. Asking puts me at the mercy of the responsiveness of the other person. In addition to all that, the other person might say no, and I'm sunk."

"It doesn't sound very productive, does it?" Matt responded. "When we share our story, we become vulnerable. We lower our defenses. Then when we ask, we ask because we can't demand and can't command, which means more weakness and more vulnerability for us. Commands and demands might work for the short term where one person has a large amount of power over another. But asking out of a vulnerable position works for the long term. When I respond to a vulnerable ask, I do so because that's what I have chosen. Because I have chosen, I'm more committed to carrying out what I have promised.

"Even though asking requires us to be vulnerable, there is power in the ask. Willard, in *The Divine Conspiracy*, makes the case that asking is so powerful that people often go to great lengths to avoid being asked.[iii] I've noticed when I'm put in charge of a volunteer effort, there are people who avoid me or don't return my phone calls because they don't want to deal with the ask. They don't want to participate but are unable to turn down the ask, so they avoid the ask. When someone does say no, I always feel the need to let them know that no is an acceptable answer because I want the relationship to continue.

"Willard illustrates the power of the ask with a familiar story about the family dog:[iv] I'm sitting at the dinner table just about to take the first bite of the homemade chocolate chip cookie fresh from the oven. As I pick up the cookie, I become aware of the dog. She's sitting on the floor next to my chair. She's alert, and her ears are perked. Her head is cocked slightly. She looks as beautiful as a dog can look. Her eyes are asking, can I have some too, please? As I take a bite, she intensifies all that she's doing to the point where either I give her some cookie, or I have to send her away because I can't handle the power of her ask. Most often I cave, and she gets some cookie.

"Speaking from my own experience with asking, it's hard to say no. I always feel bad when I say no. I want the approval of the people who are asking. One of the reasons I hate receiving calls from telemarketers is that I have to say no to them. They know I have a hard time saying no, so they push to get me to say yes. That makes my no all the harder to say and makes me never want to answer the phone again.

"Often I have to work out my yes and no in advance of the question being asked. Before going to meetings, I decide whether or not I will say yes to a request. I have to work out with Mary in which situations will we say yes to a person. If I don't work out my response to the ask in advance, I will want to say yes because asking is powerful. That's one of the reasons we have problems with our yes and no.

"Even though asking is powerful, the person asking rarely feels that power. We feel power when we make demands, give commands, and issue ultimatums. We feel weak when we ask, so we avoid it as much as possible."

"I know the feeling," Joe added. "I'm a sucker for an ask. That's part of the reason my marriage was on the rocks. I'm not a guy who can easily say no. I need Sue's approval, Sue's yes to me in order to say no to others."

"When the ask is done in the right spirit," Matt continued, "It has the power to unite. Many times I've been asked for help and have been glad to give it. In those times, I feel honored and valued that the person asking has the confidence in me to make such a request of me. As I work on the task with that person, our relationship grows.

"Again when the ask is done in the right spirit, it respects the freedom of the other person. Asking, by its very nature, means it is willing to accept a no. Because a good ask allows the person being asked to say no, there is no manipulation. When an ask is willing to accept a no, it has the power to build the person being asked. Such an ask gives a person permission to be who they are.

"Finally, an ask is a request that doesn't go away. The ask of the dog for a bite of cookie continues until the cookie is gone. When I'm asked to help on a project, even though I've said no, I continue to feel the ask until I know the team for the project has been put in place. Then I breathe a sigh of relief.

"Jesus illustrated the persistence of the ask with two parables he related to asking God. Beginning with Luke 11:5, the first parable is of the neighbor at midnight. Guests arrive at your house late. You have nothing to feed them. You knock on the neighbor's door. The neighbor says, 'Go away.' But if you keep asking, the neighbor will give you what you want not because he's your neighbor, but because of the persistence of the ask. Jesus said to ask and keep asking, knock and keep knocking, seek and keep seeking because the one who asks receives, the one who knocks has the door opened, and the one who seeks finds. I'll say more about this in a moment.

"The second parable is the parable of the persistent widow which Jesus told in Luke 18:1-8. A widow goes to an unjust judge for justice. The judge declines to help. But the widow comes back every day. The judge relents and gives justice to the widow because she's wearing him out with her requests. Jesus said, 'How much more will God respond to us when we ask?' (Matthew 7:11, author's paraphrase.) I'll say more about that in a moment also."

"Slow down a minute," Joe requested. "You keep mentioning asking in the right spirit. What is the right spirit?"

"Thank you," Matt responded, "for that ask. The right spirit or the right conditions for asking are these:

1. I have done the board removal work. That means I'm not telling a villain, victim, or powerless story. I have owned my share of the problem or the request and have dealt with my issues. I'm not pearl pushing, which means I'm not trying to fix the other person with my request. I have shared my story, being open about my hurts and hopes with the one being asked, prior to the asking. In this way, they can enter my story, follow my story, and not be shocked or surprised by the ask that is coming.
2. I have listened to their story and entered into their hopes and hurts. I'm willing to share their pain. Sometimes this comes before the ask and sometimes this comes as a result of the ask. If I'm not willing to enter their world and share their pain, I'm not asking in the manner Jesus requested.
3. I'm not trying to manipulate the person being asked. This connects with number 4.
4. I'm willing to take no for an answer. If I can't take no for an answer, then I will find myself using the ask to manipulate. If I can't accept no, and if I'm using the ask to manipulate, I have to go back to number 1 and do more board removal work to deal with my own issues.

"Let me put Jesus' words about board removal together with his words about asking so that we can see how this all works. Jesus talked about board removal. I have done the board removal work to the best of my ability.

"Jesus followed up board removal work saying to ask, seek, and knock. The Greek verb tense that Matthew recorded is continuous. This means Jesus was telling us to ask and keep on asking; seek and keep on seeking; knock and keep on knocking. As we ask and keep on asking, we will receive. If we seek and keep on seeking, we will find. If we knock and keep on knocking, the door will be opened to us.

"Despite Jesus' words, we all have had the experience of asking, seeking, knocking, and then hearing the phrase, 'Request denied.' But Jesus told us to reload and go at it again. Reloading means going back to the board removal process. As a result of my experience with the ask, seek, and knock process, have I discovered more board removal work I need to do? If I have, I need to do the board removal work and ask, seek, and knock again. I need to repeat the process until my ask is resolved.

"The board removal, combined with the ask, could lead me to a variety of places. Sometimes the ask throws me back on board removal that deals with issues of my own that I need to work through. Sometimes the ask puts me in the position of dealing with someone else's issues. For the ask to be resolved, I must work with the other person through their issues. This will usually push me back to some issues of my own. Sometimes the ask and the answer received show me that I was asking the wrong thing. Once again, I'm back to board removal work.

"Sometimes board removal and asking seems like a tedious process. It certainly takes time. It sometimes takes us places and has us deal with things when we would rather not. However, the process causes us to grow, helps us deal with the other person in a win-win perspective; and as Jesus said, if we keep at it, we'll receive what we're asking for."

"That sounds like a lot of work to me," Joe replied.

"It is," Matt responded, "but do you have a better idea?"

"No, I don't," Joe answered. "But I would have liked it a whole lot better if Jesus had worked out a way so that I could simply command and demand and people would jump to do my bidding."

"The problem with Jesus working out a way to command and demand," Matt said, "is that I don't like to be commanded and demanded. I like it a whole lot better when someone asks me, when someone trusts me, when someone takes me into their confidence. That's the way we are, which brings me to the next point of this board removal asking process Jesus laid out here. We find it in Matthew 7:12."

"Verse 12?" Joe asked. "Wait a minute, let me find it. Here it is: 'In everything, do to others what you would have them do to you, for this sums up the Law and the Prophets.' You're right—if we follow the board removal asking process, we'll end up doing the Golden Rule."

"As I think about it," Matt said, "much of what Jesus has been teaching makes it possible for us to live the Golden Rule. I would like the people I deal with to come to me when they're angry with me and try to work things out. I don't like it when they blast and blame and punish me with their anger. I like it when people who are sexually attracted to me accept the commitment I have made with Mary and seek to relate to me on other levels. I like dealing with people who can say yes and no appropriately, mean it, and live it out. When I have power over someone and am abusing that power, I appreciate them letting me know about it in nonconfrontational ways. When people consider me their enemy, I like it when they talk with me about our differences and try to do good to me even though we're on opposite sides of an issue. I like it when people ask me and tell me their thought processes leading up to the ask.

"I used to look at the Golden Rule as some random saying of Jesus that was just tossed in here. Then I looked at the Golden Rule as a good summary of the teaching of Jesus and a good way to live. But recently, I've been seeing the Golden Rule as the kingdom standard in dealing with people. I have come to the conclusion that the Golden Rule is not a summary but the apex of the kingdom teaching Jesus has been doing here. The way to live a life that exceeds the law is to treat my neighbor, respond to my neighbor, in the way I would like to be treated. All that Jesus has been leading us through are the issues we have to deal with in order to live the Golden Rule.

"I have one other Golden Rule thought. Jesus assembled this sermon in a particular order. I think there is a reason the Golden Rule comes nearly at the end. We need to see the Golden Rule in a kingdom perspective. 'Do to others what you would have them do to you.' The kingdom perspective changes my expectations of what I would like to have happen to me. Jesus is talking to us as people who have experienced the kingdom. In the kingdom, I experience grace, mercy, forgiveness, love, hope, reconciliation, and resources for living. And did I mention the incredible, out-of-proportion love God has for us? Once I have begun to experience the kingdom, which is beyond my own expectations, then my expectations for life begin to change. My expectations of life in the kingdom are that I will receive help, forgiveness, and mercy from God who is rooting for me. When I factor the kingdom into what I would like to happen to me, what I would like others to do to me, then the Golden Rule is about how I can do the kingdom thing, in the kingdom way, at the kingdom time, in this situation, with my brother or my sister.

"The problem most of us have with the Golden Rule is that we can't get past the way others treat us. Other people don't treat us in accordance with the Golden Rule, and what we want to do is treat them the way they treat us. Someone cuts us off in traffic, so we want to cut him off. We see someone we know, greet him, and he ignores us. We want to ignore him. Someone smiles at us, and we return the smile. Someone helps us, and we want to help her. The Golden Rule is about using the resources of the kingdom to get beyond the way someone has treated us to be able to treat them in kingdom ways."

"Jesus never make things any easier, does he?" Joe commented. "One of the things that has become apparent to me over and over again is that I don't have in me the resources to live in these ways. They keep going counter to how I have acted and reacted in the past. They seem to go against our natural ways of dealing with the people and the world around us. I find that to even consider acting in the ways Jesus talked about, let alone actually do them, I have to keep falling back to the first Beatitude—Help me! I certainly hope the spiritual disciplines we've begun to do will get enough of the kingdom in me that I will be able to see my behavior change so that more of the time I can act in kingdom ways."

"As you keep with the spiritual disciplines, you will begin to see your behavior change," Matt replied. "We've been looking at this board removal asking process in terms of dealing with other people. Jesus also wants us to know that this board removal asking process is how to approach God too."

"It is?" Joe asked. "Talk to me about that."

"Jesus wants us to know, as we approach God," Matt began, "that God loves us far more than we love our children. In Matthew 7:9-11, Jesus said:

> "Which of you, if his son asks for bread, will give him a stone? Or if he asks for a fish, will give him a snake? If you, then, though you are evil, know how to give good gifts to

your children, how much more will your Father in heaven give good gifts to those who ask him!

"If we, with all our issues, can do good things for our children and give our children good gifts, how much more is God, our Father in heaven, able and willing to give good gifts to us? Jesus wants us to know that God is more willing to respond to our requests of him than we're willing to ask of him. Jesus wants us to know that God is a giver of good gifts. We don't have to beg, plead, manipulate, trick, or earn good things from God. All we have to do is ask.

"All the problems we have with asking exist in prayer. In prayer, we often feel powerless and vulnerable. We're the ones taking the risk, depending on the responsiveness of God, and risking hearing no for an answer. Many of us want more control over the situation when we approach God. But there is no control, for just as in asking from people, we must depend on the character of God. But Jesus has just told us God's character. God responds to our requests with good things.

"The ask, seek, knock process applies here too. Jesus wants us to stay in conversation with God about whatever the issue is until it's resolved. In Genesis 32, we read about Jacob wrestling with God. Jacob wouldn't let go until God had blessed him. Too many times I think we stop wrestling with God just before the blessing comes. We give up on God and walk away.

"The wrestling is not about prying something out of God's hands—it's about board removal. We come to God, and we ask, but we can't see because of the board that's in our eye. God uses the asking process to help us remove the board. I've wrestled long and hard with God on many occasions because I didn't know there was a board there. I couldn't see it. Other times I've wrestled because I knew the board was there, but I didn't want it to be removed. Sometimes I've wrestled with God about another person's actions. I wanted God to remove their boards, but God was trying to get me to deal with my own boards.

"Jesus said if we stay with it, those who ask receive, those who seek find, and those who knock have the door opened.

"Prayer is not about mechanics, but about being open and honest with God about what is in our hearts. Prayer is talking with God, asking God, and working with God on what is in our hearts and what is in God's heart. Prayer is an ongoing conversation with God where each of us shares what is in our hearts.

"There are two things Willard says here that I find helpful: First, I have no relationship of which Jesus is not a part.[v] I have no conversation, no interaction with another in which Jesus is not involved. Jesus is involved in every relationship I have. I'm not alone. Even in the most difficult conversations and relationships, Jesus is with me. Part of what this means is that I can make requests on the behalf of the others. Others are a part of the life that Jesus and I share together.

"The second thing Willard says is this: 'It is God's intention that we should grow into the kind of person he could empower to do what we want to do.'[vi] God's hope for us is that we would become so consumed by the kingdom, so filled by the kingdom, so enthralled by the kingdom that our conversation with God and our requests of God would be kingdom requests. The wrestling with God in the board removal asking process is designed to help us grow into the kind of person whose heart beats after God's own heart and whose requests would take the kingdom forward.

"Having said all that, I'd like to take a look at the Lord's Prayer, found in Matthew 6:9-15.

"Jesus started the prayer by having us address God as 'Our Father.' In recent years, there have been some objections to that because some people have claimed it's sexist and indicates that God is male and that it devalues women. Others have said it's very difficult for those who have had abusive fathers to pray this.

"However, when I hear Jesus asking us to address God as Father, I hear him saying that the God to whom we are praying is the one who claims us. In order for a child to be recognized as fully belonging to the family, the father must claim the child. I see God standing in front of all creation holding each one of us high in the air and saying, 'This one is mine.'

"Our Father God is the God who claims us. God has created us, and then he claims us. God is not like Dr. Frankenstein, who is horrified by what he has created, flees the building, and wants nothing to do with his creature. Rather, God, who claims us, is pleased by what he has created. He knows each one of us intimately—all that is in our hearts for good or evil and all that we have done for good or evil—and he claims us.

"Jesus wants us to know that the God who claims us—the Our Father God—loves us, roots for us, wants the best for us, and eagerly awaits the time when we come and talk. So as we pray, we're entering into conversation with the great creator God who claims us and loves us far beyond what we think we're worth."

"That's very helpful," Joe replied. "As I have begun praying and calling God 'Father,' I have wondered about my own dad. I haven't confused the two. I never called my dad 'father,' but occasionally I have wondered if God would get angry with me and beat me like my dad did. I have balanced that with the words of the angel from the Christmas story, 'and on earth peace to men on whom [God's] favor rests' (Luke 2:14b). As I hear those words, I feel God's embrace."

"That's good, Joe. You're really beginning to understand how God is your loving Father. Let's continue," Matt said. "The second phrase of the Lord's Prayer is 'in heaven.' This phrase helps us distinguish the 'Father,' who Jesus was talking about, from our own earthly fathers. For years, when I prayed to the Father who is in heaven, I was praying to the Father who is a way off there somewhere far beyond the blue.

"Dallas Willard, in his book, *The Divine Conspiracy*, claims that when Jesus told us to pray to 'Our Father in heaven', he was telling us that God is not away off there somewhere, but actually in the air around us.[vii] So heaven is in the air around us. This means that God is near. Augustine said, 'God is nearer to us than we are to ourselves,' and Paul told us that in God 'we live and move and have our being' (Acts 17:28). So we pray to the Father who is here. His ear is able to hear, and his arm is able to help. God is actually present with us. This phrase reminds us of that.

"We need to be reminded. It's easy to think when things don't go our way, or we're feeling down or lonely, that God is nowhere near. It's also easy to think that God has gone away somewhere when we listen for him and hear nothing, or hope to feel his presence and don't. It's good to remember that our senses are not always accurate indicators of the nearness or farness of God.

"So when we pray, Jesus wants us to know we're praying to the great creator God who claims us in the presence of all creation as his dearly loved children, and this Father is not an absent father, but a very present father.

"The third section of the Lord's Prayer is where Jesus told us to pray 'hallowed be thy name.' To hallow something is to honor, respect, revere, or hold in awe. So how do we hallow God's name? How do we hallow God's name as we pray? One way we can do this is to give thanks to God for his mighty acts of creation and salvation, both in world history and in our own personal history. Another way we can do this is to give thanks to God for who he is by praying through the names of God given throughout the Bible. Some of those names are: The God Who Provides, The God Who is There, The God Who is My Strength, The God Who is My Victory, and The Most High God.

"Another way to hallow God's name is to act in ways that hallow his name. God's name is hallowed when we do what he asks us to do. So God's name is hallowed when we love our enemies, do acts of kindness to those who harm us, and forgive those who hurt us. God's name is hallowed when we visit the sick, welcome the stranger, and feed the hungry.

"God's name is hallowed by our words. God's name is hallowed when we use our words to build up, encourage, and affirm others. God's name is hallowed when we share what God has done in our lives. God's name is hallowed when we're able to engage someone far from God in conversation about God, so they move a step or two closer to God.

"To hallow God's name is a whole lifestyle that comes when, in my heart, I honor, revere, and respect God. As we pray 'hallowed be thy name,' let us pray that we can live with integrity so that the honor, reverence, and respect for God that is in our hearts shows up in our lives. Maybe we need to pray that God would help our 'hallow' for him to grow.

"When we pray, 'your kingdom come, your will be done on earth as it is in heaven,' what are we asking? We're asking for the kingdom—for all that we have been working on these last fourteen weeks. I tend to think of this specifically in those five points from Greeley:

1. Change your life, for the kingdom of heaven is at hand.
2. The day of salvation has dawned.
3. The principle sign of the kingdom and its salvation is God's loving mercy.
4. The kingdom will triumph.
5. Since we have heard about the Good News, we must rejoice.[viii]

"To pray, 'your will be done on earth as it is in heaven' is to pray to be an agent of God's kingdom. It's to pray that God will use me to bring his kingdom to the world in which I live. It's to pray that I will be as attentive to God's leadings and directions in bringing his kingdom to the world as the angels are to God's commands, the sun is to His bidding, and the seasons are to His wishes.

"'Give us this day our daily bread.' Daily bread is the stuff we need in order to live. It's food, clothing, housing, transportation, and communication. It's health. It's a job and income. It's hope, love, joy, forgiveness, and freedom. It's a good night's sleep. Daily bread is the physical, emotional, and spiritual sustenance we need to not just survive, but to thrive in this life God has given us. Sometimes we don't think to pray about these things. We're paying the bills, and life goes on—but Jesus instructs us to ask God for daily bread.

"When we ask God for daily bread, it reminds us that God is the source of supply. The company that signs my paycheck is not the source of my daily bread—it's the instrument God is using at this time. My health and my sleep are not because of some medicine, vitamin, or supplement I'm taking—they are gifts from God, and he may be using a pill or supplement to improve my health. My emotional and spiritual well-being are gifts from God as well.

"When we start to think that the job, the medicine, or our own actions are the source of our daily bread, we begin to lose bread. We begin to wonder if our job pays enough and if we're healthy enough. Something could happen so that our job disappears or our health worsens, and then what? Life is full of what-ifs and unseen twists and turns. Life is simply larger than our ability to provide daily bread.

"When we remember that God, who is larger than life, is the source of daily bread, we can rejoice in it. God's supply of daily bread to us is not limited by the economy, the stock market, or which political party holds power. God is able to supply even when it looks like all sources of supply have dried up. We're able to rejoice in God who supplies and face life without worry and anxiety.

"'Forgive us our debts as we also have forgiven our debtors.' With this phrase, Jesus has stopped praying and has gone to meddling. The prayer is no longer between God and us. Jesus has enlarged it to take in our relationships with other people. In addition, Jesus tied our relationships with others directly to our relationship with God. Each relationship influences the other.

"To show us how serious he is about our forgiving one another, Jesus told us God will not forgive us unless we forgive. I don't know about you, but I want God's forgiveness more than anything. If God were not to forgive, I wouldn't make it.

"But even with that, many of us have a difficult time forgiving one another and sometimes even forgiving ourselves. Forgiveness means I pay another's debt out of my own resources. I release them from the debt, and they are free to go. They don't have to pay. The truth is they can't pay. Sometimes we think the debt is larger than our resources. When it is, we can ask God for the resources to pay the debt. As we make the decision to pay the debt, God makes the decision to send the resources to heal our hearts.

"Sometimes we withhold forgiveness because we think if we forgive, they'll just do the same thing to us again and again. We think that withholding forgiveness prevents them from harming us in the same way again. It doesn't. It just makes our lives miserable. After we forgive, we need to take steps to change our behavior so that the same thing doesn't happen again and again. We think withholding forgiveness is somehow leverage to get them to change. It isn't. We can't change anyone else. The only change we can make is in ourselves with God's help.

"Forgiveness keeps us in tune with God and provides the resources to us so that we can make the changes to prevent the offense from occurring again.

"'And lead us not into temptation.' I'm not sure what Jesus had in mind with this petition. It seems strange to ask God to not lead us into temptation because that doesn't seem like the kind of thing God would do anyway. Some have argued that Jesus was having us pray that God not lead us into hard testing.

"Whichever it is, temptation or hard testing, I don't want to find myself in either. The reason I don't want to find myself in either situation is I know that I won't do well. I'm vulnerable to temptation. I find if testing is difficult, I don't stand up well under it. I have no trouble praying for God to lead me away from temptation and hard testing.

"When I pray this part of the prayer, I find myself praying that God would prevent me from doing dumb stuff. I pray that God would prevent me from acting out of anger or hurt or misunderstanding. I pray that God would help me not act in ways that would make a bad situation worse. I pray that God would help me act out of his grace and his kingdom resources and not out of my weaknesses.

"I find it helpful to pray that God would keep me out of situations where I'm tempted. If there's a particular temptation I'm dealing with, I find it good to pray that God would keep me from certain locations, people, and materials that help trigger the temptation. I ask God to give me the wisdom to flee temptation when it arises and not stand there looking at it. I pray that God would bring people around me to offer support and that God would help me deal with the root of the temptation. As I deal with the root of the temptation, I find that the temptation leaves.

"'But deliver us from the evil one.' I think of the words of the Christmas carol: 'God rest you merry, gentlemen, let nothing you dismay. For Jesus Christ our Savior was born upon this day, To save us all from Satan's power when we were gone astray: O tidings of comfort and joy, comfort and joy. O tidings of comfort and joy.'

"Jesus has come to break the power of Satan in our lives. What does that look like? It looks like Jesus freeing us from the powers and forces in our lives that are stronger than we are. In Jesus, we find the higher power we need to break the addictions of alcohol, drugs, sex, porn, food, or spending that send our lives spiraling out of control. In Jesus, we find the healing for the hurts that lead us into addiction. In Jesus, we find the strength to overcome the fear and anxiety that prevent us from acting. In Jesus, we find deliverance from the dysfunctional relationships that bind us. In Jesus, we find the help to set aside the thought patterns and habits that rob our lives. In Jesus, we find the one who is able to cast the demons out.

"Jesus has come to protect us from the power of Satan. Jesus brings order to chaos. Jesus brings meaning to the same old, same old and transforms it into something new. Jesus protects us from the randomness of life—strange accidents, weird illnesses, being in the wrong place at the wrong time. Jesus also gives us the power to say no.

"To access the power of Jesus over Satan, all we have to do is ask: 'Jesus, please deliver me.' However, as we pray, Jesus may ask us to do some things to help make the delivery happen. We may have to face some fears or make some choices that seem both terrifying and impossible. But Jesus will help with that too.

"I see you have been busily scribbling notes as I have rambled on here. I want to invite you to join me in a Saturday ritual. Sometime on Saturday, pray the Lord's Prayer for the church."

"How do I do that?" Joe asked.

"Start with 'Our Father,'" Matt replied, "and pray that everyone who comes to worship Sunday will feel claimed by God, valued by God, and loved by God. Then pray 'in heaven' and ask that each person who comes to worship on Sunday would feel God's presence and God's nearness during the service. Go through the whole prayer for the church."

"I'll give that a try and see what happens," Joe said. "Are we going to do a spiritual discipline this week?"

"We sure are," Matt responded. "How about prayer since we've been talking about that? On Saturday, pray the Lord's Prayer for the congregation. On one other day, set aside an hour to pray. Use some of that time to thank God, some to praise God, some to listen, some to talk to God about what's on your heart, some to pray for others, and some to pray a passage of scripture."

"How do I pray a passage of Scripture?" Joe asked.

"Take a passage, and pray it back to God," Matt said. "Let's take Psalm 23 for example. It starts with, 'The Lord is my shepherd.' Pray, 'God, please be my shepherd.' The next line is, 'I shall lack nothing.' Ask God to provide the things you need."

"Okay, I think I have it," Joe replied. "I'll give it a shot."

Then they prayed for each other. As they parted company, Joe began to think about all the board removal work that had been going on in his life. With the future visits to the counselor, Joe could see lots more board removal work coming. Since he was already heavy into board removal work, Joe decided some more asking wouldn't hurt. On the way home, he asked God to help him with his feelings about his dad.

CHAPTER 15

HOUSES OF ROCK OR SAND

Matt was whistling as he walked into the coffee shop. His step was light. His energy level was up. He hadn't felt this good in weeks. He got coffee and chocolate chip cookies for Joe and himself. Joe came in as Matt was going to the table. When Joe got to the table, ready with his cup of steaming hot coffee, Matt looked at him and said, "Mary suggested we get chai tea and scones tonight."

Joe laughed uproariously.

"That," said Matt, "was my exact response. We're guys. We do coffee and chocolate chip cookies, not chai and scones. Women just don't understand."

"You seem in good spirits tonight," Joe responded.

"I am," Matt replied. "My interview went well. It just felt good to walk into corporate America again. It felt good to be walking in the midst of deadlines, budgets, quarterly goals, department infighting, and people working together to turn out a product that will be bought by millions of consumers which in turn provides a livelihood for tens of thousands of people."

"I think you've been out of work too long," Joe said.

"I don't have the job yet," Matt replied. "It was just the first interview. There will be several more, but so far, I like the company, its values, and its goals. I had a talk with their head HR guy. Next time I get to talk with the Vice President I would report to, but so far, so good. How did your counseling session go?"

"It wasn't nearly as much fun as your interview," Joe responded. "It was very difficult. The counselor asked me to describe the first time I remember my dad beating me. I did. I thought the counselor was going to ask me how I felt about that. I thought that was what they did, so I had all this feeling stuff ready to talk about, but he didn't ask me about feelings at all.

"He asked me why I thought my dad beat me. I told him he beat me because what I did wasn't good enough. I told him he beat me because it was impossible to please my dad. He told me that was a very good explanation for an eight-year-old child. Then he told me I'm an adult now and asked me to give him an adult explanation for why my dad beat me. That was hard. I couldn't give him any other explanation. Then he talked with me about my relationship with my dad being frozen in time with my childhood memories. He said that unless I could come up with some other explanations as to why my dad beat me, I wouldn't be able to deal with him as an adult. I would still be acting like an eight-year-old child. I would be hiding from him and trying to punish him by cutting him out of my life. He asked me again for an adult explanation. I still couldn't do it. Then he asked me if I had ever talked with my mom about why he beat me. I told him I had never asked her. She used to try to comfort me as a child by saying someday I would grow up and understand, but I have never understood. He gave me homework. I'm to come up with an adult explanation for why he beat me, and I'm to talk with my mom about it. I haven't done either assignment. Maybe I'll call Mom tonight after we're done. I've been asking God for help."

"It sounds like you have some work to do," Matt said encouragingly. "It doesn't sound like pleasant work either. You've been stuck there a long time, and it will take some work on your part to get going, but I have faith in you and in Jesus. I'm sure you'll get it done."

"On a more upbeat note," Joe said, "Sue is continuing her AIDS research. She wants us to give some money to help support an orphanage. She doesn't understand all the factors involved in the efforts to prevent AIDS from spreading or the research to find a cure, but she does understand children in an orphanage who have lost their parents to AIDS. She has begun to do some work to find an orphanage that's caring for AIDS orphans. Like I said last week, it's great to see her digging into something beyond the next three-day sale at the mall."

"I'll be interested to hear what she digs up," Matt replied. "Tonight, we're going to finish up with the Sermon on the Mount. As I said when we began studying Jesus' teaching in these chapters, I'm amazed at his brilliance. All the issues we face in life are contained here in these words. The insight into the human heart as it functions and the alternatives Jesus put forward are just amazing. Prior to Jesus, there was nothing like this. Since Jesus, we have tried to understand it or dismiss it, but no one else has come up with anything like it. Whenever people have tried to live out what Jesus taught, they experience the life change, the heart change, he talked about and pointed to. I often think about the changes that are still available to occur in my life if I could get more of Jesus' teaching into my life. I think about how different the world would be if we, who call ourselves by Jesus' name, would consistently live out these kingdom teachings of Jesus.

"Just imagine what could happen in our own city if all the people in just one of the churches lived as though the kingdom message of Jesus were true. What would happen if a group of people acted like the kingdom of heaven is near and that God has drawn close to love, heal, redeem, restore, forgive, pardon, and help? What would happen if a group of people actually lived out the blessedness of the Beatitudes and received all the resources of the kingdom when they asked for help, had the strength to gracefully move through change, had their power under Jesus' control, hungered and thirsted for relationships that work and managed to have them, had integrity, offered mercy, brought heart change to conflict, and were willing to take a hit for the kingdom? What would happen if a group of people actually accessed kingdom resources to use their anger to bring reconciliation, sexuality to bring blessing and kept soft hearts in their marriage, knew when and how to say yes and no, could bless the people who misuse their power and love their enemies, live for an audience of one, treasure the kingdom, pursue the process of board removal and asking in all their relationships, receive good gifts from God, and treat others like they want to be treated?"

"Yes," Joe agreed, "that would be incredible. But the thing that hits me is that all this is just incredibly difficult. It seems like everything Jesus had to say is counter to how we naturally respond. We want the blessedness of the Beatitudes, but we want the resources, strength, control, right relationships, and all of the rest on our terms. We find it so much easier to use our anger for punishment and revenge, to use our sexuality for lust, to let our hearts grow hard in our marriages, to say yes and no to the wrong things at the wrong times, and all the rest. To actually be able to live all this stuff out requires a complete rewiring of our systems. It requires me to tell different stories to myself about what is happening and what it all means. It takes a different kind of heart. When Jesus talked about change, he wasn't talking about something as simple as changing my socks. He was talking about completely changing the thoughts, structures, dreams, reactions, and treasures of our lives. He wasn't talking about improving our hearts, he was talking about a complete makeover from the inside out.

"Now that you have helped me see what is possible, my inability to do it myself is particularly frustrating. The first Beatitude, I need help, combined with the spiritual disciplines are providing enough of the kingdom resources to flow into my life that the change can happen, but even that isn't easy. First, I have to see what Jesus asks of us, and then when I do, I face the pain and frustration of being so far from what he asks of us. Then, as the kingdom resources come, I have to open my heart in ways that are risky and vulnerable. Yes, Jesus provides the resources for the change to come, but it seems they only come after I expose myself and risk rejection and misunderstanding or even pain. He opens my fears and hurts for all to see before the change comes. It takes an incredible amount of courage and trust to go forward with Jesus.

"Sometimes I think the main reason I go forward with him at all is it just hurts too much to stay the way I am. I certainly don't want to deal with my dad, but it hurts more not to. When I talk with you, I get glimpses of the end result and know that's what I want. So I think what you described would be incredible, and I would love to be part of something like that, but the process of getting that way is the most difficult thing I've ever done."

"You're right," Matt replied. "Someone said the problem with Christianity is not that it has been tried and found ineffective, but rather it has been tried and found difficult. To go forward with Jesus is to come face to face with our finiteness, frailties, and failures. With Jesus, there is no place to hide; but if we have the courage, and if we have the nerve, the change he works in us is incredible.

"As we enter in this last part of the Sermon on the Mount, let's review just a little. What is the kingdom of heaven?"

"The kingdom of heaven," Joe answered, "doesn't have geographic boundaries. The kingdom of heaven is where God, his values, and his resources are present. The kingdom of heaven is brought near by Jesus."

"Good answer," Matt responded. "I'm impressed. So where is the kingdom?"

"The kingdom is near," Joe answered, "and to those who ask, the kingdom takes up residence in our hearts."

"You've been paying attention," Matt said. "We've been talking about what life in the kingdom looks like. What's one thing about the kingdom that surprises you?"

"I've been surprised by a couple of things," Joe replied. "The first is that as valuable as it is, Jesus is just giving it away. The Sermon on the Mount is free. Today, someone would charge hundreds of dollars a seat for a seminar to explain it and then want you to sign on to the tape series for another couple of hundred dollars. The second thing is the small, simple, almost insignificant way the kingdom works. It's quiet, still, and unassuming, and I don't quite know how to describe it, but a dream just happens, an insight comes, and there's no hype, no trumpets. It just is, and either you get it, or you miss it."

"What is something about the kingdom you have found helpful?" Matt asked.

"The whole thing," Joe replied. "I can't pin down just one. It's a different way to approach the world. It's a different set of values. It brings with it the power to live out those values. It brings forgiveness and another chance and hope. It's like a fresh wind. It's there for the taking. Jesus just offers it up, and when I said I wanted it, he gave it. It's just amazing."

"Jesus began to wrap up the Sermon on the Mount," Matt said, "with these words from Matthew 7:13-14:

> "Enter through the narrow gate. For wide is the gate and broad is the road that leads to destruction, and many enter through it. But small is the gate and narrow the road that leads to life, and only a few find it.

"What do you suppose that narrow gate is?

"As we ask those questions of Islam, Buddhism, Judaism, Hinduism, and what I call American civil religion, we find different answers to the questions. We find different promises. We find different destinations. We find different ways of traveling. What Jesus promises with the kingdom is not offered by anyone else, anywhere else. No one else makes the claims or the promises or has the final destination that Jesus does. I'm not saying here Jesus is better or even Jesus is right, but just Jesus is different. Jesus didn't come saying he's better or he's right. Rather, he came saying the kingdom of heaven is near—enter in. Jesus is not interested in arguments about better and right. He wants us to enter the kingdom. When we do, our concern is not about better and right, but rather, the kingdom is incredible, won't you try it too?"

"Let me ask a couple of questions," Joe interrupted. "Just where do Islam and all the rest lead? What are their roads about? What is American civil religion?"

"We'll visit Islam and all the rest in a few weeks," Matt replied. "American civil religion is the name I've given the belief system that says, 'If you're a good person, or at least better than someone else, and do good things—more good things than bad, or at least more good things than someone else—when you die, you'll go to heaven.' We'll talk about that in a few weeks also.

"One of the things I like about Jesus is that he said the road to life is open. No one has blocked it. There is no gate that demands a toll. Even though he said only a few find the road that leads to life, it is there to be found.

"After the narrow gate, Jesus used four pictures to make his final point. Let's look at them in Matthew 7:15-27.

"Watch out for false prophets. They come to you in sheep's clothing, but inwardly they are ferocious wolves. By their fruit you will recognize them. Do people pick grapes from thorn bushes, or figs from thistles? Likewise every good tree bears good fruit, but a bad tree bears bad fruit. A good tree cannot bear bad fruit, and a bad tree cannot bear good fruit. Every tree that does not bear good fruit is cut down and thrown into the fire. Thus, by their fruit you will recognize them.

"Not everyone who says to me, 'Lord, Lord,' will enter the kingdom of heaven, but only he who does the will of my Father who is in heaven. Many will say to me on that day, 'Lord, Lord, did we not prophesy in your name, and in your name drive out demons and perform many miracles?' Then I will tell them plainly, 'I never knew you. Away from me, you evildoers!'

Therefore everyone who hears these words of mine and puts them into practice is like a wise man who built his house on the rock. The rain came down, the streams rose, and the winds blew and beat against that house; yet it did not fall, because it had its foundation on the rock. But everyone who hears these words of mine and does not put them into practice is like a foolish man who built his house on sand. The rain came down, the streams rose, and the winds blew and beat against that house, and it fell with a great crash."

"Here we go. How do you tell the difference between a wolf in sheep's clothing and a sheep?"

"That's easy," Joe answered. "They act differently. A wolf eats sheep. Sheep eat grass. The wolf would be the one not eating grass, but eyeing the sheep and eating the sheep."

"You're good," Matt replied. "So in terms of the kingdom, its values and lifestyle, what is Jesus saying?"

"I answered the first question," Joe said. "It's your turn. I'm hoping the next question will be an easy one."

"Alright," Matt responded. "A wolf or a false prophet is someone who twists, ignores, adds to, or subtracts from the words of Jesus about the kingdom. They do so because they will profit from people following them and not following Jesus. Further, they do not live out the teaching of Jesus in their own lives. We often think about this in solely religious terms, such as the minister who is in it for the money. But Jesus is talking life, not just religious life. So let's take McWorld for instance. What does McWorld promise?"

"McWorld promises," Joe answered, "status, freedom, and self-worth through stuff and money so that I can buy what I want when I want and do what I want when I want. I'm a person of worth because of the stuff I can buy and the assets I have."

"As we saw a couple of weeks ago," Matt answered, "and as I have experienced in my life, it's a false promise. So if it's a false promise, who benefits from my believing the false promise and going full speed ahead into McWorld? All the people who own the companies from which we buy stuff and all the people who own their stock benefit from my participation in McWorld are the benefactors. If I can convince you that buying a fully-loaded new car from my car company every two years is vital to your health, well-being, attractiveness, worth, and goodness as a human being, then you will buy the car from me. If in the midst of convincing you, I know full well that your health, well being, attractiveness, worth, and goodness as a human being aren't enhanced by the purchase of the car from my company, and if the reason I want you to buy the car is to get your money, then I'm a wolf. Further, I'm a wolf because I have convinced you to invest time, energy, and money in my car that you could have invested in the kingdom where there is health, well-being, worth, and the rest. I, the wolf, have been feeding off your very life.

"Often we want to limit the false prophets and wolves Jesus talked about to the religious world. But a maker of false promises, who benefits from those who believe the lie, is a wolf no matter what the context. Buy from me, elect me, follow me, believe in me, and I will give you your heart's desires. Jesus said the way to sort through all the claims and the promises is to inspect their fruit."

"I never thought of it that way," Joe replied. "I can see that for years I was wolf food. I bought all kinds of stuff for my wife and family because I thought the purchases meant I was a good husband

and father. I spent long hours working hard to buy all those things and was never home. When I was home, I was tired and lacked patience with my children and wife. I yelled at them a lot. While I bought them nice stuff, I was not nice to them when I was around. I suspect tennis shoes at half the price of the hot brand and a dad who had time, energy, and patience for his nine-year-old child would be a much better way to go than working extra hours to buy the hot brand because everyone else had the hot brand."

"That brings us to the next picture," Matt said, "which is inspecting the fruit on the tree. What do you think Jesus would consider good fruit?"

"I think," Joe responded, "Jesus had in a mind a life that looks like what he had been describing in the past couple of chapters. Good fruit would be someone who is salt and light, loves his enemies, works the spiritual disciplines, plays for an audience of one, and uses anger for reconciliation. I think good fruit goes back to what we were saying about the narrow way. Good fruit is produced by hearing the words of Jesus, seeking to understand them, and then putting them into practice."

"What about the next picture?" Matt asked. "People were calling Jesus, 'Lord, Lord,' and telling him to look at all the great things they did in his name, and Jesus said: 'I never knew you. Away from me, you evildoers!' What was Jesus trying to tell us?"

"That sounds pretty harsh to me," Joe replied. "Here are these people doing all this good stuff in his name, and Jesus called them 'evildoers'? I don't understand."

"Listen closely to what is going on," Matt said. "They prophesied, they cast out demons, and they performed miracles in Jesus' name. That's what they did. In fact, it's all about what they did. What did Jesus say was missing? He never knew them. The relationship is missing. Jesus used hyperbole here to say he didn't care what they did—they didn't build a relationship with him. If we don't have a relationship with Jesus, then we don't know what he says, and we can't do what he says. If there is no relationship, we're just guessing about what Jesus wants and trying to do it under our own steam. Jesus wants to build a relationship with us, wants to transform us, and wants to partner with us in spreading the kingdom. Based on what we've heard thus far, I would say Jesus would rather hear on that day, 'I've enjoyed our life together, and I've done everything you asked me to do.'

"I think the evildoer label attached to those who did their own thing in Jesus' name is about opportunity lost. In the book of Acts, chapter 8, Philip fled the persecution in Jerusalem and went to Samaria. Philip preached about Jesus in Samaria, healed some sick people, and drove out some demons. Lots of people believed Philip and came to Jesus. So many people were responding that Peter and John came from Jerusalem to check it out. In the midst of all the action, an angel of the Lord said to Philip to go out to the desert road. Here's the issue: Should Philip leave the revival, where things are happening, and go where God directs him to go, or should Philip trust his own instincts and stay in the revival because there is no one traveling on the desert road? Philip chose to go out to the desert road. He met an Ethiopian eunuch. He led the man to Jesus. The eunuch went home and told people about Jesus. A church was planted. That church still exists today. It's the oldest continuing church in the world. We never hear again about what happened in Samaria. Philip's most lasting contribution was not the revival but the conversation with the man on the desert road. If Philip had said, 'No, I won't go,' what would have been the opportunity cost?

"Jesus is looking at opportunity cost. These people were doing what they thought best while the work God wanted to get done went undone. God, who sees all and knows all, knows best where to deploy us for maximum impact. Who knows how much was lost because they were doing what they thought best rather than seeking out God for marching orders? Jesus knows."

"It sounds to me like this is just more of the same," said Joe. "Hear the words of Jesus, and do them."

"That's what it sounds like to me too," Matt agreed. "The last picture is the wise and foolish builder. One built his house on the rock, and the other built his house on the sand. When the storms came to each house, the one built on the rock stood. The one built on the sand collapsed. Jesus said hearing and putting his words into practice is building on the rock. Hearing his words and not putting them into practice is building on sand. Jesus' words don't do us any good if we don't act on them."

"It seems to me," Joe said, "Jesus was saying the same thing with all four pictures: Hear my words and do them."

"Just two things to wrap up," Matt began. "First, Jesus didn't tell us if we put his words into practice there will be no storms. Rather, he said if we put his words to use, then our lives will not be destroyed by the storms. We will stand.

"Second, and maybe the most important, what one thing would Jesus have you do right now to build your house on the rock?"

"I'm trying to put his words into practice," Joe replied. "I think I need to continue working out my relationship with my father, so I need to call my mother when I get home and ask some questions and face some things about my dad and about me. How about you Matt?"

"I need to see the job interview process through," Matt said, "so that I can get back to being salt and light in corporate America.

"Next week we'll start in chapter 10 of Matthew and take a look at the sending instructions Jesus gave to his disciples. Since we are about putting Jesus' words into practice, we need to start talking about what the mission project will be that Jesus will send us on.

"Let's pick a spiritual discipline to do and pray."

They chose frugality and agreed that on Wednesday neither of them would purchase anything, go in a store, shop on the internet, and they would avoid advertising as much as possible. They prayed for each other, finished their coffee, and walked out into the night. After the prayer, Joe was actually beginning to look forward to talking with his mom to learn more about his dad. He wondered what he would find, but he was confident that whatever it was, his house would stand firm.

Suggested resource:
Tom Sine, *Mustard Seed Versus McWorld*, Baker Books, 2002.

PHASE II

SENDING INTO MINISTRY

MATTHEW 10

CHAPTER 16

SENDING INSTRUCTIONS

"You look like you've been through the wringer," Matt said as Joe sat down with his coffee. "Here, take a chocolate chip cookie, and tell me all about it."

"It's not easy having your whole world turned upside down," Joe replied. "I called my mom and asked her about my dad. I thought talking with Sue was rough. That was a walk in the park compared to the conversation I had with my mom. I'm glad it was over the phone. I don't think I could have done it in person.

"I told her about the work we've been doing here with Jesus and how I said my dad was my enemy. Jesus said I'm supposed to love my enemy. I told her about the dreams I had about being abused by Dad and about abusing Dad. I told her the counselor said I need to get an adult story about the beatings I received so that I can get through this. Then I asked my mom to tell me about my dad."

"What did she say?" Matt asked. Joe took a bite of his chocolate chip cookie and a sip from his cup of steaming hot coffee before he answered.

"Mom told me I never knew Dad the way she did," Joe answered. "She told me when I was young, I never got the chance, and when I grew up, I wouldn't take the chance. She told me he was beaten by his dad. My grandfather would go out drinking and then come home and terrorize the whole family. My dad would take the brunt of the beatings. I don't remember my grandfather. He died when I was really young. I don't even remember any stories about him. Maybe they didn't tell any stories about him. I guess my kids don't have any stories about their grandpa either. I've never let them meet him.

"Mom told me Dad joined the army as soon as he got out of high school. He didn't have any money, and his grades weren't nearly as good as the ones I got. The army was his ticket out. After basic training, the army sent him to Korea. Mom said he didn't do well in Korea. In his letters to her, he wrote of being so scared he could barely function during the day and being so terrified at night he couldn't sleep. The food didn't agree with him, and he couldn't believe how cold it got. He didn't really get in any battles while he was there. Everyone stayed behind their lines, and he was never chosen to go on any raids, and he never volunteered either. He was a miserable soldier.

"Mom said he came home feeling like a failure and a coward. They were married shortly after he got back. She told me he was so proud when I was born. She said, 'He just beamed. When you were a couple of weeks old, he had me drive over to the mill at shift change. He brought all his buddies over to the car, took you out, and held you for all to see.' Mom told me she thought she was the best thing that ever happened to my dad, but that day she knew she had been replaced. Mom said he did the same thing with my brothers and sisters."

"I don't understand," Matt interrupted. "If you were the best thing that ever happened to him, then why all the beatings?"

"That was my question," Joe said. "Mom said he wanted me to be all the things he wasn't. He wanted me to be brave and strong, smart and athletic. Mom said it was like he was trying to relive his life through me. Mom said as I was growing up, his feelings about me bounced from pride to disappointment to fear and back again. He was proud of my grades and my athletic accomplishments. He would be disappointed when I failed. He would be afraid I would up end like him or afraid I wouldn't want anything to do with him. The beatings, mom said, came from the disappointment and fear. She said it was like he would go crazy. She told me she tried to stop the beatings, but he would knock her out of the way. The storm would pass, and then he would drink himself to sleep, crying, because he was so ashamed of having beaten his kid.

"Mom said he didn't know what to say to me to make it right, so he said nothing. She didn't know what to say to me either. Neither one of them had any idea how to get him to stop. She said my brothers and sisters endured some beatings too but not as much as I did.

"Then she told me, 'You don't know this, but he's still as proud of you today as the day you were born. Whenever we talk, he asks how you're doing. He's proud of what you've done in your career, and he's proud of your wife and kids. He makes me get him copies of any pictures I have of your family. He's still ashamed of how he acted when you were growing up. He figures you don't want to have anything to do with him, and he doesn't blame you. I don't think he wants anything to do with himself either. If you were to let him back into your life...' Mom choked up a little bit there, but I got the idea."

"So what are you going to do?" Matt asked. Joe drank some more coffee before responding.

"That's the same thing the counselor asked me," Joe said. "I don't know. I'm still in shock about the whole thing. All the fear and all the hate I've felt toward him all these years somehow just don't sit right anymore. I'm wondering if I've robbed him, robbed myself, and robbed my children of something, when all the time I was trying to protect us. I had no idea he was proud of me or thought I was the best thing that had ever happened to him. I thought he beat me because he was ashamed of me. To hear Mom, the beatings were about Dad and his inability to deal with what he was feeling and not about what I was doing or hadn't done. I'm having trouble coming to grips with all this. All the stuff, all the stories I've told myself about my dad may be off 180 degrees. On the night I talked with mom, I had those dreams again, where I'm the one doing the beating. It's all just overwhelming. The counselor said I need to live with all this for a couple of weeks before I do anything."

"Are you sure you want to do our regular study tonight?" Matt asked. "We could just sit here, drink coffee, and eat cookies."

"No," Joe said. "I want to do this tonight. Jesus got me into this, and I expect him to get me out of it. Oh, by the way, did you hear anymore about that job?"

"I see the Vice President next week," Matt said. "If you're sure, we'll jump into Jesus' words."

Joe nodded.

"We leave the Sermon on the Mount tonight," Matt began, "and move into the sending instructions Jesus gave his disciples in chapter 10 of Matthew. Chapters 5-7 are about the kingdom and the kingdom lifestyle. Jesus talks to us about heart and character before he talks with us about mission. If our heart and character aren't right, no matter how competently we do the tasks of mission, we'll mess it up. The effect will be what I experienced in college. I was following a car in traffic. I noticed a 'honk if you love Jesus' bumper sticker on the car. I thought, "I love Jesus," so I honked. The driver gave me the finger. If we don't get our anger, sexuality, yes and no, audience issues, love for the enemy, and all the rest under control, then our mission will self-destruct in a colorful barrage of our own dysfunction, and we'll do more harm than good. You'll notice Jesus spends much more time talking about heart and character than he does about mission. He's setting us up to succeed.

"Before we get to the sending instructions, let's look at what Jesus does in chapters 8 and 9. Can you walk me through those two chapters?"

"I think so," Joe responded. "Jesus went down the mountain and healed a guy who had leprosy. Then he went into Capernaum and healed the servant of a centurion. Jesus just gave the word, and the servant, who was across town, was healed without Jesus even being there. Then Jesus went to Peter's house and healed Peter's mother-in-law. That night, anyone in town who was sick showed up at Peter's house to be healed by Jesus. Then, Jesus gave some discouraging and troubling words to some people who wanted to follow him. After that, Jesus and his disciples got into a boat to go the other side of the lake. Jesus fell asleep, and a storm blew up that started to swamp the boat. The panicked disciples woke Jesus, and Jesus told the storm to stop. But before he did, he asked his disciples why they had such little faith. They landed on the wrong side of the lake and were met by two demon-possessed men who were shouting at Jesus. Jesus cast the demons into a herd of pigs, which ran into the lake and died. The townspeople asked Jesus to leave. And that was just chapter 8!

"Jesus did more of the same in chapter 9. He crossed back to the right side of the lake and forgave the sins of a paralytic, and then he healed the man. Everyone was amazed, but the teachers of the law were ticked because, according to the law, only God could forgive sins. Then Jesus increased the sense of scandal when he called Matthew, a tax collector, to follow him. Matthew threw a big party for Jesus, his disciples, and all his tax-collecting buddies. The Pharisees couldn't understand why Jesus accepted the invitation to have dinner with those people. The Pharisees continued to struggle with Jesus when they asked why his disciples weren't fasting. Then Jesus got back into the healing business as the woman with the issue of blood touched him, and Jesus also brought a little girl back to life. For an encore, he opened the eyes of two blind men and gave a voice to a man who couldn't speak. Matthew wrapped up chapter 9 by saying Jesus went all over, healing everyone, teaching and preaching about the kingdom, and the crowds grew and just kept coming.

"Jesus was a very busy man wasn't he? Can you imagine what it must have been like to have had Jesus travel through your town or village? All the sick people would have been healed, and through his preaching and teaching, everyone would have gotten an incredible idea of what life can be like. The joy and the hope experienced by those people in the presence of Jesus must have been incredible. If I had been one of those blind, crippled, or whatever people, and I got healed, there would have been dancing in the streets."

"I think you're right," Matt said. "One of the things you alluded to is Jesus often healed or dined with the wrong people. He healed the unclean, the outcast, the foreigner, and the insignificant, and he welcomed the outsiders. Is there any type of pattern that emerges from what Jesus has been doing? Are these just random incidents Matthew strung together, or was he trying to show us a pattern?"

"If I go back through the chapters," Joe answered, "I see that, although Matthew told us Jesus taught in the synagogue, none of the stories Matthew recorded happened in the synagogue. It all happened in someone's house, at the beach, or on the road. It looks like

Jesus used the healings to set up his preaching and teaching. He healed somebody, a crowd gathered, and then he taught."

"That's what it looks like to me too," Matt replied. "What did Jesus ask his disciples to do and why?"

"This is starting to come back to me," Joe said. "We talked about this before. This is where Jesus sent his disciples out to do exactly what he had been doing. Specifically, he said to go and proclaim the kingdom of heaven is near and heal the sick, raise the dead, cleanse the lepers, and drive out demons. As I remember saying before, it sounds impossible."

"Maybe," Matt replied, "but we'll see. Before we do, just what is that message, the kingdom is near?"

"As I remember," Joe said, "it's that God is not way out there somewhere. He loves us so much he has moved heaven. He has brought heaven and all its resources near to us. God has drawn near to help us because he loves us. Now is the time to call out to God for help because he loves us so much. The kingdom of heaven triumphs in the end, which means everything is going to be alright. The kingdom triumphs without our help, which means it doesn't depend on us, so I can rejoice. As the kingdom comes into my life, I can change and be changed because the kingdom brings with it incredible resources for life change. Speaking personally, I can say it's true, all true."

"Yes, you can," Matt replied. "You've experienced a lot of that kingdom message. How did Jesus equip his disciples for this task?"

"It doesn't look like he gave them much," Joe answered. "They were to give freely because they had freely received. They weren't to take any silver, gold, or copper, neither were they to take any luggage. They were just to go. I don't see that he equipped them at all."

"You missed something," Matt said. "He gave them authority to drive out evil spirits and to heal every disease and sickness. If they had the message that the kingdom is near, and if they had kingdom authority, then the healings and all the rest would follow. They wouldn't need gold, silver, or luggage because the people they helped would gladly take care of them.

"Jesus told them that as they entered a town, they were to look for a worthy person, or as some translations have it, 'a person of peace.' The kind of person Jesus was talking about is a person of influence. This is the kind of person who knows and is respected by lots of people. Stay with that person, said Jesus, and use their influence."

"As wonderful as the mission is—tell the people the kingdom is near, and heal everyone you can—there will be people who will object. How did Jesus say to handle them?"

"Jesus said," Joe answered, "'if anyone will not welcome you or listen to your words, shake the dust off your feet when you leave that home or town' (Matthew 10:14). Then he said something about judgment coming their way. I'm not quite sure what all that means."

"It's good news for us, the sent ones," Matt replied. "If someone doesn't welcome me or doesn't want to listen, I can move on. I don't have to convince them. I don't have to argue with them. I don't have to show them I'm right and they're wrong. I don't have to push pearls on them. I don't have to keep going over in my mind what I could have said or should have said or wonder what they really meant by something they said. If someone isn't receptive, then I get to move on. I'm just a messenger. Convincing them is God's problem. If they reject me, that too is God's problem. If there is something I need to change in my delivery of the message, God will make that plain to me. If someone is unreceptive, then I don't have to figure out all the dynamics involved. I deliver the message, and I do the mission. If people are receptive and involved, then I stay with it. If they aren't, then I move on. I find that very freeing.

"There will be receptive people, there will be unreceptive people, and there will be people who will cause trouble. Who were the people who caused trouble for Jesus?"

"It seems," Joe responded, "Jesus spent a lot of time talking about that. He said to be on your guard against men. He didn't say which men, but he did talk about being hauled in front of councils and synagogues, and floggings, and standing before governors and kings. He even said that when you're arrested, don't worry about what to say because it will be given to you (Matthew 10:19). None of that sounds very promising. I guess he was serious about that last

Beatitude, 'Blessed are those who are persecuted because of righteousness' (Matthew 5:10). Just who are the men who will cause the trouble?"

"The people who cause the trouble," Matt said, "will be people who have a vested interest in the status quo remaining as it is. Often, they have some type of power or position they feel is being threatened by the message of the kingdom. In the book of Acts, Paul regularly had trouble with the Jews of the local synagogue. Luke, the writer of the book of Acts, tells us the problem was jealously. The synagogue was quiet, and the Gentiles were largely uninterested. Then Paul would show up, and the synagogue would be stirred up with the message that the Messiah had come, and his name was Jesus. Paul insisted that the Messiah's kingdom extended to the Gentiles in town too. The Gentiles would want to know more, and the synagogue would be packed. The Jews would object, and the synagogue would be closed to Paul. Paul would rent a hall, it would fill with people, and the synagogue would be empty again. The Jews would then run him out of town. They felt threatened.

"At other times, Paul was run out by the local merchants. In Ephesus, so many people became Christians and stopped buying idols, stopped sacrificing to idols, stopped buying magic books and cards, stopped visiting fortune tellers and the like, that people involved in the idol trade began to go out of business. It was such big business in Ephesus that the merchants rioted.

"Sometimes the person who feels threatened is the family patriarch or matriarch. If the family scapegoat comes to Christ and begins to stand up, then everyone who has been avoiding responsibility for the failings of the family has to own up. That is not a pleasant picture. Those who have been on the favorable side of a dysfunctional relationship aren't about to let go without a fight. I went to college with lots of people who came to Christ at the school, went home with the wonderful news, only to have their families be furious with them. One Christian in the family can wreck everything. That one Christian makes me aware that I'm not right with God, and the changes in that one person's life mean there is no excuse for changes not happening in my life. Often, that Christian doesn't even have to say anything about the other people in the family, just his or her presence upsets everything. If the power structure, whether it's family, religious, economic, or civic, works with you, wonderful. If the power structure chooses to be threatened and works against you, then there will be all kinds of trouble. The good news is God can and does use the trouble to advance his kingdom.

"When the trouble comes, what did Jesus say to do?"

"It looks like he said the disciples were to do a couple of things," Joe answered. "When we're on trial or on the spot, we're not to worry about what we'll say because God will speak through us. We're to stand firm, and not deny Jesus, no matter who comes against us. When persecuted, we're to flee to another town. It sounds like there are lots of towns and some will be accepting and some won't. We are to expect the same treatment Jesus received. We're to fear God, who holds our eternal destiny in his hands, not men, who can kill the body and not the soul. That all sounds bleak."

"Yes, it does," Matt agreed. "No one can accuse Jesus of sugar coating or minimizing. He wants us to know that if we're in kingdom mission with him, then there are risks involved. He said the very nature of his mission turns people against one another. Even though the angels sang about peace on earth when he was born, his mission brings strife. The strife comes because not everyone will accept the message of the kingdom. Some of those who don't accept the message of the kingdom turn on the ones who do. Jesus made it very plain that we have to choose whose acceptance we want. Some of us have to choose between God's acceptance and the acceptance of a mom or dad, or brother or sister, or a child, or even a spouse. Those are hard choices, but Jesus said that is part of it, and we must choose. Jesus said if we can't choose him over these other relationships, then we're not worthy of him.

"I get the idea here that Jesus was serious about his mission, about us and our choices, and about our ability to carry out his mission. Jesus didn't seem to be interested in people who weren't all in with him. I think it comes back to our hearts. Jesus had been talking heart stuff in the Sermon on the Mount. Here he continued with it. If we aren't in it with all of our hearts, we aren't going to make it. Pressure will come, it will show our wavering hearts, and we'll bail.

But if we're in it with all of our hearts, when pressure comes, then we'll make it through.

"What did Jesus say is the end result of the mission?"

"He seemed to be saying," Joe replied, "there will be distress and strife for us and for others. He said those who go through with the mission receive acknowledgement by his Father in heaven. I suspect some people will hear and believe, and some people will be healed and helped.

"Do we find out what happened when these twelve went out?"

"We do," Matt answered. "Matthew didn't tell us, so we have to look at the other gospels. In Mark 6:12-13, we read: 'They went out and preached that people should repent. They drove out many demons and anointed many sick people with oil and healed them.' In Luke 9:6, we read: 'So they set out and went from village to village, preaching the gospel and healing people everywhere.'

"In Luke 10, we see that after Jesus sent the first twelve men out, and after they returned, he sent seventy-two others. The same instructions were given to them as were given to the first twelve. Let's read about them in verses 1 and 17:

> After this the Lord appointed seventy-two others and sent them two by two ahead of him to every town and place where he was about to go.
>
> The seventy-two returned with joy and said, "Lord, even the demons submit to us in your name."

"They went out and things happened as Jesus said they would. Now, I would expect this with the twelve—Peter, John, and the rest of them. They were the first string. But I'm very encouraged that the second group of seventy-two, people whose names we don't even know, had the same experience as the twelve. Luke tells us the seventy-two came back filled with joy, or in my words, they were pumped about what had happened.

"With the impossibility of the task, and the possibility of such dire consequences, why would any disciple accept the mission?"

"I can think of two or three reasons," Joe said. "The first is the honor of being asked by Jesus to be involved in such a way. Second, having tasted the kingdom, they wanted to pass it on. A third reason might be that they knew a particular group of people whom they really wanted to help."

"Those are all good reasons," Matt replied. "Now let's move from the pages of the gospel to the pages of our lives. I don't think Jesus gave these instructions just for that first group of disciples. I think they're for all of us who are disciples of Jesus. As we experience the kingdom, and our hearts and lives change, Jesus wants us to share the good news of what we've discovered. One of the ways we can do that is through participating in kingdom mission.

"So the question is this: How can we, today, answer that same mission to preach the message that the kingdom is near, heal the sick, raise the dead, cleanse those with leprosy, and drive out demons?"

"I remember being all freaked out about this the first time we talked about it in one of the early sessions," Joe said. "You said some things that helped me calm down, but I don't remember them. I just remember thinking that even though I can't do any of those things, except talk about the kingdom being near, maybe I could contribute. Can you refresh my memory?"

"You're going to make me do all the work?" Matt laughed. "What I think Jesus asked his disciples to do was to tell people the kingdom is near and then to act like it. The people most responsive to that message would be the most desperate. The most desperate people in Jesus' day were the sick, the relatives of the recently deceased, the lepers, and the demon possessed. These were probably also the people who thought God was the farthest away but wanted him near the most. If I tell a leper the kingdom is near, that all the resources of heaven have come near, and that God wants to heal him, I had better be ready to pray with him for healing. As those twelve, those seventy-two, and lots of people throughout history and even today have done that, God has shown up and acted in accordance with the message of Jesus—the kingdom is near.

"First, I think we need to be clear on the message—the kingdom is near. I think we are, and we'll continue to work on clarity.

"Second, I think we need to ask ourselves who around us is desperate. So who do you know, Joe, who is desperate?"

"Matt, you know very well we're living in suburbia, and no one in suburbia is desperate," Joe said with a wry grin. "Desperate people are poor and live in the inner city or in some far away country. Desperate people do not live in the 'burbs. That's what all of us living in the 'burbs want everyone else living in the 'burbs to believe. But the truth is, the 'burbs are full of desperate people. I know—I was one.

"Who are the desperate people I know? My buddy at work who just heard he has cancer; the neighbor down the street whose husband just left her; the guy two doors down who drinks too much; the woman across the street who lost her job. She and her husband are so far in debt their heads were barely above water on the dual income. She's afraid if she doesn't get hired soon, they might have to sell the house. Anyone who has teenagers, and any teenager who has parents, is desperate.

"If I've put this together correctly, Jesus would have us find some desperate people, tell them the kingdom is near, and help them access kingdom resources to deal with their desperation. Just how do I do that? Do I walk up to the woman across the street and say to her, 'The kingdom is near. Let's pray about your job and your finances'?"

"Let's remember what we learned a couple of weeks ago," Matt said, "about pearl pushing and the Golden Rule."

"Oh, all this stuff is supposed to work together?" Joe asked while Matt just shook his head. "Let's see about the Golden Rule. How would I like to have someone approach me? Maybe I should go over there and tell her I'm sorry she lost her job. I could ask if there is anything I could do to help. I could mention there are some resources I have found helpful when I'm having trouble, and if she would like to hear about them sometime, she could let me know. If she's desperate enough, she might ask me right there on the spot. If she isn't, she might ask me in a week or two when she's feeling more desperate. Then when she asks, I can talk with her about the kingdom and its resources, how it has helped me, and how she can connect to it if she wants."

"You know more than you like to admit, don't you?" Matt commented. "Maybe you could put out a bigger net by offering a class on money management and getting out of debt, based on kingdom principles, to everyone in the neighborhood. The key is to find desperate people for the best response. Do you suppose if we get involved in kingdom mission we'll encounter any unreceptive people?"

"I can't imagine not finding some unreceptive people," Joe responded. "If we do, we say, 'Thank you for your time,' and go on."

"That's right," Matt replied. "Do you suppose we'll encounter any opposition?"

"I suspect we might," Joe answered. "I can imagine some red tape getting in the way somewhere or maybe the family member of a person who is being helped being unhappy with us, but I can't imagine us getting thrown in jail."

"You never know, stranger things have happened," Matt said. "Do you suppose we'll experience the same kinds of results the first disciples did?"

"I have no idea, but it would be really neat if we were able to genuinely help someone find their way into the kingdom and see the kingdom work in their lives the way I see it working in mine."

"If that were to happen, what do you think we would gain from the experience?" Matt asked.

"That would be so cool," Joe responded. "I think it would be awesome to be used that way. The thought of being used by God—being in the right place at the right time and doing and saying the right thing—to accomplish God's purpose in someone's life is amazing. I'd be as pumped as those seventy-two were. I'd probably want to load up and go again."

"From my own experience," Matt added, "I can say ditto to that. But some other things happen as well. I learn how to work in partnership with God. My confidence in God is much higher, my faith is much deeper, and my spiritual growth and development are used more and more by God.

"So what do you want to do for a mission project?"

"I have no idea," Joe replied.

"Let's work on that some," Matt said. "Here are some questions for you to consider:

1. Who are the desperate people you see? Different people see different types of desperation.
2. Is there anything you're passionate about? If you could change one thing about this community what would it be?
3. Have you been used by God in the past? If so, what did you do, and would you like to do it again?
4. What are your spiritual gifts?
5. Is there someone you like who is doing something you would like to help them with?
6. Have you asked God what he would have you do? Is there anything you feel called to?"

"Those are good questions, and right now, I don't have an answer for them," Joe said, "but I bet I can come up with something before next week. What are you going to do?"

"I haven't thought much about it either," Matt replied. "I guess we both have some work to do. Let's turn now to our spiritual disciplines. How did you do with frugality?"

"I almost didn't make it," Joe said. "On my way to work, Wednesday, I pulled into the parking lot here for my usual cup of coffee for the road. As I got out of the car, I remembered we weren't going to purchase anything that day. Then I looked at my gas gauge and saw I was nearly out. As I pulled out of the parking lot, I calculated that if I made no extra stops and behaved myself, I would probably be all right until the next day. At work, Frank asked me to go to lunch. I said I couldn't, and he asked why. I told him about what we were doing, and he asked a bunch of questions. We had a good talk, and I got to share some of the kingdom stuff I've been learning. Frank wants me to let him know when I can do lunch because he'd like to hear more about the kingdom. In the afternoon, one of my kids called and asked me to pick up something on the way home from work. Normally, I just get whatever it is, but this time, I told her she would have to wait a day. She asked why, and I told her. She told me I was weird. I took it in stride because she's a teenager. I told Sue what I was doing, and she decided to try it too.

"Sue and I talked Wednesday night about it. Neither of us realized how much purchasing and consuming were a part of our lives.

It was a good day, but next time I'll need to do a little advance planning with my social calendar and gasoline purchases. How did it go for you?"

"My day was not nearly as eventful as yours," Matt answered. "But like you, I'm always amazed at how much purchasing and advertising is a part of our lives. It's such a big part, but we don't even think about it. Which spiritual discipline would you like to do next week?"

"Let's do secrecy," Joe said. "That's the one where we do things for people without them knowing it, right?"

"That's it," Matt replied. "Let's also continue praying the Lord's Prayer for the church."

After praying together, it was time to go. Joe left thinking about his dad and mission projects, and somewhere on the way home, they ran together. Joe wondered if there could be some connection between his dad and a mission project. He didn't know, but he did know he certainly was thankful some people had been in mission with him. Without their touch, he might not have made it.

CHAPTER 17

THE HOLY SPIRIT

It had been a grand and glorious day. The worship service that morning had been inspiring for Matt. Sunday dinner had been particularly good—Mary had outdone herself. Matt's team had even won the ball game he had dozed through that afternoon. As Matt walked into the coffee shop, he felt himself looking forward to the time he would spend with Joe that evening. Matt ordered his coffee, found their usual table, and sat down. He was glad to have a couple of minutes to just enjoy the moment. The hot coffee, other people at other tables in conversation, the sound of coffee cups clanking against each other, the art on the wall, the fireplace across the room, all seemed to embrace Matt in the moment to say *life is good*. Soon Joe joined Matt and brought with him two chocolate chip cookies, which made life even better.

"How did the interview go?" Joe asked.

"I think I'm almost employed," Matt said. "I had a great conversation with Vince, the Vice President. The division they're hiring me into has had trouble hitting their targets. It seems something always happens to mess things up. I suspect there is a large amount of dysfunction within that division and, to a degree, in the culture of the corporation, but they seem intent on ferreting out the dysfunction so that they can increase their market share and grow forward. We talked about compensation, and what they offered is very generous. That means I'll be able to increase my generosity. Mary was excited about that. All that stands between me and the job is a background check and reference check. I should hear next week about when I'll start."

"That's great," Joe replied. "I just hope they don't uncover that ax-murderer charge from a few years back."

"Very funny," Matt said. "Has Sue found an orphanage to support?"

"She did," Joe answered. "I connected her with one of the ladies from church who is into that kind of thing. They came over here one morning last week and had tea and scones or something. Sue found out the church helps support orphans in a village in Kenya. Sue learned a lot that day. She learned that Africans don't like orphanages because it takes the child away from the family and the land. She also learned that orphanages are too expensive to operate, so typically, an African village in Kenya has their own ways of caring for the children that keep them close to the land and pass on the traditions and heritage of their families. It's just with all the AIDS orphans, those systems have been overwhelmed. Jo, from church, told her about a missionary the church supports who raises money to help support the village systems that care for orphans. Sue sent him one hundred dollars. This week she got a letter back from the missionary with some pictures of the village and what her money is helping to accomplish in caring for the orphans. There was even a thank-you note from a little girl. The missionary also referred her to a web site that more fully explains what's going on, what he's doing, and how we, in America, can help. Sue is busy plotting where the next one hundred dollars is coming from.

"In addition, Joan asked Sue to be part of the team that is raising AIDS awareness in the church. Sue has never been involved in church before. She attends some of the services with me but grew up without church and mostly lives without it too. To my surprise, she accepted Joan's invitation. She's a little nervous about attending the first team meeting, but she's excited to be doing something about AIDS orphans in Africa."

"That's pretty amazing," Matt said. "I'm always surprised at the variety of ways God shows up in people's lives and how he touches them. He certainly is beginning to work in Sue's life. I wonder what will happen. So how about you? What's happening with your dad, the counselor, and you?"

"I'm still pretty messed up about the whole thing," Joe said. "I'm getting more comfortable with what my mom told me last week. I'm becoming convinced that getting in contact with my dad would be a good thing. At the moment, I don't how, when, what to say, or even what I want to happen. I still need to work through the past. The past still stands between my dad and me. The counselor gave me this past week off to process. I see him this week, and I guess we'll start on processing some of the past so that I can go forward some more."

"I think you have come a long way," Matt responded. "If I can do anything to help, please let me know."

"Trust me," Joe replied, "you are. Just letting me bounce some of this stuff off you each week is a big help. So what are we up to tonight?"

"We're going to spend tonight," Matt answered, "and the next few weeks, getting ready for the mission project we're going to do. After Jesus begins to get a kingdom heart and kingdom lifestyle into us, he sends us out in mission. Last week we looked specifically at the instructions of proclaiming the message that the kingdom is near, healing the sick, raising the dead, cleansing those who have leprosy, and driving out demons. If the kingdom is indeed near, then from what we know about the kingdom, those kinds of things will follow. I'm very comfortable when the expectation is that Peter and John will do these things, but I'm very uncomfortable if the expectation is that I am to do these things."

"I know the feeling," Joe said. "The first time we talked about this, I told you this is Joe we're dealing with and not Peter or John. As we have talked about what a mission like this might look like today, I'm still not comfortable I can pull it off."

"You're right—we can't," Matt replied. "On our own, we can't. We can't do God's business on our own resources. Tonight we're going to talk about God's resources for kingdom mission and how we access them so that ours becomes a mission possible.

"Let's start with Matthew 10:1. There we read: 'He called his twelve disciples to him and gave them authority to drive out evil spirits and to cure every kind of disease and sickness.' The twelve are John and Peter and all the rest. The first question is this: Is the call to kingdom mission and the authority to drive out evil spirits, heal disease and sickness just given to the twelve for that one mission, or just given to the twelve for their lives, or is there the expectation that everyone who is a disciple of Jesus gets called to kingdom mission and gets kingdom authority to pull off the mission?"

"That's a good question," Joe added. "I'd sure like to know the answer because right now I feel I have no power, no authority to accomplish any kingdom mission."

"My answer to that question," Matt answered, "is that the call to kingdom mission and the authority to accomplish kingdom mission is given to anyone who is a follower of Jesus. We saw last week, in Luke 10, that Jesus sent seventy-two other nameless, faceless disciples, about whom we know nothing, with the same kingdom mission and the same kingdom authority as the twelve.

"In John 14:12 Jesus said, 'I tell the you the truth, anyone who has faith in me will do what I have been doing. He will do even greater things than these, because I am going to the Father.' Jesus' words, 'I tell the truth,' were used when he wanted his disciples to sit up and pay attention. Jesus didn't want us to miss what he was about to say. Next Jesus said, 'anyone who has faith in me.' I don't see any limitations around anyone who has faith in Jesus. Jesus didn't say, 'anyone of you twelve who has faith in me' or 'anyone who lived in the same time period as Jesus lived.' Jesus just said, 'anyone who has faith in me.' If I have faith in Jesus, that 'anyone' is me. If you have faith in Jesus, that 'anyone' is you."

"I was afraid of that," Joe said.

"If you're afraid of that," Matt replied, "it gets worse. In Matthew 28:18-20, Jesus gave the Great Commission, which reads:

> Then Jesus came to them and said, "All authority in heaven and on earth has been given to me. Therefore go and make disciples of all nations, baptizing them in the name of the Father and of the Son and of the Holy Spirit, and teaching them to obey everything I have commanded you. And surely I will be with you always, to the very end of the age."

"There Jesus said to the twelve to make disciples of all nations, and among other things, to teach these new disciples to obey everything Jesus commanded the first twelve. The sending instructions in Matthew 10 are certainly part of what Jesus commanded the first twelve to do. It looks here like Jesus has every intention that the first twelve pass these instructions on to all the rest of the people who would become disciples of Jesus across the globe and down through the ages.

"The next thing we need to look at is this: Did the disciples pass on these instructions, and did those who followed Jesus, because of their efforts, engage in kingdom mission with kingdom authority? Since we have these instructions today in the gospels of Matthew, Mark, Luke, and John, and in the book of Acts, we know that they have been passed on. As we read the book of Acts, we find people in addition to the first twelve involved in kingdom mission using kingdom authority. Philip and Paul are two who stand out. Down through the centuries and around the globe, there is documented history of people being engaged in kingdom mission using kingdom authority. You can take my word for it or you can dig through the history of the church in mission yourself.

"Today, we continue to see disciples of Jesus involved in kingdom mission using kingdom authority. There are still people who proclaim the message that the kingdom is near. Our church does that. People still pray, and the sick are healed. Sometimes we see that in dramatic fashion and other times it happens more slowly. The dead are still raised. Every now and then a story comes back from Africa about somebody being raised from the dead. It happens here too, only we often don't recognize it. How many people have stories of having died, and they're gone for a few minutes, and then come back? Doctors can't explain it. How many of those people had someone praying for them that they would live? We don't know. We put our sick people in hospitals and monitor what the doctors do, but we don't pay attention to what the prayers do. Once again, it doesn't seem very dramatic, but yet it happens. Demons are still cast out, even if a lot of us wouldn't recognize a demon if it were right in front of us. I don't have any experience with that sort of thing, but there are people I know and trust who do. Lepers are still cleansed.

"All of that is just the beginning. People are freed from addictions, marriages are restored, finances are put in order, jobs are found, forgiveness is offered and guilt removed, dysfunctional relationships are mended, abuse is stopped, and the list goes on.

"So can we agree that people today are involved in kingdom mission using kingdom authority?"

"Yes," Joe answered, "we can agree on that. But how do we move from people today to you and me? Where does this kingdom authority and kingdom power come from? How do I get it into my life so that I can use it to do kingdom mission?"

"You're good," Matt said. "That's exactly where I was going next. The answer to your question is the Holy Spirit."

"The Holy what?" Joe asked. "I'm still new to all this. Just what is it you're talking about?"

"The Holy Spirit," Matt continued, "is not an it. The Holy Spirit is the third person of the trinity. The New Testament writers use a *he* pronoun when they refer to the Holy Spirit. I see it in your eyes—you're going to ask, 'What's the trinity?' I thought so. In Matthew 28:19, Jesus said we are to baptize 'in the name in the Father and of the Son and of the Holy Spirit.' Father, Son, and Holy Spirit are the trinity. The concept which is difficult is that God is three—Father, Son, and Holy Spirit. Yet, at the same time, God is one. The Father is God; the Son, Jesus, is God; the Holy Spirit is God. All that makes God to be God is in the Father and the Son and the Holy Spirit. Don't ask me to explain it anymore because I'll get lost. All I know is God is three and one at the same time. God is far more complicated and complex than we are, and if I could explain everything about God, then God wouldn't be God."

"I won't ask you for anymore explanations of the trinity," Joe replied, "but can you tell me more about the Holy Spirit?"

"That," Matt responded, "I can do." Let's look at some of the New Testament passages about the Holy Spirit. Let's go to Acts 2:38-39. It reads:

> Peter replied, "Repent and be baptized, every one of you, in the name of Jesus Christ so that your sins may be forgiven. And you will receive the gift of the Holy Spirit. The

promise is for you and your children and for all who are far off—for all whom the Lord our God will call."

"Peter said this at the end of his very first sermon on the day of Pentecost. The response to the message of Jesus' death and resurrection is to change directions, receive forgiveness in the name of Jesus, be baptized, and receive the Holy Spirit. The Holy Spirit is the birthday gift everyone receives on the day they come to Christ. The Holy Spirit is God come to dwell in our hearts to make the change we want possible. The Holy Spirit is the one who gives us the kingdom hearts. The Holy Spirit's presence is who we feel when we feel God moving in us. Everyone who has come to Jesus has received the Holy Spirit."

"So when we prayed that day," Joe said, "and I asked Jesus to come into my life, and I felt the love, acceptance, forgiveness, joy, and peace all rolled up together, what I was feeling was the Holy Spirit?"

"Yes, you felt the presence and work of the Holy Spirit that day," Matt replied.

"If that was the Holy Spirit, then I have felt him, heard from him, and responded to him a lot these past few weeks," Joe said.

"That's right," Matt said. "Let me talk some about what the Holy Spirit does. In Acts 1:8 Jesus said, 'But you will receive power when the Holy Spirit comes on you; and you will be my witnesses in Jerusalem, and in all Judea and Samaria, and to the ends of the earth.'

"The Holy Spirit is the kingdom authority to carry out kingdom mission. The Holy Spirit is the power that accomplishes the kingdom mission. The Holy Spirit is God within us working through us to do the kingdom mission. The Holy Spirit is the power to bear witness to Jesus. Jesus said, 'the kingdom is near.' The Holy Spirit provides the power to do the kingdom thing at the kingdom time in the kingdom way. The Holy Spirit provides the kingdom words at the kingdom time so that we can speak for Jesus in the kingdom way.

"In case you're wondering, the word Jesus used for *power* in this verse is the Greek word that our word *dynamite* comes from. So we're talking about POWER, in all caps. All the POWER of

God, who created the cosmos with his words, parted the Red Sea, brought sight to the blind, cleansed the lepers, set the captives free, and brought Jesus back from the dead is the Holy Spirit POWER Jesus was talking about."

"If we're talking about all that POWER, how come I feel so powerless?" Joe asked.

"Hang on to that question, and we'll come back to it," Matt responded. "Let's continue talking about what the Holy Spirit does. In John 14:15-18, 25-27, Jesus said this about the Holy Spirit:

> "If you love me, you will obey what I command. And I will ask the Father, and he will give you another Counselor to be with you forever—the Spirit of truth. The world cannot accept him, because it neither sees him nor knows him. But you know him, for he lives with you and will be in you. I will not leave you as orphans; I will come to you.
>
> "All this I have spoken while still with you. But the Counselor, the Holy Spirit, whom the Father will send in my name, will teach you all things and will remind you of everything I have said to you. Peace I leave with you; my peace I give you. I do not give to you as the world gives. Do not let your hearts be troubled and do not be afraid.

"In this passage, Jesus called the Holy Spirit 'another counselor.' The Greek word for counselor used here is *paraclete*, and translated, it means *one called alongside to help*. It's a term from the Greek courts. When someone went to court, he was assigned a paraclete. It was the paraclete's job to walk the person through the legal system of the court. The paraclete made sure the person was in the right place at the right time. The paraclete made sure the person understood how the court functioned. The paraclete would make sure the court fully understood the case from the side of the one to whom he was assigned. The paraclete would make sure the person fully understood the decision of the court. The paraclete was called alongside to help someone through the court.

"Jesus said the Holy Spirit is called alongside of us to help us. Help us with what? Jesus referred to the Holy Spirit as *another* paraclete. In the word *another*, Jesus was referring to himself. The Holy Spirit is called alongside us to help us in the same way Jesus has been doing. The Holy Spirit is alongside us to love us, forgive us, save us, redeem us, heal us, help us, teach us, send us, equip us, to state our case in heaven, and to make sure we understand what God is telling us from heaven's throne. Further, by using the word *another*, Jesus wanted to make sure we understand there is no quality drop off from his being alongside us to the Holy Spirit being alongside us.

"When Jesus left the earth, he did not strand his current disciples nor all the ones who would follow in his footsteps. He sent the Holy Spirit to continue doing all he had been doing in the lives of his disciples. He sent the Holy Spirit to be with us forever. The Holy Spirit will not leave nor abandon us.

"Jesus further illustrated the task of the Holy Spirit in this passage by telling us one of his jobs is to teach us and remind us of all Jesus said. Specifically, Jesus said, 'But the counselor, the Holy Spirit, whom the Father will send in my name, will teach you all things and will remind you of everything I have said to you.' The Holy Spirit was the one who made it possible for Matthew, Mark, Luke, and John to record what Jesus said and did. The Holy Spirit is the one, today, who continues to teach us all we need to know and continues to bring to mind what Jesus said and did so that we can be his disciples.

"In John 16:5-16, Jesus told us more about the Holy Spirit's job. Let's read it:

> "Now I am going to him who sent me, yet none of you asks me, 'Where are you going?' Because I have said these things, you are filled with grief. But I tell you the truth: It is for your good that I am going away. Unless I go away, the Counselor will not come to you; but if I go, I will send him to you. When he comes, he will convict the world of guilt in regard to sin and righteousness and judgment: in regard to sin, because men do not believe in me; in regard to righteousness, because I am going to the Father, where you can

see me no longer; and in regard to judgment, because the prince of this world now stands condemned.

"I have much more to say to you, more than you can now bear. But when he, the Spirit of truth, comes, he will guide you into all truth. He will not speak on his own; he will speak only what he hears, and he will tell you what is yet to come. He will bring glory to me by taking from what is mine and making it known to you. All that belongs to the Father is mine. That is why I said the Spirit will take from what is mine and make it known to you.

"In a little while you will see me no more, and then after a little while you will see me."

"Here, Jesus said the Holy Spirit's presence with us and among us is a better deal for us than Jesus himself staying with us in person. I have to admit there are lots of times I would like to sit down with Jesus face to face, ask him some questions or get some advice and guidance, and get his answers back to me in good old English through my ears. So there are times I wonder if we do have a better deal.

"But then I come back to reality. The U.S. Center for World Mission says 33 percent of the world's population, which is a number just north of two billion people, are Christians. Christianity is far and away the largest religion in the world. So if there are two billion other people in the world who want to sit down and talk with Jesus face to face, I would have to take a number. The number might be so high I might not live long enough to make my appointment. If, in my talk with Jesus, I ask him to do something, it wouldn't get done because of the other two billion who are waiting to see him. Further, if Jesus were physically sitting right here with us tonight, and when we left you invited him home with you, and I invited him home with me, one or both of us goes home alone."

"I see what you mean," Joe replied. "The sheer logistics of Jesus physically meeting with two billion people is impossible. So I guess we do have a better deal. You're saying, because of the Holy Spirit, I have direct access whenever I want and as often I want. I've never gotten a busy signal when I've prayed. You're also saying I can feel the presence of the Holy Spirit at my house while you, at the same time, are feeling the presence of the Holy Spirit at your house. If all two billion call out at once, everyone gets connected all at the same time. That's mind boggling. Even more mind boggling than that is I get personal attention that is tailored to me. I have no idea how the Holy Spirit keeps the records of two billion plus accounts straight."

"In addition to those two billion plus," Matt said, "the Holy Spirit is in the lives of all people everywhere on the face of the planet drawing and wooing them to Jesus. I need to move on to the next thing, or my circuits are going to fry from trying to get my mind around all this.

"Another task the Holy Spirit has is to give us the correct information on sin, righteousness, and judgment. The Holy Spirit is the one who shows us the truth that sin kills, who lets us know what sin is, and who makes it possible for us to feel the guilt so that we have the opportunity to turn from the sin before it's too late. Where in our culture of materialism do we find the message that happiness is not another possession away, our worth does not equal our bank account, and appearance does not equal status? The Holy Spirit is the one who helps us see the emptiness of that life. The Holy Spirit is the one who shows us what the good life, righteousness, is. The love, joy, peace, patience, kindness, goodness, gentleness, faithfulness and self-control of the Holy Spirit are the characteristics of the good life as we build a quality soul, not obtain quality stuff. The Holy Spirit is the one who sets us straight on judgment. Judgment is not about good and bad stuff we have done. Judgment is about relationships. Did we develop a relationship with God through faith in Jesus? Did we love God with all of our heart, soul, mind, and strength? Did we love our neighbors as ourselves? The task of the Holy Spirit is to guide us into truth about all this and the rest of life for that matter.

"The final task of the Holy Spirit, as Jesus explained in this passage, is to tell us what he hears from Jesus. He speaks the words of Jesus directly into our hearts. He also takes from the resources of Jesus, which are all the resources of the kingdom, and brings them to us. So the Holy Spirit, who has direct access to us, has direct access to Jesus and makes sure all Jesus wants us to know and all Jesus wants us to have is available to us."

"Sounds like the Holy Spirit is busy," Joe said.

"Sure does," Matt replied. "Let's turn to Romans 8:1-8, 12-17 where Paul talks about his experience of the work of the Holy Spirit. Let's read it:

> Therefore, there is now no condemnation for those who are in Christ Jesus, because through Christ Jesus the law of the Spirit of life set me free from the law of sin and death. For what the law was powerless to do in that it was weakened by the sinful nature, God did by sending his own Son in the likeness of sinful man to be a sin offering. And so he condemned sin in sinful man, in order that the righteous requirements of the law might be fully met in us, who do not live according to the sinful nature but according to the Spirit.
>
> Those who live according to the sinful nature have their minds set on what that nature desires; but those who live in accordance with the Spirit have their minds set on what the Spirit desires. The mind of sinful man is death, but the mind controlled by the Spirit is life and peace, because the sinful mind is hostile to God. It does not submit to God's law, nor can it do so. Those controlled by the sinful nature cannot please God.
>
> Therefore, brothers, we have an obligation—but it is not to the sinful nature, to live according to it. For if you live according to the sinful nature, you will die; but if by the Spirit you put to death the misdeeds of the body, you will live, because those who are led by the Spirit of God are sons of God. For you did not receive a spirit that makes you a slave again to fear, but you received the Spirit of sonship. And by him we cry, "Abba, Father." The Spirit himself testifies with our spirit that we are God's children. Now if we are children, then we are heirs—heirs of God and co-heirs with Christ, if indeed we share in his sufferings in order that we may also share in his glory.

"This is one of the great passages of the Bible. Here we see the Holy Spirit sets us free from the law of sin and death. What is the law of sin and death? Simply stated, if I sin, then I die. The Holy Spirit sets me free by offering forgiveness for sin by paying the death penalty for me through Jesus' death and resurrection. And, and this a big *AND*, the Holy Spirit sets me free by changing my heart so that I'm able to not sin. As we follow the leading of the Holy Spirit, who gives us a new heart, we're able to live a life of love that exceeds the law. As we follow the lead of the Holy Spirit, we discover life—the kingdom life—and peace.

"Paul went on to tell us that to be led by the Holy Spirit is to be a son of God. If we are not led by the Holy Spirit, we are not God's sons. If we have questions about that, we can ask. The Holy Spirit testifies to our spirits that we are God's children. How does that work? I can't explain it except to say that I know. Oral Roberts explained it this way: How do I know? 'I just know that I know. I know that I know that I know.'[i] The Holy Spirit has put that knowing in me and puts that knowing into all who are led by him. The Holy Spirit, along with testifying to our Spirits that we are God's children, gives us the ability to call God *Father*. But it's more than that. The Holy Spirit has called God not just Father, but *Daddy*. The Holy Spirit creates the intimate relationship of a small, dearly loved child with his or her proud, loving, smiling dad for us with God. The Holy Spirit draws us close to God and makes possible our trust of God and our love of God as we respond to the love of God for us that has always been there.

"A few verses later, beginning in verse 26, Paul told us the Holy Spirit helps us in our weakness. We often don't know how to pray. The Holy Spirit helps us pray. The Holy Spirit searches our hearts and brings forth the issues and the emotions that are troubling us so that we can see them clearly and pray about them. Further, the Holy Spirit prays for us himself in ways we cannot. The Holy Spirit, in the role of paraclete, takes the deep issues of our hearts straight to the Father himself, pleads our cause with the Father, and brings to us the help we need.

"Let's look at one last passage. This one addresses your question from earlier, which was: If the Holy Spirit is all this and does all this, why do I feel so powerless, and why am I not able to do all those incredible things Jesus talked about?"

"Good, I was wondering when you were going to get that," Joe replied. "With all you've laid out so far, this Holy Spirit stuff sounds like an incredible deal. If all this is true, and if it all works this way, then there is really nothing that can stop us from living a kingdom life and doing kingdom mission. So how does it work? How do I get more of this in my life?"

"Paul told us how," Matt said. In Ephesians 5:18, we read: 'Do not get drunk on wine, which leads to debauchery. Instead be filled with the Spirit.' As we saw earlier, all of us receive the Holy Spirit when we come to Jesus. The question is what we will do with the Holy Spirit.

"Will we follow his leading and prompting, or will we ignore his leading and prompting? The more we follow his leading and prompting, the more leading and prompting we receive, and the more the Holy Spirit moves and works in and through us. The less we follow the Holy Spirit's leading and prompting, the less leading and prompting we will receive, and the less the Holy Spirit moves and works in and through us.

"Will we say of the Holy Spirit, 'This is good stuff. I want more. Please fill me'? Will we do what it takes to get more of the Holy Spirit into our lives and increase our capacity to have more of the Holy Spirit in our lives? There are at least four things I can think of that will get more of the Holy Spirit into our lives and increase our capacity for the Holy Spirit. They are:

1. Ask God to fill you with the Holy Spirit. This goes back to the first Beatitude: 'I can't make this happen, but God, you can. Please fill me with the Holy Spirit.'
2. Work the spiritual disciplines. These are the things that create space in our lives for the Holy Spirit. They increase our capacity for the Holy Spirit so that when God pours the Holy Spirit into us, there is a place for the Holy Spirit to be. It would be terrible to have God pour a fifty-gallon barrel of Holy Spirit on us, and we only had place for a tablespoon, and all the rest of the Holy Spirit ran off.
3. If there are things we are doing that we know we are not to be doing, we need to stop doing them. We need to ask for

help to stop. Living contrary to the kingdom, when we know better, prevents, blocks, and hinders our ability to respond to and receive from the Holy Spirit. If we are in the process of dealing with lifestyle issues that are contrary to the kingdom, we are participating with the Holy Spirit. But if we haven't started, we are resisting the Holy Spirit.
4. If there is something we know the Holy Spirit wants us to do that we haven't done, then we need to begin to do it. As in number 3, we are either participating or resisting the Holy Spirit.

"Let me say a word about how I have experienced the work of the Holy Spirit. The way I *want* the Holy Spirit to work is like this: I feel his presence and power, and then I pray for someone to be healed of cancer. But then, I seldom experience that.

"What I typically experience is that I find myself in a conversation with someone. That person mentions he just found out he has cancer. I feel for him and ask him questions about what kind of cancer he has, how bad it is, and what kind of treatment he's going through. He begins to answer. Then I get a Holy Spirit nudge: 'Ask if you can pray for him.' I think about what to pray. Then the kingdom stuff comes to mind. Jesus sent his disciples out to heal all kinds of sickness and disease. Cancer certainly falls into that category. But I can't heal cancer. I'm not sure I have enough in me that if I were to pray, God would heal the cancer. But the Holy Spirit has nudged me to pray for him. So I take the risk. When we get done talking about his cancer, I take the risk and ask if I can pray for him. I never get turned down. So I pray and ask God to heal his cancer. Sometimes I feel something, and I'm sure God has begun to heal him. Other times I feel nothing, and I'm sure my prayer was worthless.

"I have learned my feelings are a poor indicator of God's action. There have been times when I felt like my prayer accomplished nothing, but then people thanked me profusely for the prayer and told me how much it meant to them and how much help they received. Likewise, there have been times when I prayed and felt like God was really working, but I saw no evidence or got no feedback.

"I can't say I have prayed for anybody with cancer, and then they told me the next day they were cancer free—they received a miracle. But I can say a lot of the people I have prayed for have recovered from the cancer. They have survived the surgery, the chemo, and the rest and have come out clean. Has my prayer affected the outcome? Who's to say it hasn't? If I hadn't prayed, they could have died the next day. We don't know. But there are other times I have prayed with people about different kinds of things, and it has been easy to draw a straight line from the prayer to the positive outcome of the situation.

"There are situations I get into simply because people know I'm a Christian. Someone asks me for help, and I know that, as Jesus' follower, this is something I'm to help with. I help with it not because I feel competent or feel led but because I know it's something Jesus said to do. I do my best, and pray my best, and usually pray under my breath, 'God, I hope you show up and do something because if you don't, I will fall on my face, and your kingdom will be put back a hundred years because of my inadequacies.'

"I have learned that when I'm prompted, or when an opportunity presents itself, I need to act in a kingdom way whether I feel the power to do so or not. God is often doing things I don't know about in the situation, and he has involved me because what I have to offer in the situation is what the person needs at that moment. So I do my best to be myself, to do the kingdom thing as best I understand, and to trust God to take care of the rest, even if I never know what was going on or what happened as a result of my kingdom action.

"As I'm sure you have learned following Jesus, going with the leadings of the Holy Spirit usually puts us in a situation where we have to risk. If we take the risk, kingdom stuff happens. Holy Spirit stuff happens. We get to be a part of it.

"Next week, we'll talk some more about Holy Spirit stuff as we look at the fruits of the Spirit, the gifts of the Spirit, and how all that works. To wrap up tonight, let's talk about mission projects and pray for each other to be filled with the Holy Spirit."

And they did. Matt talked about a mission project he wanted to do with a guy named Mark, from church, to provide support for people looking for a job. Joe thought he might coach a basketball team in the church's youth league. The league was set up for two to four of the ten players on the team to be church kids and the rest to be kids they invited to be on the team who weren't church kids. Then, they prayed for each other to be filled with the Holy Spirit.

As Joe left, he wondered what risk he would be asked to take next. He wondered if he would see any kingdom work, any kingdom good, accomplished in his mission project. As Joe drove out of the parking lot, it occurred to him again that life with Jesus was about being asked to take one risk after another. But so far as Joe could see, Jesus was in each risk and was doing some incredible things in Joe's life. Joe thought, if Jesus keeps showing up, I can keep risking. He thought he wouldn't have to wait long for the next risk.

CHAPTER 18

HOLY SPIRIT: GIFTS & FRUIT

It was cold outside. It was the kind of cold that made the car run poorly. Joe's car never did warm up on the way to the coffee shop. As Joe shivered across the parking lot, he hoped they could get a seat near the fire. Just inside the door, Joe found Matt, who was stomping the snow off the bottom of his shoes and the cold out of his feet.

"It makes you glad we live in this part of the country, doesn't it?" Joe commented as he knocked the snow off his shoes.

"Sure does," Matt said. "It lets me know I'm alive. Put your money away. I'm buying tonight."

"Did you win the lottery?" Joe asked.

"No," Matt replied. "Starting Wednesday, I'm a working man again."

"Congratulations," Joe said. "It has been a while coming. When did you find out?"

"On Thursday, they called me to come in to meet Kelly, the Division Head," Matt answered. "He's in the food chain between Vince, the Vice President who interviewed me, and me. Vince thought it would be a good idea if Kelly and I talked before he officially hired me. I thought that was a good idea too and wondered why Kelly was not included in the interview process. There may be a little more dysfunction going on there than I thought. Anyway, Kelly and I hit it off. They never did find the ax-murderer charge in the background checks, so I start Wednesday."

Coffee with Matt & Joe

By the time Matt had finished telling his story, he had bought and paid for two coffees and two chocolate chip cookies. Both men sat a moment warming their hands on the coffee mugs, letting the steam from the hot coffee warm their faces.

"How did your week go?" Matt asked.

"I wanted to kill my boss," Joe said. "He called my cell phone during dinner on Wednesday. I went to answer it, but Sue wouldn't let me. She said, 'Whatever it is, it can wait until after dinner.' I started to remember what we had been saying about yes and no and how I tend to say yes to the wrong things. So I called him back after dinner. There's a project we've been working on that's due in a couple of days. We went through a check list early that morning to make sure we had everything covered. It turns out we didn't. He had missed something and wanted me to come in and work on it that evening to make sure we were going to hit our deadline.

"I have always jumped when he called, but that night I didn't. I thought about deadlines. I looked at the kids, and I had promised them I would do some things that night. I thought about how many more work deadlines there would be in my life and how short the time was that I would still have the kids around home. The yes and no of Jesus was still ringing in my ears. So I said, 'No.' My boss was furious, but I held my ground. I told him I would come in early the next morning. I did and discovered that Gary had taken care of that item two days before. My boss was just nervous about the project and wanted me to come hold his hand the rest of the night. I didn't get fired, my boss didn't say anything to me about it the next morning, and I had a great night with my kids."

"Good for you," Matt said. "How did you do with the counselor?"

"It was hard," Joe replied. "I think this whole process is the hardest thing I have ever done. I can't explain it very well. The counselor talked about a father whose son was the best thing that ever happened to him. He talked about a son who wanted more than anything else to be loved by his dad. He talked about the paradox of this dad beating his son and this son hating his dad. I had all these feelings of anger, hate, love, and pity all going on at the same time. I was a basket case. I cried a lot as we talked about it. I hate to cry. At the end, the counselor began to pray for healing for the dad who was beating his pride and joy and healing for the son who was hating the dad he wanted to love and be loved by. He told me my healing would start with mercy and forgiveness, and we would talk about that next week. He was very hopeful. I just hope he knows more than I do because I don't see any way through this. I guess I just have to wait and see."

"I guess so," Matt agreed. "I'll wait with you. While we're waiting, let's talk about some more Holy Spirit stuff. Let's start off talking about the gifts of the Holy Spirit."

"The Holy Spirit is gifted or has gifts or gives gifts?" Joe asked. "Which one do you mean?"

"All three," Matt replied. "The Holy Spirit has all the resources needed to do kingdom mission. The Holy Spirit delights in giving gifts to us so that we can do kingdom mission. In 1 Corinthians 12, Paul talked about them. He started the chapter by telling us he didn't want us to be ignorant about spiritual gifts. Then in verse 7, he gave us a definition of spiritual gifts. Would you read that?"

Joe read Paul's words, "'Now to each one the manifestation of the Spirit is given for the common good.'

"Can you tell me what that means in English?"

"I'll try," Matt answered. "Let's take it apart a little at a time. Paul is writing to the church in Corinth, a city in Greece. So who is the 'each one' to whom Paul is talking?"

"I assume," Joe replied, "they are the people who are part of the church in Corinth."

"Yes," Matt continued, "they are people in Corinth, who are disciples of Jesus. They have invited him into their hearts, are learning his teaching, and are trying to do what his words say.

"Each of these people has been give a manifestation of the Holy Spirit. You're thinking, 'Just what is a manifestation of the Spirit?' A manifestation of the Holy Spirit is the Holy Spirit making himself visible. In this verse, Paul said the Holy Spirit makes himself visible through each person who is a disciple of Jesus.

"When the Holy Spirit makes himself visible, what does that look like? The Holy Spirit makes himself visible by doing certain things through a disciple of Jesus, and that's referred to as gifts of the Holy Spirit. In 1 Corinthians 12, Paul listed some of the gifts:

Wisdom, knowledge, faith, healing, miraculous powers, prophecy, discernment, tongues, and interpretation. We'll look at a more complete list in a couple of minutes.

"I remember teaching an adult Sunday school class a few years back. A visitor from out of town came to the class that day. He came up and talked with me after the class. He told me he was having a problem in his spiritual life and wanted my help. I told him I would help him if I could. I was wondering why he wasn't talking to Rev. Jim. After telling me his story, he asked me if I could tell him his problem. As soon as he finished speaking, the word *pride* jumped into my mind. I didn't know this man, and I had no reason for thinking that, but there it was in my head. So as gently and graciously as I could, I asked him if pride was his problem. He said that was it, exactly. He just needed to hear it from someone else. That insight was a Holy Spirit manifestation called the gift of knowledge. The Holy Spirit gave me that insight. I didn't do that on my own. It was exactly the piece of information the man needed at that time to go forward in his life with Jesus."

"That's kind of weird and cool at the same time," Joe said. "So a gift of the Holy Spirit is the Holy Spirit doing something through a disciple of Jesus which that person couldn't do on his own. You're telling me there are specific things the Holy Spirit does. I think I'm with you, but I'm going to need a lot more detail to get on board with this. If this is something the Holy Spirit does with all followers of Jesus, what does he do through me? I think I have an idea of what he does through you."

"You're on track," Matt replied. "I'll try to get your questions as we go along, but let's finish Paul's thought here. The manifestation of the Holy Spirit is given to each one for the common good. The Holy Spirit is not interested in egos here. The Holy Spirit is interested in using each of us to contribute to the common good. In Jesus, through the Holy Spirit, we all have something to offer for the common good. That means all of us are needed, and all of us have something to contribute.

"Let's look a little closer at what these Holy Spirit gifts are for. In this verse, we learned they are for the common good. Paul talked again about Holy Spirit gifts in Ephesians 4:11-16:

> It was he who gave some to be apostles, some to be prophets, some to be evangelists, and some to be pastors and teachers, to prepare God's people for works of service, so that the body of Christ may be built up until we all reach unity in the faith and in the knowledge of the Son of God and become mature, attaining to the whole measure of the fullness of Christ.
>
> Then we will no longer be infants, tossed back and forth by the waves, and blown here and there by every wind of teaching and by the cunning and craftiness of men in their deceitful scheming. Instead, speaking the truth in love, we will in all things grow up into him who is the Head, that is, Christ. From him the whole body, joined and held together by every supporting ligament, grows and builds itself up in love, as each part does its work.

"What is the purpose of the gifts in this passage?"

"If by gifts," Joe answered, "you mean apostles, prophets, evangelists, pastors, and teachers, then the purpose is to build the body of Christ. It looks like some gifts are given to help us grow, or grow a group of us, so that we can know Jesus and be able to do what he wants us to do as we love and care for each other."

"You're good," Matt said. "In 1 Peter 4:10, Peter said, 'Each one should use whatever gift he has received to serve others, faithfully administering God's grace in its various forms.'

"In this verse, we see the purpose of the gifts is to administer God's grace in its various forms. Grace is God's help given freely by God because he loves us. The gifts of the Holy Spirit are the Holy Spirit's way of making sure God's help, in all the ways that God helps, gets to the people who need the help when they need the help. The gifts are the ways the Holy Spirit gives to each of us to help and to serve each other.

"In Acts 1:8, we read, 'But you will receive power when the Holy Spirit comes on you; and you will be my witnesses in Jerusalem, and in all Judea and Samaria, and to the ends of the earth.'

"The gifts are one of the ways in which we receive the power of the Holy Spirit to be witnesses to Jesus throughout the earth.

"The final passage I want us to look at here is from Matthew 10:1, 5-8:

> He called his twelve disciples to him and gave them authority to drive out evil spirits and to cure every kind of disease and sickness.
> These twelve Jesus sent out with the following instructions: "Do not go among the Gentiles or enter any town of the Samaritans. Go rather to the lost sheep of Israel. As you go, preach this message: 'The kingdom of heaven is near.' Heal the sick, raise the dead, cleanse those who have leprosy, drive out demons. Freely you have received, freely give.

"What is the purpose of the gifts of the Holy Spirit here in Matthew?"

"Matthew doesn't explicitly mention them," Joe replied. "But given what we have been talking about, the gifts of the Holy Spirit are probably the authority, the ability, or the power to actually do the kinds of things Jesus told the disciples to do."

"You're really good at this," Matt responded. "Let's look again at who has been given these gifts of the Holy Spirit that work for the common good, building up the body of Christ, administering the grace of God, bearing witness to Jesus, and announcing the nearness of the kingdom. We already looked at 1 Corinthians 12:7, which says that every disciple of Jesus has been given gifts of the Holy Spirit. In 1 Corinthians 12:27, further down the passage, Paul said this, 'Now you are the body of Christ, and each one of you is a part of it.'

"Paul had just finished a long passage in which he talked about how each part of the body does different things. Yet, each part is important to the body. In the same way, all disciples of Jesus are the body of Jesus. Each of us does different things and has different gifts, but each of us is vitally important to Jesus to accomplish all he desires. To be part of the body of Christ is to be gifted by the Holy Spirit.

"So that means you, Joe, have been given one or more of the gifts of the Holy Spirit. That means the Holy Spirit has chosen to work through you in some particular ways. To better understand what the Holy Spirit is up to in your life, let's take a look at all the lists of Holy Spirit gifts in the New Testament and give some definition to them."

"I'd really like to look at that," Joe said. "Then I'd like you to help me figure out which ones the Holy Spirit has given me."

"Okay, let's do it," Matt replied. "In 1 Corinthians 12:8-10, the first list is given to us. There we find gifts of wisdom, knowledge, faith, healing, miraculous powers, prophecy, discernment, tongues, and interpretation. Paul continued the list in verses 28-29. There we find apostles, prophets, teachers, helps, and administration. Ephesians 4:11 has some more. In addition to the gifts that were already listed, evangelists and pastors are added. Romans 12:6-8 adds serving, encouraging, giving, leadership, and mercy. The last list is in 1 Peter 4:9-11. That list adds hospitality.

"Let me go back through the lists in alphabetical order and give some definition to these twenty-two gifts.

"**Administration** is the gift that it takes to make an organization run. These people are good with plans, policies, procedures, and programs. They can set them up, or they can run them, or they can improve them, or they can measure them to see how well they work. They know how to get things done. Specifically, they know how to do this in a church, and they are passionate about the church's goals and objectives. Some of the people at the church who chair the administrative committees have this gift.

"**Apostleship** is like the twelve apostles. They went out and started new churches. The gift of apostleship is the Holy Spirit working through someone to start new ministries and new churches, either at home or halfway around the world. Church planters and missionaries are often people with the gift of apostleship.

"**Discernment** is the gift to know the difference between truth and error. Discernment is also about being able to know who someone is and what their motives are. I met a man once with this gift. He shook my hand, talked with me for minute, and then he proceeded to tell me what gifts I had and that I did a good job with them. Apart from the Holy Spirit, this man had no way of knowing that. I have been in meetings at church when we were about to go forward with a proposal from a company about a purchase when someone said there was something wrong with it. We stopped and did some more investigation and found a problem that would have been disastrous. Discernment is also about knowing whether or not what someone is saying and doing is from God.

"**Encouragement** is the gift of being able to encourage others and to build them up. Encouragers are very positive people. They tell us good things, true things about ourselves. They tell us to keep going. I love talking to people with this gift. I always feel great when I finish a conversation with one of them. They usually have the knack of knowing when I'm very discouraged, or they know, without my telling them, what is discouraging me.

"**Evangelism** is the gift of being able to talk to people about Jesus in such a way that the person can make a positive response. I know a lady who has this gift. It seems every conversation she has takes a spiritual turn and ends up about Jesus. Sometimes people just ask her stuff. Other times she turns the conversation that direction, and people aren't offended, but rather, are interested. I can try for a week to get into one of these conversations, and she gets in one in minutes.

"**Faith** is the ability to act on God's promises believing God will do what he has promised. All of us have faith to some extent, but the gift of faith is different. The gift of faith usually is about a person who knows God is going to fulfill a specific promise in an impossible situation. They don't panic, they act on what they know God is going to do, they wait for it, and it happens. I remember a girl in college who told me that a friend had told her she would marry a certain man. The guy was not interested in this girl. He was living on the other side of the country, dating someone else at the time. But she remained patient and confident and never approached this man. Two years after she graduated and he left the country, he called her. Today they have been married thirty years and have six children.

"**Giving** is the gift people have who love to give to God and his purposes. They aren't all rich people, but they love to give. Their only regret is that they don't have more money to give. Also, these people seem to have the knack to know just how much is needed, when it's needed, and where it's needed.

"**Healing** is the ability to pray for people, and they recover from whatever ails them, physically, emotionally, or spiritually. Sometimes we see people with this gift on TV. Sometimes it is the petite elderly woman on Sunday morning who comes up to me and says, 'You look like you don't feel well. Can I pray with you?' She does, and the flu starts to lift. Sometimes when this kind of person prays, there is an instant healing. Sometimes the healing isn't instant, but recovery begins at the moment of the prayer. Sometimes the healing is in the form of a booster that speeds up or strengthens the processes already at work.

"**Helps** is the gift people have who show up to help. Often they don't even need to be told what to do, they just know and go do it. When we have dinners at the church, we always need a setup crew, but we never schedule a cleanup crew. When cleanup time comes, there's one person who knows what needs to be done, and people just start putting away tables, washing dishes, and cleaning up. The one person who knows what needs to be done just kind of walks around to make sure everything happens. The people just cleaning up have the gift of helps. They are the behind-the-scenes kinds of people who often don't think they have much to offer, but without their helping hands, so much would go undone.

"**Hospitality** is the gift of being able to welcome the stranger. People with the hospitality gift often are good with food, like to entertain, and open their homes. People with this gift have a knack for knowing who is a stranger, approaching that person, and helping them feel welcome. I have a friend at church who had been talking with me before the service started on a Sunday morning but left me stranded in mid-sentence to go welcome someone he didn't know.

"**Knowledge** is a gift we talked about earlier. It's being given a piece of information or knowledge by the Holy Spirit that advances God's work in someone's life. Jesus used this gift in John 4 when he was talking with the woman at the well. She told him she didn't have a husband, and Jesus told her the rest of the story. She had six husbands, and the man she was with when Jesus spoke with her was not her husband.

"**Leadership** is the gift of being able to move people together toward the future to which God is calling the group. Churches that take initiatives to move beyond the status quo to accomplish something which God has called them to do either have a pastor or influential lay person with the gift of the leadership who rallies the troops and gets them all working together in the same direction.

"**Miracles** is the gift of praying and seeing supernatural kinds of things happen. Sometimes it's a miraculous healing of cancer, or sum of money or resource that appears out of nowhere at the right time, or a family ending a feud, or a weather pattern being averted. Miracles are unexpected, unplanned, and are so big only God can pull them off. A person with this gift always seems to be involved in these kinds of things.

"**Mercy** is the gift that helps in times of crisis or trouble. Mercy people show up at the hospital, fix meals and visit the sick, and are always asking about people on the prayer list. They offer comfort when a loved one is lost and are counted on when life falls apart.

"**Prophecy** is the gift of speaking for God. It's not about telling the future. It's about delivering a message from God. Usually a prophet speaks an insight which carries with it either a warning about what will happen if change doesn't occur or an encouragement to make the change. The insight and the warning or encouragement that go with the insight aren't something the person with the gift would have come up with on his own.

"**Shepherding or pastor** is a gift of caring for the spiritual well-being of a group of people. They have the ability to nurture and encourage people to grow spiritually. Many of the men and women who pastor churches have this gift.

"**Teaching** is the gift of being able to take the words on the page of the Bible and make them come alive and be understandable. They are able to help people grasp the concepts of God in such a way that they can understand them and put them into practice. It's what I hope is going on here on Sunday nights with the two of us at this coffee shop.

"**Tongues and Interpretation** are two gifts I would like to put together. Tongues is the gift of being able to speak, worship, or pray in a language that one doesn't know. Sometimes it's a language that is unknown, from a human perspective, and sometimes it's another language that other people speak, like German, that was not learned by the speaker. This gift has two uses. When used privately, it encourages, supports, and builds the individual who is praying or speaking in tongues. The gift often brings before God issues of the heart that are difficult to put into words. When used publically, it must be accompanied by the gift of interpretation. Sometimes a public message in tongues, along with the interpretation, is a message of encouragement and hope or a word of warning or rebuke for a congregation or an individual.

"**Interpretation** is the ability to understand the message the Holy Spirit is communicating through the gift of tongues. Someone with this gift hears the person speaking a message in tongues, and they understand the message and are able to deliver the message in English or whatever is the native language of the listeners. In 1 Corinthians 14, Paul gave specific directions for how this is to work in a worship service.

"I remember the first time I was in a worship experience where this went on. It seemed really weird to me, but I had the sense something was happening. Since then, I have been in various services through the years where the whole congregation has prayed together in tongues or sometimes sang in tongues, or where there was a message or two in tongues and interpretations. Sometimes it's done well and enhances the service, and sometimes it's done poorly and damages the service. At that point, it's like anything we do in a worship service. For instance, a musician can greatly enhance a service or wreck one.

"**Wisdom** is the gift of being able to apply God's truth and principles in specific situations. These people just seem to know what to do. When asked, they give excellent advice. They seem to understand how God works and what that means for the decisions we face."

"There certainly are a lot of spiritual gifts. This list you went through, is that all of them?" Joe asked.

"People debate about that," Matt answered. "Some people add some gifts about intercession, which is praying for other people, or craftsmanship, which is building stuff, or communication, which is using the arts. I don't know if the list is complete, but I know that, at least, it includes those things. The other thing I know is that whatever gifts we need to accomplish a task God has called us to do, the Holy Spirit will find a way to provide it."

"Are you telling me the Holy Spirit has given me one of these gifts?" Joe asked.

"Yes," Matt replied. "He has probably given you more than one. These gifts often work or appear in clusters of two or three. For instance, if someone has the gift of wisdom, chances are there is a gift of knowledge and possibly teaching to go with it. Sometimes leadership goes together with administration and faith. Sometimes faith, miracles, and healing go together. Sometimes helps, mercy, and giving go together. The Holy Spirit gives us these gifts as he chooses how he will work through each of us."

"How do I find out which ones I have?" Joe asked.

"There are a few ways to find out," Matt responded. "The first way is to ask this question: How has God used you in the past?"

"I'm brand new to all this," Joe answered. "I'm not sure I've been used by God. God has certainly been answering my prayers and doing things to change my life and get it in order, but I'm not sure I've been used by God to do anything for anyone yet."

"That's probably true," Matt replied, "but that will be changing very soon. Another way to find out what gifts you have is to take a spiritual gifts survey. You can find lots of them online by going to your favorite search engine and typing in *spiritual gifts survey*. The way they work is that they have a series of questions or statements about how the gifts work that you match with your experience. Generally, they have you put a number from 0-5 indicating how much the statement sounds like you. At the end of the survey, you total up your score, and you can see which gifts have been at work in your life. These surveys are most helpful for people who have been in ministry and mission for a while. It allows them to see how God has been working through their lives and helps them to focus. Let's take a survey this week and bring it back, and we'll see what it indicates.

"A third way to find out what gifts you have is to ask this simple question: Did any of the gifts stand out to you as we went through them? Were there some you were particularly interested in or that seemed to speak to you?"

"As you mention that," Joe said, "there were a couple that caught my attention. Helps and mercy seemed really interesting to me. I like to help people, and I always feel drawn to people who are in trouble."

"That's a start," Matt replied. "The best way to find out which gifts you have is to get involved in mission and see how the Holy Spirit shows up. You'll get a chance to do that with the basketball team you're going to coach."

"Which ones do you have?" Joe asked.

"There are three gifts the Holy Spirit seems to use in my life a lot," Matt answered. "They are teaching, encouragement, and shepherding. Through the years, depending on the circumstances, there have been other gifts that have surfaced and then gone away. I suspect, as I start my new job, I will find the Holy Spirit working in me in some different ways yet. The Holy Spirit is the one who gives the gifts or decides what he is going to do through you. So through different seasons of your life, some gifts come and go, but I've discovered there is a core way the Holy Spirit works through me that has been consistent through years."

"Are these spiritual gifts the same as our talents?" Joe asked.

"No," Matt responded, "they're different. A talent is something we're born with. A spiritual gift comes into my life through my second birth or conversion to Jesus. Someone may be a teacher, born with a talent for teaching and a desire to teach. They may teach second grade or college physics. The spiritual gift of teaching is a specific teaching gift to be able to teach the things of God from the Bible. Having a teaching degree doesn't qualify that person to teach the things of God. The spiritual gift of teaching is the Holy Spirit working through that person to lift up the things in that text that God wants the students to know in a way the students feel God at work. Someone may be a school teacher and have the spiritual gift of teaching too, but the two are not the same. The talent is wired into us at birth and works through our mind and body. The spiritual gift is the Holy Spirit at work through us using our mind and body to accomplish his tasks. Often though, the spiritual gift works in conjunction with our natural talents. The Holy Spirit doesn't often take a shy person, scared to death of public speaking, and call him to teach three thousand people."

"Okay, that helps," Joe replied. "I'll fill out this form, get involved in coaching, and see what happens. Is there anything else?"

"Yes, there are a couple of other things," Matt said. "I want to talk about the spirit in which to use the gifts, some things to avoid, and then wrap up talking about the fruit of the Holy Spirit."

"Sounds like I need to warm up my coffee then," Joe replied. They both stood up, stretched, and got some more coffee.

When they returned to their seats, Matt began to talk, "The way in which we use the gifts is as important as the gift itself. By our own poor attitude, we can destroy the work the Holy Spirit is trying to accomplish. In 1 Corinthians 12, Paul talked about the gifts and what they are. In chapter 14, Paul talked about using the gifts during worship services. But in chapter 13, Paul said that if we don't use the gifts in love, it doesn't matter which gifts we have or what we can do with them. The Corinthians thought the gifts were cool and that some gifts were more important than others. Those who had certain gifts looked down on those who didn't have those gifts. Paul wanted us to understand that the gift we have is not nearly as important as the manner in which we use it. Without love, we're wasting everyone's time and damaging our relationships with God and others.

"Along those lines, we're encouraged to avoid **gift envy**. Gift envy is when I think my gift is not as good as someone else's gift. I look at my gift of teaching and say, 'I wish I had the gift of healing. If I had the gift of healing like Dave does, then I could really help people. If I had the gift Dave has, I would be really spiritual. If I had Dave's gift, then God could really use me. There's not much God can do with the gifts I have. I wish I had Dave's gift.' Don't go there.

"We also need to avoid **gift projection**. Gift projection is the opposite of gift envy. Gift projection says, 'If Dave were really a good Christian, he would have my gift of teaching. Until Dave gets my gift of teaching, he won't really grow and blossom as a Christian. God only works through people with teaching gifts. If Dave would only let me, I could help him get my gift. Dave would be so much better off and so would the kingdom if he had my gift.' Don't go there either.

"Let me say that self-esteem is not gift based. We are not worth more or less based on the gifts we have. The Holy Spirit has given us these gifts because of who we are, the situations we find ourselves in, the people we know, and the way the Holy Spirit wants to use us. The Holy Spirit doesn't like people with teaching gifts more or people with helps gifts less. That has nothing to do with the gifts we have been given. Sometimes I wonder why God doesn't throw his hands up in the air and just walk away from the whole lot of us.

"What we need to do with the gifts and with everything else is love, and love some more. We need to love people who have gifts like ours. We need to love people who have gifts that are different from ours. We need to love the people whom the Holy Spirit wants to serve through us. We need to love, love, love."

"I think I get all that," Joe said. "But I have a question: Just how do the gifts work?"

"I get myself in a ministry situation," Matt replied, "and they just happen. They show up when we need them. They are powered by the Holy Spirit, but my faith is involved too. Faith is acting on what Jesus said. Faith is acting on a prompting or a leading from the Holy Spirit. If I don't act, I won't see the gifts in operation. I have to put myself out on a limb for God. I have to do what Jesus said or follow the prompting even though I know I can't pull it off. As I follow and get in over my head, the Holy Spirit shows up through the gifts and uses me in spite of myself and my inadequacies. Many are the times I've been on my way to talk with someone about something and have prayed, 'God if you don't show up, I'm sunk. I have no idea what to say or how to respond.' Amazingly, God has never hung me out to dry. Through the years, it has become easier to take risks for God in the areas of my giftedness because I have a track record of watching God show up and do his thing through me. Each time it happens, I'm energized and can't wait to do it again. Prayer and the spiritual disciplines are very important to this process. They create the openness for us to receive the prompting and follow the words of Jesus, and they also make it easier to respond to God in the midst of the situation and see him at work."

"So," Joe said, "you just wander in and somewhere along the line God shows up, stuff happens, the kingdom is advanced, and someone is helped. Sounds like quite a ride to me. But I guess it's not much different from what I have already been experiencing. I try to do what Jesus said. I step out there over my head, risk, and he shows up. It's pretty amazing."

"Let's look at the fruit of the Holy Spirit for a minute," Matt said. "The gifts are about what God does through us, the fruit is about what God does in us through the Holy Spirit. Paul wrote about this in Galatians 5:19-26. There Paul talked about the acts of the sinful nature and the fruit of the Spirit. Let's turn there and read:

> The acts of the sinful nature are obvious: sexual immorality, impurity and debauchery; idolatry and witchcraft; hatred, discord, jealousy, fits of rage, selfish ambition, dissensions, factions and envy; drunkenness, orgies, and the like. I warn you, as I did before, that those who live like this will not inherit the kingdom of God.
>
> But the fruit of the Spirit is love, joy, peace, patience, kindness, goodness, faithfulness, gentleness and self-control. Against such things there is no law. Those who belong to Christ Jesus have crucified the sinful nature with its passions and desires. Since we live by the Spirit, let us keep in step with the Spirit. Let us not become conceited, provoking and envying each other.

"The first list is what human nature does when left to itself. We could break down some of the words, but I think you get the idea. While we may not engage in all of these behaviors, or all of these behaviors at one time, two or three of them are enough to trash a life and the lives of the people around us. We find ourselves being unable to stop ourselves from doing the things on the list even when we want to very badly. I don't want to be jealous. I want to stop. I try hard to stop, but the jealousy gets out when I'm not looking or when I'm tired or overloaded or…I need help to stop. More than help, I need a heart change.

"The second list is the change the Holy Spirit creates in human nature. When the Holy Spirit gets a hold of our lives, these are the things he does to us. We can't will joy into our lives any more than we can will jealousy out. Joy is there or it isn't. The Holy Spirit puts joy in us. We're able to increase these character traits in our lives through continued openness and receptivity to the Holy Spirit brought on by practicing the spiritual disciplines. Wouldn't you like to have more of this going on in your life? I would. Wouldn't you like all your dealings to be with people like this? I would."

"I would too," Joe said.

"Do you remember what Jesus said about salt and light?" Matt asked. "If we put ourselves in situations where the gifts of the Holy Spirit are at work in us and we act out of love and our character displays the fruit of the spirit, I think our saltiness and wattage would increase a lot."

Joe agreed. Then they talked about their experience with secrecy and chose fellowship for the next week. They prayed for each other and their mission projects. Joe wondered on his way home how the risks he would be taking in his mission project would be any different from the risks he was taking to get his life together.

CHAPTER 19

HOW TO SHARE THE GOSPEL

The arctic air mass had not yet receded. Matt was glad it was single digit temperatures for only a few days a year. He was wearing his long underwear, thermal socks, and several layers under his heaviest coat to fight off the cold. He felt like a toddler so bundled up in a snowsuit he couldn't walk, only waddle. As Matt came in the door, he quickly spotted Joe near the fire warming his hands on his coffee mug. Matt soon joined him with his own mug of steaming hot coffee.

"How are you faring in your war against the elements?" Matt asked.

"Not well," Joe answered. "I had a water pipe burst in the garage. I forgot to shut it off when I was doing my fall clean up. What a mess. How about you, how are you doing?"

"It was so cold the other day," Matt replied, "my snow blower wouldn't start. I had to shovel the drive. I rolled the snow blower inside before I went to work. It started fine when I got back home. How did it go with the counselor this week?"

"I think some day it will get easier, but that day doesn't look like it will be anytime soon," Joe said. "The counselor talked with me about mercy. He said the same kinds of things about mercy that you did. He told me mercy was forgoing judgment and punishment to offer forgiveness in order to work on resolving the issues or problems. He told me that what my dad did was wrong. He said the issue I need to deal with is not my dad's actions but my reactions to my dad. He asked me if I want to continue judging and punishing my dad for his actions or if I want to forgive him so that I can rebuild my relationship with my dad and resolve the issues.

"He told me I wouldn't be condoning my dad's actions by forgiving him, nor would I be giving him permission to continue to act that way. Rather, he said forgiveness was acknowledging my dad hurt me a lot but freeing him from the responsibility of repairing the damage. The counselor asked me if my dad could undo the harm or repair the damage. I said there was no way in the world my dad could ever pay enough to make right what he did. The counselor told me to stop trying to make my dad pay. I asked, 'Who will pay? Who is going to make this right?' The counselor replied, 'Not your dad, not you, and not me. The only one who can make it right and repair the damage is God.' The first step the counselor wanted me to take was to let my dad off the hook and to ask God to fix the damage in my life and my dad's life. He told me to pray every day for my dad's well-being and healing, and for my own.

"The first day was tough. I didn't want to pray for my dad's well-being and healing. I wanted to pray for his punishment, but I managed to choke out a 'God bless Dad.' I've been doing it most of the week. Yesterday was the first day it wasn't a giant struggle to pray for my dad. I think I'm getting closer.

"How about you? How were your first days on the job?"

"I love corporate America," Matt said. "I decided this time I'm going to be focused on being God's man in this company, Widgets International, Inc. I want to infiltrate my Widgets International with the kingdom. So I prayed for Kelly, my boss, and Vince, my Vice President, on the way to work. I prayed for all the people who report to me. I prayed for the company. I prayed God would cause Widgets and the people working for them to prosper. I prayed they would work well together. I have a thirty-minute commute to work. Instead of listening to music or the news, I'm using the time to pray for the company. I pray God would help me do a good job, use me to bless the people I work with, and use me to advance the kingdom in the company. I've been spending time trying to figure out how to add value to Kelly. I found the usual array of miscommunications, bureaucratic redundancy, and red tape. I'll figure all that out after I figure out who reports directly to me, and what they're doing. I have five of them and have met three. The other two are out of town at other Widget plants, and I'll see them next week. Did I mention I love corporate America?

"Let's get to Jesus. This week we're going to look at some ways to proclaim the kingdom and share the gospel. To start with, we're going to look at four passages to see how this was done in the New Testament. We're going to look at the words of Jesus twice, Peter once, and Philip once. In the first passage, in John 4:1-42, we're going to look at how Jesus was sharing the faith and proclaiming the kingdom when he talked with a Samaritan woman at a well just outside the town of Sychar.

> The Pharisees heard that Jesus was gaining and baptizing more disciples than John, although in fact it was not Jesus who baptized, but his disciples. When the Lord learned of this, he left Judea and went back once more to Galilee.
>
> Now he had to go through Samaria. So he came to a town in Samaria called Sychar, near the plot of ground Jacob had given to his son Joseph. Jacob's well was there, and Jesus, tired as he was from the journey, sat down by the well. It was about the sixth hour.
>
> When a Samaritan woman came to draw water, Jesus said to her, "Will you give me a drink?" (His disciples had gone into the town to buy food.)
>
> The Samaritan woman said to him, "You are a Jew and I am a Samaritan woman. How can you ask me for a drink?" (For Jews do not associate with Samaritans.)
>
> Jesus answered her, "If you knew the gift of God and who it is that asks you for a drink, you would have asked him and he would have given you living water."
>
> "Sir," the woman said, "you have nothing to draw with and the well is deep. Where can you get this living water? Are you greater than our father Jacob, who gave us the well and drank from it himself, as did also his sons and his flocks and his herds?"

Jesus answered, "Everyone who drinks this water will be thirsty again, but whoever drinks the water I give him will never thirst. Indeed, the water I give him will become in him a spring of water welling up to eternal life."

The woman said to him, "Sir, give me this water so that I won't get thirsty and have to keep coming here to draw water."

He told her, "Go, call your husband and come back."

"I have no husband," she replied.

Jesus said to her, "You are right when you say you have no husband. The fact is, you have had five husbands, and the man you now have is not your husband. What you have just said is quite true."

"Sir," the woman said, "I can see that you are a prophet. Our fathers worshiped on this mountain, but you Jews claim that the place where we must worship is in Jerusalem."

Jesus declared, "Believe me, woman, a time is coming when you will worship the Father neither on this mountain nor in Jerusalem. You Samaritans worship what you do not know; we worship what we do know, for salvation is from the Jews. Yet a time is coming and has now come when the true worshipers will worship the Father in spirit and truth, for they are the kind of worshipers the Father seeks. God is spirit, and his worshipers must worship in spirit and in truth."

The woman said, "I know that Messiah" (called Christ) "is coming. When he comes, he will explain everything to us."

Then Jesus declared, "I who speak to you am he."

Just then his disciples returned and were surprised to find him talking with a woman. But no one asked, "What do you want?" or "Why are you talking with her?"

Then, leaving her water jar, the woman went back to the town and said to the people, "Come, see a man who told me everything I ever did. Could this be the Christ?" They came out of the town and made their way toward him.

Meanwhile his disciples urged him, "Rabbi, eat something."

But he said to them, "I have food to eat that you know nothing about."

Then his disciples said to each other, "Could someone have brought him food?"

"My food," said Jesus, "is to do the will of him who sent me and to finish his work. Do you not say, 'Four months more and then the harvest'? I tell you, open your eyes and look at the fields! They are ripe for harvest. Even now the reaper draws his wages, even now he harvests the crop for eternal life, so that the sower and the reaper may be glad together. Thus the saying 'One sows and another reaps' is true. I sent you to reap what you have not worked for. Others have done the hard work, and you have reaped the benefits of their labor."

Many of the Samaritans from that town believed in him because of the woman's testimony, "He told me everything I ever did." So when the Samaritans came to him, they urged him to stay with them, and he stayed two days. And because of his words many more became believers.

They said to the woman, "We no longer believe just because of what you said; now we have heard for ourselves, and we know that this man really is the Savior of the world."

"Now let's ask some questions of this passage. What is said?"

"What is said?" Joe repeated. "Jesus and this woman got into a conversation about water, race, gender, religion, and her life. One moment the conversation was about water from the well, and the next moment the conversation was about living water. One moment the conversation was about the ordinary mundane stuff of life, and the next it was about spiritual stuff, and God, and how we relate to him. How did Jesus do that?"

"Good question," Matt replied. "For Jesus, everything had a spiritual connotation, so every conversation he had turned that direction. I know people for whom everything has a sexual connotation. No matter what I talk about with these people, every word contains sexual innuendo. They turn every conversation into flirting or talking about when they've had sex and with whom. How do they do that? That's what's on their minds and in their hearts. That's what dominates their imagination, and that's what they would most like to be doing. There are guys I know who turn every conversation to the topic of cars or sports. They are uneasy unless the discussion turns to the big game that either just ended or is just coming up. When the conversation turns that direction, they relax and have a lot to say.

"Jesus was able to shift the conversation from literal water to living water because his mind and heart were filled with the kingdom. Jesus dreamed kingdom dreams. Jesus thought kingdom thoughts. Jesus imagined kingdom things. Jesus imagined the people he encountered in the kingdom. He imagined the changes that would happen in their lives. He imagined the love they would receive and the incredible people they would become as the kingdom got a hold of their lives.

"Because Jesus was filled with kingdom thoughts, dreams, and imagination, the shift from literal water to living water was natural for him. He may have done it without even thinking about it. Because it was natural for him and he was comfortable with the subject matter, the woman was able to talk with him about living water in ways she probably had not talked with even her closest friends.

"I don't think Jesus sat at the well talking to himself about what he would say if someone came by. I think he just sat and waited for someone to come by to help him get a drink. Because he was so full of the kingdom, when someone did come by, Jesus turned the conversation to living water. It's who he was.

"Now look at the disciples. They went into the town to buy lunch. They came back with lunch and had no spiritual conversations with any of the Samaritans with whom they came in contact. Why didn't they have any spiritual conversations? It wasn't in them. There wasn't enough kingdom in their hearts to turn their minds from lunch, prejudice, or fear to spiritual things.

"So let me ask, how do people go from being like the disciples, with not enough kingdom in their hearts to capture their imaginations and minds, to having enough kingdom in them so that when they talk it just comes out of them?"

"Why do you get to ask all the hard questions?" Joe said. "I think it probably has to with the spiritual disciplines. As I spend time daily, and probably some significant unhurried time, in one or more spiritual disciplines, the kingdom would take greater root in my heart, move to my imagination, and come out of my mouth. It seems to me some of the spiritual disciplines are geared to engage the imagination, like meditation, and others, like fellowship, are geared to engage the mouth.

"So I think the answer to my original question, how did Jesus do that, so I can know how to do that, is based on how much kingdom is in me. I can enter conversations similar to the one Jesus had with the Samaritan woman by having my heart, mind, and imagination filled with the kingdom, just like Jesus."

"When we're filled with the kingdom," Matt responded, "every encounter and every conversation has spiritual significance and can take a kingdom turn. That is what was said in the passage. What was done in the passage?"

"I'm not sure what was done here," Joe answered. "Jesus and this woman talked, and the rest of the passage is about the response from that conversation."

"Tell me about the response to the conversation," Matt prompted.

"The woman became convinced Jesus was the Messiah," Joe said. "She went back into town and told everyone she had met the Messiah, why she was convinced he was the Messiah, and that he was just outside of the town at the well. It seemed like the whole town went out to see Jesus. When they met Jesus, they too became convinced he was the Messiah. They asked him to stay, and he did, for two days."

"Are there any spiritual gifts at work here? Do you see any fruit of the spirit working?" Matt asked.

"I don't know," Joe replied. "We talked about that stuff last week, but I'm still trying to get my mind around the concepts."

"I see a couple of spiritual gifts at work," Matt said. "I see the gift of evangelism working. It's that gift of the Holy Spirit that helps

Jesus weave his way through the conversation with the woman once he got started. I also see the gift of knowledge at work. It was knowledge Jesus had about her life, given to him by the Holy Spirit, that was the turning point in the conversation for the woman. Notice how the Holy Spirit's action, of giving Jesus the knowledge about the woman, at the right time, made the difference in the conversation.

"I see some fruit of the Spirit at work too. There was the love Jesus had for this woman that got him to engage her in the conversation. There was patience as Jesus followed the woman's attempt to get him off track. There was gentleness as Jesus shared what he knew about the woman. This expression of the fruit of the Spirit kept both Jesus and the woman in the conversation.

"What can we take from this account to help us in sharing the gospel and proclaiming the kingdom?" Matt asked.

"I think I can handle this one. It looks to me like there are a few things to help us," Joe replied. "First, we need to fill ourselves with the kingdom through the spiritual disciplines so that we can approach every encounter and every conversation looking for spiritual connotations so that we can help people make spiritual connections.

"Second, it seems like we don't have to reach everyone. Jesus reached just one person, and she brought the whole town to him. If we reach the people we can reach, and have the spiritual conversations we can have, the people we're talking with will reach the people they know and use us as a resource to help them reach their friends and neighbors. I suppose, depending on the person, that could be two or three people, or as with Jesus, it could be the whole town.

"Third, it looks like even the most insignificant or most unlikely person can make a huge kingdom difference, so that makes each encounter spiritually significant because who knows what kind of kingdom impact that person could make."

"You have good instincts, Joe," Matt said. "Let me tell you about how unlikely it was that this woman would have made such an impact. This woman came alone to the well at midday. In those days, women went to the well to get water for the household in the cool of the morning or the cool of the evening, not in the midday heat. The trip to the well was a social event. Women would gather in herds, the way women do, and go together talking about whatever the women of that day talked about. So the woman Jesus talked to was alone in the noon heat. Why? Maybe she didn't want the company of the other women, or maybe the other women didn't want her company. Whatever the reason, it seems unlikely that this woman could influence the whole town.

"The other thing we learn about this woman is she has been divorced five times. Even by today's standards, that's a lot of failed marriages. If I met someone divorced five times, I would wonder what was going on. But for this woman, it was even worse. In those days, a woman couldn't divorce a man. That means this woman had five men who had married her and thrown her away. I can't imagine how low her self-esteem must have been and how wrecked her life was. We discover further that she was living with a man, but he didn't think enough of her to make her an honest woman. Whatever arrangement they had was clearly not to her advantage. As far as the town was concerned, this woman was the very bottom of the pecking order.

"Let's look at the next account. We're familiar with this one. It's the passage we're working from now. Let's look at the first part of it, Matthew 10:1, 5-8:

> He called his twelve disciples to him and gave them authority to drive out evil spirits and to heal every disease and sickness.
>
> These twelve Jesus sent out with the following instructions: "Do not go among the Gentiles or enter any town of the Samaritans. Go rather to the lost sheep of Israel. As you go, preach this message: 'The kingdom of heaven is near.' Heal the sick, raise the dead, cleanse those who have leprosy, drive out demons. Freely you have received, freely give.

"What was said?"

"We have to read between the lines on this one, don't we?" Joe commented. As Matt nodded in agreement, Joe went on. "I suppose the disciples told someone or some group of people in the towns and villages that the kingdom is near."

"That's a good supposition," Matt replied. "What was done?"

"People were healed of diseases and sicknesses, and evil spirits were driven out," Joe answered.

"What type of response occurred?" Matt asked.

"Once again, I have to guess," Joe said. "I would say as people were healed, evil spirits were cast out, and people were helped, people would have believed the message of the disciples about the kingdom being near."

"Do you see evidence of the gifts of the Holy Spirit or fruit of the Spirit at work?" Matt asked.

"Let's see if I can answer it this time," Joe replied. "Would the gift of healing and maybe miracles be at work? Were the fruits of love, and maybe joy, and possibly goodness present?"

"I'll buy it," Matt said. "What can we take from this account to help us?"

"I see two things," Joe responded. "First, in this instance, kingdom word and kingdom deed go together. The disciples, who were telling people the kingdom was near, had to act like the kingdom was near in order for people to believe the message.

"The second thing I see is that delegation is a good thing. There were more people, towns, and villages than Jesus could personally reach, so he trained his disciples to join him in the task."

"Good," Matt replied. "Let's look at the next one. We find Peter and John, in Acts 3:1-11, going to the temple to pray. Here's what happened:

> One day Peter and John were going up to the temple at the time of prayer—at three in the afternoon. Now a man crippled from birth was being carried to the temple gate called Beautiful, where he was put every day to beg from those going into the temple courts. When he saw Peter and John about to enter, he asked them for money. Peter looked straight at him, as did John. Then Peter said, "Look at us!" So the man gave them his attention, expecting to get something from them.
>
> Then Peter said, "Silver or gold I do not have, but what I have I give you. In the name of Jesus Christ of Nazareth,

walk." Taking him by the right hand, he helped him up, and instantly the man's feet and ankles became strong. He jumped to his feet and began to walk. Then he went with them into the temple courts, walking and jumping, and praising God. When all the people saw him walking and praising God, they recognized him as the same man who used to sit begging at the temple gate called Beautiful, and they were filled with wonder and amazement at what had happened to him.

While the beggar held on to Peter and John, all the people were astonished and came running to them in the place called Solomon's Colonnade.

"What was said here?"

"A lot," Joe said. "To start with, Peter and John talked to the beggar. They told him they didn't have silver or gold, but what they did have they would give him."

"That's enough to start with," Matt responded. "Then Peter acted like the kingdom was near, grabbed hold of the man's hand, and helped him to his feet. The lame man stood up, completely healed.

"What kind of response followed?" Matt asked.

"The man started running around the temple area praising God," Joe replied. "He caused enough of a ruckus that people wondered what was going on. Then the people recognized him as the lame beggar at the temple gate and became really curious. As a crowd began to gather around the lame man, staring in amazement, Peter began to talk.

"He explained how the lame man was healed. Peter was rather blunt in accusing them of killing Jesus, but then softened his approach by saying they acted in ignorance. Then he offered all of them forgiveness, refreshing, and blessing if they would turn to Jesus. I looked a little further down the page and it said many believed them, and the number of men grew to about five thousand. I would say that was a lot of response."

"Did you see any spiritual gifts at work here or fruit of the Holy Spirit in action?" Matt asked.

"Yes," Joe answered. "The gift of healing was at work as Peter healed the lame man. I think the gift of evangelism was at work as

Peter spoke to the crowd about Jesus in a way they could respond. Was the fruit of the Spirit at work? Maybe love was at work as Peter and John cared enough about the lame man to stop, listen to him, and then help him. Maybe some patience was practiced by Peter as he reined in his speech and allowed that the people acted in ignorance and now was a time for them to turn to Jesus."

"What can we take from this account to help us as we share the faith and proclaim the gospel?" Matt asked.

"It looks like Peter just gave a kingdom response to a human need," Joe said. "The lame man needed to be healed, and Peter knew there was healing in the kingdom and offered those kingdom resources. It looks like if we offer kingdom resources, we'll get to share the faith or proclaim the gospel to someone."

"I hope you're up for one more," Matt said. "Let's look at Philip in Acts 8:26-38:

> Now an angel of the Lord said to Philip, "Go south to the road, the desert road, that goes down from Jerusalem to Gaza." So he started out, and on his way he met an Ethiopian eunuch, an important official in charge of all the treasury of Candace, queen of the Ethiopians. This man had gone to Jerusalem to worship, and on his way home was sitting in his chariot reading the book of Isaiah the prophet. The Spirit told Philip, "Go to that chariot and stay near it."
>
> Then Philip ran up to the chariot and heard the man reading Isaiah the prophet. "Do you understand what you are reading?" Philip asked. "How can I," he said, "unless someone explains it to me?" So he invited Philip to come up and sit with him. The eunuch was reading this passage of Scripture:
>
> "He was led like a sheep to the slaughter,
> and as a lamb before the shearer is silent,
> so he did not open his mouth.
> In his humiliation he was deprived of justice.
> Who can speak of his descendants?
> For his life was taken from the earth."

The eunuch asked Philip, "Tell me, please, who is the prophet talking about, himself or someone else?" Then Philip began with that very passage of Scripture and told him the good news about Jesus.

As they traveled along the road, they came to some water and the eunuch said, "Look, here is water. Why shouldn't I be baptized?" And he gave orders to stop the chariot. Then both Philip and the eunuch went down into the water and Philip baptized him.

"I know the drill," Joe said. "What was said? Philip was told by an angel to go out to the desert road. Philip did. On the desert road, Philip came upon a Eunuch reading some scripture in his chariot. I guess he must have been reading it out loud because Philip asked the man if he understood what he was reading. The man said, 'How can I?' and asked Philip to explain it. Philip did.

"What happened? As a result of their conversation about what the prophet was saying, the Eunuch gave his life to Christ and was baptized. I guess that was the response too.

"What spiritual gifts and fruit were at work? This one was as dramatic as the last couple of stories. Looking at the list of spiritual gifts here, I would guess the gift of teaching was at work as Philip walked the man through the Old Testament passages about the Messiah and related them to Jesus. Once again, I see love, and patience, and maybe kindness and gentleness at work.

"What can I take from this account to help me? I guess when God gives you direction, it would be a good idea to do what he says because he has something all set up for you."

"Let me do a little summary here," Matt began. "In each case, spiritual gifts combined with the fruit of the Spirit made the difference. Without the Holy Spirit working through the gifts and the fruit, Jesus wouldn't have made the connection with the woman at the well and then the whole town, the disciples wouldn't have been able to do what they did when they were sent out by Jesus, Peter wouldn't have been able to heal the lame man and lead a couple of thousand people to Jesus that day, and Philip wouldn't have been able to adequately respond to the Eunuch's question. It's a good idea to discover what our spiritual gifts are and get in places and situations where we can use them. When we use them, the Holy Spirit shows up, and kingdom stuff happens.

"So through the spiritual disciplines, we need to do what we can to keep open our lines to the Holy Spirit. We need to get what help we can from our brothers and sisters in Christ, who have the same gifts as we do, to learn how the gifts work so that we can be effectively used.

"Another thing that seems to run through each account is everyone was making a kingdom response to a human need. We need to tune in to the people around us. We need to listen because that's how we become aware of human need. Once we're aware of the need, we can offer a kingdom response. So as much as we need to open our lines to the Holy Spirit, we need to open our lines to the people around us.

"One more thing is present in all these accounts: Each act has a domino effect. Jesus' encounter with the woman at the well led to the whole town coming to him. Jesus' work with the disciples led to their ability to affect lots of towns and villages. Peter's healing of the lame man dominoed into a couple of thousand people responding to the good news about Jesus. Philip's encounter with the eunuch led to that man sharing his discovery about Jesus with his friends and neighbors in Ethiopia, and that led to the start of a church that is still in existence today. We need to watch for the dominoes to fall. We also need to be aware that these encounters are high stakes encounters. Not only are we dealing with the eternal destinies of the men and women we encounter, but that encounter sets up encounters for countless other people.

"Bill Hybels and Mark Mittleberg, in their book, *Becoming a Contagious Christian*, talk about six different evangelism styles they find in the New Testament. A lot of us are nervous about evangelism, sharing the gospel or proclaiming the kingdom, because we've tied the concept to practices or approaches we're uncomfortable with. For instance, the thought of going door to door, making cold calls and trying to share the gospel, to lead a complete stranger to Christ, on his doorstep, makes me very nervous. But on the other hand, being engaged in a mission project like running a support group for guys looking for jobs at the out-placement job center, and in the course of the support, praying for them or asking how they're doing spiritually, is something I'm looking forward to. So let's take a look at these six styles and find the ones we're comfortable with.

"The first style is Peter's confrontational style. Peter was a direct, sometimes blunt, and often bold sharer of the gospel. But that fit Peter's personality. In Matthew 16:15, Peter answered Jesus' question, 'Who do you say I am?' by saying that Jesus is the Christ. Moments later, as Jesus told them what it meant to be the Christ, Peter was in Jesus' face, telling Jesus he had it wrong and couldn't do it that way. Jesus had to back Peter down. Then Peter's first sermon, recorded in Acts 2, was on the day of Pentecost. In that sermon, Peter was confrontational. In verse 36, Peter plainly told his hearers, 'Therefore, let all Israel be assured of this: God has made this Jesus, whom you crucified, both Lord and Christ.' That sounds like in-your-face evangelism to me. There are some people who won't respond to the gospel until someone gets in their face with it.[i]

"This style doesn't fit me. But then I'm not a direct, in-your-face kind of person. Does it fit you?"

"No," Joe said, "I'm not that kind of guy, either."

"The second style is Paul's intellectual approach," Matt continued. "Paul used logic and reasoned arguments with evidence to support his case. He dealt with tough questions and defended the gospel against misconceptions. His letter to the Romans is a long, sustained argument. In his message to the philosophers in Acts 17, he carefully built his case point by point using their own poets and their own experience with life to lead them to consider Jesus.[ii]

"This is a style I'm comfortable with. I have the spiritual gift of teaching, and this fits that gift very well. I like explaining things, answering tough questions, helping people work through issues, and helping people see that the reasons to believe Jesus far outweigh the reasons to disbelieve Jesus."

"This one doesn't fit me either," Joe said. "I don't think I know enough to do this kind of thing. I'm always glad when someone can do this, but it's beyond me how to put that type of presentation together."

"The third style is the blind man's testimonial approach, found in John 9," Matt explained. "Jesus healed a blind man on the Sabbath. The Pharisees were very upset because they considered healing to be work, and one didn't work on the Sabbath. Since one wasn't supposed to work on the Sabbath, Jesus couldn't possibly be from God. The Pharisees investigated the healing, trying to discredit Jesus. Finally, they asked the blind man, who could now see, what he thought of Jesus. The blind man replied, 'One thing I do know. I was blind but now I see! If this man were not from God, he could do nothing' (verses 25 and 33). The Pharisees were insulted by the man's disrespect for their authority and threw him out, but they could not argue with the man's testimony.[iii]

"Someone's personal experience is a powerful tool. You see the impact of the gospel in that person's life right in front of you. This is a style I use as one of the pieces of evidence in the intellectual approach I like to use."

"I feel more comfortable with this one," Joe replied. "I can tell my story. That's no problem. God has certainly done a lot for me in these last few months, and if my story can help someone, I'm more than glad to share it."

"I'm glad we hit one that fits you," Matt said. "The fourth style is Matthew's interpersonal approach. Jesus called Matthew out of the tax collector's booth to come and follow. Matthew did. One of the first things Matthew did was to throw a party for all his tax collector buddies so that they could meet Jesus too. Matthew used his personal relationships to share the gospel. His style was to relate to people, to spend time with them. As I spend time building relationships with people who have yet to come to faith in Jesus, I'm building trust and credibility. As a result of the trust and credibility, I can offer kingdom resources when they ask me to help with a problem. Or, when I make an invitation to a worship service, a small group, or some type of special program at the church, they'll accept the invitation because of the friendship. Polls regularly show that 25 percent or more of people who don't go to church would attend if invited by a friend. Other polls show that anywhere between 70 percent and 90 percent of people who have come to Christ as adults did so through a friend or relative."[iv]

"I like that one," Joe responded. "It fits my experience with you, and I'm a people person, so I can use my contacts and networks to connect with people."

"The fifth style is the Samaritan woman's invitational approach," Matt continued. "She had an experience with Jesus. She went to her friends in town and basically said, 'Jesus is outside the town at the well. Come with me and see for yourself.' A person with this kind of style is always inviting people to 'come with me and see.' They have the full minivan for the special events at the church, or they're the ones waiting at the door for their friends to come."[v]

"My wife, Mary, uses this style. She always has someone on her arm when there is something special going on at church. Her group always has an empty chair to remind them to invite someone to come with them to fill the empty chair. She's very good at filling the empty chair in her small group."

"I can see how that style is effective," Joe said, "but it's not for me."

"The last style is Dorcas' service approach," Matt began again. "We read about Dorcas in Acts 9:36. She was well known in her community for helping the poor and doing good works for everyone. These people like to serve others. They see a need in someone's life, and they do something about it. Fixing a meal, visiting a hospital room, repairing a car, and offering some home improvement help are just some of the ways to serve. This is the approach Jesus had the disciples use in Matthew 10, and this is the approach we're using with our mission projects. As we offer help through our mission projects, we're doing two things: One, we're helping someone with something they can't do themselves. Two, we're building relationships. This often leads the person being served to ask, 'Why are you doing this for me?' and we get to answer. Sometimes it leads to strong enough relational ties that we can invite the person we're serving to something where they can hear the gospel and experience more of the Christian community. Helping someone produces a very powerful effect in their lives."[vi]

"That sounds simple enough," Joe replied. "I can do that."

"Good," Matt commented. "We're both going to get the chance to do that.

"I want to talk for a minute about writing your own story, your testimony. There are three points it needs to cover. Point one is what you used to be like before you came to Jesus. Point two is how you came to Jesus. Point three is the changes Jesus has made in your life. The other thing about the testimony is that it needs to be three minutes or shorter. Part of what we'll do next week is to share a three-minute testimony with each other, so spend some time working on it this week.

"Let's go back to the service approach for a minute. There's a question there I want to spend some time on because, as we do our mission projects, we most likely will hear it. The question is: Why are you doing this for me? For example, let's say you're coaching a basketball team of teenagers in the church league. Seventy-five percent of them aren't church kids. About halfway through the season, after you've spent time with them in practice, games, and doing devotions, one of the boys on the team asks, 'Are you getting paid to do this?' You respond, 'No.' Then the boy asks, 'If you aren't getting paid, then why are you doing this?'"

"How do you answer?"

"Because Matt is making me do this mission project." Joe laughed.

"Wrong answer, try again," Matt responded, shaking his head and smiling.

"How about this?" Joe answered. "God loves you, and this is a concrete way I can show God's love to you."

"Good answer." Matt smiled. "That answer opens the door to all kinds of conversational possibilities. It raises lots of questions for the teenage boy. Who is this God who loves me? How can I learn more about him? Is this love real? If God loves me, why is there bad stuff going on in my family? How do you know God loves me? How do you know God? He might ask some of those questions. He might not. He might not say anything for a couple of weeks, and then he may just start asking a bunch of questions. When he does, just be yourself and answer the questions out of the evangelism style that fits you best. It's all right to say 'I don't know' to a question."

"That's good to know," Joe said. "So basically, I just answer the questions as best as I can, be myself, and watch to see what God will do. I think I can do that."

"In *Becoming a Contagious Christian,* Bill Hybels tells about being on a sailing trip. He got invited to a party on another boat. As he was leaving the boat, one the people asked Bill, 'I've always wanted to ask a Christian what it means to become one. Can you tell us?' Bill figured he could count on them for about a 45-second attention span in which to give his answer.[vii] In a similar situation what would you say?"

"What would I say?" Joe echoed. "Nothing like putting a guy on the spot. Let me ponder that a moment. While I'm pondering, I'll get you a chocolate chip cookie."

When Joe returned with chocolate chip cookies, Matt said, "You stall well. What did you come up with?"

"All I can do is share my experience," Joe said. "So my answer would be, 'The way I became a Christian was I prayed this prayer, "Jesus, please come into my life, forgive me for the way I've messed up my life, help me live differently, and I'll follow you." When I prayed that prayer, I felt forgiven, loved, joyful, and at peace, all at once. Since then, as I have followed Jesus—read his words and tried to put them into practice—he has done many good things in my life. If you would like to do it, I can help you get started with that prayer right now or anytime you would like.' So how did I do, and what did Bill say?"

"You did well," Matt said. "You briefly shared your experience and invited them to join you. Bill went at it a little differently. He talked about *do* versus *done*. Religion is about the things I do to try to gain God's favor and forgiveness. The only problem is that there's a lot of doing involved, and I never know when I've done enough. Christianity is about *done*. It's about what Jesus did for me. He died for me and rose again for me so that I could be forgiven, set free, and have a new life. It's about what Jesus has done for me. The way to access what Jesus has done is to invite him into your heart, ask for forgiveness, a new life, and promise to follow him."[viii]

"I did do all right, didn't I?" Joe replied.

"Yes, you did," Matt agreed. Another way to have this conversation is with *The Bridge Illustration*. It's something you can draw on your napkin as you talk. You can find it online at www.navigators.org."[ix]

"I'll check it out," Joe said.

"Let me say a word about sharing the gospel, pearl pushing, asking, and the Golden Rule," Matt continued. "We have to ask permission to share the gospel or else we're pearl pushing. If we pearl push, the gospel will be rejected every time. If we ask, then the gospel has a chance to be heard. When someone wants to stop or says they need to think about it, grant that time, and then ask if you could talk some more in a week. Always think how you would like someone to treat you if you were hearing this and trying to make sense of it.

"Some people are ready to make a commitment the first time I talk with them. Some people need time. Some people need to work through obstacles. We take each person where they are, and through asking and the Golden Rule, we help them move closer to the day when they're ready to come to faith in Jesus."

"I guess listening to the other person is as important as what we say about Jesus," Joe replied. "I know your listening to me was a very important part of my beginning to follow Jesus."

They prayed for each other, chose the spiritual discipline of solitude, and went out into the cold. Joe wondered if he would get to use what they were talking about on his upcoming mission project.

Suggested resource:
Bill Hybels and Mark Mittelberg, *Becoming a Contagious Christian*, Zondervan, 1994.

CHAPTER 20

OBJECTIONS TO THE GOSPEL

Joe was already seated at the table enjoying his cup of steaming hot coffee when Matt came in. Matt got some coffee and came over and joined him.

"I see you already got some chocolate chip cookies," Matt said by way of 'hello.'

"Yes, I did," Joe replied. "You look like you're tired. Have they been working you overtime already at Widget?"

"Not exactly," Matt answered. "One of my direct reports, John, is a younger guy. He left early on Friday because his mom is in the hospital. I asked him to keep me posted. Saturday she took a turn for the worse. He called me Saturday evening to let me know things didn't look good. I've been looking for an opportunity to be God's man at Widget. I thought hospitals aren't really my thing, but I'll go down and see John at the hospital. When I got there, his mom had been put in intensive care. Only immediate family was allowed in and then only for a limited time, so there was lots of sitting in the waiting room. I sat with John and waited.

"He was surprised to see me. After talking about the game, the weather, and his mom's medical condition, he thanked me for coming. He was genuinely touched. He told me some other people at work knew his mom was in the hospital, but no one had ever come down to the hospital to visit. Then John surprised me by asking me why I came. I said, 'This may surprise you, but I care what happens to you and your family.' John was curious, and he said, 'I've just met you. You're my boss. I've known lots of other people at Widget for a lot longer, and they haven't come. Why do you care?'

"I remember thinking that what I said next could be crucial. God had opened a door for me in this man's life, and God was giving me a chance to be his man at Widget. I quickly prayed, 'Give me help with the right words' because I hadn't foreseen this conversation coming. I told him I care because God cares about him, and I'm just trying to be God's arms and legs, hands and feet.

"He asked me if I went to church, and I said I did. He said he didn't, but it was cool that I went. Then he said, 'I've always wanted to ask a church person why they think Jesus is the only way to heaven and why they don't think Buddhists, Hindus, Muslims, or Jews are going to make it.' I was thinking to myself, 'Couldn't he have started with an easier question?'"

"What did you say?" Joe asked.

"We'll get to that later on," Matt replied. "We had a good conversation around that topic. When we finished, he said, 'Those are some new ideas that I need to think about.' I said to him, 'If it's alright with you, maybe we can talk some more about that in a week or so.' That was agreeable to him, and then I asked if it would be alright if I prayed for his mom and his family. He agreed, and I prayed. He thanked me again for coming. I didn't get back from the hospital until early on Sunday morning. So how's it going with you this week?"

"Sue continues to amaze me," Joe said. "She wrote to the missionary that she sent the money to, asking what she could do here to help him there. She hasn't received a response back yet. Next week the AIDS awareness team she's on at church is having a dinner to raise awareness. They have a video they'll be showing that tells the story of AIDS devastation in Africa, and they have some after-dinner activities planned to help bring the information home. I don't know what they're doing because she wants me to experience it like everyone else. Do you have your tickets for the dinner yet?"

"No, I haven't," Matt answered.

"This is your lucky day," Joe replied. "I just happen to have tickets here for you and your family! Let's talk about the lesson for this week. You said we're getting into objections to the gospel, what's that about?"

"Before we get there," Matt responded, "did you work up your testimony?"

"Yes, I did," Joe said. "I'm not sure this is exactly what you asked for, but let me give it a shot: My life wasn't working. My marriage was on the rocks and the demands from my boss were out of control. I felt like I couldn't do anything right. My kids didn't like me. They were right. I didn't like myself either. I came over here one night to get away from the phone and the big fight I had just had with the kids and Sue. I sat staring into the steam rising from the coffee, but there were no answers there, no hope there. I wanted change, but I didn't know how to change or even what to change. That night, you saw me sitting there and came over and sat down. I didn't know you well then. Our sons had been on a soccer team a year ago, and I had talked with you some on the sidelines. You sat down and said, 'You look like things aren't going so well.' You asked me if I wanted to talk, and I said, 'No.' I wasn't going to spill my guts to someone I barely knew. You said that was okay, then you invited me to church by saying you had found answers and you would be praying for me. Then you went and joined your friends. The invitation put a new idea into my head—church. I thought, 'What do I have to lose?' So I went to church, and you left your family and came and sat with me. Over the course of the next several weeks, you answered a bunch of questions for me about God, church, and Jesus. Then you helped me pray the prayer to invite Jesus and all the stuff of heaven into my life. Jesus came into my life and brought love, forgiveness, hope, peace, and lots of help.

"Before coming to Jesus, I was full of guilt and shame about the things I had done that I thought were right. They seemed like good ideas at the time, but all those things had blown up on me. I thought they were right, but they just made a mess out of my life. I felt like the world's biggest loser and didn't know how to fix anything. My marriage was on the rocks. My kids didn't like me. My relationships with my extended family were a mess. The only relief I found was in the bottle at the bar I would occasionally stop at. That was very temporary relief and often caused more trouble.

"Since coming to Jesus, life has changed. I have peace in my heart. The guilt and shame are gone. I can look at myself in the mirror. I learned what I needed to do to patch things up with Sue, and the marriage is better than it has been in years. I'm getting along better with my kids. I've found the strength to say no to my boss. I'm working on my issues with my dad. I feel that my best years are now ahead of me. I still have a lot of work to do, but I know everything is going to be alright.

"Is that the kind of thing you were looking for?"

"That's great," Matt said. "It covered how you came to Jesus, what life was like before and after coming to Jesus, and you did it in just under three minutes."

"Do I get to hear your testimony?" Joe asked.

"Sure," Matt replied. "I was interested in this girl when I was in college. She attended an on-campus church that was made up entirely of college students. The minister was supported by area churches. Since Jennifer was going to be there, I thought I would go. So I went on a Tuesday night, and there were a couple hundred college students there. I liked what the minister had to say and how he said it. Maybe a dozen or so people I didn't know engaged me in conversation. I thought, *this is a pretty cool place.* I had gone to church growing up, but I never connected with what went on there. Here, it was different. They were drawing me in. I came back again and again. I started to make friends and got involved. I liked what they had to say about how God has a plan for your life and wants to use you to change the world. They talked about dating, money, marriage, classes, prayer, Jesus, reaching your dorm for Jesus, and mission projects. I found myself wanting what they had. One of the guys I met helped me pray to invite Jesus into my life. I lost track of Jennifer but hung on to Jesus.

"Before Jesus, I was self-centered, easily hurt, lacked confidence, and had no direction for my life. Since coming to Jesus, I've become God-centered and other-focused, have gained confidence and direction, and am far less easily hurt. During the nearly thirty years I've followed Jesus, he has not let me down. He has brought me through storms, healed hurts in my life, given me a wonderful wife and family, and has used me to help a lot of people. I wouldn't trade my time with him for anything in the world. I intend to follow him for the rest of my days. I can't imagine life without Jesus."

"Jennifer?" Joe asked. "I guess God does work in mysterious ways."

"I just want you to know," Matt said, "that I'm far from the only guy who has bumped into Jesus because he was chasing a girl. Most of us find our stories unremarkable, but I have discovered over the years that other people are fascinated by our stories. This doesn't mean I have license to talk about myself for hours on end, but God does use our stories to reach others.

"Okay, let's move on to the lesson and your question. Objections to the gospel are issues, obstacles, questions, and concerns people have about God, the Bible, or the Gospel message itself that they need to have answered before they can move forward. I have a list here of some the most common ones I've encountered. They are:

1. Being a Christian would be the end of any kind of fun, adventure, or excitement. Life would be over.
2. Does being a Christian mean I have to wear a loud sports coat, wear Jesus buttons, have Jesus bumper stickers on my car, engage only in Jesus talk, and generally be loud and obnoxious?
3. Isn't Christianity just a bunch of myths and legends that aren't really true?
4. How can you believe the Bible? It's full of contradictions.
5. I don't want to hear about God because a friend of mine died a terrible death of cancer. If God were good, he wouldn't have allowed that to happen.
6. What about all the starving children in India?
7. Aren't all religions the same?
8. If Jesus is the only way, and all the Buddhists, Hindus, Moslems, and Jews are going to hell, how is that fair?
9. What about all the people who have never heard of this Jesus? Are they going to hell too? God must be bigger than that, so there must be ways to heaven other than Jesus.
10. What if I call out to God, and he doesn't respond to me?

11. If I were to take seriously what you say, I'd have to make some changes in my life. I'm not sure I want to change.

"If you were talking with someone about Jesus, and they asked one of these questions, how would you respond?"

"I'd say, 'That's a really good question,'" Joe replied, "'but I have no idea how to answer that. Let's call my friend Matt and find out what he has to say.'"

"You could do that." Matt laughed. "But what if I don't answer my phone?"

"I guess," Joe replied, "we both would be stuck."

"Let's take a look at three of these questions and work on some answers so that you don't have to worry about losing my phone number," Matt said. "Which ones would you like to look at?"

"Let me look over the list again," Joe responded as he ate some of his chocolate chip cookie. "How about number five, which talks about cancer; number eight, which talks about Buddhists, Hindus, and the rest; and lucky number nine, about what happens to all the people who have never heard of Jesus?"

"I'm glad," Matt smiled, "you picked the easy ones. Seriously, those three are the tougher ones to deal with. Let's get started and dig in to number five. Let me state the objection again: 'I don't want to hear about God because a friend of mine died a terrible death of cancer. If God were good, he wouldn't have allowed that to happen.' This question, or objection, is basically asking, 'Why do bad things happen to good people?' Occasionally, it's stated the other way which is, 'Why do good things happen to bad people?' The classic way of saying that is, 'Why do the wicked prosper?' Sometimes it's stated this way, 'Either your God isn't all that good and loving because bad things happen to good people, or your God is good and loving but isn't all that powerful because he can't stop bad things from happening.'"

"How would you deal with that issue?"

"I don't have arguments for those things," Joe answered, "so I would have to say, 'I don't know,' or 'Let's call Matt.' I'm assuming you have a response, or maybe I could share my story saying, 'I don't know about all these things, but this is what God has done in my life.'"

"Those are good responses. Let's see if we can come up with some answers," Matt said. "First, we tend to overestimate our goodness, acting like we're saints and thinking God should be indebted to us for how good we've been. We just are not as good as we like to think we are.

"Second, we tend to underestimate our own responsibility for the troubles we're in. I had a friend whose father died at age sixty-six from lung cancer. He had been a chain smoker for forty years. My friend, in his grief, blamed God for his dad's death and turned away from God. The man had been killing himself for forty years and finally succeeded. How is that God's fault? How many times did someone talk to this man about his smoking? How many opportunities did he have to quit? Did he ever call out to God for help to quit and make choices to prolong his life?

"I knew a lady in her third bad marriage. She married alcoholics who beat her, took her money, and complained she wasn't working hard enough. She was blaming God for her bad marriages. I asked her if she had prayed about these marriages. I asked if she talked to anyone about whether any of these three men she married were good husband material. She said no to both questions. So I asked, 'How, then, are your bad marriages God's fault?' I figure in my own life maybe 90 percent of my troubles are a result of my own choices and actions. The other 10 percent are just the stuff of life.

"I know that sounds like a hard thing to say. The more I understand the kingdom lifestyle Jesus described, as recorded in Matthew 5-7, especially the parts about yes and no, board removal, asking, and the Golden Rule, the more I find myself responsible for the troubles I have.

"A third factor in all this is human free will. We cause trouble for one another by what we do. I think we would all agree the world would be a better place if God limited the free will of other people. We like to think, 'I don't need my freedom limited, but other people do.' Yet if our freedoms are limited, our humanity is diminished, because we're the total of our choices.

"I believe when we fully take the human factor into account, much of the human suffering that happens through natural disasters, child abuse, and things like cancer, about 90 percent of the bad things could be eliminated through making different choices.

"Now what about that remaining 10 percent? We have to ask God some questions. Does God promise anywhere in the Bible that bad things will not happen to good people? The book of Proverbs and some of the Psalms seem to come close. However, the book of Job challenged the thought process that God spares the righteous from having troubles in life. Jesus said his followers would be persecuted. Jesus told us to build our houses on the rock because the storms will come. If we build on him, our lives will still be standing when the storm passes. Jesus told his disciples, in John 16:33, that in this world, they would have trouble, but he has overcome the world. Many of the Psalms were written by people in the midst of the storms of life crying out for help.

"In Ecclesiastes 9:11-12 we read:

> The race is not to the swift
> or the battle to the strong,
> nor does food come to the wise
> or wealth to the brilliant
> or favor to the learned;
> but time and chance happen to them all.
>
> Moreover, no man knows when his hour will come:
> As fish are caught in a cruel net,
> or birds are taken in a snare,
> so men are trapped by evil times
> that fall unexpectedly upon them.

"I know, nice thoughts. We assume life is supposed to be just good times, and when bad times come to us, somehow God has done us wrong. But the message of the Bible is that good times and bad times come to all of us. The stuff of life is good times and bad times. What choices we will make? What will we do in the good times, and what will we do in the bad times?

"The choice God wants us to make with our lives is to invite him into our lives to do our lives with him with help from his resources. God would like us to give him thanks in good times and enjoy them. God would like us to call out to him for help in bad times, and cling to him while the storm passes. Sometimes it's the good times that will cause us to call out to God. So much good has happened to us, it's more than we deserve, and we look up to God to ask, 'Why are you blessing us in this way?' Sometimes it's the bad times that will turn us to God to ask for help. Of course, we can, in the bad times, take the advice of Job's wife, and 'curse God and die' (Job 2:9). In the good times, we certainly can say it's our own doing that's causing things to go well. What choices will we make?

"A final thought here is to ask, 'Does God have a plan for the bad times? Can we find a way to thrive in the bad times, or at least after we survive, will we be able to use the bad times?' Jesus tells us if we hear his words and do his words, we'll survive the bad times. Romans 8:28 says, 'And we know that in all things God works for the good of those who love him, who have been called according to his purpose.' The promise in that verse is not that the bad times are good, but that God can use the bad times to bring good to our lives. James 1:2-4 says:

> Consider it pure joy, my brothers, whenever you face trials of many kinds, because you know that the testing of your faith develops perseverance. Perseverance must finish its work so that you may be mature and complete, not lacking anything.

"The struggles and the bad times of life grow us.
"In 2 Corinthians 1:3-11 Paul writes:

> Praise be to the God and Father of our Lord Jesus Christ, the Father of compassion and the God of all comfort, who comforts us in all our troubles, so that we can comfort those in any trouble with the comfort we ourselves have received from God. For just as the sufferings of Christ flow over into our lives, so also through Christ our comfort overflows. If

we are distressed, it is for your comfort and salvation; if we are comforted, it is for your comfort, which produces in you patient endurance of the same sufferings we suffer. And our hope for you is firm, because we know that just as you share in our sufferings, so also you share in our comfort.

We do not want you to be uninformed, brothers, about the hardships we suffered in the province of Asia. We were under great pressure, far beyond our ability to endure, so that we despaired even of life. Indeed, in our hearts we felt the sentence of death. But this happened that we might not rely on ourselves but on God, who raises the dead. He has delivered us from such a deadly peril, and he will deliver us. On him we have set our hope that he will continue to deliver us, as you help us by your prayers. Then many will give thanks on our behalf for the gracious favor granted us in answer to the prayers of many.

"In this passage, we see Paul's response to hard times. He called out to God and found help, comfort, and deliverance. His reliance on God increased. He discovered that God's work in his life during the hard times made it possible for Paul to help others through hard times they were having.

"I can speak personally to this issue. These are not just words on the page, but they are my experience too. Mary and I lost our first child, a daughter, to crib death. Mary went to check on Christy one morning, and she wasn't breathing. Mary did what she knew to do, but Christy didn't respond. She called 911, and me. We prayed hard, but the paramedics couldn't get her to breathe either. She was gone. We were devastated. We blamed ourselves, each other, and God. We got past blaming and began to accept the unacceptable. We cried out to God for comfort and healing, and we clung to each other. God brought us assurance that he was taking good care of Christy. God brought healing to our hurts, wiped the tears from our eyes, and gave us hope for future children. It was a couple of years before we tried to have a child again. Then when we did, we were afraid, but there was no more crib death. Through all of that, we have grown closer to God, have been able to help others, have grown immensely ourselves, and are looking forward to the day we will be with Christy again.

"I don't like bad times, but I have discovered they are a way to experience the goodness of God, his grace and help, in a way that cannot happen when the sun is shining all the time.

"Often, when someone asks this question, they have experienced some deep hurt. They need us, first, to ask about what has happened to them and to hear their story. Then after that, we can share how God has helped us with our hurts and begin to unpack how life works."

"All of that was pretty heavy," Joe said. "I'm sorry. I didn't know about your little girl. But you're right—no one wants tough times to come. It does seem to be much easier just to blame God than to work through all this. But if hard times are part of life, it doesn't make sense to waste them. Are questions eight and nine this rough too?

"That all depends," Matt replied. "Question eight is, 'If Jesus is the only way to heaven, is everybody else—the Hindus, the Buddhists, the Moslems, the Jews, and whoever else—going to hell? And if so, how is that fair?'

"To start with, let's get Jesus' picture of heaven. What is heaven? The book of Revelation talks about a wedding, a bride prepared for her bridegroom, and a grand wedding feast. The wedding is a marriage between Jesus and his followers, whom he dearly, desperately, outrageously loves. Jesus is the bridegroom, and we, collectively, are the bride. There is a grand celebration that is out of this world, but the heart of the celebration is that there is now a new, deeper intimacy between Jesus and his followers. We know him better. We experience his love more fully. Our lives become wrapped up in his life more fully, more closely. And as a result of this, our love for him and each other grows incredibly. In this sense, heaven is the grandest of the fairy tale endings, where the handsome prince marries Cinderella, whom he has saved from the evil stepmother; and they live happily ever after in a grand marriage, where the hopes and dreams of the human heart are fulfilled in Jesus, and where he heals all our hurts. What is heaven? Revelation also talks about heaven as a grand city where the gates are made of pearl, the foundations and the walls of the city are built of dazzling gem stones, and the main street of the city is gold. Into this city, all the kings of the earth will bring the best they have, and the nations will be honored—not unlike the Olympic Parade of Nations. In this city, there will be no more dying, sickness, or sorrow, and all the tears will be wiped away. The nations will be healed, and all will live in peace with one another. There will be no night in the city, no sun, moon, or street lights, and neither will there be any temples or churches in this city, for God, himself, will be with them. He will be their God, and they will be his people. They will see him face to face. And God, himself, will wipe the tears from their eyes and heal each one. All of this implies that our God, the awesome God, whose creativity, imagination, engineering, tenderness, and love, who created this grand world in which we live with him, now has a grander world in mind for us, where we will dwell with him, and will know him, and will be known by him for all the rest of eternity.

This is tied up with the Christian concepts of judgment, hell, and heaven. Christian judgment is based on what we have done with Jesus. Have we believed Jesus and acted on what he has said? If we have believed Jesus and have acted on what he has said, three things will have happened in our lives: We will have invited him into our hearts to forgive our sins and make us right with God; we will have had a relationship with Jesus where we have come to know and love him; and we will have been doing the things he asked us to do, namely, we will have cared for those around us, and we will have invited them to be his followers too. For the one who has not believed Jesus, who has not acted on what Jesus has said, hell awaits. For the one who has believed Jesus and has acted on what he said, Heaven awaits. Entrance to heaven is not about being a good person and doing good things. It's about what we do with Jesus. Being a good person, and believing Jesus and acting on what he said, are two entirely different things. Jesus laid all this out very plainly in John's gospel.

"Heaven is an incredible place. Jesus, himself, invites us all to come. 'Put your belief in me,' he says, 'because I will not only show you the way through the gate, I am the way' (John 10:9, author's paraphrase).

"Is Jesus the only way to get to this place? Let's ask this question: Are the Hindus trying to get to heaven? Let's see. Hinduism has been around for thousands of years, coming out of the Indus River valley of Persia, and has no main teacher or personality that directed it. Hinduism has thousands of gods. Hinduism, like Buddhism, believes that one is reincarnated, again and again, forever. The goal of Hinduism is to get off the wheel of life. When one comes to Moksha, which is the understanding that one's purpose, one's goal, is to be one with Brahman, one begins to get off the wheel of life. Brahman is the cosmic force, energy, or power, behind the universe. Brahman has no personality but is a force. To be one with Brahman is to be absorbed back into Brahman. The Hindus describe that state this way—it's like a drop of water being absorbed into the ocean. It ceases to exist, as an individual drop is wholly and completely indentified with, and becomes part of, the ocean.

"The concept of being like a drop of water absorbed back into the ocean, and ceasing to exist as an individual drop, doesn't sound at all like heaven, where individuals live in a community of love and joy with God and each other.

"Let's ask the same question of the Buddhists. Buddha was born in 563 B.C. His name was Sidharta. Sidharta was raised by wealthy parents in a beautiful house inside a compound with high walls. Sidharta's parents wanted to keep the world out so that no negative experiences would mar their boy. As a man, however, Sidharta's first experience outside the walls was to see someone die. From that experience, Sidharta concluded that life was filled with pain, sorrow, and suffering. Sidharta had a Hindu background and believed in reincarnation. Life is a wheel, and one lives, dies, and is reincarnated, again and again and again, forever and ever. If life is full of suffering, pain, and sorrow, this reincarnation is a curse because one is doomed to suffer forever unless one can figure out how to get off the wheel of life. Buddha devised an eight-fold path that taught the way off of the wheel was to distance oneself from attachment and desire, because attachment and desire cause pain, suffering, and sorrow. It would take many reincarnations to accomplish getting off the wheel, but it is possible. Getting off the wheel is to enter a state called *nirvana*. It's a peaceful, resting state. The Buddhists describe nirvana this way: It's like snuffing out a candle. What happens when a candle is snuffed out? The flame is extinguished—existence ceases—there is no more pain, sorrow, and suffering.

"What the Buddhists hope to achieve is to cease existing, period. That is different from what the Hindus want. Further, that is very different from heaven. Heaven is where the pain, suffering, and sorrow are healed and cease so that we can live in joyful community with God and each other forever.

"Let's look at Judaism. The Jewish sects don't agree with one another. One faction believes that when one dies, that's all there is. Some others think there will be a messianic kingdom, the world to come, and a judgment based on what one did with God's law. Those are the concepts, but the details aren't very specific. Eternity and what happens after we die were not something with which the Old Testament was concerned. Those concepts are particularly absent from the first five books of the Old Testament, the books of Moses, on which Judaism is based. It's hard to tell, but I do know the Jews don't want to spend eternity with Jesus. They don't think he's the Messiah.

"What do the Moslems believe? Islam has concepts of Judgment, hell fire, and Paradise. On Judgment day, each stands before Allah and is judged according to what one did during his/her life on earth. If one's bad deeds outweigh one's good deeds, then one is banished to hell fire for punishment and/or destruction. If one's good deeds outweigh one's bad deeds, then one is ushered into Paradise. What is the Islamic Paradise? According to the Qu'ran, it is the real success, the house of eternity, the house of lasting joy and happiness, the house where there is no sorrow, no pain, and no death but just pleasure and enjoyment, and above all, there is in Paradise the pleasure of Allah on its inhabitants. More specifically, Paradise is described as a garden in which flow rivers of water incorruptible: Rivers of milk, of which the taste never changes; rivers of wine, a joy to those who drink; and rivers of honey, pure and clear. In it there are for them all kinds of fruits and grace from their Lord. It's drinking wine and never getting drunk. It's eating and drinking from dishes and goblets of gold. It's wearing silk clothing, and sitting on thrones and couches, and having lots of beautiful women. I think this sounds a little better to men than to women. But after a moment's thought, a woman would finally have someone to do the cooking and cleaning, the laundry, and run the errands. The Islamic emphasis seems to be that Paradise is Allah's gift to those who have done lots of good deeds in this life. That gift appears to be a giant party where one can indulge in all kinds of sensual pleasures without consequence. It's sex without complications, wine without getting drunk, and chocolate chip cookies without calories. All this comes with luxury and lots of servants.

"While Paradise and Heaven may look similar on the surface, a closer look shows them to be very different. Both have the element that the pain and sorrow of this life are gone. Paradise is a sensual delight, where one gets to indulge all one's senses and appetites to one's desire without consequence or restraint. Heaven is a joyful community of love with God and one another—the emphasis is not pleasure but fullness of relationships.

"Let's review a moment. Christianity is about a bottom line of living in joyful community with Jesus and his followers forever. Hinduism is about a bottom line of ceasing to exist as an individual and being absorbed back into the great world spirit or force. Buddhism's bottom line is about ceasing to exist like a candle with its flame extinguished. Judaism is about continuing to be the community Moses created. Since Moses didn't talk much about life after death, Judaism struggles with the concept. Islam's bottom line is an endless party of sensual pleasure.

"If we grant for a moment that each is a live option, then I would say we have four very different options and four very different ways of getting to those options."

"I never thought of it that way before," Joe said. "I always thought everybody wanted to go to heaven, and they just had different names for it. I thought the talk about Jesus being the only way was like arguing about who was a better running back, Jim Brown or Walter Payton. But that's not it at all, is it?"

"You're right," Matt responded. "Jesus is the only one who talked about heaven. Jesus is the only one who told us how to get to heaven. Jesus did not say, 'I'm right, and everyone else is wrong.' Jesus introduced the concept of heaven to a weary world and said if you want to go heaven, then follow him, and he will lead you there. If you don't want to go, that's your choice. If you're Buddhist, you aren't going to heaven. Buddhists aren't about heaven and don't want to go. They're trying to get somewhere else entirely. If you're a Hindu, you aren't going to heaven. Hindus aren't about heaven and don't want to go. They're trying to get somewhere else entirely. The same is true of the Moslems and the Jews.

"Jesus told a story, in Luke 14:15-24, where he compared the kingdom of heaven to a great banquet hosted by a certain man who invited many guests. When the day of the banquet came, all of the guests made excuses, and none of them came. So the man's servants were sent out into the highways and the byways to get people to come to the banquet. Jesus wanted us to understand that not everyone wants to go to heaven.

"C. S. Lewis wrote a little book, *The Great Divorce*. In it, a bus pulls up to the bus station in hell. The destination for the bus is Heaven. The fare is free. Although there are lots of people milling around the bus, when the bus leaves, it's far from full. When the bus arrives outside the gates of Heaven, not everyone actually gets off the bus. The gates of Heaven are open, and all one needs to do is to walk in. Those who get off, walk around some outside the gates, but everyone gets back on the bus to take the return trip to hell. No one actually enters the gates of Heaven.[i]

"Is it possible that God is far more willing for us to enter heaven than we are?"

"It seems that way, doesn't it?" Joe commented. "God sent Jesus to tell us about heaven and to pay the price so that we could go there. All we have to do is accept what God has done."

"Let me look at the hell side of the question a moment," Matt continued. "We have a sin problem. We want to make sin God's problem and say, 'We're good enough as we are, but God is narrow-minded and judgmental. If God were really all that loving, he would just accept us, sin and all.'

"Here's the sin problem: *Sin* is an archery term that means missing the mark. I take my best shot at the bulls-eye and miss. Sometimes I miss the mark because my best shot isn't good enough. Sometimes I miss the mark because I'm tired. Sometimes I miss the mark because I'm angry. Sometimes I miss the mark because I want to miss the mark. Each time I miss, I damage someone's life with my actions. This damage causes me to feel guilt and shame. The miss, the guilt, and the shame mark me. I can't face God. This is what happens in Genesis 3 with Adam and Eve. They sinned. They did what God asked them not to do. As a result, when God walked through the garden, they hid. God asked them why they were hiding. They told God they were naked. They had something to hide from God. When God asked who told them they were naked, Adam sold out Eve, and Eve sold out the serpent. In the moment that Adam sold out Eve, what happened in that relationship?"

"I would say it was irreparably damaged," Joe answered. "If I remember the story right, didn't Eve get Adam to eat the apple? I bet Adam was irreparably damaged by Eve's actions, which is why he was hiding from God."

"That's correct," Matt said. "We have Eve missing the mark and damaging Adam. We have Adam missing the mark and damaging Eve. We have both Adam and Eve hiding from God, unable to face him. If God takes no action, what will happen?"

"From my own experience," Joe replied, "I would say one of three things. First, Adam and Eve would go to opposite ends of the garden, build walls to keep each other out because of the damage that has been caused, and each would continue to hide from God. Second, they might try to repair the damage to each other by doing good things, but in the midst of doing good things, they would inflict more damage, never be able to do enough, and wonder if they could ever be acceptable to God or each other again. Third, one might try to make it up to the other, but the other would say it isn't enough and not accept the gifts or actions, and they would each try to convince God that the other was unlovable."

"None of those scenarios is what God wants," Matt continued, "so God acted. What Adam and Eve needed, and what we all need, is someone to pay for the damage we've caused. Jesus did just that when he died on the cross. He paid the price for the damage. His death bought each of us forgiveness. His death paid for the damages, which means if I let him, he will repair the damage in my heart, so I can forgive the one who did the damage. Further, it means Jesus paid the price for the damage I have caused, so I can be forgiven, so my debt can be paid, so I can stand in God's presence free and forgiven. Finally, it means the Holy Spirit enters my heart to make it possible for me to not sin.

"Heaven is where we live with God face to face and with one another in joyful, loving community. Without Jesus paying the price for me, I can't stand before God. It's not that God would throw me out, it's that I can't face God. I would flee the gates of heaven. Further, without Jesus paying the price for me, I wouldn't be able to live in joyful, loving community. I would mess it up and stomp out of heaven, mad at the people there.

"One more thing: Whenever someone is injured or something is damaged, the first thing we say is, 'Someone's going to pay.' Someone has to pay for the damage I've done. If I don't allow Jesus to do it, then I have to pay. The penalty is death.

"Without Jesus, I flee heaven because I couldn't face God, couldn't live in community with the people there, and I would be under the death penalty. If I flee heaven, the only place left is hell. God acted by sending Jesus so that this doesn't need to happen to me.

"How do Hinduism, Buddhism, Islam, or Judaism deal with the sin problem? Judaism offers a ritual asking forgiveness and a promise to make things right with the damaged parties. That helps, but the damaged hasn't been paid for yet. Islam says if we ask Allah to erase the bad things we've done from his book, he will. But this doesn't address the damage done to others. Buddhism and Hinduism do not address the sin problem. They talk about Karma. I create bad karma when I do bad things. It may take several lifetimes to work off bad karma. During those lifetimes, I have probably added to my bad karma. I think before the end of one lifetime, I could accrue an eternity's worth of bad karma and never work out of it.

"Hell is not the result of God's arbitrary judgment. It's the result of our action. God is doing everything he can to save us from it. The only problem is that we have to let him."

"That brings us to question nine, doesn't it," Joe said. "What about those people who have never heard of Jesus? Are they going to hell?"

"2 Peter 3:9 says, '[God] is patient with you, not wanting any to perish, but all to come to repentance,'" Matt quoted. "God is rooting for us. In Acts 14, Paul healed a lame man in Lystra. The people thought he was one of the gods and prepared to make sacrifices to him and Barnabas. Paul got them to stop with these words, recorded in verses 15-17:

> "Men, why are you doing this? We too are only men, human like you. We are bringing you good news, telling you to turn from these worthless things to the living God, who made heaven and earth and sea and everything in them. In the past, he let all nations go their own way. Yet he has not left himself without testimony: He has shown kindness by giving you rain from heaven and crops in their seasons; he provides you with plenty of food and fills your hearts with joy."

"In every culture and in every place, God has not left himself without testimony. God has left enough testimony everywhere that people may call out to him for help.

"This is the message of the first Beatitude, 'Blessed are the poor in spirit.' I know I'm not right with God. I know I've caused damage I can't repay. I know I'm lost and can't save myself. I need God's help. I don't how God will do it, but I can't do it. God honors the prayer asking for his help. If someone has prayed that prayer and thrown themselves on God's mercy, then when they hear about Jesus, they will embrace him because they will see him as the answer to their prayer.

"In Romans 4, Paul talked about the faith of Abraham. Abraham didn't know about Jesus. God had made a promise to Abraham. The fulfillment of that promise was Jesus. Abraham never saw Jesus, but he believed God would keep his promise. All who have never heard of Jesus have the option of the faith of Abraham to call out to God, who has left testimony to himself in all cultures. They call out to God and trust him to find a way to save them. Abraham and those who have his faith believe in the promise of God to be fulfilled in Jesus. We, who have heard of Jesus, believe in the promise of God to Abraham fulfilled in Jesus to save us. All history looks to Jesus.

"The faith in the promise to come may get me in heaven at the end, but the faith in the promise fulfilled begins to fill me with the stuff of heaven now. Faith in the promise fulfilled is so much better that faith in the promise to come that I need to do what I can to help make the promise fulfilled known everywhere for all who are calling on God to be saved.

"There's a lot to think about here," Joe said. "If it's true, and I think it is, then I need to get off my spiritual duff and find ways to communicate to my friends and neighbors about Jesus because without him, they're lost. He came so that they don't need to be lost."

"I'll be looking forward to watching that happen for you, your friends, and neighbors," Matt replied. "Take a sip of coffee because I have one more thing I want to run by you before we go. I want to talk a minute about the modern mindset, which as much as anything, is the religion of North America for those of us who are boomers and older. The modern mindset believes:

- Humans are basically rational.
- Humans are basically good.
- God is uninvolved.
- Morality is based on reason.
- Life can be managed by reason.
- Science and education are our hope for solving problems.
- All problems are solvable; progress is inevitable.
- Natural religion philosophy teaches all religions are basically the same.[ii]

"What are the problems this mindset poses to someone accepting the gospel?"

"If someone believes this," Joe answered, "then there's no need for Jesus. This is the stuff I thought was reality in high school and college. I didn't realize it was a mindset option. I thought, for a long time, it was just the way reality was. As I watched it break down in my own life, I thought there were cracks in it, but I didn't know there were other ways of looking at life.

"This modern mindset is not at all compatible with the kingdom as Jesus taught us is it?"

"No," Matt said, "it isn't. One of the reasons many boomers aren't in church is no one has helped them build a bridge from the modern mindset to the kingdom. Lots of kids grew up in church and the beginnings of faith, but went off to college and weren't prepared to deal with professors, authors, and philosophers who promoted the modern mindset."

"How do we help people get past this?" Joe asked.

"One of the ways is just laying it out like I did just now," Matt responded. "When we see it like this, we can see from our own experience it just doesn't hold up to reality. Another way is to help people discover in their own lives how the modern mindset doesn't work by just simply asking questions. The questions are:

- From your experience, can life be managed by reason?
- Are humans basically rational?
- Do you think all problems are solvable, and progress is inevitable?

Just ask questions, and people will take it apart for themselves.

"In dealing with any objection, leave room for God to work. You don't have to wrap the package up tight.

"Sometimes people use objections to avoid making a decision about Jesus. If you suspect that is what is going on, gently ask, 'If we could get answers for all your questions, would you invite Jesus into your heart and follow him?' Often that will get the person to tell the truth. Many times people will raise one objection after another because of a moral issue in their life they know isn't right but don't want to change."

The objections were finished and so were the coffee and the chocolate chip cookies. They prayed for each other and chose service for their spiritual discipline. As Joe left, he began to feel an urgency to engage his family and friends in spiritual conversations about Jesus and the kingdom. He began to wonder where Sue was with all this. He wanted her to be able to experience what was happening in him, and that community of joyful love Matt talked about wouldn't be the same without Sue. How could he talk with Sue about this stuff in a way that she would be interested? He didn't know, but he thought the first Beatitude would be a good way to start.

Suggested resources:
C. S. Lewis, *The Great Divorce*, MacMillan Publishing Company, 1946, HarperOne/HarperCollins Publishers, 2009.
S. Mark Helm, *Is Christ the Only Way?* Judson Press, 1985.
Don Richardson, *Eternity In Their Hearts*, Regal Books, 1981.
Philip Jenkins, *The Next Christendom: The Coming of Global Christianity,* Oxford University Press, 2002.
Michael Green, *Evangelism Through the Local Church*, Tomas Nelson Inc., 1992.
George Hunter, *Church for the Unchurched*, Abingdon Press, 1996.

PHASE III

PARABLES

MATTHEW 13

CHAPTER 21

SEEDS, SOWING, & SOILS

Matt spotted Joe in the parking lot. He put his hands into the shoulder-high pile of snow next to him and pulled out a softball-sized white projectile. He lobbed it in Joe's direction, landing it two feet in front of him, and laughed as Joe's shins were covered in its powder.

"Hey!" Joe yelled across the parking lot, "I spent all afternoon clearing this stuff out of my drive. I don't need any more coming my direction." Joe quickly brushed himself off and stepped inside the coffee shop before Matt could reload.

When they were seated with their coffee, Joe said, "What I could really use is some beach time in the islands with some sand between my toes, not snow down my boots."

"You gotta love it," Matt replied. "I find it very disheartening to think that spring training is scheduled to begin in a couple of weeks. Before you know it, we'll be listening to baseball, then we'll be watching baseball, and then we'll be playing baseball in the backyard with our kids. It's like summer is half done."

"There's something wrong with you," Joe said.

"How is it going with the counselor and the stuff with your dad?" Matt asked.

"The counselor asked me to pray for my dad," Joe answered, "and I have been. I've been praying for dad for 2½ weeks now. The first three or four times it was very difficult. But I'm starting to look forward to it. I've been praying God would bless him. I've been praying God would heal the hurt in my dad that caused him to treat me the way he did when I was growing up. As I have been praying that, it seems like my own wounds are starting to heal. My desire to see him seems to grow each day. I have no idea what I would say to him. As I have been working with the counselor, it seems my fear has shifted from being afraid of dad to being afraid of what I might say or do to him. It feels weird, but the counselor says that often happens. I've got a long way to go, but I feel like I'm making progress, getting a step or two closer each day.

"How's your coworker's mom doing?"

"It seems that after I left the hospital that night," Matt said, "John's mom took an unexplained turn for the better. Two days later she was moved from ICU back to a regular room. I think she's going to a skilled nursing facility for a few days to do some rehab, and then she'll be ready to go home. John says the change in her was very remarkable.

"I had some coffee with John on Friday. He told me he was thinking a lot about what I had to say about Jesus being the only way to heaven. He was also thinking about how the other religions don't offer a way to heaven because that isn't where they want to go. John said that got him to thinking about where he wanted to go. Prior to our conversation, John said he had only vague notions of a heaven with gold streets, lots of clouds, harp players, and good people. He wasn't sure he was interested in that and wasn't even sure he believed there was such place; but a place where tears were dried, hurts were healed, everything made sense and was alright, where people could live in a grand city, where the best of all the cultures and the treasures of all the tribes were celebrated, and where the people lived in peace with one another, fascinated him. The only thing that bothered him was God. Could God really be the center of a city with such life, joy, and peace? Could God really welcome him? He had always thought of God as narrow and judgmental, some kind of cosmic killjoy, who would take the fun and excitement out of life, with a sour face and a bunch of rules and regulations. I told him I thought of God that way for a while too, but once I got to know him, I found God was quite different from what I thought. John asked if we could talk sometime next week about what I thought God was like. I said, 'Sure.'

"How are your preparations coming for your mission project?"

"We had a league organizational meeting this week," Joe replied. "I get a list of kids next week, and practice starts the following week. They gave us devotional materials for each practice and game. They did some teaching on prayer so that we could pray effectively and comfortably with the kids. They gave us some coaching and strategy pointers and went over the league rules. Then they told us, when we get two weeks into the season, to call the parents of all the kids we have on the team. They said to tell each parent something good about their kid and that we're glad their kid is on our team. They told us those phone calls really connect with the parents. I'm looking forward to getting started and so is my son.

"How about your project?"

"Mark and I are going to start our job search support group next week," Matt said. "We have six guys we know for sure are coming and maybe some others. At the first meeting, we'll have everyone tell their story about losing their jobs and where they are in the process of finding another job. We'll pray for everyone's efforts. Then in the following weeks, we'll deal with some of the emotions everyone is feeling, talk about God's will, the role of work in life, and keep praying for each other. Like you, I'm looking forward to getting started.

"Speaking of getting started, tonight, we move into the third major teaching section of Jesus, the parables of the kingdom, found in Matthew 13. These parables help us see how God is working as we participate in kingdom mission. Before getting started with the first parable, which is the Parable of the Sower, let's look at what happens in Matthew 11 and 12.

"In Matthew 11, John the Baptist had some of his disciples ask Jesus if he was the one they were waiting for. You're right—that seems like a strange question for John the Baptist to ask. He was the one who baptized Jesus and who proclaimed to anyone who would listen that Jesus was the one. But at the time of the question, John was in prison. Maybe John was asking out of prison discouragement. Maybe John was asking because he had expectations of things that Jesus would do, that Jesus had not done yet. How did Jesus answer the question?"

"He said, 'The blind receive sight, the lame walk, those who have leprosy are cured, the deaf hear, the dead are raised, and the good news is preached to the poor'" (Matthew 11:5), Joe answered. "It sounds like he was using the testimonial approach with John. All this stuff is happening. What do you think?"

"That's exactly what he was doing," Matt added. "All the miracles mentioned are things the Messiah was expected to be able to do. It's not like anyone else was doing this stuff, so Jesus just told the men to look around and report what they saw.

"Evidently, out in the crowd around Jesus, there were questions about him and John the Baptist. The next thing Jesus did was talk to the crowd about John. He told them John was the Elijah who was to come. That was a connect-the-dots statement. If John was Elijah, who was the forerunner of the Messiah, what does that make Jesus?

"Then Jesus addressed what I call the whiney generation. Some people didn't like John the Baptist because he was a religious extremist, and yet the same people complained because Jesus ate and drank too much. After that, Jesus criticized the cities in which he had done most of his work to date because there wasn't change. They saw those incredible miracles and heard the amazing teaching, but Jesus was upset because after all that, there was no change."

"It doesn't sound like Jesus was having a good day in chapter 11," Joe commented. "As I look at chapter 12, things don't seem to get any better. In chapter 12, the Pharisees hassled him about his Sabbath activities and got mad enough at him that they began to plot how to kill him. Later in the chapter, after Jesus healed a demon-possessed man, who was blind and mute, the Pharisees said Jesus could do this because he was the prince of demons. After that, the Pharisees wanted Jesus to do some outrageous sign to prove he was the Messiah. Haven't they been paying attention? Didn't they see the same things John the Baptist's disciples saw? The chapter wraps up with a scene involving Jesus' mother and brothers. I don't understand what's going on there."

"The family came to take Jesus home," Matt replied, "because they thought he had lost his mind. They wanted him to come home and rest. I don't know what the brothers thought about him, but Mary knew who he was. The fact that Mary was there indicates to me that, like John the Baptist and the Pharisees, she didn't think Jesus was acting in a Messiah-like manner either. But Jesus didn't go. Rather, he redefined family as 'those who do the will of my Father in heaven.'"

"So Jesus had two rough chapters," Joe said in reflection. "People were disappointed in him. He was disappointed in them. They accused him of awful things and thought the worst of him. He said some hard things also, but he kept talking to them and kept trying to get them to see. I wonder if Jesus thought it was easier to open the eyes of a blind man than to get the Pharisees to see.

"Chapter 13 opens with Jesus going to the lake on the same day as the conflict with his family and the Pharisees. I wonder what state of mind he was in."

"We read large crowds gathered around him," Matt answered. "There were so many crowds Jesus had to get in a boat and push out from the shore just a little to be able to talk to them. The people in these crowds were very different from the Pharisees and his family. They seemed to hang on his every word and want more. I'm not sure how much they understood of what he said, but they wanted to hear him. Their eagerness to hear seemed to change the mood from the previous two chapters. He told seven parables in this chapter. Most of them started with a description of what the kingdom of heaven is like, and then, off Jesus went into his story. We're just going to look at the first one tonight, so let's read the Parable of the Sower and its explanation (Matthew 13:1-23):

> That same day Jesus went out of the house and sat by the lake. Such large crowds gathered around him that he got into a boat and sat in it, while all the people stood on the shore. Then he told them many things in parables, saying: "A farmer went out to sow his seed. As he was scattering the seed, some fell along the path, and the birds came and ate it up. Some fell on rocky places, where it did not have much

soil. It sprang up quickly, because the soil was shallow. But when the sun came up, the plants were scorched, and they withered because they had no root. Other seed fell among thorns, which grew up and choked the plants. Still other seed fell on good soil, where it produced a crop—a hundred, sixty or thirty times what was sown. He who has ears, let him hear."

The disciples came to him and asked, "Why do you speak to the people in parables?"

He replied, "The knowledge of the secrets of the kingdom of heaven has been given to you, but not to them. Whoever has will be given more, and he will have an abundance. Whoever does not have, even what he has will be taken from him. This is why I speak to them in parables:

"Though seeing, they do not see;
though hearing, they do not hear or understand.

In them is fulfilled the prophecy of Isaiah:

"'You will be ever hearing but never understanding;
you will be ever seeing but never perceiving.
For this people's heart has become calloused;
they hardly hear with their ears,
and they have closed their eyes.
Otherwise they might see with their eyes,
hear with their ears,
understand with their hearts
and turn, and I would heal them.'

But blessed are your eyes because they see, and your ears because they hear. For I tell you the truth, many prophets and righteous men longed to see what you see but did not see it, and to hear what you hear but did not hear it.

"Listen then to what the parable of the sower means: When anyone hears the message about the kingdom and does not understand it, the evil one comes and snatches away what was sown in his heart. This is the seed sown along the path. What was sown on rocky places is the man who hears the word and at once receives it with joy. But since he has no root, he lasts only a short time. When trouble or persecution comes because of the word, he quickly falls away. What was sown among the thorns is the man who hears the word, but the worries of this life and the deceitfulness of wealth choke it, making it unfruitful. But what was sown on good soil is the man who hears the word and understands it. He produces a crop, yielding a hundred, sixty or thirty times what was sown."

"We're just going to talk about the first parable tonight. Next week, when we look at the rest of these parables, we'll learn why Jesus told them. So let's ask some questions of this parable. What do we learn about the sower?"

"He sows seed," Joe answered.

"Yes, but look a little closer. Is there anything odd or unusual about this particular sower?" Matt pushed.

"Now that you mention it," Joe responded, "some of his actions do seem odd. This sower goes out and sows the seed everywhere. The farmers I know are very careful to plant their seed in the good soil of the prepared, plowed field. But this sower sows on the pathway, in the rocks, among the thorns and the weeds, and on the good soil. Either he's a careless sower, or he passes no judgment on the ability of the soils to actually support the seed. Because he scatters his seed everywhere, he seemingly has no concern about his seed supply. He doesn't act like he's going to run out. He seems to think he has an endless supply."

"That's good," Matt complimented. "So what is the seed? Is it wheat or corn or something else?"

"It's something else," Joe said. "Jesus told us in the explanation the seed is the message of the kingdom. I suppose the message of the kingdom would be: The kingdom of heaven has drawn near—change."

"Yes," Matt replied, "although, I'd like to play it out a little more. The message of the kingdom is that in Jesus we can be reconciled with God and live in the kingdom here, now, today.

"What do we learn about the soils?"

"The pathway soil," Joe responded, "is hard. The birds eat the seed. Jesus said if anyone hears the message and doesn't understand it, the evil one comes and snatches away the seed. How does that work?"

"I've had the experience of talking with some pathway people," Matt said. "The conversation turns to spiritual things, and I get a chance to talk a minute about Jesus; and as I talk, I see no lights on—their eyes are glazed. They have no idea what I'm talking about, and they aren't particularly interested in finding out. They're nice people, but they're without a clue when it comes to God. After the conversation but before they have a chance to think about what was said, the evil one arranges for some circumstance to occur so that the mood is broken and the conversation is forgotten or overshadowed by the next thing.

"The people who are like the rocky soil are different. They're glad to hear the gospel. They respond quickly. They jump in with both feet, but their response lacks depth. Just like plants in rocky soil wither under the sun because they have no root, these people quickly lose interest when things become difficult. I knew a businessman like this. He received Jesus. He started coming to church and joined a small group I was in. He was really into it. Then one day, he just dropped off the face of the earth. He didn't show at church or small group. He didn't return phone calls. When I finally was able to track him down, I discovered things at work had changed, and he threw all his energy there.

"What about the thorny soil?"

"Those people," Joe replied, "according to Jesus, get a good start and put down roots. But life gets in the way. They're worried about too many things, McWorld tricks them, and they don't bear any fruit. What does that look like?"

"There are a lot of people I know who are like this," Matt answered. "They have faith in God, and they are good people. But rather than trusting God with the worries of life, they take all the worries on their own shoulders and try to deal with them by themselves. They're people who haven't discovered the first Beatitude. They also get caught up in the McWorld race to have more, do more, and get more because they think that status, achievements, wealth, and possessions will validate their lives. Because they're full of worry and striving, they have no time to be a kingdom influence. To be honest, because of the worry and striving, being a kingdom influence is the last thing on their minds. They're just trying to make it through the day. Their lives look no different than those who have never received the kingdom message at all. No fruit.

"I like the good soil people Jesus talked about. They're the people who hear, receive, and understand—they act on his word. These people bear lots of fruit—a hundred, sixty, or thirty times what was sown."

"What is the crop Jesus talked about?" Joe asked.

"I think the crop," Matt said, "is the kingdom working in a person's life to develop kingdom character and to do kingdom mission in a way that plants kingdom seeds that cause other people to want to follow Jesus too. Rev. Jim walked me through all this a few years ago. Since then, I've taken about fifteen others through this, including you and the two guys I'm working with now. What was sown in me is reproducing in the lives of other people. Seven or eight of those early guys are doing the same thing I'm doing. They have each taken five or six guys through, who are getting ready to take more guys through. I'm thinking, when I hit twenty, I'll have a family reunion of the people I've taken through Jesus' kingdom training, and the people they've taken through, and the people they've taken through. I'd really like to see how many, who, and what has happened through their lives.

"Which one of the soils do you think you're most like?"

"I'm not good soil yet," Joe said. "I haven't reproduced. But I would like to think I'm on my way to becoming good soil. I've been trying to do the things Jesus said or asked me to do. It has been hard sometimes, but Jesus always seems to show up and do his work. I'm looking forward to becoming good soil.

"I have a question. If a person is pathway soil, are they always that way, or can they change?"

"I believe they can be changed," Matt replied. "I don't think we change the kinds of soils we are, I think that's the Holy Spirit's job. As we saw last week, God is not willing for any to perish. Someone who is pathway soil is so lost they don't even know they're lost. I believe the Holy Spirit is at work arranging circumstances, relationships, and conversations to soften the hard soil of the pathway so that they can receive the seed. In the rocky soil, I believe the Holy Spirit is at work removing rocks or breaking them so that a person's response can go deeper. I believe the Holy Spirit is at work on the thorns of worry and wealth, to pull them up by their roots, so that a person can become good soil. I believe the Holy Spirit works on the good soil to increase and improve the harvest.

"Just because someone is pathway today, doesn't mean tomorrow, or ten years from now, he will still be pathway. Maybe the reason the sower sows the seed in all the soils is that today, and with this seed, the soil may be changing.

"In this parable, who is the sower?"

"That's easy," Joe answered. "The sower is Jesus."

"Is it?" Matt responded. "What happens to the parable if *we* are the sowers?"

"If I'm the sower," Joe said thoughtfully, "then the whole parable changes. It's not about Jesus working in my life, but rather it's about me in kingdom mission. The four soils become the kinds of people I will encounter in kingdom mission. The four soils are the kinds of responses I will be receiving."

"So if we are the sowers, based on the parable," Matt continued, "I shouldn't be surprised or discouraged if some people show no response at all, if some people respond quickly and drop out quickly, or when some people get bogged down with life and don't live up to their potential; but I will rejoice when I hit good soil, and the seed has a hundred-fold harvest or even ten-fold.

"Jesus talked about four different kinds of soils or four different responses to the kingdom message. How many of these four soils produce a harvest?"

"Just one," Joe answered.

"What do you suppose Jesus was trying to tell us?' Matt asked.

"Maybe we shouldn't be discouraged," Joe replied. "Maybe only 25 percent of our effort is going to pan out. Maybe it's the old 80/20 rule. Twenty percent of the soil is going to produce eighty percent of the harvest. Maybe he wants us to be encouraged because the thirty, sixty, or hundred-fold harvest is a huge payoff."

"What's the most important thing a sower can do?" Matt asked.

"I think we said a sower doesn't change the type of soil," Joe said, "so maybe the most important thing a sower can do is go sow. The sower in the parable doesn't spend any time trying to identify what kind of soil he's sowing in. He just goes and sows."

"That's right—our job is not to fuss with the soils or analyze them," Matt added. "Our job is to sow. In the words of Bill Hybels, Jesus wants us to be seed-sowing fools.[i]

"This leads to other questions: What kind of sower am I? Does the message about sowing just bounce off me? Do I get excited about sowing and go sow, but as soon as someone gets upset with me or gets angry about God or the church, do I wither away and stop sowing? Do I have good intentions but never get around to sowing because I have too much work to do, too many family activities, and there is never time or energy? Or am I out there being a seed-sowing fool?

"If we are to be seed-sowing fools, how do we sow the seed?"

"I think I sow the seed," Joe said, "by living a kingdom lifestyle as described by Jesus in the Sermon on the Mount. By living this way, I'm going to get into a lot of conversations. I think I sow seed by being involved in kingdom mission. I'm looking forward to being with those boys in my league and getting to know their parents. I think I sow seed by getting in situations where my spiritual gifts are being used. I think I sow seed by displaying the fruit of the Spirit in my character. I suspect the first Beatitude is part of the answer too, which is to pray: 'I want to sow seed, but I need your help. Please set me up in seed-sowing situations so that I can sow seed.'

"As I listen to myself, it sounds like I need to develop a seed-sowing lifestyle, where the first thing I think in the morning is what seeds I'm going to get to sow today, and pray, 'Father please give me seed-sowing opportunities today.' Then I spend the rest of the day looking at the world through seed-sowing glasses. Are there seed-sowing opportunities with my family? Are there seed-sowing opportunities at work? Are there seed-sowing opportunities at the gym, at the restaurant at lunch, in the grocery store and anywhere else I happen to be? That's the mentality you described Jesus had when we talked about his conversation with the woman at the well."

"That's what it takes," Matt replied. "Let's encourage one another to be seed-sowing fools, and let's report back next week with the seed-sowing opportunities we've had.

"To close us out tonight, what do we learn from this parable about how God is at work with us in kingdom mission, and what we can expect?"

"I think," Joe answered, "God has given us a whole world in which to sow seed, and it's appropriate anywhere and everywhere to sow seed. I think God has given us the seed to sow. I think we can expect that not every seed is going to take, but the ones that do will have a huge harvest. I think I can't get any more out of this parable. That doesn't mean there isn't more in there, but I don't see any more."

"That's all I see too," Matt agreed. "Let's go up to the counter and see if we can sow any seeds as we get some chocolate chip cookies."

They went up to the counter. They didn't find a chance to sow seeds, but the chocolate chip cookies were good. As they ate, they kicked back and talked about guy stuff—cars, the game, projects at home—and enjoyed one another's company. Then they prayed for each other, for their mission projects, and to become seed-sowing fools.

As Joe drove out of the parking lot, he was glad for the time he and Matt spent together every Sunday evening. Matt had become a big part of his life, and Joe thought that was a good thing.

CHAPTER 22

WEEDS, SEEDS, TREASURE, & NETS

"My, what a difference a week makes," Matt said when he found Joe in the coffee shop. "Last week you were pelting me with snow balls in the parking lot, and this afternoon the temperature hit the mid-forties. I didn't know whether to work on my tan, play golf, or mow the yard."

"Wait a minute!" Joe laughed. "I was pelting you with snowballs? I seem to remember I was the one running for cover. It sure did feel great outside this afternoon. I waded through the mud and standing water in the back yard to pick up some limbs that came down in the last big storm.

"I saw Mary talking with Sue last night after the dinner and program on AIDS in Africa. They aren't planning to crash us tonight to force tea and scones on us are they?"

"No," Matt replied as he took a bite of his chocolate chip cookie. "Mary was very much taken by what is happening in Africa. The fourteen million AIDS orphans got her attention. Our house has always been open to the neighborhood kids, and Mary has a way of adopting the strays. Mary was talking with me later about doing something to help at least a few of those orphans. She said one of the reasons she took that job she did was so that we could have money to use for kingdom purposes. She said it's time we start doing something. I agreed with her. So one of the things we're going to do is

Coffee with Matt & Joe

give some money to help raise some AIDS orphans. Mary wants some more information before we give because she wants to make sure her gift counts. So I guess we're going to join you and Sue in the AIDS orphans business."

"Great," said Joe. "Sue was really pumped after the dinner. In addition to Mary, there were probably a dozen other people who came up to her wanting to give, but wanting more information. She started to work this afternoon looking for the kind of information people were asking for. Her interest in this still amazes me.

"Did you get your mission project started? Did you have your first meeting?"

"Yes, we did," Matt answered. "Mark and I were pleased to have six guys and two women out for the first job finders support group meeting. I think only one of them is actively involved in a church. Mark and I each shared briefly how we had lost our jobs and how long it took us to find another job. Then we had the others in the group share how they lost their jobs and how long they had been unemployed.

"I forgot how much you can learn about someone by listening to the story they tell. We heard several victim stories and some villain stories. Only one person told a healthy story, where she accepted some responsibility for the job loss as well as placing some responsibility on the management. We had planned to deal with some emotions the first night, but as Mark and I heard the stories, we looked at each other and changed plans. We talked about the stories we tell ourselves. We talked about the villain story, the victim story, and the helpless story. We talked about the board removal work Jesus asked us to do, which involves taking responsibility for our part in the things that happen in our lives. It was a difficult concept to communicate, but as Mark shared how he wasn't able to go forward with his job search until he got his story straightened out, people began to understand. Mark asked me to close by praying for all who came and for their job search. Since I had the last word, I asked if each of them would pray for their former employers this week. I said, 'If you aren't used to praying, that's okay. Just give it a try, and ask God to bless your former employer.' No one rushed out. People hung around and talked with each other, Mark, and me for nearly another half hour. It was good. I can hardly wait until next week.

"Did you get the names of the kids on your basketball team?"

"I did," Joe said. "Bob, my son, was real excited about who was going to be on the team with him. I call the kids tomorrow night for the first practice. I explained to Bob this team was about more than playing basketball. I told him that along with basketball, I wanted to communicate to the players that God loves them and wants to help them with their lives. It occurred to me that although Bob has come to church with me a few times, this was the first spiritual conversation I ever had with him. Bob asked me if it's really true God loves us and wants to help us. He said he thought God, if he existed at all, lived way out there somewhere, didn't care about us at all, and probably didn't even think about us because he has so many other things to do. After the way I've been raising him, I'm not surprised he thinks that way. So I shared my testimony with my son. He said he noticed a difference in me but didn't know what it was and didn't know how to ask me about it. Maybe I'm going to influence my own son as much as the other kids on the team. I've been praying for each of the boys on the list, and I'm looking forward to the calls tomorrow night.

"Did you talk any more with that guy at work?"

"John?" Matt replied. "We had some more coffee on Thursday. John asked me what I thought God was like. I told him I thought God was like Jesus. Jesus spent a lot of his time helping people by healing them and teaching them. I said I think God wants to help us with our lives by giving us the resources to do for us what we can't do for ourselves and to teach us how to live more productively. I mentioned that Jesus got invited to a lot of parties. It seemed once people met Jesus, they wanted to have him around. I think once we get to know God, we want to have him around and spend time with him. I went on some more. John was blown away by the concept. He had never connected God with Jesus and really knows little about either, but the idea that God could add value to our lives was a totally new idea to him. I gave him the Bible I have in my office, asked him to read John's gospel, and said we could talk some more. He said that sounded good to him. We'll see what happens.

"How's it going with the counselor?"

"It's still uncomfortable," Joe responded. "The counselor asked me point blank what I was afraid I would say or do if I were to sit down with my dad. As he asked me the question, the dreams flooded my mind with images of my kicking my dad until he stopped moving, then kicking him some more. I shared that with the counselor and went on to say I would yell at him, demanding an answer for why he treated me the way he did. I said I was afraid that after yelling at him, I wouldn't wait for his answer before I began to punch and kick him without mercy.

"Then the counselor asked me what I would like to have happen if I sat down with my dad. I said I'd like to know why he beat me. I'd like to know if he hated and despised me like I've thought all these years, or if what my mom said was true—he thought I was the best thing that had ever happened to him. If what mom said was true, then I want to know why things happened the way they did.

"The counselor asked me two more questions after that. First, he asked me what I need to do so that I won't lay into my dad like I'm afraid I will. Then, he asked if I would be able to handle my dad's answers to the questions. The answer I gave to the first question was that maybe I need God to do some more healing, and maybe I would need someone else present to help me stay under control. The answer to the second question was, 'I don't know.' The counselor prayed with me about those two questions and then gave me homework to pray about those questions myself.

"As I left the counselor, I was thankful that whatever I've messed up in my relationships with my children, those relationships are in far better shape than the relationship I have with my father. I shared with you a conversation Bob and I had. I couldn't imagine having the same kind of conversation with my dad.

"So what do we have on tap tonight?"

"Parables," Matt replied. "We looked at the Parable of the Sower last week in Matthew 13. Tonight we're going to look at the other six parables Jesus told in that chapter. Here we go with the first one, which is called the Parable of the Weeds. It's in verses 24-30:

Jesus told them another parable: "The kingdom of heaven is like a man who sowed good seed in his field. But while everyone was sleeping, his enemy came and sowed weeds among the wheat, and went away. When the wheat sprouted and formed heads, then the weeds also appeared.

"The owner's servants came to him and said, 'Sir, didn't you sow good seed in your field? Where then did the weeds come from?'

"'An enemy did this,' he replied.

"The servants asked him, 'Do you want us to go and pull them up?'

"'No,' he answered, 'because while you are pulling the weeds, you may root up the wheat with them. Let both grow together until the harvest. At that time I will tell the harvesters: First collect the weeds and tie them in bundles to be burned; then gather the wheat and bring it into my barn.'"

"Is there anything unexpected that happens in the parable?"

"Yes," Joe answered. "I see two unexpected things. The first is that someone would go to the trouble to get weed seed and then go out in the middle of the night and plant it. I mean, you gotta stay up nights thinking to come up with something like that. The second unexpected thing is almost as shocking to me as the first. The owner says to let the weeds grow and sort it all out at harvest time. I understand his concern about pulling up the wheat, but to sit and do nothing would drive me crazy. I guess they didn't have crop dusters that spray the fields for bugs and weeds."

"It drives me crazy too," Matt agreed. "What does this parable tell us about the kingdom?"

"I think the parable tells us there are forces at work besides the kingdom," Joe replied. "I don't know exactly what those forces are or how they work, but other things are going on besides the kingdom.

"I think the parable tells us that sometimes we can do everything right, and things still get messed up. The servants prepared the field and sowed the wheat. They did their jobs and probably did them well. But even with their best efforts, the enemy came at night, when no one was looking, and sowed the weeds. I sometimes feel that way. I do something, and do it well, and suddenly there's trouble. Where did the weeds come from? Does the parable tell us anything else?"

"Yes," Matt said. "The owner isn't worried about his wheat. He's not afraid the weeds are going to cause the wheat to cease being wheat. The owner trusts the harvest and judgment process to sort everything out. He knows that in the end, he will be able to tell the wheat from the weeds, and the weeds will not overcome the wheat during the growing season. Something else here that is helpful is the kingdom is about planting seeds, not pulling weeds. Not everything has to be perfect. In spite of all the imperfections, the harvest comes, and the wheat bears fruit. The enemy actions were not able to prevent harvest time and the growth of the wheat.

"What are we to do as a result of the parable?"

"The first thing that jumps out at me," Joe answered, "is that we're not to spend all of our time pulling weeds. I don't have to go around making sure everyone is doing everything just right. I don't have to push pearls. I can trust God with the judgment to make everything right. I can also trust God that the crop he's planting and the work he asks us to do can withstand the enemy's attempts to destroy it. I suppose I can be patient with others and their efforts and even myself."

"Something else that occurs to me," Matt added, "is that I don't have to spend my time deciding who is a weed and who is wheat. They will show me by their actions. This is like another one of Jesus' parables where he said a good tree can't bear bad fruit, and a bad tree can't bear good fruit. Even though the weeds and wheat may look alike for a while, they show what they are by their fruit at harvest. This gets me out of judgment mode. When it becomes apparent what a person is by his actions, then I can act appropriately.

"I suppose this means, at some point, someone is going to try to mess up, or actually succeed at messing up, whatever kingdom stuff I'm doing for God. I need to keep going and keep doing my kingdom work. I need to keep doing what it is God has called me to do, not go off pulling weeds. I can trust God with the weeds. He knows and will take of the problem, and if he wants me to do anything about the weeds, he will tell me. I find that to be very freeing.

"As his disciples asked him to explain the parable, in verses 36-43, Jesus' explanation gives cause for self-examination. He wants us to ask ourselves if we are weeds or wheat. He wants us to know there is a judgment coming, and we will have to account for ourselves. Are we weeds or wheat? I think Jesus made very clear, at the end of the Sermon on the Mount, the difference between weeds and wheat. Those who are wheat are those who hear his words and do them. Those who are weeds are those who hear his words and don't do them. The judgment on those who are weeds is terrible. They are thrown into the fiery furnace where there is weeping and gnashing of teeth. The wheat, however, will shine like the sun in the kingdom of their father. Jesus ends this explanation with one of his signature closings, 'He who has ears, let him hear.'

"Many have tried to soft pedal, down play, explain away, or protest this judgment picture. Yet, it's a concept Jesus used several times. He wants us to understand that this life matters, and we have to give an account for it to the One who made us. We do not live to ourselves. Our lives are not our own."

"I have to admit," Joe said, "this sounds harsh. While I certainly want to be wheat and am trying to be, I'm not comfortable with his words here. Can you say some more about them?"

"Judgment is not my favorite subject either," Matt replied, "but I'll try. Judgment says my life is important to God. My life is so important to God that he has taken a personal interest in it. Whether the judgment is negative or positive, at this point, doesn't matter. What matters is that my life, all of our lives, are important enough to God that he examines them.

"I remember writing a long paper for a class in college. We had to have references, bibliographies, footnotes, and no typos. This was before personal computers. I spent hours working on that paper and paid one of the girls in the apartment next door a month's worth of pizza money to type it and make it look pretty. I had to rush to class to get it in on time. The prof gave us the papers back two weeks later. All mine had on it was a check mark in the upper right hand corner of the title page. There was not a mark, not a comment on the entire rest of the paper. I'm not even sure he read it. I was furious. I had put forth all that time and effort for nothing. A paper that received an *F*, all marked up in red, with comments written all over it, would have been a whole lot better than the wasted effort of it not even being read.

"God values each of us enough to read our lives. He reads every word, every nuance, and even reads between the lines.

"Jesus said the angels will weed out of the kingdom everything that causes sin and all who do evil. As we saw a couple of weeks ago, sin is an archery term that has to do with missing the mark. Each time I miss the mark, I cause damage to another and to myself. The damage I cause is beyond my ability to repair, so this damage results in hurts and wounds in the lives of other people that cause them to miss the mark in their anger and pain, and then guilt and shame in my life cause me to further miss the mark. The penalty for missing the mark is death. That may sound harsh, but that is exactly the penalty we have tried to collect from each other down through history. Damage is caused. As soon as the cry of pain ends, the cry of vengeance begins. That cry shouts loudly, 'Someone has to pay.' The payment that is demanded is death. We kill the offending party and, sometimes, his or her family, friends, and neighbors.

"I have a hard time hitting the mark even when I'm having a good day, but according to Jesus, there are people who go about deliberately trying to get me to miss. Sometimes they distract me just before I release my shot, and sometimes, they foul me by grabbing my arm or bumping into me. Some people are so subtle about it I don't even know they have messed me up, and others are so crude there's no doubt about their actions or intent. I think we can all agree that if death is the penalty for those who miss the mark, and the damage is irreparable by us, then those who cause others to miss the mark should have an even greater penalty.

"I should think so," Joe agreed. "I bet those who do evil are the people who live looking to inflict damage or those so self-absorbed they don't even care about the damage they're causing. They should get nailed too."

"The only problem is," Matt replied, "to some extent or another, we're all guilty of doing those things. In my younger, less wise years, people came to me for advice, and I loaded them up to do more damage. There have been times when I have been like a bull in a china shop, not caring whom I harmed or why—I just wanted what I wanted when I wanted it.

"God's judgment for this behavior is the burning fiery furnace. The image Jesus used here is of weeds being burned. Weeds are burned because they're without value and are harmful. In other places, Jesus used the concept of Gehenna. Gehenna was the garbage dump outside Jerusalem. In it was a fire that burned 24/7, so anyone could take out their trash anytime. The judgment of God on a life that behaves as we have been talking about is as if God were saying, 'I gave you the gift of life, and you have taken something of supreme value and trashed it. You, by your own actions, have made your life worthless and toxic.'

"Jesus wants us to understand that God knows exactly what we've done. God is not ignorant of our lives. God can't be bribed, bought off, blackmailed, or manipulated. Nor does God wink at our actions and give us a pass because we're cute, handsome, smart, rich, or whatever. God is the judge of all the earth, and he does what is right.

"As we have seen before, one of the reasons Jesus came to planet earth is to declare the love of God to us who deserve to die. God doesn't want us to end up on the trash heap of eternity. Jesus died on the cross to pay the penalty for us. As we ask Jesus to pay the penalty for us, accept his actions on our behalf, and live into the change that the kingdom brings, the judgment God makes on our lives is different. For in Jesus, we increase the value and the worth of the gift of life that God has given us. A life of increasing value is a life that resembles the kingdom lifestyle Jesus laid out in the Sermon on the Mount and is involved in kingdom mission as Jesus described in Matthew 10.

"The weeping and gnashing of teeth Jesus talked about, going on in the fiery furnace, is the sound of people whining and complaining because of the judgment passed on their lives. They maintain the judgment of God on their life was unfair, they didn't deserve what happened to them, and on and on. I picture it not much different than the professional basketball player protesting a call against him. The replay is up on the big screen for all to see the obvious foul, but the player maintains he didn't do it.

"The warning of the coming judgment is an act of mercy on the part of Jesus. He warns us what is coming so that we don't have to go there. But we must act on his words. Let him who has ears to hear, hear. Some of us do hear. Others refuse to believe that such judgment awaits. Still others refuse to believe that such a judgment could be rendered on their lives because they aren't ax murderers.

"I'm glad it's not my job to do the judging. I'm also glad it's not my job to convince people that this judgment scene Jesus described is real or how it will all play out. I just sow the seed. I just share what Jesus said. The rest is between them and God. I'm also glad, as somber as this whole judgment thing is, God is not willing that any should perish. However, God does give us a say in what happens in our lives and to our lives, and while God is not willing that any of us should perish, some of us choose to perish anyway. That's a tragedy I think breaks God's heart.

"Had enough? I thought so.

"Let's look at the next parable, in 13:31-32:

> He told them another parable: "The kingdom of heaven is like a mustard seed, which a man took and planted in his field. Though it is the smallest of all your seeds, yet when it grows, it is the largest of garden plants and becomes a tree, so that the birds of the air come and perch in its branches."

"What unexpected thing happens in this parable?"

"The unexpected thing I see in this parable," Joe answered, "is how such a small seed can grow into a large plant. Sue was doing something with mustard seeds early this week, and they are very small. I'm always amazed by how a huge oak tree comes from just a little acorn."

"What does this tell us about the kingdom?" Matt asked.

"It starts small but grows big," Joe said.

"Let's expand on that for a minute," Matt continued. "I'm not all that familiar with mustard plants, so let's talk about oak trees. An oak tree comes from a single acorn. How many acorns does a full size oak produce each year?"

Joe shrugged his shoulders.

"I have no idea either, but my guess is hundreds. I know at least that many fall on my deck from the oak tree out back every year. Now suppose, this year, every acorn from the oak tree in my back yard is planted and becomes an oak. How many acorns will be produced by those trees? How many more trees will be produced from those trees? It staggers my imagination, and I'm just thinking of the acorns from the first oak tree for just one year, but this process goes on throughout its lifetime. So from a small seed, we get this huge tree, and the seeds for a kazillion more, over the course of a few years.

"The kingdom of heaven is like that. It starts small, grows big, and produces lots of seeds that will continue producing the kingdom over and over and over. There is no kingdom shortage. The kingdom runs an economy of abundance, not scarcity.

"Do you remember, three weeks ago, we talked about the domino effect with the kingdom? Jesus talked with the woman at the well. The woman at the well brought the whole town. Who knows the influence that town had on the region? This kingdom expansion began with a small, insignificant question, 'Will you give me a drink?' (John 4:7) to perhaps the town's most insignificant person.

"What are we to do as a result of the parable?"

"Don't despair over small beginnings," Joe replied. "I think, also, it means I don't have to reach the whole world with the kingdom in significant ways. All I have to do is plant a kingdom seed in a person's life. It can begin in very insignificant ways. So as we talked a couple of weeks ago, all I have to be is a seed-sowing fool, and the kingdom will have a huge impact. I can be a Johnny Appleseed for the kingdom."

"Let's look at the next parable," Matt said. "It's in verse 33:

> He told them still another parable: "The kingdom of heaven is like yeast that a woman took and mixed into a large amount of flour until it worked all through the dough."

"Let me do a little background work with this parable. The large amount of flour the New International Version uses here is actually a measure. The Greek text says, 'three satas,' which is a half bushel of flour. To say it another way, that is about 50 pounds of flour or enough to feed 100-150 people."

"I've got the first question,' Joe jumped in, "What unexpected thing happens? This is like the last parable. Something so small has a huge influence. But yet, it's different too. In the last parable, the small thing grew into a big thing. In this parable, the small thing has an influence over a large thing.

"I know—what does this parable tell me about the kingdom? The kingdom is powerful stuff. Just a little bit has a huge influence.

"I feel the last question coming. Here it is: What are we to do as a result of the parable? Just a little bit of the kingdom changes the entire situation. I don't have to unpack the whole kingdom or explain everything. All I have to do to have a kingdom impact is to say a kingdom word or do a kingdom act and stand back. The kingdom will take off from there.

"Something else that has occurred to me from these two parables is that the kingdom is not expanding or growing in some loud, noisy, flashy way. The seed develops into a plant underground and grows slowly, to our way of thinking. The yeast does its thing, and we don't really see it all happen. It just works. So as a result of my kingdom efforts, I might not see anything happen for a while, or it may appear slowly. I will want to speed up the process, but I have to keep my hands off, be patient, and let the kingdom work."

"You're getting really good at this," Matt complimented Joe. "Maybe there is some kingdom rattling around in you somewhere. Let's look at the next parable, found in verse 44. This is one of my favorites.

> "The kingdom of heaven is like treasure hidden in a field. When a man found it, he hid it again, and then in his joy went and sold all he had and bought that field.

"Since it's one of your favorites," Joe said, "you can unpack it."
"Alright," Matt replied, "I will. The unexpected thing is the man finding treasure in a field. He's kind of like a man who finds a

winning lottery ticket on the sidewalk. The man hides the treasure again, and in his joy, sells all he has to buy the field so that he can have the treasure. When the purchase of the field is complete, the man celebrates because the treasure in the field is worth far more than what he paid for the field. He also celebrates because the treasure in the field is worth far more than all his assets. He got the treasure for a bargain. There is no way he could have paid full price for the treasure. Now he has more than he ever dreamed he would have.

"The kingdom is like that treasure hidden in a field. The value of the kingdom is that God has drawn near with all the resources of heaven to help us because he loves us. Among other things, in the resources of the kingdom are the ways to get the most out of this life and the help to pull it off. We talked about all this in terms of the Beatitudes. Those with the kingdom have it made.

"This parable tells me the kingdom is found by people who weren't looking for it. They just stumble across it. God, in his goodness and love, has put the kingdom in places where people can stumble over it. If they stop to look at what they have stumbled over, they will make a stunning discovery.

"What am I to do as result of this parable? Since I've found the treasure, I need to stay focused on its resources so that I can live life with the joy of one who has a great treasure. Maybe if I live a life of joy, I might be what someone stumbles across.

"The next parable is similar to this one. We find it in verses 45-46:

> "Again, the kingdom of heaven is like a merchant looking for fine pearls. When he found one of great value, he went away and sold everything he had and bought it.

"Take a shot at it, Joe."

"Here goes," Joe replied. "It's similar to the last one. A man finds something of great value, sells all he has, and makes the purchase. But there are some differences. The merchant has been looking for a fine pearl. It doesn't look like the merchant gets the pearl for a bargain. He pays full price but is glad to pay it.

"There's not as much unexpected in this parable as the others. Maybe what's unexpected is that the merchant finds what he's looking for and is able to actually have it. I know a lot of people who don't know what they're looking for. I was one of them. I know others who know what they want, but it's always just out of their reach.

"I think what this parable tells us about the kingdom is that it's able to stand up to scrutiny. The merchant knew his pearls. I imagine the merchant looking at this fine pearl with a magnifying glass looking for flaws. I imagine him holding it up to the light and examining it from every angle. The kingdom, after careful examination, is the treasure it appears to be.

"Maybe what we're to do as a result of the parable is to encourage those who know what they are looking for to closely examine the kingdom."

"Okay," Matt said. "Let's take a look at the last parable. It's found in verses 47-50:

> Once again, the kingdom of heaven is like a net that was let down into the lake and caught all kinds of fish. When it was full, the fishermen pulled it up on the shore. Then they sat down and collected the good fish in baskets, but threw the bad away. This is how it will be at the end of the age. The angels will come and separate the wicked from the righteous and throw them into the fiery furnace, where there will be weeping and gnashing of teeth."

"There doesn't seem to be much that is unexpected here with the net and fisherman. Maybe the unexpected part is that we will be sorted just like the fish. Maybe the unexpected part is there is a judgment coming.

"Part of what I think this tells us about the kingdom of heaven is that its arrival on the planet, in the person and work of Jesus, calls for decision. I have to decide what to do with the kingdom. That decision is the most crucial decision I will ever make. To decide for the kingdom is to accept and receive the love and resources of God and to order my days in alignment with God's values and mission.

To decide against the kingdom is to reject the love and resources of God and to align my days with values and mission other than God's. One way brings blessing, the other brings cursing. One way brings life, the other way brings death.

"Like the parable of the weeds, this parable calls us to be ready for the judgment. This parable calls us now, today, to decide for the kingdom. This parable calls me to ask if I'm living a life of value to the kingdom and if not, to ask what changes need to be made. It's another wake up call.

"If we combine all the parables we have looked at tonight and add the Parable of the Sower, what is Jesus trying to tell us?"

"I'll give it a try," Joe responded. "Be a seed-sowing fool who is not discouraged by ground that doesn't bear fruit, who keeps sowing even though weeds come up in the field, who is confident of the power of the small seed and its effects, who rejoices in the great treasure he has found in the seed, and who is living life in harmony with the seed he sows. I need to be about kingdom business and planting kingdom seeds, all the while remembering that whatever happens, the kingdom is the best thing that has ever happened to me, and to trust God to sort it all out in the end."

"That's a good summary of it," Matt commented. "To look at it from another angle, I hear Jesus telling us God is at work in giving us good seed, preparing the soil, guaranteeing the harvest, and straightening everything out at the end. I like that I don't have to pull weeds, that I don't have to make the judgment calls, that the kingdom is like treasure, that small beginnings can have big endings, and that we have plenty of advance notice for judgment day."

"You promised last week," Joe remembered, "that you would talk about why Jesus used parables instead of coming straight out with what he had to say. So what is the deal with all these stories?"

"This stuff is hard to understand," Matt replied. "These parables are the clearest way to say the things Jesus was communicating. As difficult as it is sometimes to get at what's going on in the parable, I think we would have missed altogether what Jesus was trying to say if it weren't in a story. This is the kingdom in a child's picture book. If Jesus had put the kingdom in a text book or philosophy book, it would have been lost. Eugene Peterson, in his translation of the Bible, *The Message,* in Matthew 13:11-17, says it this way:

> He replied, "You've been given insight into God's kingdom. You know how it works. Not everybody has this gift, this insight; it hasn't been given to them. Whenever someone has a ready heart for this, the insights and understandings flow freely. But if there is no readiness, any trace of receptivity soon disappears. That's why I tell stories: to create readiness, to nudge the people toward receptive insight. In their present state they can stare till doomsday and not see it, listen till they're blue in the face and not get it. I don't want Isaiah's forecast repeated all over again:
>
>> Your ears are open but you don't hear a thing.
>> Your eyes are awake but you don't see a thing.
>> The people are blockheads!
>> They stick their fingers in their ears
>> so they won't have to listen;
>> They screw their eyes shut
>> so they won't have to look,
>> so they won't have to deal with me face-to-face
>> and let me heal them.
>
> But you have God-blessed eyes—eyes that see! And God-blessed ears—ears that hear! A lot of people, prophets and humble believers among them, would have given anything to see what you are seeing, to hear what you are hearing, but never had the chance."[i]

"I get it," Joe said. "I guess my prayer is to ask God to cause my ears to hear and my eyes to see that I might not miss what God is trying to show me."

"That's my prayer too," Matt replied.

They chose sacrifice for their spiritual discipline, prayed for each other and their mission projects, and then left for another week of sowing kingdom seed in the wide world.

PHASE IV

GETTING ALONG WITH EACH OTHER

MATTHEW 18

CHAPTER 23

LIFE TOGETHER: CHILD CARE

Joe hustled into the coffee shop. He was running a few minutes late. On his way out the door, Sue had asked him to run an errand. He always hated it when she did that, but he couldn't very well turn down dropping off a DVD about AIDS at Rick and Marcia's house. Of course, they wanted to talk to him for a few minutes, so he was feeling a little frazzled when he finally sat down with his cup of steaming hot coffee and a chocolate chip cookie at the table with Matt.

"I can almost reach out and touch spring," Matt said. "It makes me sad winter is about gone. I'll probably only get to use my snow blower once more. I saw the geese return, and the blue herons are back. In addition to that, I heard a spring training game on the radio Thursday, which is the surest sign of spring I know."

"You're a sick man," Joe said, relieved that Matt wasn't harassing him about being late. "I'm looking forward to getting my mower out of the shed and starting it for the first time. Did you get to talk to John at work?"

"I did," Matt answered. "There was a lot of stuff that went on at work this week. I think it's my second mission project, but I'm not complaining. I wanted to be God's man in corporate America, and I'm getting the chance. I had lunch with John on Wednesday. He had actually read some of John's gospel, three or four chapters. He had some questions. John asked if he was reading it right because it looked like the beginning of chapter one was saying that Jesus was

God come to live among us as a human being. I told him that was exactly what the text was saying. He asked me if that was possible. I told him to read on and see for himself. He said he would.

"On Tuesday, I had my second meeting with Kelly and the other four project mangers. I guess, at the first meeting we had, they were on their best behavior because a new kid was in class. Ed came in a whole lot later than you did tonight. Jane kept leaving the meeting to answer her cell phone. Tom was emailing during the meeting. Phil used the time to clip and file his finger nails. Kelly was called out of the meeting twice by his secretary. I got the distinct impression that everyone, including Kelly, thought this meeting was a waste of time. As all that was going on, I remembered Vince, talking about some dysfunction and how this division was underperforming. Kelly noticed my amazement and told me afterwards I would get used to it. I didn't say anything to Kelly, but I don't want to get used to it, so I have been praying for that group and asking God to show me how to help them become a team. I don't have any answers yet, but that's my big project. Until we can work together around that table, it won't matter how my team performs, the division will still underperform.

"How's your basketball team?"

"I'm excited about my guys," Joe said. "We might even win some games. But I know what you're saying about that meeting at work. I have ten guys excited about being on a team, even though they're far from being a team. I have a couple of big guys, a couple of little guys, one guy can shoot, and nobody plays defense. I think I managed to connect every name with a face and each name and face with their basketball skills. Did I mention we have a lot of work to do?

"I had fun with the devotion. Did I mention the devotion materials they gave us to use are from John's gospel? So I'm going through the same thing with the guys that you are with John. The devotion was to ask the guys what they thought about God and what God was like. Most of them said they thought God was far away, and he didn't care much about them. A couple of them had some God stories to tell from a grandparent, but mostly, they didn't know what to think about God. I told them I went most of my life without giving much thought at all to God. I told them I did most of my talking about God on the golf course after bad shots. Then I said, recently, all that has been changing. I took them to John 1:17 which says the law was given through Moses, and grace and truth were given through Jesus. They all knew about the law, the big Ten. They could only tell me three or four of the commandments, but they got the concept. They had no idea what grace and truth through Jesus was about. I told them *grace* means help freely offered from God. I told them the truth about people is that we need lots of help. Then I told them the truth about God is that he loves to help us. Through Moses, we get the law from God. Through Jesus, we get help from God. The idea that God would want to help us was a new concept for these guys. I told them about some of the help I have received from God through Jesus. Then I prayed for them and their families. It was a good night.

"How did the second night of your support group go?"

"We had a couple more people out," Matt answered. "We had a good night with them. We welcomed the new people and got their stories. Then we talked about emotions. The guys were like, 'Emotions...what are those?' But the women helped us. Everyone felt rejection, anger, loss, and worthlessness. We talked about those feelings in terms of the grief process of shock, denial, anger, bargaining, and acceptance. We also talked about how emotions are the energy that gives us motion. When we have lots of emotions happening all at the same time, sometimes we get confused and don't know what to do. Sometimes, in a loss, the emotions are negative and conspire to take us into a downward spiral of blame, self-pity, and depression.

"We talked about how to take control of these emotions and use them to take us in a positive direction. We talked about three ways to do this. First, let go of blame, either of ourselves or others, for the situation we're in. Second, ask this question: In what areas of my life does this situation show me I have an opportunity for growth? Third, begin to dream and imagine what to put in the empty space. Then we talked about the first two Beatitudes. Some of the people were on their way to making good use of their emotions. A couple were headed toward bitterness, one couldn't let go of anger toward the man who fired him, and one was depressed. We asked for prayer requests, and Mark prayed for everyone.

"One of the women, who was headed toward bitterness, talked with me a little while after we were done. She asked about Jesus. She had been attending church in her early thirties, but she got upset with women working in the children's ministry, and left, and hasn't been back; but she said she often wonders about the *God* side of church and if she's missing something. I invited her to come to church with us and see. She said she might."

"That's cool," Joe said. "You'll never guess what my counselor told me last week. He told me he wanted me to write a letter to my dad asking him if we could get together. I couldn't believe it. We had been doing all this talk about feelings, history, and reexamining stories. I didn't think he would actually get around to having me contact my dad."

"Isn't that the reason you're seeing the counselor?" Matt asked.

"Well, yes," Joe answered, "but I didn't actually think we would get around to doing that anytime soon. I know I've been working toward this for a couple of months now but to actually do it surprised me."

"Yes, I can see it did," Matt commented. "But have you written the letter?"

"You're getting as pushy as the counselor," Joe replied. "I have it written. It's a short letter. I told dad it has been a long time, but I'd like to see him if that's alright with him. I asked him to reply by letter."

"Have you sent it?" Matt asked.

"I already have a mother and a wife," Joe responded. "I'm going to put it in the mail box tomorrow morning."

"Maybe we could put it in the mail box on the other side of the parking lot tonight," Matt suggested.

"Maybe we could, but the letter is at home," Joe said. "Before it gets any hotter in here, what is Jesus up to this week?"

"I like the way you changed the subject," Matt replied. "Jesus is shifting gears tonight, just like you are. Last week, we finished the parables of the kingdom. This week, we move on to Jesus' fourth teaching section about kingdom community, where he talked about our life together. We find that in chapter 18 of Matthew, but before we get there, let's look at what Jesus did in Matthew 14-17."

"Knowing Jesus," Joe said, "I bet he did a lot. Let me look. Chapter 13 ends on a bit of a sour note. Jesus told the crowd all those amazing parables, and then he went to Nazareth. It looks like he taught the same kinds of amazing things because the people were amazed. But the amazement went south. It says they took offense at him. I guess not everyone is happy when the home town boy makes good.

"Chapter 14 doesn't start any better. The first thing I see is John the Baptist got beheaded. If I'm reading it right, it looks like John was executed because of some kinky dysfunctional family plot. Herod, the king, married his brother's wife. At least I assume he married her. There is a footnote in my Bible that says this woman, Herodias, was the daughter of the third brother. So Herod was married to his niece, whom he took from his other brother. No wonder John the Baptist was giving him grief. At a big birthday dinner, Herodias's daughter danced in such a way that Herod promised her anything, up to half his kingdom. I bet she wasn't performing a ballet.... The daughter asked her mom what to ask for, and Herodias said, 'The head of John the Baptist' (verse 8). So as not to lose face in front of his dinner guests, Herod had John's head brought on a platter. This looks like something straight out of a prime time soap opera."

"Yes, it does," Matt agreed. "When Jesus was given the news, he took his disciples and withdrew by boat hoping to get some time to grieve. But the crowds followed him around the coast and met him when he landed. Jesus, being Jesus, healed the sick among them, and by that time it was late. The disciples asked about dinner arrangements. Jesus said, 'You give them something to eat.' But the disciples said, 'We have here only five loaves of bread and two fish' (verses 16,17). The fives loaves of bread were five barley rolls, and the two fish were like sardines. We're told in John's gospel the food is actually some boy's lunch, which he gave to Jesus. So Jesus fed the crowd with the five loaves and the two fish. Matthew tells us the crowd was five thousand men plus the women and children with them. Further, Matthew tells us everyone ate and was satisfied, and there were twelve baskets of leftovers. This miracle is the only one recorded in all four gospels. It made quite an impact."

"I wonder if he can do that with coffee and chocolate chip cookies?" Joe asked. "This next part is one of my favorites. Jesus sent the disciples back out onto the lake in a boat. He dismissed the crowd and went up on a mountainside by himself to pray. In the middle of the night, Jesus noticed the disciples hadn't made it across the lake yet because of a strong wind. This part amazes me. I guess just like any son of God, Jesus just started walking on the water to go out to the boat. I can't even walk on water when it's frozen. The disciples saw him and freaked. So would I. Peter said, 'Lord, if it's you, tell me to come to you on the water' (verse 28). Jesus called Peter out of the boat. Peter got out of the boat, and he actually walked on the water too. Can you imagine telling this to your wife and kids when you got home the next day? 'Hi, honey. Guess what we did last night. Jesus and I were out walking on the water....' Peter did well until the wind started to blow harder, and then Peter saw what he was doing, and I can picture him saying to himself, 'Fisherman don't walk on water.' Then he started to sink. Jesus pulled him back up, they got into the boat, and then the weirdest thing happened—the wind stopped. Everyone in the boat worshiped Jesus, saying, 'Truly you are the Son of God' (verse 33). Feeding the five thousand plus and then walking on the water, Jesus just amazes me. Just when I think there isn't anything new for Jesus to do, he just blows me away. I do wonder, though, if I were in the boat, if I would have gotten out or stayed in."

"In chapter 15," Matt continued, "Jesus was being hassled by the Pharisees over what was clean and unclean. The Pharisees' position was that what is on the outside can make you unclean on the inside. Jesus claimed uncleanness comes from the heart, not food and the digestive system. The disciples didn't get the principle and asked about it. Jesus was surprised they didn't get it and asked them, 'Just how dense are you?' (Matthew 15:16, author's paraphrase.)

"Then they left that area to go to gentile country. A gentile woman, whose daughter was possessed by a demon, came to ask Jesus to heal her daughter."

"I saw that," Joe said. "What Jesus did with her is very un-Jesus-like. He didn't answer. The disciples asked him to send her away because she was annoying them. Finally, Jesus engaged her in conversation and healed her daughter. What's the deal here?"

"I think," Matt answered, "Jesus continued the clean and unclean discussion for the sake of his disciples. They were in gentile country, which was unclean. They were dealing with a gentile woman, who was unclean. You noticed Jesus didn't answer the woman. Now, notice the disciples' reaction. They didn't urge Jesus to help her. They had urged Jesus to do something about the hungry crowd, but they had no compassion, no mercy for this woman. They wanted Jesus to send her away. I think the conversation Jesus had with the woman was what the disciples were thinking. The Messiah was only for Israel. It's not right to take what belongs to the children of Israel and give it to gentile dogs. I wonder if he winked at her, or maybe there was something in his tone of voice that encouraged her, because she didn't give up. Jesus healed her daughter, and then he complimented her on her great faith. Never do we hear Jesus complimenting a Pharisee on his faith. I think Jesus was trying to show them a contrast between great faith in an unclean person and no faith in a clean person. I think Jesus was trying to get the disciples to think differently about clean and unclean. He was trying to show them the old definitions for clean and unclean were incorrect.

"Next, people got hungry again. So Jesus fed a crowd of four thousand men, plus the women and children, from seven loaves and a few fish. He did this after teaching and healing all their sick and disabled. It would have been a grand afternoon. The crowd got to hear some amazing Jesus stories, and the blind got to see, the lame walk, the mute speak, and the crippled were made whole. Then everyone got to eat Jesus' food.

"Please notice how chapter 16 begins. The Pharisees and Sadducees came to Jesus and wanted him to show them a sign from heaven to prove he was the Messiah. The sign I think they wanted was for Jesus to cause manna to come from heaven and feed the people the way Moses did. But as I read it, I have to ask if they missed what just happened. Jesus miraculously fed two large crowds. The blind received sight. That was something they believed only the Messiah could do. In all the miracles of the Old Testament, no blind people ever got their sight. Actually, I believe the Pharisees and Sadducees were very well informed about what Jesus had been doing. I think they wanted Jesus to jump through their hoops, and he wouldn't. Anyway, he told them they would get no sign 'except the sign of Jonah' (verse 4). In another place, Jesus told his disciples that just 'as Jonah was three days and three nights in the belly of a huge fish,' he would be 'three days and three nights in the heart of the earth'" (Matthew 12:40).

"It looks like things really began heating up between Jesus and the religious leaders," Joe commented. "After that, Jesus managed to get some alone time with his disciples. That seemed to be a miracle in itself. Jesus asked them who they thought he was. Peter responded, 'You are the Christ, the Son of the living God' (Matthew 16:16). Jesus gave Peter a gold star for his answer. Then he talked about building his church and the gates of hell. Can you talk about that for a minute?"

"Sure," Matt replied. "Jesus is the builder of the church. The church is not a building but rather a gathering of people who are disciples of Jesus. Jesus said the gates of hell could not prevail against a gathering of his disciples. The picture here is of hell as a fortress with barricaded doors, with people trapped inside unable to leave. The disciples of Jesus are the battering ram knocking down the gates of the hell. Hell can't stop them. With each blow of the battering ram, the foundations of hell shake. Most people in churches have the image backwards. They picture the church as the fortress with hell battering the gates, and they are hoping the gates hold."

"That helps," Joe said. "As soon as the disciples identified Jesus, he began to tell them what it meant to be the Messiah, which was to suffer, die, and rise again. But the disciples didn't understand. Peter told Jesus it wouldn't happen that way, and Jesus had to back Peter off.

"Chapter 17 has a weird beginning. Jesus took Peter, James, and John up a mountain, and at the top, Jesus was transfigured. Everything got white and bright, and Moses and Elijah showed up. Then there was a voice from heaven, and the disciples fell to the ground, terrified. After Jesus reassured them, he told them not to tell anyone about it until after the resurrection.

"When they got back down the mountain, Jesus drove a demon out of a boy the disciples couldn't help. He sounded a bit put out with them. Then, Jesus closed the chapter by doing something that really hurts: Jesus paid taxes. I like the way he raised the money to do it though. I'm doing my taxes in a couple of weeks. Maybe I'll go fishing and see if I can catch anything that helps."

"Maybe I'll come too," Matt replied. "All of that brings us to chapter 18 where Jesus talked about life together. It starts with the disciples asking Jesus, 'Who is the greatest in the kingdom of heaven?' Who is the greatest? Where does that question come from?"

"I've never really thought about it," Joe responded. "I know our whole culture is built on being number one. I know I'd rather be on the top of the pecking order than on the bottom. So where does the question come from?"

"It comes straight out of the insecurities of the human heart," Matt said. "It comes straight from the garden of Eden. As we talked about this before, we said Eve handed Adam the forbidden fruit. They both ate. They both saw they were naked. They both hid from God. They both had something to hide. God asked Adam why he was hiding. Adam's response was, 'I ate the fruit, but it was Eve's fault' (Genesis 3:12, author's paraphrase).

"Adam admitted his shortcoming but tried to compensate for it by claiming he was better than Eve. The relationship Adam had with God was gone. Adam knew he didn't measure up anymore, and he thought this meant God didn't love him anymore. He wanted the love back. He thought if he could show he was better than Eve, maybe God would love him again.

"We see this again in Adam's children, Cain and Abel. Abel presented a more pleasing sacrifice to God than Cain did. Abel is number one, so Cain thought, in God's eyes. God likes Abel best. Cain, in all of his insecurity and striving to be loved and accepted, thought God could only love number one. Cain killed Abel so that he would be number one.

"Behind all the striving to be number one, to be the greatest, is the attempt to show God we're better than everyone else, so he should love and accept us. We know who we are and what we have done. We can't erase it or change it. We're stuck with it. Since we can't change it, our next option is to look better than the next guy. If I can be number one at something, anything, then I can say to God, 'I may be messed up, but I'm better at this than anyone else in the world. That must mean, God, you have to accept me and love me.' Our desire to be on top of the pecking order, to be the greatest, is all about propping up our low self-esteem and convincing God, others, and ourselves that we're loveable and acceptable.

"The sad part of all this is that God already loves us. We don't have to be number one. Because God loves us, he sent Jesus to make a way to change our hearts and pay for the damage our past has done to others and ourselves. God's love is not a nonrenewable resource. God has an endless supply of love that far exceeds the love needs of each member of the human race. He lavishes this great love on each of us who will stop striving and just accept it.

"The disciples brought all of this to Jesus when they asked him, 'Who is the greatest in the kingdom of heaven?' What kind of answer did Jesus give them?"

"In verses 3 and 4," Joe answered, "Jesus said, 'I tell you the truth, unless you change and become like little children, you will never enter the kingdom of heaven. Therefore, whoever humbles himself like this child is the greatest in the kingdom of heaven.'

"I'm familiar with this kind of answer from Jesus. It makes absolutely no sense. How can being great have anything to do with little children? The thing about being humble doesn't make sense either. I'm greater than you because I'm more humble than you? This is typical of Jesus. I didn't say I understand what he was talking about. I just said I'm familiar with this kind of answer. So what was he trying to say?"

"Let's unpack it by looking at the status and place of little children in the world in which Jesus lived," Matt said. "In that world, children had no status and no rights. They were treated as property more than as people. The old saying that children are to be seen and not heard is an upgrade from the position of children in the ancient world. I have a friend who says that you don't become a real person until you're age twenty-one. Before that, he would say you have no feelings, no thoughts, and nothing you do counts because you aren't a real person yet. While I think he's kidding, that certainly was the reality for children in the ancient world. In that day, children were never held up as a role model for anything."

"Okay, so children are at the bottom of the list," Joe summarized. "But that doesn't help me. How does becoming like a little child, who has no status and no rights, cause someone to become the greatest in the kingdom of heaven? I still have a big disconnect here."

"Little children don't have status or rights," Matt replied, "but neither do they seek status or rights. Little children are oblivious to all that. Little children aren't interested in who is number one or winning. I remember teaching my children to play chess. They didn't care about winning the game. They would move their game pieces in ways that made no sense if they wanted to win the game. I would ask them, 'Why did you move that piece?' Each child would respond, 'I like moving that piece.'

"Hang on to that for a minute. Let's talk about the kingdom of heaven. In the kingdom of heaven, there is no shortage of love and acceptance. God, the king, lavishes us with so much love it's beyond our ability to receive it all. God loves us more than our capacity to receive love. I have pictured God sitting on a talk show host's chair saying, 'It's true—I love people too much.' God loves us more than we think we're worth. Further, there's nothing we can do to cause God to love us more than he does right now, and there's nothing we can do to make God love us any less than he does right now. I have another friend who tells me, 'God loves you, and there's nothing you can do about it.'

"This love God has for me is not dependent upon my performance. This love God has for me is not dependent upon my being better than someone else. Winners and losers, beautiful and ugly, good and bad, popular and unpopular are all loved the same by God.

"In the garden, Adam assumed his eating the apple caused God not to love him anymore. Adam assumed wrongly, and the rest of us have followed his bad assumption. God did not love Adam any less. Adam, however, felt separated from that love because of the guilt and the shame he felt for having eaten the forbidden fruit. Adam had no way to remove the guilt and the shame, and he had no way to repair the damage in his relationship with God caused by eating the forbidden fruit.

"But God, in his great love, has made a way to remove the guilt and the shame and repair the damage caused by our actions. Jesus came to die on the cross for us, to pay the price, to repair the damage, so that we could be forgiven. Jesus came to absorb our guilt and shame so that we could be free of it. As we accept what Jesus did on the cross and ask him to work in our lives, we become able to stand in the presence of God free and forgiven, and we feel his great love for us and can begin building a relationship with him. This work Jesus did on the cross and wants to do in each life, is offered to each of us for free. All we have to do is ask for it. Winners and losers, beautiful and ugly, good and bad, popular and unpopular all have the same access to the work Jesus did because all are loved by God. It doesn't matter if we're the professional baseball team that has won more championships than we can count or if we're like the little league team that has never won a game—God loves us. God does not value winners over losers.

"Here comes the disconnect. In God's kingdom, there is no number one. In God's kingdom, there is no greatest. The question the disciples asked, about being the greatest in the kingdom of heaven, makes no kingdom sense in the same way the answer Jesus gave makes no sense to us.

"The answer Jesus gave essentially says that the greatest in the kingdom of heaven is the one who is the least concerned about being the greatest. Little children have no concern about being the greatest. They are loved, and they are enjoying the world in which they live and they love."

"Wait a minute," Joe said, "that just doesn't make sense. How can I strive to be the greatest in the kingdom if the greatest isn't concerned about being great?"

"That's the point," Matt replied. "Give it up. Live in the love of God. Love one another. Do your best to do what God asks you to do. That's all there is. There is no one-upping. There are no winners and no losers in the kingdom."

"Give it up?" Joe asked. "I hear what you're saying about the kingdom and the love of God for us, and if I work at it, it makes sense. But having it make sense in my head is a long way from feeling it in my heart. This is a completely different approach to life. I know everything Jesus told us is completely different from everything else I've learned, but I used what Jesus said about anger in my quest to be number one. I processed that in terms of it being a better way to deal with anger, and I reasoned that if I can actually do this, I'll be better than all those people who don't even know what they're supposed to do with anger. So now the motivation is all different."

"That's right," Matt replied. "Having given up my quest to be number one in order to gain God's love and acceptance, I now live in his love and attempt to put into practice what Jesus said about anger because I love God and because I love other people. Applying Jesus' teaching about anger helps me to love in the way that I am loved.

"What Jesus said here, about not being able to enter the kingdom unless you become like a little child, is very similar to his statement in John 3: Unless we are born from above, we can't even see the kingdom (verse 3, author's paraphrase). Both statements imply that we need to start again. Both statements imply that our current mindset and assumptions are so contrary to the kingdom that the only way to connect is to throw it all out and start again. There is no way to connect with the kingdom as long as we try to number-one our way in. It's only when we accept the work of Jesus, on the cross, done for us, that we can enter the kingdom.

"In Matthew 20:20-28, Jesus had to deal with the issue again. This time the mother of James and John asked that Jesus give them the best seats in the kingdom, or in effect, declare them to be the greatest in the kingdom. The rest of the twelve heard about it, and Jesus had a big family squabble on his hands as they all began trying to out-number-one each other. Jesus stopped it by saying the greatest in the kingdom is the one who is servant of all. The whole reason to be number one is so that you don't have to serve anyone, but rather have others serve you. Once again, Jesus gave a disconnect answer because to be number one is a disconnect to the kingdom.

The greatest and the kingdom are like oil and water. They are mutually exclusive. The more concerned I am about being great in the kingdom, the more kingdom growth I need. The less concerned I am about being great in the kingdom, the more the kingdom is already in me.

"Now this doesn't mean I don't work hard for God and do my best. It means I'm working from love rather than trying to gain love. As you said earlier, the motivation is different.

"Having said all that, here's a question for you: What kind of change must occur in my heart for me to embrace this?"

"I think," Joe said, "this is the same kingdom change we've been talking about all through the Sermon on the Mount. If the kingdom of heaven moves into my heart with the incredible love of God and the amazing resources of heaven, then I can abandon my quest for status and the number-one ranking. When I'm sure of my place with God, then status is irrelevant. If I'm living for an audience of one and I know that audience is smiling upon me, then it doesn't really matter what you do. I don't have to one-up, because I'm secure. This is just such a different approach to life and dealing with other people. Most of what I've processed to this point has to do with getting my relationships in order. But the idea of being in a group and not having to be number one, in some way, shape, or form, just hadn't occurred to me. I suppose it didn't occur to the disciples either."

"Let's look at verses 4-14," Matt continued, "and see how this plays out in our life together.

> Therefore, whoever humbles himself like this child is the greatest in the kingdom of heaven. And whoever welcomes a little child like this in my name welcomes me.
>
> "But if anyone causes one of these little ones who believe in me to sin, it would be better for him to have a large millstone hung around his neck and to be drowned in the depths of the sea. Woe to the world because of the things that cause people to sin! Such things must come, but woe to the man through whom they come! If your hand or your foot causes you to sin, cut it off and throw it away. It is better for you to enter life maimed or crippled than to have two hands or two

feet and be thrown into eternal fire. And if your eye causes you to sin, gouge it out and throw it away. It is better for you to enter life with one eye than to have two eyes and be thrown into the fire of hell.

"See that you do not look down on one of these little ones. For I tell you that their angels in heaven always see the face of my Father in heaven.

"What do you think? If a man owns a hundred sheep, and one of them wanders away, will he not leave the ninety-nine on the hills and go to look for the one that wandered off? And if he finds it, I tell you the truth, he is happier about that one sheep than about the ninety-nine that did not wander off. In the same way your Father in heaven is not willing that any of these little ones should be lost.

"The first thing Jesus said about our life together is that we are to welcome a little child. Jesus feels personally welcomed when the little children are welcomed, and Jesus feels personally unwelcomed when little children aren't welcomed.

"In the next phrase, the term little children becomes little ones. I think Jesus is expanding the circle. Little ones are those in the church, since Jesus is talking directly to his disciples and their life together, who have no status. They are those without voice, vote, power, or influence. I think that the little ones without voice, vote, power, or influence also exist in the larger community of our towns and cities, schools, and work places.

"So the welcome extends to all those without voice, vote, power, or influence. When we looked at the passages about sharing the gospel, we saw that two of the passages involved kingdom resources being offered to people without voice, vote, power, or influence. We are to seek out those people and welcome them wherever we find them. The rest of society, in their desire to be number one, has little use for these little ones whom God loves.

"Jesus went on to say that we aren't to harm them, drive them away, or cause them to fall. Whatever our plans, we are to include them and grow them. The picture Jesus painted of those who mistreat the people without voice, vote, power, or influence is not pretty.

Hell awaits such people. Here again, Jesus used the language about cutting off one's hand or foot if it is a cause of sin in regard to these little ones. The last time we heard that language was in relation to our sexuality. I wonder if Jesus was telling us that the drive to power is as difficult to manage without his help as the sex drive.

"I suppose another way to say this is that anything that gets in the way of my relating to those without status, voice, vote, power, or influence must be eradicated. Yes, it's that important to welcome and care for those without voice, vote, power, or influence. In Matthew 25, Jesus painted a judgment picture based on how those without voice, vote, power, or influence are treated, but we will get there later.

"Jesus told us not to disdain them, not to look down our noses at them. This sounds dangerously close to contempt to me. When we dehumanize those without voice, vote, power, or influence, we're one step away from our shunning of them becoming active harm. When we take that step we say, 'After all, we can't reason with people who have no voice, vote, power, or influence. The only thing they understand is violence. We have to run them off.'

"Jesus closed out this section by giving us two pictures of God's feelings for those without voice, vote, power, or influence. First, God has assigned the angels closest to him—those who see his face—to care for these little ones.

"Second, Jesus compared God's feelings for those without voice, vote, power, or influence to a shepherd who leaves the ninety-nine sheep to look for the one that was lost. God doesn't want them to be lost or to perish and has assigned resources to help them and expects us to do the same."

"Jesus sounds pretty serious here, doesn't he?" Joe commented. "I guess we are our brother's keeper."

"Yes, we are," Matt said. "Let's bring this home. In our church, who are the people without voice, vote, power, or influence?"

"The little children, like Jesus said," Joe answered, "are that way. Maybe the elderly, who are in a nursing home or a hospital, are in that category too. I think the visitors, people brand new to the church, don't have any voice, vote, power or influence."

"That's a good start," Matt replied. "From hanging around our church for a few years, I'd like to narrow in on the children. The infants have lots of grandmas and moms looking out for them, so I wouldn't put them on the list. I would put the toddlers on the list. In our church, it's hard to get people to work with the two and three year olds. I would put seventh and eighth graders on the list too. We have difficulty finding people who will work with them. Also, I've noticed it's difficult to find people to work with the special needs children. The rest of the people you mention, I think, belong on the list. There is one more type of person: In every church, there are what I call the social misfits. They are nice enough people, but either they lack the social initiative to dive into a group, and they get left out unintentionally, or they lack social skills, and people keep their distance.

"So how do we apply all Jesus said to our church and our lives?"

"I think it means I'll see you in the toddler room next Sunday," Joe said. "Then I'll hang around in the gathering area looking for people who are alone. People cared about me when I was new, and the least I can do is care for someone else who is new.

"I bet I can apply these words of Jesus to every social setting I'm in, from the basketball team I'm coaching, to work, to the soccer league, and to our subdivision."

"Yes, you can, and you'll be surprised what happens when you do," Matt said.

They chose submission as their spiritual discipline and prayed for each other. Before they left, Matt and Joe looked around the coffee shop for anyone who looked like they lacked voice, vote, power, or influence. They noticed a well-dressed elderly lady sitting by herself, so they went over to say hello.

CHAPTER 24

LIFE TOGETHER: OFFENSE & TOGETHERNESS

"How did things go with Grace?" Joe asked as he got settled in with his cup of coffee.

"She and Mary hit it off really well," Matt replied. "Since Mary's mom died a few years back, she has been looking for an older lady to involve in her life. While she has not been looking for another mother, she has been looking for someone in that generation because she misses the sense of history and wisdom in a person of that age. Mary still can't believe we found Grace just sitting by herself last Sunday. Mary thinks Grace must have been pretty desperate to talk to a couple of gruff looking characters like us."

"I found it hard to believe too," Joe said. "But like she told us, Grace lives alone in a big old house, her children all moved away, and her husband is dead. She was waiting to meet a friend who didn't make it to the meeting. But I guess when you live alone and don't have anyone to talk with, you will talk with anyone. Even guys like us."

"Grace and Mary gave each other their life histories over lunch one day last week, and they talk on the phone every couple of days," Matt added. "At this rate, I wouldn't be surprised to find another plate at Easter dinner at our house.

"What I want to know is did you mail the letter to your dad, and did you get a response back?"

"I thought you would never ask," Joe answered. "I sent the letter on Monday. My hand was shaking a little as I put the letter in the mailbox. Yesterday, I got a letter back."

"What did it say?" Matt asked.

"He wrote," Joe replied, "that he had been waiting for a letter or phone call or something from me for the last two decades. He asked that we meet somewhere near him because he doesn't get around as well as he used to, and he doesn't drive at night anymore. He suggested a park, a diner, or even his house. I haven't written back yet, but I'm thinking about suggesting we meet at the end of the month at the diner for a cup of coffee. I'm both excited and scared to death at the same time. Yet, as I read his letter with the shaky handwriting, I had this sense of peace from God that this was a good thing, and everything is going to work out alright. So I'm going to write back tomorrow and mail the letter."

"Good for you," Matt said encouragingly. "This has been a long road for you, but you're close to the end of it. I'm proud of you for not bailing."

"As you know," Joe responded, "it hasn't been easy. Even though I feel God's hand in this, I suspect there's more difficulty to come. But enough of that. What's going on with your mission project?"

"One of the guys in the group got a job," Matt exclaimed. "When we parted last week, he told us he had an interview and asked us to pray that it go well. Mark and I have always prayed for their job efforts, but he was the first one to actually ask us to pray for something specific around a job. So we all celebrated with him. We talked about hope. We talked about how to keep going when the job search process keeps turning up dead ends. We gave everyone a chance to share some discouragement and some hope. This week, everyone asked us to pray for their job search. Marge, the lady who talked with me last week after the meeting, talked with me again. She shared that she has been sour on life for a long time and thinks maybe she needs to get an attitude adjustment. She asked me to pray about that. She told me she didn't come to church last week, but she was working on it, and I would see her there sometime soon. I told her I would save her a place.

"How's your team doing?"

"We have our first game next week," Joe replied. "Two practices before the games is all we get. They don't look much like a team yet, but they've figured out where the basket is, and they do act like they have teammates. The devotion this week was from John 1, where Andrew and John were pointed to Jesus by John the Baptist. Andrew and John approached Jesus, and Jesus said to them, 'What do you want?' (John 1:38) They asked him where he was staying. Maybe there's some deep significance to that, but it sounds pretty lame to me. So the question for the guys was this: If you could ask Jesus a question, what would it be? After some wise-guy questions about girls, they got serious. One guy wanted to know if Jesus could tell him why his mom and dad divorced. Another guy wanted to know which college to go to. Someone else wanted to ask if his life had any purpose to it. Someone else, with a little Bible background, wanted to ask Jesus why he died on a cross. Another wanted to ask Jesus if there really is a heaven and if his grandma is there. I told them those were all good questions. Then I prayed and gave the questions to Jesus. After I was done praying, I asked them to come back next week and tell me if they had received any answers.

"What does Jesus have for us tonight?"

"For lack of better terms, I would say Jesus is giving us a grievance policy tonight," Matt said. "By this time, the disciples had been given plenty of opportunity to annoy one another, cross one another's lines, and generally tick one another off. What does Phillip do with Andrew when Andrew thinks he's further up the kingdom pecking order than Phillip? What does John do with Peter when they're on a mission project and Peter messes up in a way that puts the whole project at risk?"

"I give up—what?" Joe responded, "And what are we to do?"

"Let's look at Matthew 18:15-20 and see," Matt said.

> "If your brother sins against you, go and show him his fault, just between the two of you. If he listens to you, you have won your brother over. But if he will not listen, take one or two others along, so that 'every matter may be established by the testimony of two or three witnesses.' If he refuses to

listen to them, tell it to the church; and if he refuses to listen even to the church, treat him as you would a pagan or a tax collector.

"I tell you the truth, whatever you bind on earth will be bound in heaven, and whatever you loose on earth will be loosed in heaven.

"Again, I tell you that if two of you on earth agree about anything you ask for, it will be done for you by my Father in heaven. For where two or three come together in my name, there am I with them."

"You're right," Joe commented, "It does have a policy manual kind of feel about it. Can you walk me through what it all means?"

"I'll give it a try," Matt answered. "As we get into this, we need to remember this is not the first thing Jesus taught his disciples. This passage builds on everything that has come before, so we'll be drawing on past sessions to unpack this.

"Jesus started with the concept of what to do when a brother sins against you. Let's review sin for a moment. Sin is an archery term that means missing the mark. So to sin against someone is to miss the mark in that person's life. My action needs to hit the bull's-eye, but it doesn't even hit the target. Each miss causes pain and damage in a person's life. The further my miss is from the bull's-eye the greater the pain and the greater the damage.

"Let's create a scenario to help us walk through this. Billy and Bob are doing a mission project together. Let's say they coach one of the basketball teams together. Billy agrees to get practice started, while Bob stays out in the parking lot to talk with the parents for a few minutes to try to build some relationships with them through which some ministry can happen. Billy shows up at practice twenty minutes late. Bob has to stop meeting parents in the parking lot to go in and start practice because boys in a gym easily get in trouble. Bob is angry that Billy is late. Bob feels abandoned. Bob doesn't know if he can count on Billy. Trust has been broken. Bob is frazzled from trying to do two things at once. He didn't feel right about leaving his post in the parking lot, but he couldn't leave the boys alone in the gym. In the gym with the boys, he feels he's missing prime parent-connection time. It wouldn't be too bad, but this isn't the first time Billy has stranded Bob at the beginning of practice.

"Let's add Jesus' words to the scene at this point, 'If your brother sins against you, go and show him his fault.' Bob needs to talk to Billy about what has been going on. Drawing from the early teaching of Jesus, what needs to happen before Bob sits down with Billy?"

"Bob needs to do some board removal work first," Joe replied. "Bob needs to examine the stories he's telling about Billy's lateness. If he's telling a villain story, 'Billy is irresponsible and always has been,' things will turn ugly. Or if Bob tells a victim story, 'I was just doing my part of the job, and Billy messed everything up,' or even if Bob justifies his feelings by saying, 'Based on what Billy did, I had no other choice,' trouble will come. So Bob needs to get his story straight. As Bob tells his story to Billy, he needs to be sure not to jump to any conclusions about why Billy is late. He needs to allow Billy to tell his side of the story."

"You're right—Bob needs to do some board removal work," Matt agreed. "In addition, notice that Bob, the party who was sinned against, has the responsibility for initiating the conversation. Bob is not to sit and stew while waiting for Billy to notice something is wrong. Bob is to take the initiative and track down Billy.

"Bob needs to come to the conversation with resolution and reconciliation in mind, not punishment for Billy's shortcoming or a pearl for Billy to swallow that will fix him."

"Okay, so having done the prep work, Bob is supposed to approach Billy one-to-one and show him the problem. Peterson, in *The Message,* translates it this way, 'If a fellow believer hurts you, go and tell him—work it out between the two of you.'[i] If Billy is responsive, then life is good—the issue is resolved, the relationship is restored, and the two can continue working together.

"Now if Billy isn't responsive, won't listen, and won't resolve the issue, then there's trouble. At this point, Jesus said to take two or three witnesses. Once again, let's look at a quote from Peterson's translation, 'If he won't listen, take one or two others along so that the presence of witnesses will keep things honest, and try again.'[ii] Once again, if Billy is receptive, then life is good. If Billy is not receptive, then things escalate one more level.

"This time, Bob is to tell it to the church. I don't think that means to get up during a worship service and air the issue, although I suppose arrangements could be made to do that. I think it needs to come to some official gathering that speaks on behalf of the church, like a board, or elders, or some such group. Then that group communicates the issue to everyone. Bob is to tell it to the church. Jesus, however, didn't say how or in what setting to tell it to the church. I guess we have to figure that out ourselves. Once again, if Billy responds, life is good. If Billy doesn't respond, then he is to be treated like a pagan or tax collector."

"That sounds harsh," Joe said.

"I think it sounds harsher than what it is," Matt replied. "We'll look at that more closely in a few minutes. What would happen if we followed the procedure outlined here by Jesus?"

"Let me think for a minute," Joe pondered. "What would happen? I think just having the procedure in place and encouragement to use it would help Bob and others in his position a lot. What are we supposed to do when someone's actions mess things up? Ignore it, and hope it will go away? Be nice, and smile through the hurt? Ream the offending party? Gossip behind their backs? This spells it out. If I'm Bob, I go talk to Billy. If I have done the board removal work and am looking for reconciliation and resolution, then I have a good chance. It would present an opportunity for growth in both Billy and Bob. If I've done the board removal work, then I'm aware that I might be contributing as much to the problem as the other person is.

"Would anything else happen?"

"Yes," Matt continued, "there would be some other things. This procedure builds a way to control the behavior. If I'm Billy and don't like Bob talking to me about being twenty minutes late, I don't get to sound off to everyone. If I think Bob is way off base, I move to stage two and have some witnesses listen to us hash it out. The job of the witnesses is to keep us honest and push us if we're telling bad stories to ourselves.

"The other thing I think is going on is that the procedure doesn't leave me anywhere to hide. If I'm Billy, and I'm in the wrong, and I cry foul at stage two, chances are I'm in denial about my behavior. That means I have some issues I need to work through that I don't want to face. Step three, taking the issue to the church, cuts off my escape route. Now I have been exposed. Everyone now knows my dysfunctional behavior. Now, no one will let me get away with it. If I choose to stay in the church, then what I'm offered is healing, help, and the opportunity to grow and change, which is exactly what Jesus offered pagans and tax collectors. Peterson does a good job with the tax collectors and pagan line. Listen to how he translates it, 'If he won't listen to the church, you'll have to start over from scratch, confront him with the need for repentance, and offer again God's forgiving love.'[iii]

"Like I said, there's no place for me to hide. I have to face my issues in this supportive, loving community, or I have to get out because they won't let me get away with it anymore. It's both scary and helpful.

"But unless we have a healthy way of dealing with the issues that arise between us, we wreck the community Jesus envisioned for the church. Gossip and anger will run rampant. There will be no order, no discipline, and no accountability. Growth in the kingdom will not occur, and people will talk about us for all the wrong reasons.

"Why wouldn't we do this?"

"That's easy," Joe answered, "If I'm Bob, and I do this, I can't complain about Billy. I can't get revenge. There are no paybacks. I can't sulk or pout. If I'm Bob, to do what Jesus is talking about means I have to grow up. I'm also risking my rightness with this procedure. It could turn out, as I follow the process, Billy might be right, and instead of insisting that he change, I might have to apologize and change. There's another risk here. In the first stage of this, where it's just Bob and Billy, Billy could really go off. I might be afraid of facing the other person's anger when I bring up the issue, I might be afraid of hurting him, or I might be afraid of being rejected. It's also possible the other person might try to emotionally hurt me or threaten me in some way. It takes strength to do the board removal work and talk to someone face to face. It's much easier to talk about him behind his back."

"What kind of change is necessary in someone to be able to work this process?" Matt asked.

"It's that kingdom change we've been talking about all along," Joe replied. "If I'm the offended party and the kingdom change hasn't occurred in me, then there's no way I'll even consider this. But if the kingdom change is occurring within me, and I'm trying to use my anger for reconciliation—I'm trying to love, learn from, and forgive my enemies—and I'm doing board removal work, then I'll give this a try. I may need to ask for some kingdom help, but that's alright."

"Let me say another word about the tax collector and pagan line," Matt said. "In some traditions, that has been taken to mean you excommunicate someone or kick them out of the church. After all, you wouldn't want pagans and tax collectors in your church. But we have to look at how Jesus treated pagans and tax collectors. He hung out with them. He didn't try to run them off. He wanted to offer the kingdom to them.

"In terms of Billy, if he refuses to listen to the church, the church still welcomes him and offers him love and healing and a chance to grow and change. Now as that is occurring, no one involves Billy in a task that requires him to be on time because everyone knows he's twenty minutes late for everything. If Billy responds at some point, begins to grow and change, and starts to demonstrate he can be on time, then at some point someone will need to trust him with a mission opportunity that depends on Billy being on time.

"What Jesus has said here is vitally important. If we can't work this procedure with one another, then whatever communities, whatever teams form to accomplish kingdom purposes, will either self-destruct, or will settle in for a long slow death as issues get ignored or aren't dealt with. Either way, the kingdom purposes for which we're called together aren't accomplished. People who need us to storm the gates of hell to set them free remain imprisoned. Our own hearts become less open and responsive to the kingdom, and we begin to shrivel.

"If we can make it work, nothing is impossible for us. That's what Jesus wants us to see in the next couple of verses. Let's look at his words (Matthew 18:18-20):

"I tell you the truth, whatever you bind on earth will be bound in heaven, and whatever you loose on earth will be loosed in heaven.

"Again, I tell you that if two of you on earth agree about anything you ask for, it will be done for you by my Father in heaven. For where two or three come together in my name, there am I with them."

"This is pretty powerful stuff, but notice that these words are spoken about a group. The *you* that Jesus uses in the binding and loosing passage is *you* plural. He's speaking to the entire group of disciples. If the lot of you can get your act together to agree on what you would like to have bound and what you would like to have loosed, it will be done. I'm not quite sure what happened next. Maybe Jesus took a good look at the quarreling, self-centered, self-serving, ambitious group he was addressing and thought it would be too much to ask to get them all on board. So he said if only two of you can get it together, then whatever you ask for will be done for you. For when two of us or three of us are together for Jesus, Jesus is with us, and all that Jesus did becomes possible for us.

"For years, I've struggled with this passage. Often, it has been applied to prayer meetings. People have expected that just because they've agreed on a prayer request and have prayed, then boom, like magic, it should have suddenly happened. That's not quite what Jesus had in mind here.

"Once again, we need to remember this is not the first thing Jesus told his disciples. To more fully understand what Jesus was telling us here, we need to remember what he has already told us.

"The first thing I think we need to remember is what Jesus said about asking, seeking, and knocking. He said it was a process. He said we need to ask and keep on asking, seek and keep on seeking, knock and keep on knocking. Only then will we receive what we ask for, find what we seek, and have the door opened to us. We combined those words of Jesus with what immediately followed about board removal. What we ask for and seek often can't be given to us until we change. So the board removal process is about asking questions of myself: What do I need to do to change, what do I need to do differently, so that this request can be granted?

"When two or three or a dozen join together in this process, participate in board removal, and willingly engage one another around each other's faults and failings in the manner we have been describing, then the opportunity for me to see the changes I need to make, my willingness to make those changes, and the support I receive in making those changes goes way up. If that is true for everyone in the group who is pursuing the same request or the same goal, imagine the kingdom resources that would be unleashed upon the world.

"As we engage in that process, we do so with Jesus. Jesus, who knew the power of board removal and change in regard to prayer—that is asking God—and asking other people, is with us to guide the process and grant the requests as the change occurs. As we work the process as individuals and as groups, we grow into the kinds of people and groups whom God could empower to do whatever we want to do.

"Psalm 133 begins with these words, 'How good and pleasant it is when brothers live together in unity!' The psalm ends a few short lines later with, 'For there the LORD bestows his blessing, even life forevermore.'

"It is good and pleasant when we dwell together in unity, but unity is not something that just happens. Unity is work. It's the work of board removal, asking, seeking, knocking, and working through the offenses and disappointments with each other as we follow Jesus together.

"Patrick Lencioni opens the introduction to his book, *The Five Dysfunctions of a Team,* with these words:

> Not finance. Not strategy. Not technology. It is teamwork that remains the ultimate competitive advantage, both because it so powerful and so rare.
>
> A friend of mine, the founder of a company that grew to a billion dollars in annual revenue, best expressed the power of teamwork when he once told me, "If you could get all the people in an organization rowing in the same direction,

you could dominate any industry, in any market, against any competition, at any time."

Whenever I repeat that adage to a group of leaders, they immediately nod their heads, but in a desperate sort of way. They seem to grasp the truth of it while simultaneously surrendering to the impossibility of actually making it happen.

And that is where the rarity of team work comes into play...The fact remains that teams, because they are made up of imperfect human beings, are inherently dysfunctional.[iv]

"Lencioni describes the dysfunctions of a team as lack of trust, fear of conflict, lack of commitment, avoidance of accountability, and inattention to detail. He spends the rest of the book talking about how to overcome those dysfunctions so that a team can work in unity.

"Now let me ask a question: What would a kingdom team accomplish using the kingdom resources of board removal, asking, and working through offenses with Jesus as a part of the team? I think they would accomplish the impossible on a regular basis.

"How pleasant it is when brothers dwell together in unity, or a kingdom team works kingdom stuff using kingdom resources to deal with self and one another. There the Lord bestows his blessing, even life forevermore. Life is given for the team and for everyone the team touches."

"You're right about teams," Joe agreed. "I've been on a couple of athletic teams and one work team where everything clicked. On those teams, there was always at least one, and often more than one, member who pushed the others to do more than we thought possible. We yelled and screamed at each other, hung out with each other, and conquered the world together. Chemistry was great. I still talk with some of those guys from high school.

"I never thought about teams and the power of teams in this context though. But I see what you mean—a team is only as strong as its weakest member and its leader. A kingdom team, where everyone is working on the kingdom lifestyle and using kingdom resources, has the opportunity for even the most ordinary of individuals to grow and develop into highly functioning, highly achieving teams. With kingdom teams, we don't need a superstar or two. Since Jesus is part of the team, and all the resources of the kingdom are available to anyone or any team who asks, all we need to do is to be meek—to be put under the control of Jesus. As everyone helps everyone else do that, everyone grows and develops, and the team is able to accomplish more.

"That's a good question you asked. What could I do if I were part of a highly functioning kingdom team? What would that look like? What would be accomplished? Who could be helped? How would the community change?"

"In the midst of that dreaming," Matt began, "Peter brought everyone back down to earth with this question: 'Then Peter came to Jesus and asked, "Lord, how many times shall I forgive my brother when he sins against me? Up to seven times?"' (Matthew 18:21) I can hear the wheels grind to a screeching halt. No longer is the focus on what the team can accomplish. Now, the focus is on how long I have to put up with these guys before I can trade them from my team and get guys who are much better teammates.

"Peter thought he was being generous. The rabbis debated about how many times one was to offer forgiveness. Some said three or four. Nobody said seven. So Peter was expecting a pat on the back for his willingness to forgive seven times before removing someone from his team.

"Peter, however, was shocked by the answer Jesus gave. 'Jesus answered, "I tell you, not seven times, but seventy-seven times"' (Matthew 18:22). Some passages translate the number seventy-seven as seventy times seven. In addition, some commentators make the assumption that the number Jesus uses is a per-day number. Some other commentators assume it's the same sin. So if I'm Bob, the question is how many times do I have to forgive Billy for being twenty minutes late? Since Jesus says 77 times, or 70 times 7, which is 490 times a day, the answer appears to be as many times as Billy is late.

"Now before you throw up your hands like Peter and say, 'This is ludicrous,' let's remember this is not the first thing Jesus said to his disciples. Let's go back and review forgiveness.

"Forgiveness is Bob not holding Billy responsible for repairing the damage his lateness has caused. Forgiveness is Bob recognizing that Billy can't pay the price and releasing him from having to pay the price. Forgiveness is Bob being willing to the pay the price for Billy's damage. If the damage is more than Bob can pay, he asks God for the resources to finish the payment.

"Forgiveness is not about becoming a door mat for people to walk on and abuse anytime they want. Forgiveness is not the healing of the hurt caused by the damage but the first step toward healing. Forgiveness is not reconciliation but the first step toward reconciliation. Forgiveness does not change or fix the other person's behavior but is the first step toward changing the other person's behavior.

"Forgiveness is not the end of the matter for Bob and Billy but only the first step toward resolution and reconciliation.

"If you remember from the board removal stuff we did, we have to ask some questions of Bob. Billy is out of control, but what is Bob doing that this continues to happen? Bob can't change Billy's actions, but Bob can change his own actions. As Bob changes his actions and reactions, then Bob won't give Billy the opportunity to keep sinning against him. So if Bob needs to forgive Billy seventy-seven times today, Bob needs to change as much as Billy does.

"As soon as Bob votes Billy off his team, Bob loses his opportunity to grow through Billy's actions, and Billy loses his opportunity to grow through Bob's actions. Chances are the next person Bob adds to his team will bring some action that will need Bob's forgiveness. If Bob keeps trading team members, he will never change his behavior. Likewise, if Billy keeps getting traded, he won't change either.

"I think Jesus' answer, forgive your brother seventy-seven times, is like saying, 'The two of you need to keep at it with one another until you get this thing worked out. If you don't work it out, then you will keep changing teams and team members and never work it out. It takes staying with it seventy-seven times to work it out. If you work it out now, you'll save yourself lots of time and pain, and you won't waste kingdom opportunities.'

"Then Jesus told a story to drive his point home (Matthew 18:23-35):

"Therefore, the kingdom of heaven is like a king who wanted to settle accounts with his servants. As he began the settlement, a man who owed him ten thousand talents was brought to him. Since he was not able to pay, the master ordered that he and his wife and his children and all that he had be sold to repay the debt.

"The servant fell on his knees before him. 'Be patient with me,' he begged, 'and I will pay back everything.' The servant's master took pity on him, canceled the debt and let him go.

"But when that servant went out, he found one of his fellow servants who owed him a hundred denarii. He grabbed him and began to choke him. 'Pay back what you owe me!' he demanded.

"His fellow servant fell to his knees and begged him, 'Be patient with me, and I will pay you back.'

"But he refused. Instead, he went off and had the man thrown into prison until he could pay the debt. When the other servants saw what had happened, they were greatly distressed and went and told their master everything that had happened.

"Then the master called the servant in. 'You wicked servant,' he said, 'I canceled all that debt of yours because you begged me to. Shouldn't you have had mercy on your fellow servant just as I had on you?' In anger his master turned him over to the jailers until he should pay back all he owed.

"This is how my heavenly Father will treat each of you unless you forgive your brother from your heart."

"I think Jesus meant what he said about forgiveness. It's only because God constantly forgives us, so that we can get it right with him and others, that we aren't destroyed. God expects us to offer others what we have received from him.

"Notice that Jesus didn't give up on his team. I'm sure there were many times when Jesus wanted to trade Peter, but he didn't. Jesus kept the team together and gave them the tools to grow from where they were to become a team that literally changed the history of the world. The question for us is this: If we would stay with Jesus, the task, and one another, what could we do? But I think the real question is this: Will we ask God for the courage, the nerve, the vulnerability, and the strength to stay with it?"

"I hear you," Joe said. "Do you suppose we could become part of such a kingdom team as you've been talking about?"

"By the time Jesus is done with us at the end of Matthew we will," Matt smiled.

That satisfied Joe for the moment. They chose a spiritual discipline and prayed for each other. As Joe drove away, he began to wonder just what Matt meant when he said they would become part of a kingdom team.

Suggested resources:
Eugene H. Peterson, *The Message*, NavPress, 2002.
Patrick M. Lencioni, *The Five Dysfunctions of a Team: A Leadership Fable*, Jossey-Bass, 2002.

PHASE V

UNTIL THE END

MATTHEW 24-25

CHAPTER 25

UNTIL THE END: PART I

As Matt walked across the parking lot, he wondered what kind of shape he would find Joe in. He wondered if Joe had sent the return letter to his father and actually set a date for the meeting. Matt had spent a lot of time praying for Joe to work his issues out with his dad, and now that the time was getting close, Matt hoped Joe wouldn't stall.

Matt entered the coffee shop and spotted Joe, already with his coffee. Matt purchased his own cup of coffee and two chocolate chip cookies and went over to his seat across from Joe.

"The girl at the counter says she's going to start charging us rent," Joe said.

"If rent means purchasing more chocolate chip cookies," Matt replied, "I'm all for it. How's it going? Did you get that letter off to your dad?"

"Yes, I did," Joe answered. "I set a date for us to meet at the diner at the end of the month, just two weeks away. Now that I've done it, I'm not sure it was a good idea. I'm thinking about sending another letter and canceling the whole thing. I'm not sure I can get through it. Maybe it's better to just to leave everything the way it is. I'm afraid. I don't know where it's coming from or what it's about, it's just there. Maybe I should just walk away from the whole thing."

"I was afraid you were going to say that," Matt said. "Often big changes like this come with a wall of fear. We get right up next to the change, just about ready to make the change, and fear shows up.

Fear has a way of gathering all the old negative emotions, repackaging them, and using them to create a wall to keep us from making the change."

"That's funny," Joe replied. "That's exactly what my counselor said. He told me to stay the course. He told me to take a deep breath and just step through the fear like it was beads in a doorway. He said when I do that, the fear will go away. He said it's the last hurdle I need to cross before I can be reconciled with my dad. I told him, 'Thanks, but that doesn't make it any easier.'"

"No, it doesn't," Matt agreed, "but at least you know it's something you can step through, and on the other side is the reconciliation you've been working toward for the last several months. I'll be praying for you to get through the fear.

"How did your basketball team do in their first game?"

"They got clobbered!" Joe laughed. "It was evident that it was everyone's first game, including the officials. But a couple of guys on the other team were less nervous than anyone else. We lost by twenty. When we got down by fifteen, my guys started yelling at each other, blaming each other, and yelling at the refs.

"After the game, we had to do some team building work. I remembered some of the of board removal work we talked about. So I asked if yelling at each other helped us play better, if yelling at the ref improved their calls, and if yelling helped them win the game. They said, 'No,' and one of them said after we started yelling, things got worse. The rest agreed with that assessment. So I asked them why they continued yelling. They said they were angry and frustrated and didn't know what else to do. I asked them if they would like some alternative behaviors. They said they would."

"What did you tell them?" Matt asked.

"I told them to ask their teammates for help," Joe answered. "They looked at me like I was crazy, and one of them said, 'But my teammates were the ones messing up.' Everyone agreed that everyone else was the problem. I point-blank asked each player if he played a perfect game. They each said, 'No.' Then I asked each of them if they were doing the best they could on their own. They assured me they were trying their hardest. Then I asked if they could do better than their best. They said, 'No.' I disagreed with them.

I said the way you can do better than your best is to ask for help, because two bests are better than one best.

"One of the guys, Jack, started to get it and said, 'Coach, you're telling me that instead of yelling at Tony to do better, I should ask Tony to help me. I said, 'Yes,' and then I asked him what he thought Tony could do to help him. Jack said, 'I got beat to the basket a lot. I could ask Tony, who is a big guy under the basket, to pick up my man when he gets close to the basket.' Tony said he could do that. Then Tony asked George for help. After that, we had a regular help fest going on.

"That led me into the devotion about what Jesus said about taking the board out of our own eye before trying to take the speck out of someone else's eye. I said, 'Because Jack asked Tony for help, everyone on the team asked everyone else for help. Next week, we're going to do better because we got help. Jack, asking for help, set up the dynamic to make us all better.' They were amazed that Jesus had said something that could help them play basketball. It was fun to be a part of that."

"I tried to do some team building, too, this week," Matt said. "Only my team was at work, led by Kelly. The last two meetings were the same as the one I told you about, with Kelly being interrupted by his secretary, Jane, taking cell calls, and all the rest disengaging in their own ways. After the last meeting, I asked Kelly why we were having these meetings. He said they weren't his idea. Vince wants the meetings. Kelly said Vince attended some seminar about the power of teams and insisted he get all his direct reports together for meetings to help us become a team. Vince even gave Kelly this stack of stuff to read, which he hasn't read, about how to do it. Before this, he thought they were doing fine with him just checking with everyone individually. I didn't tell him we both knew everything wasn't fine. He doesn't know why we need 'this team stuff,' as he put it.

"At that moment, I knew why Vince had hired me, without much input from Kelly. Vince wanted someone on Kelly's team who knew how teams were supposed to work and who had experience building teams. The only problem is I've never tried to build a team from the position of team member. I've always been a team leader. In fact, I have my own direct reports well on their way to becoming a team."

"What are you going to do?" Joe asked.

"I'm not sure, but I did take the first step," Matt replied. "I asked Kelly what it would be like if everyone was working together toward the same goal, caring about how their colleagues were doing, and able to ask for and offer help to one another. Kelly said there was no use thinking about it because his direct reports would never act that way. I told Kelly if he thought there was anything I could do to help, I would be glad to do it. Then I asked, if he didn't mind, if it would be okay if I read the material on teams that Vince had given him. He said, 'Go ahead, I can't imagine there's anything helpful in there. Since you're going to read it, let me know what it says. That way, I can impress Vince the next time I talk with him.' He's always asking me if I've looked at any of that stuff.

"I think, maybe, I've managed to get us started down the team road, even if Kelly isn't aware of it yet."

"How did your support group go this week?" Joe asked.

"It went really well," Matt responded. "The group has started to care for each other. Some had met each other during the week for coffee to talk about their job searches. This week, during our time together, they were sharing job leads with each other. When it came to the prayer time at the end, one of the men asked to do the prayer. Mark and I were really impressed at the way the group has begun to care for itself.

"This week, we move into the last major teaching section of Jesus. We find it in Matthew 24-25. In this section, Jesus talked about the end, but more importantly, what to do until the end comes. But before we get to that, let's take a look at what has happened to Jesus since chapter 18.

"In chapter 19, some Pharisees hassled Jesus about divorce. The answer Jesus gave them caused the disciples to think it was better not to marry. After they left, some moms wanted Jesus to bless their children, but the disciples told the moms Jesus was too busy to deal with children."

"Maybe I missed something," Joe interrupted, "but two weeks ago, didn't we hear Jesus tell us how important children are in the kingdom and how we have to become like them to enter the kingdom?"

"Yes, we did," Matt replied, "but the disciples haven't been able to put that information into practice yet. Following that, a rich young man came to Jesus to ask what good thing he must do to get eternal life. A lot went on in the exchange between Jesus and this man. The man ended up walking away from Jesus because Jesus told him to sell all he had, give to the poor, gain treasure in heaven, and follow him. The disciples were completely baffled by Jesus because they thought being rich was a sign of God's blessing. The thought had never occurred to them that riches could get in the way of what God wants for us. In this man's case, riches took him away from what he said he wanted, eternal life. Jesus was and is eternal life, the possessor of it and the giver of it. Jesus offered this man what he said he wanted, but the price was too high for him. He couldn't leave his possessions. Chapter 19 was a tough chapter for the disciples. They misunderstood Jesus all the way through the chapter.

"Chapter 20 begins with a parable Jesus told to follow up his words at the end of chapter 19. There's no note about whether the disciples understood, but Jesus has been in trouble with the Unions ever since. The parable is about a landowner who hired workers for his vineyard at harvest time. He hired workers in the morning and in the afternoon. When the day's work was done, he brought all the workers together. He paid the ones who worked the least amount of time the same as he paid the ones who worked the longest. There was a great outcry. But the landowner said he paid everyone what he promised to pay them when they hired on. Jesus wrapped up by saying, 'So the last will be first, and the first will be last' (verse 16). I don't know about the disciples, but I find it to be a difficult parable.

"Another crucifixion and resurrection prediction from Jesus was given to the disciples so that they would understand when it all happened.

"Next, we read that the mother of James and John asked Jesus to give her sons the best seats in the kingdom. Uproar came from the rest of the disciples when they heard about it, and Jesus had to repeat his teaching about the greatest in the kingdom being servant of all.

"All this happened on the way to Jerusalem. As they were leaving Jericho, the last stop before Jerusalem, two blind men called out to Jesus to have mercy on them. Jesus asked them what they wanted. They told him they wanted to see. Jesus healed them, and they followed him into Jerusalem. I don't think they followed quietly.

"I think, maybe, the healing of the two blind men before entering Jerusalem was Jesus' way of asking us if we can see. Those in the religious establishment awaiting him in Jerusalem claimed to see, yet they were blind. They didn't recognize Jesus. Those two blind men knew who Jesus was even without their sight.

"Joe, can you walk me through Holy Week?"

"I'll try," Joe replied. "Chapter 21 opens with Jesus riding into Jerusalem with all the crowds cheering and Jerusalem asking, 'Who is this?' (verse 10)

"Once in Jerusalem, Jesus went straight to the temple and ran out all the merchants and money changers selling animals for the sacrificial system. With the temple cleared, the blind and the lame came to Jesus to be healed, and the children sang his praises. The chief priests and the teachers of the law were ticked. Jesus spent the night in Bethany.

"Monday began with Jesus cursing the fig tree. I don't get that—what's going on?"

"Mark and Luke also record this event," Matt answered. "I think Luke gives us the best help toward understanding. Luke gives us the idea that Jesus was acting out his judgment of the temple. The fig tree looked like it should have figs with all its leaves. The temple and all its activity looked like it was about the things of God, but it wasn't. God wasn't at all pleased at how it was being operated. Jesus' cleansing the temple on Palm Sunday was just the beginning. Just as Jesus cursed the fig tree, so the temple was about to be cursed. In the year 70 A.D., the Romans destroyed Jerusalem and the temple. It has never been rebuilt. The sacrificial system on which the temple was built was destroyed also and never reinstated."

"I think I understand now," Joe said. "After Jesus entered Jerusalem on Monday morning, he went back to the temple. It looks like, during the next couple of days, the various religious factions in Jerusalem took their turns trying to discredit Jesus by asking questions that were supposed to trip him. Jesus wasn't tripped. As each group finished their questions, Jesus had questions, parables, stories, and woes for them that exposed their true motives. Finally, they reached the point when they decided it wasn't safe to ask him anymore questions, and they left him alone. But even though they left him alone, they weren't finished. They began to plot how they could kill him."

"As Jesus was leaving the temple," Matt picked up the narrative, "his disciples were talking with him about what beautiful stones the temple had (Luke 21:5). The temple in Jerusalem was one of the wonders of the ancient world. It was the largest temple in the world and was made of stone that was dazzling white. When the sun shone on it, you couldn't look at it because it was so bright. Jesus, however, carpenter that he was, was not impressed by the temple and its buildings. He told the disciples the temple would be destroyed, and not one stone would be left on another.

"Later, the shocked disciples asked him about this while they were sitting on the Mount of Olives. The Mount of Olives is across the Kidron Valley from the temple. They were sitting on the side of the mountain at eye level with the temple. While looking at it, they asked Jesus, 'When will this happen, and what will be the sign of your coming and of the end of the age?' (Matthew 24:3) There are three questions there, but the disciples asked it as one question because they couldn't imagine a world without such a magnificent temple.

"As we look at the answer Jesus gave them, we need to remember Jesus was answering three questions, not one.

"In Matthew 24:4-14, Jesus painted a rather bleak picture. Let's look at the passage:

> Jesus answered: "Watch out that no one deceives you. For many will come in my name, claiming, 'I am the Christ,' and will deceive many. You will hear of wars and rumors of wars, but see to it that you are not alarmed. Such things must happen, but the end is still to come. Nation will rise against nation, and kingdom against kingdom. There will be famines

and earthquakes in various places. All these are the beginning of birth pains.

"Then you will be handed over to be persecuted and put to death, and you will be hated by all nations because of me. At that time many will turn away from the faith and will betray and hate each other, and many false prophets will appear and deceive many people. Because of the increase of wickedness, the love of most will grow cold, but he who stands firm to the end will be saved. And this gospel of the kingdom will be preached in the whole world as a testimony to all nations, and then the end will come.

"False prophets, wars and rumors of wars, earthquakes, famines, and persecution are all part of the picture. I believe what Jesus gave us here is a general picture of the history of the planet from his time until the end. In every age, there have been false prophets."

"Excuse me," Joe interrupted, "but could you help me with what you mean by a false prophet. Are you talking Jim Jones and the Kool-Aid, the Moonies, the Branch Davidian guy, and people like that, or something else?"

"Yes," Matt replied, "I'm talking about them and others. There is always somebody somewhere claiming to be the Messiah. Right now, there is some guy in Florida who claims to be Jesus, who has a bunch of people following him. But I'm also talking about movements and philosophies too. Jesus said to beware of false prophets and false Messiahs. A prophet is someone who speaks forth a message from God. A false prophet is someone who claims to have a message from God, but doesn't. The term *Messiah* is the Hebrew form of the Greek word *Christ*. The term literally means *anointed one*. One who is anointed is chosen for a task. The kings of Israel were anointed by God for the task of ruling the people. A prophet could be anointed by God to deliver a particular message. What task has the Messiah, the Christ, been chosen by God to do? The Messiah is the one chosen by God to fulfill the promises he made throughout the Old Testament. Some of those promises are to bring blessing to all people, to be the one who forgives sin and removes sin, to give us a new heart, to reconcile us to God, to bring healing, to show us how to live, and to give us the power to pull it off. A false Messiah would be someone not chosen by God, claiming to do any one of these things and more.

"False prophets and false Christs are those who claim, 'This is the way, walk in it.' I believe there are religious false prophets and Christs like the people you named. I believe there are economic false prophets and false Christs. The whole McWorld system claims life is about getting stuff, and if you just have enough stuff, you will be blessed and have it made. That's false, yet McWorld has convinced us that is how life works—sounds like a false prophet and false Messiah to me. Likewise, there are prophets telling people how to manage their relational lives, emotional lives, parenting lives, marriage lives, and work lives that are just false. People follow these prophets, found in religion, psychology, education, self-help, and pop culture, and they wreck their lives."

"I see what you mean," Joe said. "We focus our attention on the religious false prophets and swallow McWorld without giving it a second thought. Probably the false prophets who do the most harm are the ones we don't even know are false because we haven't paid enough attention to Jesus and what he taught to know what is true and what is false. This whole concept is scary. I was on my way to destroying my life by doing what I thought was right based on the stuff in the culture around me. I didn't even know I was trashing my life until it was nearly too late."

"The next thing Jesus talked about," Matt continued, "was political unrest. Wars and rumors of wars, and nation rising against nation, for better or worse, is history. Earthquakes and natural disasters, along with famines and plagues, are part of our history too. I think Jesus was telling us that because Germany may go to war against England, or Israel may go to war with Iran, we're not to think the end is near. He called these things 'the beginning of birth pains.'

"Jesus talked about persecution of his followers, people following false prophets and being deceived, wickedness increasing, and the love of many growing cold. Once again we have world history. Throughout history, disciples of Jesus have been beaten, imprisoned, and lost their lives. In the twentieth century, more people died because they were Jesus' followers than all the previous centuries combined. Each generation talks about how the generation that followed it is more evil than their generation ever was. Whether one generation is worse than another, I don't know; but each generation seems to come up with its own take on how to be evil. Jesus said to stand firm until the end. Jesus said this stuff is going to happen. Don't be surprised by it.

"Jesus finished this part by saying, in verse 14, 'And this gospel of the kingdom will be preached to the whole world as a testimony to all nations, and then the end will come.' If we want to follow a thread in all this that leads to the end, it's the spread of the gospel around the globe to all the peoples living on the planet. False prophets, political unrest, natural disasters, persecution, and rampant evil are not signs of the end. They are just the playing field on which the gospel is proclaimed. The questions to be asked are not these: What does it mean that Iran may attack Israel? Why did the tsunami hit southern Asia? What about internet porn or AIDS? The question of significance for history and the end is this: Who has heard the gospel, who needs to hear, and how I can be part of the effort? The end is determined by the spreading of the gospel, not politics, plague, or wickedness.

"In Matthew 24:15-25, Jesus described a time of great suffering. Let's look at it:

> "So when you see standing in the holy place 'the abomination that causes desolation,' spoken of through the prophet Daniel—let the reader understand—then let those who are in Judea flee to the mountains. Let no one on the roof of his house go down to take anything out of the house. Let no one in the field go back to get his cloak. How dreadful it will be in those days for pregnant women and nursing mothers! Pray that your flight will not take place in winter or on the Sabbath. For then there will be great distress, unequaled from the beginning of the world until now—and never to be equaled again. If those days had not been cut short, no one would survive, but for the sake of the elect those days will be shortened. At that time if anyone says to you, 'Look, here is the Christ!' or, 'There he is!' do not believe it. For false

Christs and false prophets will appear and perform great signs and miracles to deceive even the elect—if that were possible. See, I have told you ahead of time.

"The suffering was so bad it was cut short, otherwise no one would have survived. This tribulation, as it's called, is it an end of the world thing, or is it related to something else?"

"I don't know," Joe answered. "You're the one doing the talking. I would suspect it might be an end of the world kind of thing since it follows what Jesus said about the gospel being preached everywhere."

"A lot of people suppose that too," Matt replied, "but I don't think Jesus was talking about the end of the world. Remember, the disciples asked him three different questions. He has answered one question: When will be the end of the age? The second question is about the fall of Jerusalem and the destruction of the temple. The third question is about when Jesus will return.

"I think this tribulation Jesus talked about is the fall of Jerusalem. He gave the end of the age answer first to show us the general flow of human history. I think this is the answer Jesus gave to the fall of Jerusalem because it's part of the flow of human history. It's part of the wars and rumors of wars, and all the rest. The other reason I think Jesus was talking about the fall of Jerusalem is because he told us that's what he was talking about. Here, in Matthew, he mentions Judea, and Judea's capital is Jerusalem. In Luke's gospel, in chapter 21, we read the same passage. There, Jesus was asked the same question about the temple. In verses 8-19, Jesus talked about the false prophets, the wars, the persecutions, and the encouragement to stand firm.

"Luke 21:20 begins with, 'When you see Jerusalem being surrounded by armies, you will know that its desolation is near.' Let's look at the whole passage, Luke 21:20-24:

"When you see Jerusalem being surrounded by armies, you will know that its desolation is near. Then let those who are in Judea flee to the mountains, let those in the city get out, and let those in the country not enter the city. For this is the time of punishment in fulfillment of all that has been written. How dreadful it will be in those days for pregnant women and nursing mothers! There will be great distress in the land and wrath against this people. They will fall by the sword and will be taken as prisoners to all the nations. Jerusalem will be trampled on by the Gentiles until the times of the Gentiles are fulfilled.

"This terrible time in Jerusalem occurred in 70 A.D. when the Romans got tired of the endless Jewish revolts. Rome wanted peace. The way Romans achieved peace, throughout the long history of their empire, was to create a desolation and call it peace. Roman legions were dispatched to Jerusalem, and Jerusalem was totally destroyed. As Jesus said, 'not one stone will be left on another' (Luke 21:6). The suffering and the bloodshed that went with that destruction was horrific. Ann Rice, in the notes on her research for *Christ the Lord: Out of Egypt*, says we have yet to come to grips with the magnitude of the suffering and death for the Jewish people during that time.[i]

"Many people believe Jerusalem is the key to the end of time. Maybe it is. But what I hear Jesus saying is the gospel proclamation is the key to the end of time, and the destruction of Jerusalem is just one of the many things that happen on the way the to the end. If Jesus had not been specifically asked by his disciples about the temple, I doubt Jesus would have included it in his talk about the end. There are many people who disagree with me about this, but that's alright. There's only one way to know, and we'll all find out in due time.

"Once again, however, Jesus warns his disciples to beware of false prophets. When times are hard, we have a tendency to believe anyone or anything offering hope.

"Let's pick up Jesus' words again with Matthew 24:26-31:

> "So if anyone tells you, 'There he is, out in the desert,' do not go out; or, 'Here he is, in the inner rooms,' do not believe it. For as lightning that comes from the east is visible even in the west, so will be the coming of the Son of Man. Wherever there is a carcass, there the vultures will gather.

"Immediately after the distress of those days

> "'the sun will be darkened,
> and the moon will not give its light;
> the stars will fall from the sky,
> and the heavenly bodies will be shaken.'

"At that time the sign of the Son of Man will appear in the sky, and all the nations of the earth will mourn. They will see the Son of Man coming on the clouds of the sky, with power and great glory. And he will send his angels with a loud trumpet call, and they will gather his elect from the four winds, from one end of the heavens to the other."

"The point Jesus was making here, with all the dramatic language, is no one is going to have to wonder whether or not he has returned. Jesus said his return will be very public, like lightning flashing across the sky. He will come on the clouds. He will come with power and great glory. There will be a trumpet sound and angels everywhere. As obvious as a dead carcass is to vultures, so obvious will the return of Jesus be to humanity.

"The reaction of the peoples of earth at the return of Jesus is mourning. I don't know about you, but I won't be mourning. I'll be jumping up and down shouting, 'Yesssssssss!' I'll be looking for the angel who's supposed to gather me up. I'll be ready. I suppose there will be mourning from the peoples of the earth who are not ready. They're not happy to see Jesus because they're living in opposition to him and in avoidance of him.

"Based on what Jesus has said so far, what do you think he wants us to know?"

"It looks to me," Joe said, "like the high points are: He's coming back, beware of false prophets, and preach the gospel everywhere. I think he mentions false prophets at least three times, so I bet that's important."

"You're with the program," Matt responded. "Let's look at the next section of it, Matthew 24:32-41:

"Now learn this lesson from the fig tree: As soon as its twigs get tender and its leaves come out, you know that summer is near. Even so, when you see all these things, you know that it is near, right at the door. I tell you the truth, this generation will certainly not pass away until all these things have happened. Heaven and earth will pass away, but my words will never pass away.

"No one knows about that day or hour, not even the angels in heaven, nor the Son, but only the Father. As it was in the days of Noah, so it will be at the coming of the Son of Man. For in the days before the flood, people were eating and drinking, marrying and giving in marriage, up to the day Noah entered the ark; and they knew nothing about what would happen until the flood came and took them all away. That is how it will be at the coming of the Son of Man. Two men will be in the field; one will be taken and the other left. Two women will be grinding with a hand mill; one will be taken and the other left.

"In these verses, Jesus told us the time of his return is completely unpredictable. Yet, in the midst of that unpredictability, there are some signs that will show us we're getting close, like a fig tree and summer. What are those things? The destruction of Jerusalem is one of them. Even though that occurred in 70 A.D., we're closer today than before it happened. The gospel will be proclaimed to all the peoples. We're gaining on that task, I think. However, with the coming of each new generation, the challenge grows again.

"Jesus said something here that has puzzled people ever since he said it. He said this generation will not pass away until all these things happen. Did he mean the generation of Peter and John and the rest of the disciples? They did see the resurrected Jesus in all his power and glory. They lived during the time when Jerusalem fell and the temple was destroyed. But his return in the clouds was not something they saw. The word *generation* also means *race*. Is Jesus saying there will be Jews, which is what those first disciples were, until the end comes? I'm not certain, but I think he meant Jews.

"Whatever he meant, he also wanted us to understand that no one knows when the end will come. It will be like Noah's flood. As this disaster was overtaking the world, life was going on as usual. No one seemed to know what was happening. When Jesus returns, life will be going on as normal. No one will be ready or expecting it to happen at that moment. It just happens, and where there are two people, one may be taken and the other left, depending on who they are. But it happens without warning or time to change what we're doing.

"After having laid all this out, Jesus made his point, which was what he wants us to be doing until the end comes, whenever that is. We see that point in Matthew 24:42-51:

> "Therefore keep watch, because you do not know on what day your Lord will come. But understand this: If the owner of the house had known at what time of night the thief was coming, he would have kept watch and would not have let his house be broken into. So you also must be ready, because the Son of Man will come at an hour when you do not expect him.
>
> "Who then is the faithful and wise servant, whom the master has put in charge of the servants in his household to give them their food at the proper time? It will be good for that servant whose master finds him doing so when he returns. I tell you the truth, he will put him in charge of all his possessions. But suppose that servant is wicked and says to himself, 'My master is staying away a long time,' and he then begins to beat his fellow servants and to eat and drink with drunkards. The master of that servant will come on a day when he does not expect him and at an hour he is not aware of. He will cut him to pieces and assign him a place with the hypocrites, where there will be weeping and gnashing of teeth.

"If you were asked what Jesus wants us to do between now and the end, what would you say?"

"What do you mean *if*," Joe replied. "It looks like I'm being asked now. What does Jesus want us to do? It looks like he wants us to keep watch. He could return anytime, so he wants us to be ready. The way to be ready is to do what he asked us to do, like the faithful and wise servant."

"What did he ask us to do?" Matt pushed.

"All the stuff we've been talking about," Joe answered. "Act on the message that the kingdom is near, and access the change the kingdom brings so that we can live a kingdom lifestyle, like the one Jesus described in Matthew 5-7; be in kingdom mission as Jesus described in Matthew 10; and engage in kingdom community as Jesus talked about in Matthew 18. He may have something else by the time we're done studying, but that's what I know. If I'm doing those things, I think I'll be ready to greet Jesus when he comes."

"I think you will too," Matt said. "I think the chief concern of Jesus for the long run of history is that the good news of the kingdom is to be proclaimed in word and deed, and we are to spend our time doing it."

"Jesus didn't give us maps and charts and lists of signs to watch for. Basically, I think Jesus meant something like this: The end is coming. You have work to do. The best way to be ready for the end is to do the work, not to try to figure out the time of the end. All the time you spend trying to figure out when the end will be can be better used by trying to spread the good news of the kingdom.

"I don't find Jesus telling us to pray for the end. In college, during finals week, we used to pray hard Jesus would come. That way we wouldn't have to take the exams. Jesus didn't tell us to pray for the end. He told us to do what he has asked us to do. I think Jesus told us what he told us so that we wouldn't be surprised or distracted when a false prophet, war, natural disasters, or persecution come. I think Jesus told us all these things so that we could keep our hands to the tasks no matter how messed up things look like they might be.

"Jesus continued this theme in chapter 25 as he told three parables. We'll look at two of them next week and the third one in the following week."

"Works for me," Joe said.

They prayed for Joe's meeting with his dad, for their mission projects, and for the stuff Matt had going on at work. They picked a spiritual discipline, urged each other to be wise and faithful servants, and went out into the parking lot. Matt left feeling uncomfortable, as though his wise and faithful servanthood was going to be brought into question soon and maybe expanded. But he had no idea what that was about. All he had was a quiet unrest. He wondered if another chocolate chip cookie would help, but instead, he began the drive home.

Suggested resource:
Ann Rice, *Christ the Lord: Out of Egypt*, Ballantine Books, 2008.

CHAPTER 26

UNITIL THE END: PART II

It had been a beautiful day in the neighborhood. The temperature was warm. The sun was shining. The sky was blue. Joe was whistling as he walked into the coffee shop. He was wondering what he would learn from Jesus with Matt's help and how things were going for Matt. After he ordered his coffee and got a couple of chocolate chip cookies, he went over to a couple of teenagers he knew from the neighborhood and rattled their cages. Then he saw Matt come in. Joe waved the chocolate chip cookies at him, then went over and got a table.

As Matt got settled in, Joe asked him, "Who was that lady sitting with your family at church today?"

"That was Marge," Matt answered, "the lady from the job hunting support group who said she might come. I almost missed her. I was eating a donut, drinking some coffee, and hounding some high school kids about their love lives before the service started. I saw her out of the corner of my eye near the entrance, looking a little lost and a lot tentative. I excused myself from the high school kids and wondered for a moment, *where's Mark when you need him?* Then I remembered Mark had taken his family on a little weekend trip. Fortunately, one of the greeters had engaged Marge in some conversation by the time I got there. I said hello and invited her to come and sit with my family. She accepted. I just hoped Mary had picked a row where there was room for one more. She had.

"It's different being in the service with someone who hasn't been there before, who came because you invited her. I kept hoping there wasn't going to be anything to make her cringe or cause her to be uncomfortable and not want to come back. I had a hard time getting into the service because I was praying so hard the service would get into her. I think God answered my prayers because at the end of the service, she thanked me for the seat, chatted with Mary for awhile, and told me she would be back next week."

"That's cool," Joe said. "Hey, it's all set."

"What's all set?" Matt asked.

"I'm meeting my dad next Saturday morning at the diner for coffee," Joe replied. "I'm scared to death but kind of excited too. I just I hope I don't back out. I hope he doesn't either. Sue volunteered to come along, but I told her I needed to go by myself the first time.

"How's the team stuff coming with Kelly?"

"I've been praying a lot about how to go forward with that," Matt responded. "I read through the stuff Vince gave me, and it's good stuff. Some of it was from Patrick Lencioni's books, *The Five Dysfunctions of a Team*[i] and *Silos, Politics and Turf Wars*.[ii] I'm going to use some of it with my team. Friday, in passing, Kelly asked me if I had read any of it and if it was any good. I said I had read some of it, and it was some of the best stuff on teams I had ever read. Kelly was surprised. Then he asked me if I thought any of it would work with our team. How do you answer that loaded question? I managed to respond, 'I don't know. I haven't been here long enough, but I don't think it would hurt us.' Kelly muttered something noncommittal and then surprised me by saying maybe he had better look at it. So I dropped the materials off to Kelly as I was leaving on Friday. I wonder what will happen next.

"How did your basketball team do?"

"They almost won this time," Joe answered, "which is a huge improvement. At practice, we talked about how to give the kind of help each player said he needed. So during the game, they gave each other the kind of help they needed. We had the lead for awhile. Then in the last three minutes of the game, they forgot what they had been doing and stopped helping each other. Each player tried to win it by himself. We ended up losing by six. We talked about it afterwards, and they all said they stopped helping and asking for help. I think we'll win next week.

"I made my calls to the parents of the players and told them how much I enjoyed having their sons on my team. I didn't have to lie either. I was surprised by the reactions of the parents. Some seemed to breathe a sigh of relief that their son wasn't in trouble. Some were surprised that anyone noticed their son. I had two parents, whose boys are new to the league, ask me if I got paid to do this. When I told them I didn't get paid, they were amazed. So I got to have two conversations that included the phrase, 'This is a concrete way for me to show your son God loves him.' I think a couple of the parents are going to treat me with a little more respect now. But more importantly, I think some of the parents are starting to think a little more closely about God than they did.

"So what kind of trouble is Jesus going to get me into tonight? Last week I learned the world is going to end, Jesus is going to return, no one knows for sure when that will happen except it seems to be tied to spreading the kingdom message, and I need to be ready. So all I know for sure is that the world didn't end last week. What do we have tonight?"

"Tonight, Jesus continues," Matt replied, "with the theme he started last week about getting ready, being ready, and staying ready. To flesh out his idea, Jesus told three stories. We'll look at two of those stories this week and the last one next week. The first story is the Parable of the Ten Virgins, which we find in Matthew 25:1-13. Let's look at it:

> "At that time the kingdom of heaven will be like ten virgins who took their lamps and went out to meet the bridegroom. Five of them were foolish and five were wise. The foolish ones took their lamps but did not take any oil with them. The wise, however, took oil in jars along with their lamps. The bridegroom was a long time in coming, and they all became drowsy and fell asleep.
>
> "At midnight the cry rang out: 'Here's the Bridegroom! Come out to meet him!'

"Then all the virgins woke up and trimmed their lamps. The foolish ones said to the wise, 'Give us some of your oil; our lamps are going out.'

"'No,' they replied, 'there may not be enough for both us and you. Instead, go to those who sell oil and buy some for yourselves.'

"But while they were on their way to buy the oil, the bridegroom arrived. The virgins who were ready went in with him to the wedding banquet. And the door was shut.

"Later the others also came. 'Sir! Sir!' they said. 'Open the door for us!'

"But he replied, 'I tell you the truth, I don't know you.'

"Therefore keep watch, because you do not know the day or the hour.

"I know, nice ending. Before we get to the ending, let's get the details. There are ten virgins waiting for the bridegroom to come. Five are wise, and five are foolish. As the story opens, we don't know who is who. The bridegroom delays, the virgins fall asleep, and some run out of oil for their lamps. Those who run out of oil go to get some more, and while they are away, the bridegroom comes, and they get shut out of the party. The bridegroom won't let them in because he claims not to know them.

"Did you notice anything unexpected?"

"Just a couple of things," Joe said. "First, the bridegroom takes so long to come. Second, the virgins with oil don't share with the ones who don't have oil. But the most unexpected thing to me is the virgins without oil, who went to get some more oil, got shut out of the party. I'm also shocked at the words of the bridegroom to these women, 'I don't know you.' I don't understand the wedding customs of the day, but this seems overly harsh based on what has been going on."

"Yes, it does," Matt agreed, "but apparently that is in keeping with the custom of the day. William Barclay, in his commentary on the Gospel of Matthew, Volume 2, describes a typical wedding in a Palestinian village. It includes all the kinds of things that are going on in the parable, including those not present at the bridegroom's arrival being shut out.[iii] So I think Jesus told his story using a custom his hearers knew well. Jesus began this story with 'At that time the kingdom of heaven will be like…'

"What point do you suppose Jesus is making here?"

"I think," Joe replied, "you said it earlier—get ready, be ready, and stay ready. I think getting ready is not something someone else can do for me. I can't borrow your readiness. Either I'm ready or I'm not. I can't cram for readiness. Since I don't know when Jesus will return, I can't put off until tomorrow what I know today I need to do to be ready.

"So help me out here. What does the readiness Jesus talked about here look like? I don't mind taking a nap, but I don't want to be caught without the oil."

"It looks like living out what we've been talking about since the beginning," Matt answered. "Change, for the kingdom of heaven is near. Believe, act on that message, and let the change the kingdom brings sweep over your life and make your heart new, giving you the power and the ability to act in life and react to life in completely different ways. We discovered what the kingdom change looks like in Matthew 5-7. In the Beatitudes, we discovered the kingdom values. We learned a life that exceeds the law is to live in love. We saw that a kingdom life includes using anger for resolution and reconciliation, sexuality for blessing and keeping our hearts tender toward our spouses, and saying yes and no to establish kingdom boundaries in our lives. We saw kingdom ways to deal with abuses of power, how to love the enemy, fight evil with good, learn from the enemy, and pray for those who persecute us. We learned that the practice of spiritual disciplines is a way to increase our capacity for the kingdom. We saw that living for an audience of one is crucial. We learned about using our treasures for the kingdom, the kingdom itself is a treasure, and the treasure in the kingdom is God. We saw if we commit our treasures to the kingdom, then God, the king, will commit the treasures of his kingdom to provide abundantly and generously for us. We learned about board removal, pearl pushing, and asking. We saw the Golden Rule as the apex of the things Jesus taught in the Sermon on the Mount. We left the Sermon with the closing words of Jesus, that it doesn't do anything just to hear these words, we have to do them.

"In Matthew 10, Jesus sent us out on kingdom mission.

"In Matthew 13, Jesus showed us the dynamics of how God and the kingdom function in kingdom mission.

"In Matthew 18, Jesus told us about what kingdom community looks like and how we are to get along with each other.

"We saw the starting point of accessing all this kingdom change in our lives is the first Beatitude, 'Blessed are the poor in spirit, for theirs is the kingdom of heaven.'"

"I thought that was what you were going to say," Joe replied. "Here's my problem. I'm nowhere near ready. My life looks a lot more like what Jesus described than it did a year ago, but I'm a long way from being a kingdom poster boy. If you looked kingdom living up in the dictionary, my picture wouldn't be next to the definition. Maybe a few more years down the line it might, but not now. So if Jesus came today, would I be welcomed in, or would I be shut out?"

"The very asking of the question," Matt said, "is an indication you would make it through the door. Unconcern about readiness is a sign of unreadiness.

"But let me respond further. Jesus closed out the Sermon on the Mount by telling us to do what he said. So I think being ready has to do with attempting to do what Jesus said. Am I putting my heart into living this way? Am I asking for help and for kingdom change to come into my life? Am I spending time in the spiritual disciplines to increase my kingdom capacity, which, in turn, increases my ability to live out the words of Jesus? When the Holy Spirit prompts, moves, leads, nudges, or calls, do I respond and follow the Holy Spirit's direction?

"Readiness is a lifestyle of following Jesus. Readiness is present tense. The readiness question is not: Was I ready yesterday? It's not: Will I be ready tomorrow? The readiness question is: Am I ready now? Am I following Jesus today? I may know more and understand more and follow better tomorrow, but that's not the issue. I may have had some great yesterdays following Jesus, but that's not the issue. The issue is: Am I following Jesus today with the best I can offer today?

"So are you ready?"

"If the trumpet sounds right now, I'm ready," Joe responded. "It appears, then, the way Jesus sets this up, that he's looking for moment-to-moment, day-to-day readiness. I guess that makes sense because the only time I can follow Jesus, live his words and do what he asks, is right now. The present is the time in which I act. So unless I build the readiness from yesterday into today by the power of habit, yesterday's readiness means nothing today. Unless I act today in readiness, the idea of being ready on some tomorrow means nothing today either. I think I hear you saying Jesus wants me present to him and with him today."

"I think you have it, for now—" Matt laughed. "Are you ready for the next parable? Okay, we find it in Matthew 25:14-30. Let's look at it:

> "Again, it will be like a man going on a journey, who called his servants and entrusted his property to them. To one he gave five talents of money, to another two talents, and to another one talent, each according to his ability. Then he went on his journey. The man who had received the five talents went at once and put his money to work and gained five more. So also, the one with the two talents gained two more. But the man who had received the one talent went off, dug a hole in the ground and hid his master's money.
>
> "After a long time the master of those servants returned and settled accounts with them. The man who had received the five talents brought the other five. 'Master,' he said, 'you entrusted me with five talents. See, I have gained five more.'
>
> "His master replied, 'Well done, good and faithful servant! You have been faithful with a few things; I will put you in charge of many things. Come and share your master's happiness!'

"The man with the two talents also came. 'Master,' he said, 'you entrusted me with two talents; see, I have gained two more.'

"His master replied, 'Well done, good and faithful servant! You have been faithful with a few things; I will put you in charge of many things. Come and share your master's happiness!'

"Then the man who had received the one talent came. 'Master,' he said, 'I knew that you are a hard man, harvesting where you have not sown and gathering where you have not scattered seed. So I was afraid and went out and hid your talent in the ground. See, here is what belongs to you.'

"His master replied, 'You wicked, lazy servant! So you knew that I harvest where I have not sown and gather where I have not scattered seed? Well then, you should have put my money on deposit with the bankers, so that when I returned I would have received it back with interest.

"'Take the talent from him and give it to the one who has the ten talents. For everyone who has will be given more, and he will have an abundance. Whoever does not have, even what he has will be taken from him. And throw that worthless servant outside, into the darkness, where there will be weeping and gnashing of teeth.'

"I'm beginning to think Jesus didn't tell any stories with happy endings," Joe complained. "By the way, how much money is a talent?"

"A talent," Matt answered, "is the wages of a day laborer for fifteen years. So let's do some math. Minimum wage is about $7 an hour; $7 for 40 hours a week is $280 a week; $280 times 50 weeks is $14,000 a year; $14,000 times 15 years is $210,000. So a talent could be as low as $210,000, or if you use a labor rate of $20 an hour, it's a lot more."

"That's a lot of money the master is throwing around in the story," Joe said. "That would mean the servant who was given 5 talents received $1,050,000 and the servant with 2 talents received

$420,000 and the servant with the 1 talent got $210,000. Sounds like nice work if you can get it."

"You've got the money straight," Matt commented, "Do you have the rest of the details together?"

"Let me see," Joe responded. "The master leaves on a long trip. He gives all this money to three of his servants, and I get the idea they were supposed to work it for him. Each one gets what he can handle based on his abilities. That sounds good so far. Two of the servants work the money and double it. Their master returns, is happy with their efforts, and rewards them. The third servant puts his money in a hole in the ground. When the master returns, he's not happy with the third servant and has him thrown outside into the darkness where there will be weeping and gnashing of teeth. Like I said, has Jesus forgotten how to tell a story with a happy ending?"

"That's good—you have it," Matt replied. "Now, is there anything unexpected in this story Jesus tells?"

"I think so," Joe said. "We get two completely different pictures of the master, and the story doesn't refute or endorse either view. I didn't expect the treatment the third servant received. He didn't lose the money, but then his money is given to the one who now has ten talents. The third servant is thrown out. To make matters worse, Jesus called him wicked, lazy, and worthless. I can see lazy and maybe worthless, but how is this guy wicked? He didn't cheat the master—he returned the full amount. Wicked would be the guy started a drug smuggling ring, hid the money, murdered a bunch of people in the drug trade, and told everyone the master was behind it. That would be wicked. I don't see how Jesus can call this guy wicked."

"Let's unpack this some," Matt said. "First, let's look at the descriptions of the master. I think the first two servants would describe their master as a kind and generous man and a good judge of his servants' abilities. He trusted them with great amounts of money and gave them a chance to succeed. Upon observing their faithfulness with what was entrusted to them, the master entrusted them with more. They got promoted. The master told the two servants on his return, 'Well done, good and faithful servants…come and share in your master's happiness.' What more could anyone want? The servants got a chance to prove themselves and got to move up, and I think, got to be closer to the master.

"The third servant called the master 'a hard man, harvesting where [he has] not sown.' The master did not deny that assessment. The master then proceeded to act with this servant precisely as a hard man would act.

"Let me ask a question about the master. What if the master's primary purpose was something other than increasing his material assets? What if the master's primary concern was the development of his servants? What if the master's journey, and the money entrusted to his servants, was done to give them a chance to show what they could do?[iv]

"Then what do we learn about the servants?"

"The first two servants," Joe answered, "showed they were just what the master said about them. They were good. They were faithful. They took appropriate risks. I think they were even concerned about their master. The money wasn't theirs, and the profits weren't theirs. While doing a good job managing the master's money had benefit to them, it was nothing compared to the payoff the master would receive. So I think they cared about their master and his business. I think they had tied their own futures to the future of their master and were committed to his success.

"The third servant was nothing like the first two. Like his master said, he was lazy. He took no initiative. He was afraid of his master. His focus seemed to be himself. He had no love for the master or concern for his master's business. He looked like he was just putting in his hours, showing up, and marking time. I can understand the master calling him lazy, and even firing him, but how is this man wicked?"

"Erwin McManus, in his book, *Uprising: A Revolution of the Soul,* says we have a tendency to measure wickedness," Matt replied, "in terms of something we have done.[v] The master is measuring wickedness in terms of what could have been done, but wasn't. In the business world, we call that opportunity cost. The servant missed an opportunity to double his master's money. In not doubling his master's money, the master now misses additional opportunities that would have been available to him had the money been doubled.

"Further, the servant missed the opportunity to develop himself beyond where he was. This servant could have become a two-talent servant and then could have been developed like the two-talent servant into a four-talent servant. A servant who developed from a one-talent servant to two-talent servant would be able to manage far more for the master than the one-talent servant. So what the master had planned for the servant now has to be scrapped. There is one more place where the opportunity cost hit the master. The opportunity that was wasted by this servant could have been given to another servant who would have made the most of the opportunity. So this third servant robbed his master, another servant, and himself.

"Let me play this out on one more level and see if the wickedness doesn't become more apparent. Suppose the master had expectations, based on some business opportunities that were realistic, that this servant could have made his one talent two. Suppose the master was going to use those two talents to dig some wells in a part of the world where clean water for drinking and irrigation were lacking. Suppose the master had intended the clean water from those wells to bring health into a village of disease and death. Because the servant didn't work the opportunity, another fifteen people died before the master could leverage resources to dig the wells. Would the people in the village question the master's assessment of this man as wicked?

"What is Jesus telling us with this parable?"

"I think we need to make sure we work the opportunities given to us," a rather somber Joe said. "With this concept of opportunity cost, Jesus was talking about some pretty serious business. What's even scarier is that, like the servants, we aren't aware of the scope of the opportunity when it presents itself. I'm thinking about those passages we looked at when we were talking about sharing the gospel. When Peter stopped to deal with the lame man at the temple gate, he didn't know his encounter with the lame man meant two thousand people would come to Jesus in the next hour or so. When Stephan left the revival in Samaria and heeded the angel's call to go to the desert road in Gaza, he had no idea he would meet a man who would take Christianity to Ethiopia and change the destiny of that nation."

"Along those lines," Matt added, "the small stuff matters. What was it the master said, 'You have been faithful with a few things; I will put you in charge of many things.' If we want to do great things for God or be used by God in great ways, we have to be faithful with the small, seemingly unimportant things. A woman at a well, a lame beggar by a temple gate, and a lone man on a desert road all seemed small and insignificant. Yet, it was the attention paid to those people that resulted in God touching the lives of thousands of people. We often pass by the small things or the small people wishing God would give us some great or important thing to do. But God doesn't give us great, important things to do until we show ourselves faithful in the small things. The detail we give to small things, the effort we put into small things, the way we handle small things is exactly the way we'll handle large things. If we handle small things poorly, why would God give us large things? I remember coaches yelling at us in practice that the way we play in practice is how we would play in the game. If we didn't hustle in practice or play defense in practice, the coach knew he couldn't depend on us in the game to hustle or play defense. It's the same with God, except the stakes are much higher. In the kingdom, we're not talking about a ball game or a few dollars—we're dealing with the lives of men and women and their destinies for eternity.

"I think, in this parable, Jesus told us how to advance in the kingdom of heaven. God gives us small stuff. When we do well with small stuff, God gives us a little larger responsibility, and then a little more. 'You have been faithful with a few things; I will put you in charge of many things' were the master's words. Do well with the entry level tasks, and the manager will promote you. That's how it works in most companies. It's the same with the kingdom. Do well with the small stuff, the entry level stuff, and God will promote you in the kingdom.

"I wonder if being promoted in the kingdom is not about power and prestige, but simply the opportunity to deal with more women at wells, more lame beggars at temple gates, and more lone men on desert roads. I wonder if being promoted in the kingdom is about helping others to see the small stuff and the small people so that they, too, can see the opportunity and offer kingdom help and see what incredible thing God has wrapped up in this small thing or small person.

"I also think Jesus was telling us the opportunities are given by God to develop us. As we have seen, God's measure for our lives is not about who we are, but who we can become. I think God is committed to doing all he can to help us grow to be the people he sees we can become. Look at how much time Jesus spent with these twelve disciples. He continually unpacked all the stuff of the kingdom of heaven because if it could ever get a foothold in their lives, the sky would be the limit for them. What God wants us to become is less about what we can do and more about who we are. God is interested in our character. Character will grow competency, but competency will not grow character. It's in the small stuff that character is developed."

"Let me ask a question," Joe broke in. "What do you think the master would have done if the third servant had taken his one talent and put it to work and lost it?"

"I think," Matt said, "the master would have praised him for his effort. Then, the master would have helped the servant discover how he failed and where he needed to improve to do better the next time. I think the only way you can fail with God is not to try."

"Let me see if I can sum this up," Joe said. "Small stuff matters, character counts, and God is far more interested in the good we do than in the evil we don't do. That sounds to me like what Jesus said about living a life that exceeds the law. The law is about not doing harm, but love which seeks to do good exceeds the law."

"I think you have it," Matt responded. "Next week, we'll look at the last parable in Matthew 25 and put together all these parables, stories, and pictures Jesus gave us about life until the end."

"Sounds good to me," Joe replied.

Matt prayed for Joe's meeting with his dad, and Joe prayed for Matt's dealings with Kelly and his team. Together they walked out into the warm spring night, looked at the stars for a few minutes together, then each got into his car, wondering not just about the big things that were coming but what small thing God might set them up with next week.

Suggested resources:

William Barclay, *The Gospel of Matthew, Volume 2, Chapters 11 to 28*, The Westminster Press, 1975, The Saint Andrew Press, Edinburgh, Scotland, First Edition 1957.

Patrick Lencioni, *The Five Dysfunctions of a Team,* Jossey-Bass, 2002.

Patrick Lencioni, *Silos, Politics and Turf Wars*, Jossey-Bass, 2006.

Erwin Raphael McManus, *Uprising: A Revolution of the Soul*, Thomas Nelson, Inc., 2003.

CHAPTER 27

UNTIL THE END: PART III

As Matt walked across the parking lot, he wondered how Joe's meeting with his dad went. Joe had called him and asked him to pray for the meeting as he was driving to the diner. Joe had been extremely nervous Friday night and Saturday morning. *It's one thing to think about doing something and something else entirely to actually do it*, Matt thought. He hoped it went alright. As Matt opened the door, he took another look around the parking lot and still didn't see Joe's car. Matt went in, looked the place over, saw their usual table, but didn't see Joe anywhere. Matt ordered, got his cup of coffee, sat down, and waited. It was an uncomfortable wait. Matt was 95 percent certain that everything went alright for Joe, but that 5 percent uncertainty was playing with his mind as all kinds of what-if scenarios involving Joe and his dad played out. Matt couldn't remember the last time the second hand on the big clock on the wall had moved so slowly. All these past weeks it had seemed to run double time, but tonight it seemed as though each tick was an hour instead of a second.

Finally, after the second hand spent three eternities making three revolutions, Matt saw Joe walking across the parking lot. Matt began to breathe easier. Joe came in, waved at Matt, noticed the lack of chocolate chip cookies on the table, and ordered two with his coffee. As Joe sat down, Matt said, "Tell me, how did it go?"

"Hello to you too," Joe replied. "How did what go?"

"I see," Matt said, "You're going to torture me. I've been waiting since yesterday to find out how the meeting went with you and your dad. If you don't tell me, I'll eat your chocolate chip cookie."

"Okay! Okay!" Joe laughed. "I'll tell you. The best word I have to describe the meeting is *weird*. Not good weird or bad weird, just weird. My dad is not the man I remembered. I know that I haven't seen him or talked with since I was twenty-five, but I wasn't prepared at all for the gentleman who met me at the diner. I didn't recognize him. This old, feeble-looking man, leaning on a cane, came up to my table, said my name, and said he was glad to see me. I just stared at him for a moment. His hair, which had just a little gray in it all those years ago, was now white. His face was heavily lined, and he was wearing glasses, which was something I never saw. The military posture was gone. He was so much smaller than I remembered. He was shorter and lighter. His eyes lacked the fire I remember. Even though he called me by name, I had to ask, 'Dad, is that you?' He laughed and said it had been a long time, but it was him.

"He thanked me for coming. He told me he didn't deserve to be my father. He told me he was proud of me and what I had become. He showed me the pictures my mother had sent him of my family through the years. He told me they were a nice looking family. Then he told me his biggest regret in life had been losing me because of his inability to be a good father to me. He said, 'You were my pride and joy, but I had no idea of what to do with you or how to handle you. I didn't know who to ask. I was too proud to ask for help anyway. Your mother tried to help me, but she didn't know what to do with me either. I swore that I would be a better father to you than my father was to me, but I was worse. I've had a lot time to think about what I would say to you if you ever gave me the chance. To be honest, as the years rolled into decades, I didn't think I would ever get the chance. These last few years, my hope was that maybe you would come to my funeral. But now I have the chance to say it, can you forgive me?'

"As he was telling me those things, I felt like I had wasted a lifetime. I felt like I had thrown away something that was far more precious than I had ever imagined. I felt a terrible emptiness and a huge regret at the same time. There was this lump in my throat. When he asked if I could forgive him, there were tears in his eyes, and there were tears in mine when I said, 'Yes.' He started shaking with sobs, and I asked him if he could forgive me for shutting him out for a lifetime. He said there was nothing to forgive and reached across the table and took my hand. When we had both regained our composure, the waitress, who had been giving us time and space, took our order for coffee.

"After the coffee came, Dad asked me what had happened after all these years that I would want to see him again. I told him about you, me, and Jesus and the changes happening in my life. His response took me took me off guard. He said, 'So there is a God, and he cares. You don't how many nights I asked God to fix the mess I made and bring you back into my life. Every time, it felt like there was no one there, and if someone were there, it was no one who cared. I'd like to hear more some time.' Then he asked, 'So what happens now?' I told him about Sue and each of the kids, and we set a time for me to bring them to his place so that he could meet all of them. He said, 'You don't know how happy that would make me.' I told him it would be good for us too. As we parted, I gave him a hug.

"I still can't believe it. I guess I'm in shock. I see the counselor again this week, and he'll help me process through this stuff."

"Wow, that was some pretty heavy stuff," Matt replied. "I'm glad it went well. It will be interesting to see how you two go about building a new relationship."

"That's too far for me to see right now. I'm just excited about taking the grandkids to meet him," Joe said. "How did your job search group go this week?"

"Several members of the group have bonded," Matt reported, "so there's a nice core. People have been inviting others to come, so each week the group has grown. Three of the members have gotten interviews over the last couple of weeks and are waiting to hear back for second interviews. Each of those three have attributed their interviews to the prayers the group has been praying for them. We reviewed the key concepts in John Maxwell's book, *Failing Forward,* this past week.[i] Maxwell says the price of success is failure. It's the lessons we learn from failing that help us succeed.

We talked about failure in the search for a new job. We talked about the second Beatitude, 'Blessed are those who mourn, for they shall be comforted,' as meaning Jesus promises strength to get back up and go on after failing. Afterward, Marge asked me for an appointment to sit down and, in her words, 'have a serious God talk.' I was up for that. It's coming up in a couple of days.

"Did your team win?"

"Yes, they did," Joe said. "We played late Saturday afternoon. I was on autopilot after seeing my dad in the morning. I think that's why they won. The team they played only had one win, so they were more at our level. The boys continued to help each other, and this time they got rewarded with a *w*. The devotion was from John 3:16. Like me, some of them had never heard it before. It's an amazing verse, especially the 'whosoever' part. They asked me a bunch of questions about it. I'm glad I was able to answer most of them. The lights are on, and the wheels are turning. Maybe I can get them to move from help basketball to help life.

"If I'm right, I think we have the last story Jesus told tonight."

"You're right," Matt answered. "This is his last story. It's about The Sheep and the Goats, and it's in Matthew 25:31-46. Let's look at it:

> "When the Son of Man comes in his glory, and all the angels with him, he will sit on his throne in heavenly glory. All the nations will be gathered before him, and he will separate the people one from another as a shepherd separates the sheep from the goats. He will put the sheep on his right and the goats on his left.
>
> "Then the King will say to those on his right, 'Come, you who are blessed by my Father; take your inheritance, the kingdom prepared for you since the creation of the world. For I was hungry and you gave me something to eat, I was thirsty and you gave me something to drink, I was a stranger and you invited me in, I needed clothes and you clothed me, I was sick and you looked after me, I was in prison and you came to visit me.'

"Then the righteous will answer him, 'Lord, when did we see you hungry and feed you, or thirsty and give you something to drink? When did we see you a stranger and invite you in, or needing clothes and clothe you? When did we see you sick or in prison and go to visit you?'

"The King will reply, 'I tell you the truth, whatever you did for one of the least of these brothers of mine, you did for me.'

"Then he will say to those on his left, 'Depart from me, you who are cursed, into the eternal fire prepared for the devil and his angels. For I was hungry and you gave me nothing to eat, I was thirsty and you gave me nothing to drink, I was a stranger and you did not invite me in, I needed clothes and you did not clothe me, I was sick and in prison and you did not look after me.'

"They also will answer, 'Lord, when did we see you hungry or thirsty or a stranger or needing clothes or sick or in prison, and did not help you?'

"He will reply, 'I tell you the truth, whatever you did not do for one of the least of these, you did not do for me.'

"Then they will go away to eternal punishment, but the righteous to eternal life."

"Is there anything unexpected in this story?"
"Yes," Joe replied, "there are several unexpected and disturbing things going on in this story. I'm surprised that the basis of judgment is how well we take care of people who need to be fed, housed, clothed, visited, and need something to drink. It seems to me there are more significant things to do, from winning a Nobel prize, to running a great company, to running a government, to creating art, to winning championships, to inventing things that make life easier or extend our reach. But then again, maybe the most important thing we can do is to take care of one another. But still, the way Jesus put it makes it sound unexpected. I guess the people we care about the most are ones who have the ability to care for us. But the people Jesus highlighted don't seem like they would be able to do anything for us, or at least, not do anything anytime soon.

"I'm also surprised that both groups, sheep and goats, are surprised by the judgment. Maybe the biggest surprise is Jesus claimed that care for the hungry, thirsty, naked, sick, and imprisoned is care for him. The sheep aren't aware their care of the sick, hungry, the naked, the imprisoned, and the thirsty is so significant. Likewise, the goats aren't aware they haven't taken care of Jesus and that he would take personally their treatment of the sick, the hungry, the naked, the imprisoned, and the thirsty.

"I'm also surprised by the severity of the judgment on both sides. Just caring for the sick is worth blessing and admittance into the Father's kingdom? It doesn't seem like much to get in. Likewise the penalty for not caring seems equally severe—cursing and eternal fire prepared for the devil and his angels. It doesn't seem like much to be damned.

"There's something else that bothers me. The basis of judgment here is what someone does, not what someone believes. I thought we were saved by faith, not by works. Help me out here."

"I'll try," Matt said. "We are saved by faith, not by works. Works is the attempt to do enough good things to get in. Remember, we said faith is not just believing something is true. Faith is believing something is true and acting on it. If I act on the words of Jesus and invite him into my life because I want to be forgiven and to live a different life, then the Holy Spirit begins to drive my actions. The more I surrender to or cooperate with the Holy Spirit, the more I'm able to act in accordance with what the Holy Spirit desires. Paul talked about this as recorded in the first part of Romans 8. As I act out of the life of the Holy Spirit within me, I find myself taking care of the sick, visiting the imprisoned, feeding the hungry, clothing the naked, and giving drink to the thirsty. I find myself doing this as a lifestyle.

"The flip side of this is that apart from the work of God's Holy Spirit, we're unable to live this type of lifestyle. Maybe we can live this way upon occasion—I can be like that at Christmas. Or maybe, if it's someone close to me, I can care for that person. But by and large, without the work of the Holy Spirit in my life or the work of the kingdom, as we have been saying all these weeks, I won't do these things—I'll live my life according to some law, which boils down to do what you like as long as you don't harm anyone. My focus is myself. If I help too much, there won't be any left for me. The law of love, which is brought by the kingdom change in our hearts, is to do good, to help, to love. My focus is no longer myself. I can focus on others because, in the kingdom, I'm cared for with endless love.

"Jesus' story of The Good Samaritan illustrates this (Luke 10:25-37). A man is beaten, robbed, and left to die on the side of the road. Both a priest and a Levite, people of high religious character and attentive to law keeping, pass by on the other side of the road, no doubt thinking: Poor fellow—I better go fast because the bandits might still be near. According to the law, they have done nothing wrong, but according to Jesus, in the parable of The Sheep and the Goats, they're likely to end up with the goats. The Samaritan, who no one would think would do anything good, actually stops to help the man. The Samaritan is not motivated by law keeping but by compassion and love. He likely would wind up on the sheep side.

"That's helpful," Joe said. "My faith or lack of it shows in my actions. That makes sense. If the kingdom is near and if the kingdom is in my heart, then I would act differently. I couldn't help myself. With the kingdom in my heart, I would naturally find myself visiting the sick, feeding the hungry, giving drink to the thirsty, and visiting prisoners. I suspect these are some of the people Jesus meant when he urged us to care for those without voice, vote, power, or influence."

"That brings us to Jesus' main point here," Matt added. "This is the part I find most surprising, and I think the sheep and goats are surprised by it too. Jesus takes personally how we treat the sick, imprisoned, naked, thirsty, and hungry. Jesus told the sheep they took care of him. The sheep asked when they took care of him, and Jesus said that when they cared for those in need, they cared for him. Likewise, Jesus said the same thing to the goats, only in the negative—they didn't take care of him. All self-respecting goats know you take care of the people who can take care of you, and who better to take care of than the king? So they were surprised that they would have missed that chance, and they protested. But Jesus told them they didn't care for the sick, and so on, so they didn't take care of him.

"It always amazes me that the Lord of lords, the King of kings, the ruler and creator of the cosmos and all that is, identifies with the poor and downtrodden.

"Let's put these six stories, or pictures, where Jesus told about life until the end, together and see what we come up with.

"The first story is that Jesus said the time of his return will be like in the days of Noah. People will be busy with life and unaware he's about to return.

"The second story is that if the owner of the house knew the thief was coming in the middle of the night, he would have been ready for the thief.

"The third story is about wise and foolish servants. The wise servant is taking good care of his master's business and is rewarded when the master returns. The foolish servant is abusing his position and the master's business and is punished when the master returns.

"The fourth story is about wise and foolish virgins. The wise virgins are ready when the bridegroom comes, and the foolish ones aren't.

"The fifth story, about the three servants and the talents, is about two servants taking initiative with the master's resources, growing them, and being rewarded when the master returns, and the third servant doing nothing with the master's resources and being punished when the master returns.

"The sixth story is about sheep and goats, and the sheep being rewarded for caring for the king by taking care of the needy, and the goats being punished for not caring for the king by not caring for the needy.

"What do you think Jesus is trying to tell us with these six stories?"

"There seem to be themes that keep reoccurring," Joe replied. "One of the themes is that Jesus is returning, and we don't know when. A second theme is that he has certain expectations of what we are to be doing in his absence. A third theme is judgment when he returns. It's like we said when we started this section, we need to get ready, be ready, and stay ready."

"Readiness is what Jesus has been telling us about ever since we started with him," Matt said. "Readiness is responding to the message—change, the kingdom of heaven is near. Readiness is accessing and living the kingdom values found in the Beatitudes:

> "Blessed are the poor in spirit,
>   for theirs is the kingdom of heaven.
> Blessed are those who mourn,
>   for they will be comforted.
> Blessed are the meek,
>   for they will inherit the earth.
> Blessed are those who hunger and thirst for righteousness,
>   for they will be filled.
> Blessed are the merciful,
>   for they will be shown mercy.
> Blessed are the pure in heart,
>   for they will see God.
> Blessed are the peacemakers,
>   for they will be called sons of God.
> Blessed are those who are persecuted because of righteousness,
>   for theirs is the kingdom of heaven.

"Readiness is being salt and light. Readiness is living a life of love that exceeds the law. Readiness is using our anger for reconciliation and resolution. Readiness is using our sexuality for blessing and keeping our hearts soft toward our spouses. Readiness is knowing when to say yes and when to say no and sticking to our yes and no. Readiness is being able to level the playing field when power is abused, and being able to use power to help and serve. Readiness is being able to love the enemy, learn from the enemy, overcome evil with good, and pray for the enemy. Readiness is in engaging the spiritual disciplines in ways that deepen our capacity for God and a relationship with him. Readiness is using our treasure to advance the kingdom and finding treasure in the kingdom. Readiness is putting our treasure and energy into advancing the kingdom and trusting God to provide for us with the same abundance, creativity, and glory in which he provides for the birds of the air and the flowers in the field. Readiness is not judging but doing our own board removal work so that we can help others with the specks with which they struggle. Readiness is setting aside pearl pushing in favor of asking, seeking, and knocking. Readiness is realizing that God, our father in heaven, likes to give good gifts to his children. Readiness is being able to treat others they way we would like to be treated rather than the way they treat us. Readiness is not just hearing and understanding what Jesus said, but actually doing it.

"Readiness is being involved in the kingdom mission of proclaiming the good news that the kingdom is near and then using the resources of the kingdom to help people through the life struggles they face.

"Readiness is being involved in kingdom community, kingdom teams to do kingdom mission where we're able to care for those without voice, vote, power, and influence and are able to work through the hurts and pains we cause one another, forgiving each other until we all get it right.

"Readiness is committing ourselves, our time, out talents, our treasures, our hopes, and our dreams to living this way until he comes and then living it with him far better than we ever did before he returned."

"That's a mouthful," Joe responded, "and I seem to remember most of it. I seem to remember the way to get ready is the first Beatitude, which is to pray: 'Jesus, it isn't in me. Please put it in me, and make up the difference with your kingdom resources.' As we do that and work the disciplines, do what Jesus taught, the life of the kingdom grows and grows within us, and we find ourselves looking more and more like what Jesus taught and doing the things that Jesus did."

"There are two things about Jesus' picture of readiness I have always found disturbing," Matt said. "The first is that there is no middle position. Either we're ready or we aren't. It's like a woman being pregnant. She either is or isn't. There's no way to be sort of or kind of pregnant. I think readiness is about the kingdom in us, and are we moving and living in accordance with it according to what we know and understand, or aren't we? That is an everyday thing.

"The second thing that disturbs me is these stories, these pictures Jesus gives of the end, are given to the disciples. They're given to us, who are trying to be ready. Some of them raise the issue that being ready yesterday isn't good enough—I need to be ready today. The indication is that if I were ready yesterday but not ready today, I will be left out, and the door will be shut on me. I know there has been lots of theological ink spilled about this by minds much brighter than mine. I don't know about all that. All I know here is Jesus said, 'Be ready,' and being not ready is not where I want to be. So I need to live each day in readiness."

"Jesus doesn't let us off the hook, does he?" Joe commented. "Maybe he knows something about human nature. Maybe he knows how easy it is for us to procrastinate about the difficult things in life. Maybe he knows how easy it is for us to get comfortable, and how we do less and less in a comfort zone, and how hard it is for us to get out of a comfort zone, or maybe rut is a better word.

"Let me ask a question: Just what does readiness look like?"

"I think readiness," Matt replied, "asks these questions: Did I encounter the kingdom today? Did I live any of it today? Did I put my heart into it? Did I connect with Jesus today? Did I do anything in relation with him?

"A follow-up question to that is to ask what does minimum readiness look like? But that's the wrong question. The question is: What does maximum readiness look like, and how can I achieve it today? It's like this: I ask you to eat a chocolate chip cookie, which, by the way, you do very well here every week. Would you ask me how little chocolate chip cookie you would have to eat to be able to say you ate a chocolate chip cookie?"

"No," Joe answered immediately, "I'd say do I have to stop at one?"

"My point precisely," Matt followed up. "Nor do I think you would ask how little you can do to love Sue today and still be able to say you love her. You love her and look for ways to grow your heart and love her more. You look for ways to show it and live it because it's in your heart. Some days you do better at it than others. If a few days go by and you don't show it or act on it, then Sue calls you on your priorities.

"Readiness works the same way. It's a heart thing. I love Jesus or I don't. I have the kingdom in me, or I don't. I'm working for the kingdom, or I'm not. The question is not how little can I do and be ready, but rather, how can I arrange my life so that I can do more? If the kingdom is like treasure hidden in a field, if it's the best thing that has ever happened to me, why I would I want less? This is good stuff—I want more. The question, how little can I do to be ready, takes us back into the law. I did this, and I did that, and that's enough kingdom for the day, and now I can do what I really want to do. Readiness is having the kingdom be what we really want to do. Readiness is asking how I can arrange my life so that I can do more kingdom.

"I know we read these passages and are afraid we won't be ready. That's the question Jesus wants us to struggle with. It's not an action issue. It's a heart issue. Jesus wants us to guard our hearts. Proverbs 4:23 says, 'Above all else, guard your heart, for it is the wellspring of life.' The heart needs to be guarded, examined, and engaged daily. The way we lose readiness is the same way we fall out of love with our spouses. It happens a little bit at a time, so slowly we don't even notice it, until one day we wake up, and we aren't in love with our spouses anymore. One unresolved issue here, a little lack of communication there, a slight here, a distraction there, and so it goes, until we find ourselves drifted apart. We have to stay current with our spouses. We have to stay current with Jesus. Readiness is a daily thing."

"I want to stay ready," Joe said, "Will you help me keep on track with my readiness?"

"I'll help you if you help me," Matt responded.

"Deal," Joe replied. "Now about those chocolate chip cookies—"

As they ate more chocolate chip cookies, they prayed for each other, chose a spiritual discipline, and finished their coffee. *Readiness is asking, how can I arrange my life so that I can do more kingdom?* Driving out of the parking lot, that phrase stuck with Joe, and he prayed on the way home, "Jesus, please show me." With a smile on his face, he thought, *I've been here before.*

Suggested resource:
John C. Maxwell, *Failing Forward*, Thomas Nelson Publishers, 2000.

PHASE VI

THE GREAT COMMISSION

MATTHEW 28:18-20

CHAPTER 28

THE GREAT COMMISSION

It was a beautiful spring evening as Joe pulled into the parking lot. He saw Matt getting out of his car a couple of rows over. After Joe parked his car, he yelled a greeting to Matt. Matt waited for him, and they entered the coffee shop together talking about the nice weather, yard work, and baseball. The girl at the counter had to interrupt them to get their order, not that it mattered because she told them they were getting two coffees and chocolate chip cookies.

When they were seated, Joe asked Matt, "How did your serious God talk go with Marge?"

"I'm not sure," Matt answered. "God is doing some stuff in Marge's life, but I'm not sure Marge can see it. The God stuff she wanted to talk about had to do with forgiveness, although that wasn't how she phrased it. She said she has appreciated the couple of Sundays she has attended church with us and likes the upbeat, encouraging service we have there. Her issue was, 'How can God be so good and allow so many mean people to be in the world?' She told me a couple of stories of how people have hurt her through the years. She wanted to know why God allowed those kinds of people to live. She said she would like to be closer to God, but every time she tries to get close to God, there is some mean person who messes things up for her."

"What did you say to her?" Joe asked.

"I said it slowly and carefully," Matt replied, "because I didn't want her to put me in the mean person category too. I told her I don't know why God allows mean people to keep on living. Then I said, 'With God's help, I've found a way to deal with mean people.' I asked her if she was interested. I asked because I didn't want to pearl push and wasn't sure she really wanted to know. But she asked to me to go on. I talked about forgiveness, asking God for healing, praying for the person who was mean, and finding a way to do something good for that person. She had some objections, which we talked about. She closed the time by saying, 'What I have been doing hasn't been working. I want to be closer to God, and this has been in the way, so maybe I'll give it a try.' She wasn't sure it would work, but she wasn't sure it would hurt either. So I'll pray for her and wait and see what happens.

"So tell me more about your dad."

"My counselor," Joe responded, "was very pleased. But he warned me that chances are that even though my dad deeply regrets his poor parenting record, he probably hasn't done anything to change. Further, although our relationship will be very different, I'll probably have to help him understand the turmoil in his soul and show him where and how to get help with those issues. I guess sometimes our parents parent us, and sometimes we parent them. Either way, I'd like to help him to get the help to work through his issues. Sue and the kids are looking forward to seeing him next weekend. Sue always thought I had been too hard on him and is very happy we're reconnecting. I have received big husband points for this. I had no idea. I think I'll find another relative to go reconcile with.

"Speaking of Sue, I think she has figured out a way to become involved with the AIDS orphans in Africa. She had lunch last week with a couple of her roommates from college. The one lady was talking about another lady they all knew, who has a daughter who is preparing to go to Africa to work in an orphanage there. While Sue isn't sure orphanages are the answer, this was a personal contact. When she got home, she dialed the lady and got the daughter's email address. Sue is buying the daughter some lunch next week and is going to ask how she can be of support. I'm sure Mary will fill you in on all the details once Sue has them."

"I'm sure she will too." Matt laughed. "Did your team win this week?"

"What kind of question is that?" Joe replied in mock offense. "Of course we won. It was shaky, but we won. I had to call a timeout in the third quarter to remind them they needed to help each other. The devotion was good. They paid attention and asked questions. They had prayer requests, and one of the guys even volunteered to pray. After the game, one of the parents pulled me aside. He thanked me for coaching the team, told me how much his boy enjoys being on the team, and then told me his boy's general attitude had improved markedly since the first game. That was great to hear. I told the dad it wasn't something I had done—God was working through the team. He looked at me kind of puzzled and asked what I meant. So I told him how much I pray for the boys, why I'm doing this, and how much God loves those guys on the team. He looked at me like the concepts I just told him were all foreign. He thanked me again and said, 'Anyway, I just wanted you to know.' I wonder if I'll get to have some more conversations with him before the season ends."

"I bet you will," Matt said. "Tonight brings us to the last words of Jesus in Matthew's Gospel. They're found in Matthew 28:18-20. Before we get to them, let's take a look at what happened to Jesus after chapter 25."

"Since we're looking at the last words of Jesus, does this mean this is our last night together?" Joe asked.

"That depends on you," Matt replied. "We'll talk about that later on. But for now, let's track Jesus. At the beginning of chapter 26, Jesus made plans with his disciples for the Passover and predicted his crucifixion again. While that was happening, the religious leaders were meeting to plot how they could arrest Jesus away from the crowds and have him executed. Fortunately, for the religious leaders, that evening brought their plan together. Jesus was dining in Bethany at the house of Simon the Leper. During dinner, a woman broke open a jar of very expensive perfume and poured it over Jesus' head. The disciples were upset about this because the perfume could have been sold and the money used for the poor. For whatever reason, this set Judas off enough that he went and sought out the religious officials and agreed to deliver Jesus into their hands.

"On Thursday, Jesus celebrated the Passover with the disciples and instituted the Lord's Supper, giving them the bread and saying, 'Take and eat; this is my body' and then pouring the wine and saying, 'This is my blood of the covenant, which is poured out for many for the forgiveness of sins' (Matthew 26:26-28). Also during the evening, Jesus predicted the betrayal by Judas and the denial by Peter.

"After supper, Jesus and the disciples went to the garden of Gethsemane. Jesus prayed with a troubled and overwhelmed soul, asking for the cup to pass from him but wanting the Father's will to be done. As Jesus prayed, the disciples slept.

"After about an hour, Judas came to the garden with a large crowd armed with swords and clubs. It almost sounds like a lynch mob. But in the crowd were some soldiers from the temple guard and some temple authorities. Judas identified Jesus by greeting him with a kiss. Jesus prepared to go with them, but Peter took a sword and swung it, cutting off the ear of the high priest's servant. Jesus told Peter to put the sword away and said he could call twelve legions of angels to fight for him if he wanted to. A legion is 6,000 so 12 legions would be 72,000 angels. That's a lot of angels. I don't know if the other disciples got Jesus' point, but I do. He didn't have to go—he wasn't a victim here. He was choosing to go, and as I read the rest of the narrative, it appears that Jesus was doing just enough to move events along to a crucifixion. There are many places where just a word from him would have stopped the events, but he didn't say the word. There are a couple other times that if he would have been quiet, things would have been different. Jesus was not swept along by events here—he was managing the events to the outcome of crucifixion. The crucifixion, which would be followed by resurrection, would bring salvation to all of us, change history, and firmly establish the kingdom of heaven forever.

"The disciples didn't see it, or couldn't see it, and they fled for their lives.

"Jesus was taken before the Sanhedrin, which was the seventy-member council which ruled the Jews. Testimony was brought against Jesus, but they couldn't get any two people to agree on any one charge. According to the law, every charge had to be verified by two or three witnesses. Finally, the high priest had had enough and put the question directly to Jesus, 'I charge you under oath by the living God: Tell us if you are the Christ, the Son of God' (Matthew 26:63).

"If Jesus remained silent, the proceedings would have stalled and broken down. Jesus chose to answer in such a way that it sent the high priest and most of the council over the edge. 'Yes, it is as you say...In the future you will see the Son of Man sitting at the right hand of the Mighty One and coming on the clouds of heaven' (Matthew 26:64). Then all hell broke loose. The high priest cried blasphemy, the members of the Sanhedrin spit on him, struck him with their fists, and slapped him with their hands. Then they sent him to Pilate, the governor, for the death sentence.

"While this was happening, Peter denied knowing Jesus not just once but three times. On the third time, he called down curses on himself if what he was saying was not true. Then the rooster crowed, and Peter remembered what Jesus had said and went out and wept bitterly.

"When Judas saw what was happening, he went to try to undo his deed. He went to the chief priests and tried to return the money to get Jesus released. They would have nothing to do with Judas or the money. Judas threw the money at their feet and went out and hung himself.

"Pilate tried to free Jesus, but Jesus gave him no help. When the High Priest began to apply some well-positioned political pressure, Pilate gave up, but he told them he wasn't guilty of Jesus' blood and washed his hands before them. The crowd responded, 'Let his blood be on us' (Matthew 27:25).

"So Pilate had Jesus flogged and then sent him to be crucified. A flogging is forty lashes with a whip that has glass and jagged rocks tied into its frayed ends. The flogging ripped opened his back. It was not unusual for a man to die from flogging. It was in this nearly dead state that Jesus was mocked by the soldiers as a king. It's no wonder Jesus wasn't able to carry the nearly forty-pound cross to Golgotha. Simon of Cyrene was forced to carry the cross for Jesus. Jesus was crucified at nine in the morning just outside the city gates at the major crossroads so that all would see. *Golgotha* means place of the skull, and the hill behind the crossroads looks like a skull even now, in our day. Jesus was crucified between two thieves. The soldiers divided his clothing between them by casting lots. Many people came to watch. Many of them were the religious leaders who had opposed him. They came to talk trash and gloat. The thieves crucified with him joined the insults.

"About noon, things got weird—it got dark. At three, Jesus cried out in a loud voice, 'My God, my God, why have you forsaken me?' (Matthew 27:46) Some tried to give him a pain killer. Jesus cried out one more time, and died. When he died, the curtain of the temple, which separated the Holy of Holies from the rest of the temple, was torn in two from top to bottom. Don't think living room curtain, but rather, something more substantial than a stage curtain. Then there was an earthquake. But weirdest of all, Matthew said some tombs broke open, and many holy people were raised to life. After the resurrection of Jesus, they went into the city and appeared to many people. Then the Roman Centurion, who by now was terrified, was heard to say of Jesus, 'Surely he was the Son of God' (Matthew 27:54).

"When evening came, Joseph of Arimathea, a rich man who had become a follower of Jesus, went to Pilate and asked for the body. Pilate was surprised to find out Jesus was dead so soon. Usually it took people a couple of days to die on a cross. Pilate gave orders to have the body released. Joseph took the body and wrapped it in a clean linen cloth. Then he put the body in his own new tomb that had been cut out of rock. He rolled a big stone in front of the entrance. John's Gospel tells us Nicodemus helped Joseph (John 19:39). Because of the detail in John's Gospel, I wouldn't be surprised if John, himself, were there too. The women, the two Marys, and some others were there watching and, I suppose, helping.

"They had to hurry because the Sabbath began at sundown on Friday. Even though they hurried, they didn't get finished with the burial preparations. On Saturday, the Sabbath, there was no work that could be done, especially burial preparations. The Sabbath ended at sundown on Saturday. No one went to the tomb Saturday night because it was dark. Anyway, I wouldn't want to play in a graveyard with only a torch for a light. So the women went back to the tomb at dawn on Sunday, the earliest they could get there. In the meantime, the chief priests went to Pilate to ask for a Roman guard for the tomb. They didn't want the disciples to steal the body and claim Jesus had risen from the dead. Pilate sent soldiers to guard the tomb. The women were unaware of the soldiers.

"As the two Marys arrived at the tomb, there was a violent earthquake, and an angel came down from heaven, went to the stone, rolled it back, and sat on it. The guards passed out at the sight of the angel, and the women were terrified. The angel told them not to be afraid, that Jesus was risen, to go in and look, and then tell the disciples that Jesus would meet them in Galilee. The women fled from the tomb both afraid and filled with joy, and ran straight into Jesus, who greeted them and repeated the message from the angel.

"While the women were running to tell the disciples, the guards regained their senses and reported back to the chief priests what had happened. The chief priests and the elders gave the soldiers a lot of money and told them to tell people that the disciples had come during the night while the soldiers were asleep and had stolen the body."

"Wait a minute," Joe interrupted. "Do you mean to tell me that these chief priests who arranged his execution because they were at odds with him and hated him, yet at the same time claimed to be doing God's work, were still going to oppose him even though they knew he had risen? Didn't Jesus say his resurrection would prove who he was and what he was doing? And they were still going to oppose him? What were they going to do if he showed up and confronted them face to face? Didn't they see they were fighting God? To me, this is just mind boggling."

"If you think that's mind boggling, wait until you see what happened next," Matt said. "Let me set the context of the Great Commission. The disciples gathered at the mountain in Galilee following the message from the women. But the disciples were a mess, and the whole Jesus movement was in danger of collapsing. There were two resurrection stories. The official line from the networks was the disciples stole the body. The problem with that story was that it was highly unlikely the Roman soldiers fell asleep at their post. Even if they did, how would the scared disciples roll the stone away from the entrance of the tomb without waking the soldiers?

The unofficial story circulating on the internet and the talk radio programs was that some women had seen Jesus alive, that he had risen. The problem with this story was that women weren't considered credible witnesses in that day. A woman's testimony was not admitted to court as evidence. The disciples and the rest of the city that cared didn't know what to think.

"As I said, the disciples did go to the mountain. Jesus met them there. We aren't told how he arrived, just that he met them there. Now, here's the part that boggles my mind. The reaction of the disciples to the risen Lord was that they worshiped. I'm good with that. But then Matthew recorded that 'some doubted' (Matthew 28:17). I can understand that maybe the first reaction would be that this can't be real, but after some time to talk with Jesus, see the nail prints and all the rest, how could one doubt? But then again, maybe if I had been there and had experienced all that they had, my reaction might not have been much different.

"It was in this context of worship and doubt, truth and lie, rumor and shadow, opposed by the power structure of the day, that Jesus gave the Great Commission to his disciples. Let's get it in front of us. It's in Matthew 28:18-20:

> "All authority in heaven and on earth has been given to me. Therefore go and make disciples of all nations, baptizing them in the name of the Father and of the Son and of the Holy Spirit, and teaching them to obey everything I have commanded you. And surely I will be with you always, to the very end of the age."

Jesus didn't let all that was going on around him distract him, nor did he let it lower his expectations. In the midst of all the turmoil and unrest, and that was just his disciples, Jesus launched a mission through them that has changed the world. Let's look closer.

"This commission Jesus gave came in three parts. Part I is that Jesus said all authority in heaven and earth has been given to him. If Jesus has been given all authority, over who and what does Jesus have authority?"

"If I read it right," Joe answered," that would be all authority over everything."

"Over everything?" Matt asked.

"All authority in heaven and on earth would be authority over everything," Joe replied. "Jesus is the trump card. No one, or nothing, has more authority than he does. Jesus is the guy on the top of the pyramid."

"Are you telling me then," Matt clarified, "that Jesus has authority over the weather, the stock market, terrorists, cancer, multinational corporations, the President of the United States, my mortgage, and professional baseball?"

"I hadn't thought of it that way," Joe answered, "but that's what the man said. His authority, then, would be not just over religious or spiritual stuff, but over everything. So if I wanted to see someone in charge, it would be Jesus. So yes, Jesus has authority over cancer, multinational corporations, terrorists, mortgages, and even baseball."

"What do you suppose Jesus does with all that authority?" Matt asked.

"I don't know," Joe replied, "but I bet you're going to tell me."

"You're right," Matt said. "That takes us to Part II of the commission. 'Therefore go and make disciples of all nations, baptizing them in the name of the Father and of the Son and of the Holy Spirit, and teaching them to obey everything I have commanded you.' Jesus used, and uses, his authority to send his followers everywhere to be disciple makers and to clear the way for us to actually do it.

"Let's talk for a moment about what a disciple is. If you remember all the way back to the conversation that got us started, I said a disciple was someone who followed a teacher and learned the teachings in order to put those teachings into practice in his or her life. So then, a disciple of Jesus is someone who follows Jesus to learn his teachings in order to put those teachings into practice in his or her life. I've been reading Jeffrey Gitomer's book, *The Little Red Book of Selling*. At the end of the book, he talks about what to do with his material if you're serious about selling. He says to read it ten times to master the material and make it your own. If you read it ten times, he promises 'great sales, great attitude, great creativity, great relationships, great bank account, great life.'[i]

"Now if all that effort is required for something as mundane as selling copiers or time shares, wouldn't our efforts to live out the teachings of Jesus, which have eternal significance for us and those who live around us, require at least as much of our effort? What would happen if we went through these teachings of Jesus five times, ten times, fifteen times, or the rest of our lives? What would happen if we did this not just to learn the principles but to learn how to apply them and actually put them into practice?

"A disciple of Jesus, that is someone who is applying the words of Jesus to his or her life, would apply the good news or the nearness of the kingdom of heaven by embracing the change Jesus brings and inviting him into his or her heart. That person would be pursuing a kingdom lifestyle as taught by Jesus in Matthew 5-7, engaging in kingdom mission as sent by Jesus in Matthew 10 and 28, participating in kingdom community as described by Jesus in Matthew 18, and increasing in kingdom readiness as Jesus laid out in Matthew 24-25."

"I think I'm with you on what a disciple is," Joe commented. "I know the huge change that just going through these teachings of Jesus one time has had on my life. I can't imagine what I would look like if I went through them like this ten times. Or maybe I can. My life would look a whole lot more like what Jesus was describing in his teachings than it does now. That would be a bonus for everyone.

"How does Jesus want us to go about making disciples?"

"Drawing from what we've learned from Jesus," Matt answered, "we have to be salt and light to the people we would like to help become disciples. Being salt is living out the kingdom lifestyle in a way that makes people thirsty for what it is we have. Being light is being able to talk about what it is that makes us different. A second part of disciple making is being in kingdom mission. It's kingdom mission that addresses the needs in the lives of people, communicating to them that God knows, God cares, and God helps. This mission, this kindness, melts the resistance in the hearts of many, drawing them close to the God who loves them. As they respond to the mission and ask questions, we can answer. A third part of disciple making is getting into situations where the Holy Spirit can work through the spiritual gifts he has put into our lives. This, too, draws people because the Holy Spirit is at work. A fourth part of disciple making is helping people to actually cross the line of faith and pray that little prayer to invite Jesus in and to commit to follow him, just like you did. A fifth part of disciple making is engaging people in mentoring situations or small groups where they can be taught the teachings of Jesus in a way they can apply them, just like we've been doing. A sixth part of disciple making is helping them to make disciples of others. All the while, we need to treat people at each stage with the standard of Jesus, 'Do unto others as you would have them do unto you.'"

"It's not a simple process, is it?" Joe responded. "It has been messy with me. The first time I met you, I had no idea we'd be engaged in this incredible, life-changing work. But God was at work, and you hung in there. So my job as a disciple maker is to be used by God to do the same kinds of things for someone else that you did for me.

"Why is baptism a part of the process?"

"Baptism," Matt began, "is a multi-layered symbol, which is a fancy way of saying it means a lot of things at once. Let me talk about a few of them. The word *baptism*, before it was a religious word, was a word used for the dying of cloth. To baptize was to dip a white piece of cloth in a vat of blue dye. After the dipping, all the fibers of the cloth would be colored blue, and the whole piece of cloth would be blue. In baptism, the water of baptism is a symbol of the Holy Spirit. We are dipped in the Holy Spirit, all the fibers of our being are colored by the Holy Spirit, and we are no longer what we once were. We are different. In Romans 6, Paul used the waters of baptism to symbolize the death of Jesus. We go under the water and die to our old life as Jesus died on the cross. When we come up out of the water, we rise to new life in Christ just as Jesus rose to new life on Easter morning. Baptism is also a symbol of the love and grace of God working to draw us to him. It's a symbol of the saving work of Jesus in the resurrection and crucifixion. It's a symbol of the perfecting work of the Holy Spirit in our lives. It's a symbol of our commitment to Jesus. It's a public owning of Jesus by us and being claimed publically by Jesus and his people, the church."

"I had no idea," Joe replied, "that baptism was about all of that. You know I've never been baptized. Can I get baptized? What do I need to do?"

"I'm sorry," Matt said. "When we prayed the prayer that day, I was so excited that I never thought about baptism. I should have talked with you about it quite awhile ago. We'll talk to Rev. Jim and get you lined up for a baptism. We can probably do it in a couple of weeks. Rev. Jim will ask you to invite your family and friends, and there will be a lot of church people who will come. At the baptism, he'll ask you some questions that will lead to sharing your testimony. Knowing Rev. Jim, he'll probably try to organize a dinner around the event so that the church people can mingle with your family and friends."

"I think I'd like to invite my dad to come," Joe said thoughtfully.

"I think that would be a great idea," Matt added after a couple of moments. "Now, let me ask you a question. What's the 'everything' Jesus commanded us to teach?"

"That would be all the things we've been learning the last however many weeks we've been at this," Joe replied.

"Could you be a little more specific?" Matt asked.

"You mean run through everything like you did last week?" Joe answered by asking his own question.

"That's exactly what I mean," Matt responded.

"I'm not sure I can do it," Joe replied.

"It's an open book question," Matt prompted. "Give it a shot."

"Okay, I'll try," Joe said. "Here goes. Jesus began by saying the kingdom is near, change. As best I remember, that's about God loving us so much he has moved heaven here to help us, heal us, forgive us, and resource us. Part of the resources are this huge life change I've been experiencing over the last several months. Then Jesus gave us the Beatitudes, a description of what a truly blessed life is. Let me see, as Jesus continued, we're to be salt and light, to live a life of love exceeding the law. We're to use our anger for reconciliation and resolution, our sexuality for blessing and keeping soft hearts toward our spouses. Jesus helps us get our boundaries in order so that we can say yes and no to the right things at the right times. Then there was some stuff on how to deal with abuses of power, loving, learning, praying for your enemy, and overcoming evil with good. We're to use the spiritual disciplines to increase our capacity for God and the kingdom so that more kingdom can get in us so that we can more closely live the things Jesus was teaching. How am I doing so far?"

"You're doing well. Keep going," Matt encouraged.

"I was afraid you'd say that," Joe continued. "We're to use our treasure to advance the kingdom, treasure the kingdom, and allow God to provide for us as we seek the kingdom. We're not to judge but to engage in board removal so that we can be helpful. We're not to pearl push, but to ask, seek, and knock. We're to treat others as we would like to be treated. We're to beware of false prophets and teachers, and above all, we're to do what Jesus has been teaching.

"Then Jesus talked about kingdom mission. We're to share the good news that the kingdom has drawn near, and we're to act like it by healing the sick, cleansing the leper, and basically meeting human needs with kingdom resources.

"The parables are encouraging stories about how God is at work as we're in mission. I remember we aren't to give up, small beginnings can have big endings, God is at work in small stuff, there will be weeds, judgment is coming, and remember, what we have been given is a treasure.

"The next part was about kingdom community. The way to be great in the kingdom is to set aside status and the drive to be number one and use our gifts, abilities, and resources to serve one another. We're especially to care for those without voice, vote, power, and influence. When we have problems with each other, we're to work them out face to face and get help if we need it. We are to forgive each other as many times as it takes. If we can get our acts together with each other and Jesus, there's nothing that will be impossible for us.

"The last part was to get ready, be ready, and stay ready because Jesus is coming and no one knows when. But if we aren't ready, we've blown it. Readiness is about engaging the kingdom to do all the things we've just been talking about on a daily basis.

"And I suspect we all need to be in the disciple making business.

"Did I get it all?"

"You did very well," Matt said. "That's what we're to teach in order for people to become disciples.

"Who are candidates for disciple making?"

"Everyone, I would think," Joe replied. "Didn't Jesus say to make disciples of all nations or all peoples?"

"Yes, he did," Matt said. "I have noticed a tendency, though, to limit candidates for disciple making to people who are like us. People like us are those who are in the same social economic class, with the same racial background, the same moral ethical code (that is they haven't messed up in ways different than we have), and with the same educational levels. I've noticed a tendency when dealing with people who are different from us, by having a background we consider less than ours, to try to bring them up to our level before we engage in the disciple-making process. It's almost like we believe there is a minimum culture standard for disciples. I've noticed a tendency when dealing with people who are above us in their cultural setting, to assume we have nothing to offer them or that they won't be interested in being disciples because they have more money, better education, and have better jobs than we do.

"I admit that it's much easier for most of us to reach people who are like us, and people who are like us are most attracted to us. But with that admission, I believe Jesus calls us to leave the comfort zone of those who are like us and reach out to those who are not like us as well. As we do, we need to take the risk to enter their world rather than try to get them to enter our world. The apostle Paul wrote that he would become all things to all people in order to win some to Christ. Jesus, himself, left heaven and came to live among us. A big part of the disciple-making process is about leaving our worlds and our comfort zones to enter the worlds of those who are lost."

"Could you give me an example of what you're saying?" Joe asked.

"In my neighborhood, there's a house that's not well kept," Matt answered. "I think there's an alcohol problem in that house, but I'm not sure. I've only met those neighbors once. Their kids don't hang with my kids, and I never see them at any school activities. The same distance from my house is a very well-kept house. It looks better than mine. I see those neighbors out in the yard a lot. I like talking with them. I've been working on being salt and light in their lives, trying to influence them toward the kingdom. However, I've done nothing to try to connect with the people who live in the unkempt house with the problems that are there. As I reflect on the teachings of Jesus, I think I need to spend more effort on the unkempt house. That requires a good deal of risk on my part."

"So you're saying," Joe echoed, "that the unkempt, the troubled, and the desperate are candidates for disciple making. As I think back on Matthew, it was precisely these people who sought Jesus out and got help. I hear you. But you like said, it's difficult."

"That brings us to Part III of the commission," Matt continued. "As difficult and risky as this commission is, Jesus promised to be with us to the very end of the age. Jesus did not ask us to do this alone. He promised to be with us as we carry out the mission. To be honest, some of the times I have felt Jesus with me the most are the times I have left my comfort zone and risked for the sake of the mission. I'll have to think about this, but I wonder if there is a correlation between feeling the presence of Jesus and involvement in his commission."

"Let me see if I have all the parts of the Great Commission," Joe said. "Jesus has been given all authority in heaven and on earth, and he's using that authority to send us out to make disciples and to clear the obstacles to disciples out of our way. Disciple making involves being salt and light and being in mission. As people respond, we talk with them about Jesus, help them commit to him, teach them and help them apply his teachings, and then help them get in the disciple-making business. As we do this, Jesus is with us."

"That's it," Matt replied.

"So what's next?" Joe asked. "We're finished with our Matthew study, should we study the book of Mark?"

"Is that what Jesus said is next?" Matt asked.

"I think what Jesus said is next," Joe said, "is that we need to get into the disciple-making business. So how do we do that?"

"I've been thinking about that," Matt answered. "I've been thinking about that a lot. Jesus has been pushing me here. I've led a few guys like you through this, but when we get to this point, I've turned them loose and said, 'Go find someone you can do this with.' And they have, but like me, it's sporadic—it's not all the time.

"So I've been thinking what would happen if you and I got together a group of twelve like Jesus did and work through this material with them, and at the end of the material, we pair them up and get each pair to work through this material with a group of twelve they would assemble, who would then pair up their twelve and get them to gather a group of twelve they could share this material with, and so on.

"What do you think?"

"Do you mean you and me," Joe exclaimed, "helping twelve others experience the same life change I've had over the last several months? That would be incredible. If we were to do that, and those twelve paired up to work with groups of twelve, and if you and I got another group of twelve, that would result in quite a movement after a couple of years."

"I've been thinking about that too," Matt said. "We would work in a group of 12 people, and then from that 12, each person would partner with some else from the group to form 6 new groups, each of which would work with a group of 12, or 72 for the 6 groups. Those 72, in groups of 2, would work with 432, and on it goes."

"If each of those people could experience the joy and peace and forgiveness that I did," Joe continued, "and get help with the stuff of their lives and get involved in kingdom mission, that kind of thing could radically change our community. Like I said, that would be incredible.

"I'm still so new to this, do you really think I could help do something like this?"

"I think together, with the help of Jesus, we could pull it off," Matt said.

"When can we start?" Joe asked.

"I was hoping you would say that," Matt responded. "We can get started now."

Matt and Joe got a refill on their coffees and another round of chocolate chip cookies and started talking about who they could invite to be in their first group of twelve. They prayed for those people and planned to meet the next week to start talking about invitations and when the group would begin.

Matt left the coffee shop that night being more excited about following Jesus than anytime he could remember. The thought of being involved in that kind of kingdom work that would change the lives of so many people filled him with a joy and an expectation that he had rarely experienced. The thought of working with Jesus to change lives in this way humbled him and honored him at the same time. He started thinking about the people he would like to invite to be part of the group, and he wondered just what would happen in each life and whose lives they would touch. In the quietness of his car, he said, 'Thank you.'

Joe left the coffee shop feeling in over his head and overwhelmed by the task and the possibilities. But he remembered, *I've been here before.* Then he applied the very first lesson he learned from Jesus: "Blessed are the poor in spirit for theirs is the kingdom of heaven." He prayed, "Jesus, I'm in so far over my head I can't even see the surface. I can't do this, but I want to. Please help me." Joe drove home with a sense of deep peace and great expectation about what could happen in the rest of his life.

What about you? What has happened in your life as a result of your journey with Matt and Joe through the teaching that Jesus did to make disciples? What would happen if you and a partner gathered a group of twelve to journey through the teaching of Jesus with Matt and Joe? What would happen in your life, in your partner's life, in the lives of the twelve? What would happen if those twelve paired up and each pair made the journey with another group of twelve? What would happen?

When I first bumped into what Jesus was doing with his teaching in Matthew's Gospel, I thought it was a neat idea. But Jesus wouldn't let me leave it at that. He asked me if I was teaching anyone these things. I told him, "Not exactly." He asked me, "Why not?" I told him it would take a huge amount of time to process all the things he was saying and assemble them in a way that I could teach them. I remember he asked me point-blank, "Do you have anything better to do with your time?"

As you consider Matt and Joe, a partner, and a group of twelve, I know it's a significant commitment of your time and energy, and you might even have to rearrange your life and some of your goals and priorities to do it. But the question Jesus asked me hangs there for you too, "Do you have anything better to do with your time?"

Like Joe, all this may feel overwhelming, and you may not feel up to it. That's all right. In fact, that's a good way to feel at this point. I'll do all I can to give you whatever support you need to pull this off. But more importantly, Jesus is doing all he can to help you. All the resources of heaven have been assembled to help you, all the authority in heaven and on earth has been aligned to support you, and Jesus promised to be with you always as you move forward with this task. Let me leave you with the first thing Jesus taught us.

"Blessed are the poor in spirit, for theirs is the kingdom of heaven."

Thank you for reading *Coffee with Matt & Joe*.

Coffee with Matt & Joe was designed to be part of a small group experience. For maximum *Coffee with Matt & Joe* benefit, I invite you to start your own Matthew Group.

A Matthew Group is a 30-week small group study of *Coffee with Matt & Joe*, that includes study guides, spiritual disciplines, and mission projects. To get started, go to the Matt & Joe website:

www.coffeewithmattandjoe.com

I'll see you there! — Dr. Jim

Endnotes

Chapter 1
[i] Andrew M. Greeley, *The Jesus Myth* (New York: Image Books, 1973), pp. 43-44.
[ii] Greeley, p. 47.
[iii] Greeley, p. 50.
[iv] Greeley, p. 51. Greely used the word *metanoia* where I have inserted the word *change*.

Chapter 2
[i] Dallas Willard, *The Divine Conspiracy* (New York, NY: HarperCollins, 1998), p. 121.

Chapter 3
[i] E. Stanley Jones, *The Unshakeable Kingdom and the Unchanging Person* (Nashville, TN: Abingdon Press, 1972), p. 166. Used by permission of Abingdon Press.
[ii] Bill Hybels and Mark Mittelberg, *Becoming a Contagious Christian* (Grand Rapids, MI: Zondervan, 1994), pp.41-46.
[iii] Greeley, pp. 43-44.

Chapter 5
[i] Willard, p. 149.
[ii] Willard, pp. 151-154. My discussion of the anger cycle is informed by Willard.

Chapter 6
[i] Willard, p. 159.
[ii] Willard, p. 167.
[iii] Dan B. Allender and Tremper Longman III., *Bold Love* (Colorado Springs, CO: NavPress, 1992), pp. 102-104.
[iv] Willard, pp. 170-171.
[v] Willard, p. 169.

Chapter 7
[i] Willard, p. 174.
[ii] Henry Cloud, John Townsend, *Boundaries* (Grand Rapids, MI: Zondervan Publishing House, 1992), p. 59.
[iii] Cloud and Townsend, pp. 49-51.
[iv] Cloud and Townsend, pp. 57-59.
[v] Cloud and Townsend, pp. 53-56.
[vi] Cloud and Townsend, pp. 52-53.
[vii] Cloud and Townsend, pp. 270-286.
[viii] Robert Hemfelt, Frank Minirth, Paul Meier, *We Are Driven* (Nashville, TN: Thomas Nelson, Inc., 1991), pp. 304-312.

Chapter 8
[i] Walter Wink, *The Powers That Be* (Minneapolis, MN: Augsburg Fortress, 1998), pp. 99-101.
[ii] Wink, pp. 101-103.
[iii] Wink, pp. 103-105.
[iv] Wink, pp. 105-106.
[v] Wink, pp. 106-108.
[vi] Wink, pp. 151-153.
[vii] Wink, pp. 116-117.
[viii] Chuck Colson, *The Body: Being Light in Darkness* (Nashville, TN: Thomas Nelson, Inc., First Edition, September 23, 1992). Referenced by permission of Thomas Nelson, Inc. All rights reserved.
[ix] Terry Pluto, "God Speaks to Hostage, Her Captor," *The Akron Beacon Journal*, March 15, 2005, Document ID: 108E031F0C117374.
[x] Rick Warren, *The Purpose Driven Life*, (Grand Rapids, MI: Zondervan, 2002).
[xi] Wink, pp. 147-148.
[xii] Angie O'Gorman, "Defense Through Disarmament: Nonviolence and Personal Assault," in *The Universe Bends Toward Justice,* O'Gorman, ed. (Philadelphia: New Society Publishers, 1990), pp. 242-246. Story used by permission of Angie O'Gorman.
[xiii] Wink, pp. 149-150.

Chapter 9
[i] Wink, pp. 162-164.
[ii] Wink, p. 165.
[iii] Wink, p. 169.
[iv] Wink, p. 171.
[v] Allender and Longman, pp. 287-295.
[vi] Allender and Longman, pp. 299-303.
[vii] Allender and Longman, pp. 263-268.
[viii] Allender and Longman, pp. 268-283.
[ix] Pat Conroy, *The Great Santini* (New York: Houghton Mifflin, 1976).

[x] Allender and Longman, pp. 234-243.
[xi] Allender and Longman, pp. 244-254.

Chapter 10
[i] Willard, p. 188.
[ii] Willard, p. 189.
[iii] Gary Thomas, *Sacred Pathways,* (Grand Rapids, MI: Zondervan, 2000), p. 49.
[iv] Thomas, p. 66.
[iv] Thomas, p. 92.
[vi] Thomas, p. 112.
[vii] Thomas, p. 131.
[viii] Thomas, p. 148.
[ix] Thomas, pp. 170-171.
[x] Thomas, p. 191.
[xi] Thomas, p. 211.

Chapter 11
[i] Dallas Willard, *The Spirit of the Disciplines: Understanding How God Changes Lives* (San Francisco: HarperCollins, 1989), p. 156.
[ii] Watty Piper, *The Little Engine That Could,* TM & © Penguin Group (USA) Inc. Used by permission of Penguin Group Inc.
[iii] Willard, p. 157.
[iv] Willard, p. 158.
[v] Willard, p. 176.
[vi] Willard, p. 158.
[vii] Willard, p. 176.
[viii] Willard, p. 161.
[ix] Willard, p. 163.
[x] Willard, p. 173.
[xi] Willard, p. 177.
[xii] Willard, p. 188.

Chapter 12
[i] Tom Sine, *Mustard Seed Versus McWorld* (Grand Rapids, MI: Baker Books, 2002), pp. 149-165. Used by permission of Baker Publishing Group.
[ii] Sine, p. 155.

Chapter 13
[i] Dallas Willard, *The Divine Conspiracy* (New York, NY: HarperCollins, 1998), p. 225.
[ii] Willard, p. 228.
[iii] Willard, pp. 228-229.
[iv] Robert E. Quinn, *Deep Change* (San Francisco: Jossey-Bass Inc., 1996), pp. 33-34. Used by permission of John Wiley & Sons, Inc., Hoboken, NJ.

[v] Quinn, pp. 34-37.
[vi] Kerry Patterson, Joseph Brenny, Ron McMillan, Al Switzler, *Crucial Conversations: Tools for Talking When Stakes Are High* (New York: McGraw-Hill, 2002), p. 99. Used by permission of The McGraw-Hill Companies.
[vii] Patterson, Brenny, McMillan, Switzler, p. 113.
[viii] Patterson, Brenny, McMillan, Switzler, pp. 106-107.
[ix] Patterson, Brenny, McMillan, Switzler, pp. 107-108.
[x] Patterson, Brenny, McMillan, Switzler, pp. 108-109.
[xi] Patterson, Brenny, McMillan, Switzler, pp. 124-131.
[xii] Willard, pp. 218-219.
[xiii] Willard, pp. 229.
[xiv] Willard, pp. 231.

Chapter 14
[i] Dale Hanson Burke, *The Skeptics Guide to the Global AIDS Crisis* (Waynesboro, GA.: Authentic Media, 2004), p. 5. Used by permission of Authentic Media.
[ii] *Coalition Military Fatalities By Year* chart, http://www.icasualties.org/Iraq/index.aspx, September 30, 2010.
[iii] Willard, p. 234.
[iv] Ibid.
[v] Willard, p. 236.
[vi] Willard, p. 250.
[vii] Willard, pp. 67-68.
[viii] Greeley, pp. 43-44. See *The Jesus Myth*, Endnotes, Chapter 1.

Chapter 17
[i] I heard Oral Roberts preach these words to the student body in the Oral Roberts University chapel, Tulsa, OK, 1980-1983 while I was in seminary there. More information on Oral Roberts Ministries can be found at www.oralroberts.com.

Chapter 19
[i] Hybels and Mittelberg, pp. 123-124.
[ii] Hybels and Mittelberg, pp. 125-126.
[iii] Hybels and Mittelberg, pp. 126-127.
[iv] Hybels and Mittelberg, pp. 128.
[v] Hybels and Mittelberg, pp. 129- 130.
[vi] Hybels and Mittelberg, pp. 130-131.
[vii] Hybels and Mittelberg, pp. 149.
[viii] Hybels and Mittelberg, pp. 155-156.
[ix] *The Bridge Illustration*, http://www.navigators.org/resources/shared/tools/bridge.pdf.

Chapter 20
[i] C. S. Lewis, *The Great Divorce* (New York, NY: MacMillan Publishing Company, 1946) (New York, NY: HarperCollins Publishers, 2001, HarperOne, 2009).
[ii] George G. Hunter III, *Church for the Unchurched* (Nashville, TN: Abingdon Press, 1996), pp. 21-22. Used by permission of Abingdon Press.

Chapter 21
[i] Bill Hybels, *Just Walk Across the Room* (Grand Rapids, MI: Zondervan, 2006), p. 43.

Chapter 22
[i] Eugene Peterson, *The Message* (Colorado Springs, CO: Navpress Publishing Group, 2002).

Chapter 24
[i] Peterson, Matthew 18:15-17.
[ii] Peterson, Matthew 18:15-17.
[iii] Peterson, Matthew 18:15-17.
[iv] Patrick Lencioni, *The Five Dysfunctions of a Team* (San Francisco, CA: Jossey-Bass, 2002), p. vii. Used by permission of John Wiley & Sons, Inc., Hoboken, NJ.

Chapter 25
[i] Anne Rice, *Christ the Lord: Out of Egypt* (New York: Ballantine Books), 2008. Referenced by permission of Anne Rice.

Chapter 26
[i] Lencioni, see *The Five Dysfunctions of a Team*, Endnotes Chapter 24.
[ii] Patrick Lencioni, *Silos, Politics and Turf Wars* (San Francisco, CA: Jossey-Bass, a division of John Wiley and Sons, Inc., Hoboken, NJ), 2006.
[iii] William Barclay, The New Daily Study Bible, The Gospel of Matthew Vol. 2, Saint Andrew Press, Edinburgh, UK, 2001 (available in North America through Westminster John Knox Press, Louisville, Kentucky). Referenced by permission of Saint Andrew Press.
[iv] Erwin Raphael McManus, *Uprising: A Revolution of the Soul* (Nashville: Thomas Nelson Inc., 2003), p. 183.
[v] McManus, p. 184.

Chapter 27
[i] John Maxwell, *Failing Forward* (Nashville, TN: Thomas Nelson Inc., 2000). Referenced by permission of Thomas Nelson, Inc. All rights reserved.

Chapter 28
[i] Jeffrey Gitomer, *Little Red Book of Selling* (Austin: Bard Press, 2005), p. 212. Used by permission.